Critical Forms

Critical Forms

Forms of Literary Criticism, 1750–2020

ROSS WILSON

Great Clarendon Street, Oxford, OX2 6DP,
United Kingdom

Oxford University Press is a department of the University of Oxford.
It furthers the University's objective of excellence in research, scholarship,
and education by publishing worldwide. Oxford is a registered trade mark of
Oxford University Press in the UK and in certain other countries

Published in the United States of America by Oxford University Press
198 Madison Avenue, New York, NY 10016, United States of America

British Library Cataloguing in Publication Data
Data available

Library of Congress Control Number: 2023931432

ISBN 978-0-19-888111-7

DOI: 10.1093/oso/9780198881117.001.0001

Printed and bound by
CPI Group (UK) Ltd, Croydon, CR0 4YY

For Flora and Constance

Acknowledgements

Parts of Chapter 1 appeared as 'Henry James at Any Rate', *Henry James Review*, 38 (2017), 250–9; I am grateful to Johns Hopkins University Press for permission to reuse some of the material included in that article here.

The award of a Research Fellowship by the Leverhulme Trust was vital to work on this book. I offer my thanks to the Trust, and to Daniel Wunderlich, who helped with the application. The General Board of the University of Cambridge and the Council of Trinity College, Cambridge, also granted me a term's sabbatical for work towards this book, for which I am grateful.

At OUP, Jacqueline Norton was warmly encouraging of this project at its inception—as well as throughout the long process during which it actually came to fruition. Karen Raith and Ellie Collins have been extremely helpful and supportive, and I benefited enormously from the reports of anonymous readers that the Press commissioned. I greatly appreciate the care and dedication shown throughout the production process by Emma Varley, Dolarine Fonceca, and Hilary Walford.

Aspects of the central arguments of this book were presented at the following events: Late and Later James/James at Lamb House, Centre for Modernist Studies, University of Sussex (hosted by the National Trust at Lamb House, Rye, East Sussex); the Eighteenth-Century and Romantic Studies Graduate Research Seminar and the Faculty Research Seminar of the Faculty of English, University of Cambridge; the Research Seminar of the School of English Literature, Language and Linguistics, University of Newcastle-upon-Tyne; the 26th Annual Meeting of the North American Society for the Study of Romanticism (hosted at Brown University); the International Conference on Romanticism (2019, hosted at the University of Manchester); Affects in History workshop hosted by the University of York; and Fellows' Talks at Trinity and Emmanuel Colleges, Cambridge. David Ferris organized an opportunity for me to present research from this project at the University of Colorado at Boulder, for which I would like to express my gratitude. In addition, the postgraduate seminars on 'Inventing Criticism' I have taught over the past few years at the University of Cambridge have profoundly informed many of the arguments in this book. I would like to acknowledge the contribution of the students who took those seminars—especially the class of 2022.

Many friends and colleagues have assisted me during work on this book. I cannot attempt to acknowledge all of them here, but I would like in particular to thank Alex Freer for reading the typescript at an important stage in its development and for offering characteristically constructive and insightful advice. Stefan Collini also offered indispensable advice on the whole typescript, and he has been a source of wisdom, friendship, and encouragement throughout. The friendship of my colleagues in English at Trinity and Emmanuel Colleges, and in the Faculty of English, University of Cambridge, has been vital to the gestation and completion of this book. In particular, I would like to thank Christopher Burlinson, Alex Freer (again), Nick Hardy, Phil Knox, Angela Leighton, Robert Macfarlane, Joe Moshenska, Adrian Poole, Corinna Russell, Helen Thaventhiran, Christopher Tilmouth, and Anne Toner.

I thank my father, Mike Wilson, for his interest and support. Adequately to acknowledge the support of my wife, Lesley Wylie—wisest of counsellors, best of friends, inspirational example of determination in the completion of her own projects—is beyond me. Without the daily gifts of love, companionship, and sheer exuberance from our daughters, Flora and Constance, neither the completion of this book, nor much else besides, would have been possible. This book is dedicated in grateful acknowledgement to them.

Contents

Note on the Text

References to the works of Shakespeare are to *The Riverside Shakespeare*, ed. G. Blakemore Evans et al., 2nd edn (Boston: Houghton Mifflin, 1997), and references to the Bible are to the Authorized (King James) Version. Where no translation is cited in the notes, translations from texts originally in languages other than English are my own.

The following abbreviations have been adopted throughout.

CHLC III	*The Cambridge History of Literary Criticism*, iii: Glyn P. Norton (ed.), *The Renaissance* (Cambridge: Cambridge University Press, 1999)
CHLC IV	*The Cambridge History of Literary Criticism*, iv: H. B. Nisbet and Claude Rawson (eds), *The Eighteenth Century* (Cambridge: Cambridge University Press, 1997; repr. 2005)
CHLC V	*The Cambridge History of Literary Criticism*, v: Marshall Brown (ed.), *Romanticism* (Cambridge: Cambridge University Press, 2000; repr. 2007)
CHLC VI	*The Cambridge History of Literary Criticism*, vi: M. A. R. Habib (ed.), *The Nineteenth Century, c.1830–1914* (Cambridge: Cambridge University Press, 2013; repr. 2016)
CHLC VII	*The Cambridge History of Literary Criticism*, vii: A. Walton Litz et al. (eds), *Modernism and the New Criticism* (Cambridge: Cambridge University Press, 2000; repr. 2006)
CI	*Critical Inquiry*
HJR	*Henry James Review*
LRB	*London Review of Books*
ODNB	*Oxford Dictionary of National Biography*
OED	*Oxford English Dictionary*
PMLA	*Proceedings of the Modern Language Association*
TLS	*Times Literary Supplement*
VP	*Victorian Poetry*

Introduction

This is a book about the generic forms of literary criticism, and I should like to begin it with a short foray of my own into the genre of autobiographical anecdote. Somewhat over fifteen years ago, I applied for a fixed-term lectureship in the Faculty of English at the University of Cambridge (where, as it happens, I now work—but that's another story). The lectureship was to be in 'Criticism', very broadly conceived, and candidates for the position had been asked to give details of some lectures they would offer if appointed. I duly proposed a set of lectures for an optional course in the history and theory of ethical and political thought, a course oddly if venerably at that date still called 'the English Moralists'—oddly, because the course addresses topics in the history of moral and political thought since Plato and takes in a host of other non-English thinkers from Aristotle to Arendt and beyond; venerably, because it has been a fixture of the Cambridge English degree from its earliest days. My lectures would explore a series of eighteenth- and nineteenth-century *German* thinkers, from Kant and Hegel to Marx, Nietzsche, and Kierkegaard (reasoning that 'English' in 'English Moralists' had not been taken too literally for a long time, perhaps I hoped that my definition of 'German' might stretch to include the Danish theologian and controversialist as well). One of the eminences on the interview panel asked how I would account in my lectures for the significant *generic differences* between the writing of thinkers such as, for example, Kant and Nietzsche. It was a good question. I cannot now remember what I said in response—probably for the best—but it was not a convincing answer. In thinking about my proposed lectures, I had been chiefly concerned with ideas such as the categorical imperative, objective spirit, alienation and ideology, *ressentiment* (great waves of which I was about to feel when I didn't get the job), and the teleological suspension of the ethical—and what had they to do with such lowly questions as the genre of the writings in which they were set forth? Anyway, my chances of getting the job were un-teleologically suspended there and then.

That fateful question has stuck with me—in the way that questions we do not manage to answer tend to stick with us—and it has significantly shaped the ways in which I have come to think about intellectual history generally. As Jonathan Lavery has emphasized with respect to the history of Western philosophy (though the point could be extended to other philosophical traditions as well), philosophers have deployed 'myriad expository styles and literary forms', which 'play [...] organizational role[s] in the way one conceives philosophical problems and

Critical Forms: Forms of Literary Criticism, 1750–2020. Ross Wilson, Oxford University Press. © Ross Wilson 2023.
DOI: 10.1093/oso/9780198881117.003.0001

questions in the first place'.[1] It is not without regret, then, that Lavery remarks the dominance of 'the academic essay, extended treatise, and specialized anthology', a 'narrow generic range in contemporary philosophical writing [that] is exceptional in the history of philosophy'.[2] Lavery is of course not the first commentator to have noted the significance of genre, as well as style, tone, and rhetoric, to philosophical writing, nor the first to have deplored the damaging effects of their neglect. John Richetti's landmark study, *Philosophical Writing: Locke, Berkeley, Hume*, for example, pays scrupulous attention to the writing of the philosophers examined in it. Near the opening of his book, Richetti issues the following admonition:

> Philosophical writing has been treated for the last hundred years or so as if it formed part of a consecutive conversation and running debate among philosophers, a dialogue between the living and the dead, a group project or grand institute stretching from Plato to the present that has as its purpose the establishment of the transhistorical truth of things, the facts in the case. But this dialogue with the dead is a strange one, since the dead are in effect not allowed to speak their own language. Their writings are treated as if they were submissions to a modern journal of philosophy.[3]

One way to start allowing the dead to speak their own language in this 'dialogue between the living and the dead' would be to recognize that they often spoke in dialogue—as both Berkeley and Hume did, for instance, in some of their most important philosophical works. Another step towards taking the forms of philosophical writing seriously would be to recognize that submissions to modern journals of philosophy, and the 'academic essay, extended treatise, and specialized anthology' mentioned by Lavery, themselves conform to generic and stylistic expectations, however routinely questions of genre and style may be disregarded in them. Other philosophers have also been subject to the kind of sensitive literary-critical reading for which Richetti and Lavery call, as in, for instance, Willi Goetschel's refusal to treat Kant's *Critique* 'as a sort of theory stockpile' and attempt instead to recognize the significance of 'the style of stylelessness and the structure of structurelessness' in Kant's work, or in Keston Sutherland's recovery of the work of Karl Marx from a similar fate (from, that is, its transformation into

---

[1] Jonathan Lavery, 'Philosophical Genres and Literary Forms: A Mildly Polemical Introduction', *Poetics Today*, 28 (2007), 171–89 (181).
[2] Lavery, 180.
[3] John Richetti, *Philosophical Writing: Locke, Berkeley, Hume* (Cambridge, MA: Harvard University Press, 1983), 9.

'an array of undifferentiated concepts for theoretical consumption') by focusing on the central role of satire in Marx's writing.[4]

But vitally informative as these interventions have been for this project, *Critical Forms* is not about philosophy; it is about literary criticism. Indeed, both Richetti and Goetschel make sure to preserve a distinction between philosophy and literary criticism. 'The work of academic philosophers', Richetti reminds us, 'consists in examining past systems with a fiercely unsentimental clarity that excludes any literary dimension or generic conventions and that separates truth from illusion or fallacy in, say, Descartes or Berkeley. In a way,' he concedes, 'this is exactly as it should be'.[5] Goetschel is, if anything, more emphatic on this point: '[t]he literary-critical investigation of philosophical works differs from criticism of purely literary works because the former must concern itself with objective truth claims'.[6] We may leave to one side here the matter of whether or not there are 'purely literary works', along with the implication that their criticism need not be concerned with 'objective truth claims'—though it will be worth bearing these issues in mind because the overlaps between philosophy and literary criticism are often considerable and I have frequent occasion to address them in this book. Nevertheless, prevailing conceptions of philosophy and of literary criticism have differed, and the history of those conceptions has accordingly developed in different ways. Richetti's historical account is particularly suggestive on this point. He notes that the turn from ancient and medieval to modern thought is marked by a 'profound transformation of what might be called the dominant literary genres of philosophy'. Predicated on the exegesis of a body of sacred and otherwise canonical texts, and assuming a 'communal context', the older forms of 'dialogue, polemic, commentary, and disputation', which 'require, continually add to, and redefine a pre-existing philosophy', come increasingly to give way to private forms, such as 'the autobiographical meditation, the essay, and the treatise', not predicated on the assumption of communal verbal exchange. Philosophy, according to Richetti, thus moved away from a model of textual evaluation and commentary, towards one based on individual experiential observation. Philosophical writing thus becomes an increasingly transparent medium, aspiring to 'the condition of neutral scientific notation'. The transition Richetti remarks from the 'reformed but still oratorical habits of Bacon and Hobbes to the understatement, relative looseness, and plainness such as Locke cultivates' in the period that is his focus is a transition in the understanding of philosophy and thus also in the way

---

[4] Willi Goetschel, *Constituting Critique: Kant's Writing as Critical Praxis*, trans. Eric Schwab (Durham, NC: Duke University Press, 1994), 8; Keston Sutherland, *Stupefaction: A Radical Anatomy of Phantoms* (London: Seagull Books, 2011), 39.
[5] Richetti, 9.   [6] Goetschel, 10.

philosophy is habitually written and, crucially, read. Professional students of philosophy today 'read Descartes and Hume as if they were Kant'.[7]

Goetschel has given us reason to rethink our habit of reading Kant, let alone
Descartes and Hume, as if he were Kant (so to speak), and Richetti's concern is as
much with the *style* of supposedly transparent philosophical writing as it is with
the more obviously oratorical forebears of a writer like Locke. Richetti's is a persuasive account of the history of philosophical writing from which students of
literary criticism have much to learn, but there is an important barrier to transfer-
ring Richetti's model directly from the history of philosophy to the history of
literary criticism. As I mentioned above, fundamental to the transition from
earlier to later forms of philosophical writing was the shift from a conception in
which philosophy's business is engagement with texts, to one in which philosophy
is predicated upon the communication of the results of private observation and
reflection. That shift is itself accompanied by other shifts that are certainly recognizable in the history of literature and its reception—the increasing privatization
of reading, for instance—but, insofar as literary criticism must remain engaged
with those texts that go to make up the contested field of literature, then literary
criticism cannot undergo the transition away from textual commentary and
towards experiential observation and reflection in quite the way that, Richetti
argues, philosophy did. If it is the case, first, that the large-scale abandonment of
earlier forms of philosophical writing was in part a consequence of philosophy's
transition away from commentary and emendation of an existing textual tradition,
and if, second, literary criticism cannot undergo such a thoroughgoing transition
while hoping at the same time to remain literary criticism, then one consequence
may be that the range of forms for literary-critical writing have remained broader
and more continuous with an older tradition than the range of forms that has
come to typify modern philosophical writing.

It is unnecessary here to get any further into the exact nature of pre-modern
philosophy and the effects of the transition to modern thought, except to
acknowledge that the texts with which earlier philosophers engaged were often
granted a different kind of status from that routinely envisaged for literary texts. It
is nevertheless worth contemplating the way that literary criticism as a mode of
writing not only requires (to revert to Richetti's useful terms) but also adds to and
redefines the pre-existing literature on which it comments. I have just remarked
the way in which literary criticism, in contrast with philosophy as it has come to
be practised in modernity, requires a pre-existing body of texts. How, then, does
it add to and redefine that body of texts?

Even to ask this question is to assume that literary criticism is capable of
adding to and redefining literature. Such an assumption has, of course, been
contested on the grounds that the proper role of literary criticism is to observe,

---

[7] Richetti, 6–7, 16–17.

comment on, and evaluate literature, rather than to be it. As soon as the distance between literary criticism and literature is thus narrowed (or closed altogether), so the argument proceeds, then the capacity of literary criticism to observe, and so on—its capacity, that is, to criticize—is damagingly diminished. The relation of literary criticism to literature and the question of what kind of writing literary-critical writing is have been fundamental, for instance, to recent considerations of what has come to be called 'creative criticism'. Indeed, the attention given in recent years to the loose set of practices of literary-critical writing that are actively engaged in adding to and redefining (as well as commenting on and evaluating) literature itself is a key context for this book. Specifically, the theory and practice of creative criticism (if I may be allowed one final autobiographical aside) played an important role in my own professional history and thus, at least partly, in my decision to write this book: the first teaching position I actually did manage to get was at the University of East Anglia, one of the institutions where (in the United Kingdom at least) creative criticism was pioneered. More broadly and import-antly, the attention that creative criticism has garnered, alongside its actual prac-tice, may be traced to a range of intellectual, institutional, and cultural factors that have come to bear on the way that literary-critical writing is theorized and prac-tised. The belated impact of twentieth-century literary avant-gardes on the prac-tice of literary criticism, the critique of prevailing assumptions about critical objectivity and a renewed attention to rhetoric, and the impact of cultural studies and literary theory more generally have all, in different ways, had an impact not just on the conception of literary criticism, but on its practice in writing.[8] A dan-ger arising from the confluence of these factors that historians of creative criti-cism have identified and, in some cases, sought to guard against is literary criticism's dissolution into a recuperated belle-lettrism. Despite the title of Gregory L. Ulmer's early intervention in this field—'The Object of Post-Criticism'—more recent proponents of creative criticism have disavowed an alli-ance with what has come to be called post-critique (Ulmer's essay itself predates the emergence of post-critique as a clearly identifiable movement within literary criticism and theory). Far from giving up on the attempt to develop knowledge about literature and taking refuge in devotion to personally cherished books and poems instead, creative criticism, it has been claimed, engages in a thoroughgoing reconsideration of how thinking about literature happens, how literary-critical knowledge is arrived at, and on what epistemological assumptions it rests (Ulmer himself, in fact, was already concerned with 'an "epistemology" of

---

[8] See, e.g., Gregory L. Ulmer, 'The Object of Post-Criticism', in Hal Foster (ed.), *Postmodern Culture* (London: Pluto Press, 1985; first pub., as *The Anti-Aesthetic*, 1983), 83–110; Mary Poovey, 'Creative Criticism: Adaptation, Performative Writing, and the Problem of Objectivity', *Narrative*, 8 (2000), 109–33; Clare Connors, 'Creative Criticism: A Histori-Manifesto', in Irving Goh (ed.), *French Thought and Literary Theory in the UK* (New York: Routledge, 2020), 46–62.

performance–knowing as making, producing, doing, acting').[9] Advocates of creative criticism, along with defenders of the writing practices of contemporary academic critics, profess allegiance to many of the writers (Derrida, Foucault, Jameson) disavowed by the proponents of post-critique, albeit viewing those writers as having engaged, crucially, in 'a writing understood not as sceptical critique, but as an inventive practice'.[10] The point here is well taken, although the tacit assumption nevertheless of an opposition between 'sceptical critique' and 'inventive practice' cedes too much ground to the assumption espoused by proponents of post-critique that critique is merely destructive. No such opposition between critique and practice need be granted; sceptical critique is frequently an inventive practice.

The suspicion that creative criticism tends to the dissolution of literary criticism's distinctively critical claims—and, in particular, the qualified attempt to dispel that suspicion—raises the question of the professional and disciplinary status of literary criticism. The institutional sources of creative criticism—from the emergence and rapid growth of the adjacent discipline of creative writing to frustrations with the (perceived, at least) limitations placed on the allowable range of literary-critical writing taken to have resulted from the regimes of administrative audit imposed within the managerial university—have themselves been well attested. The idea that certain forms of literary criticism are professional and disciplinary, and others, not so much, has been aptly described by Stefan Collini:

> Reviews in newspapers may be literary criticism, as may introductions to paperback reprints, as may footnotes in school editions; writing a poem or novel may be a form of literary criticism, as indeed may conversations over dinner about the most recent book one has read. But that, of course, is not what we now expect from a work of this title, no that is not it at all: the word has got around that literary criticism is an academic subject, and so its history, like histories of sociology or physics, will be largely a history of Precursors and Founding Parents.[11]

The implication that the migration of literary criticism to the academy from a series of other venues—newspapers, paperbacks, schools, dinner tables—and hence literary criticism's transition from an only quasi-professional or even amateur pursuit to a professional discipline, is a significant one to which I will return—for example, in Chapter 4, on reviews. It is a deft touch of Collini's to suggest that the report of literary criticism's disciplinary status is itself a property

[9] Ulmer, 94.   [10] Connors, 51–2 (the quotation is on p. 52).
[11] Stefan Collini, *Common Reading: Critics, Historians, Publics* (Oxford: Oxford University Press, 2008; repr. 2010), 258.

of the kind of sociable conversation ('word has got around') from which literary criticism is now rumoured to have become distinct. The turn from activity to idea, from multiplicity (newspapers, paperbacks, and so on) to singularity ('an academic subject') is seen, usually with regret, to entail a reduction in attention to the variety of forms in which literary criticism is, and has historically been, done.

Yet there are good reasons to doubt whether the breach between professional and other forms of literary criticism was ever so finally decisive—or, put another way, whether literary criticism's professional constitution was predicated on its severance from newspapers, paperbacks, schools, and dinner tables. Bruce Robbins, in his treatment of the professionalization of intellectual labour, contested the assumption that a gulf separates professionals from the public, and emphasized instead that 'versions of "the public" have been *internalized* by critics and [...] these internalizations act with real force upon the profession's psychic economy'.[12] Professional literary critics are always mindful ('the profession's psychic economy'), often to the point of anxious preoccupation, of the variously constituted (and frequently fantasized) publics for which, in some ways, they write. As Robbins memorably puts it: 'Professions are not hermetically sealed, but porous. [...] Address to outsiders [...] is indispensable to professional speech.'[13] The professional internalization of publics often cast as external to the profession, and the perennial porousness of the profession itself to what is only ever provisionally external in any case, have important consequences for attempts to account for the history of the professionalization of literary criticism. In particular, positing a date for the supposed breach between free and creative critical response, on the one hand, and professional labour obedient to the protocols of an established discipline, on the other, has proved, as Robbins has shown, a tricky business. The fall into professionalism and disciplinarity from a unified and harmonious culture always ends up being pushed further and further back into the mists of time, even once a date for the catastrophe has been confidently announced.[14]

If there never was a time when criticism's creativity was wholly unencumbered, a time when professional and disciplinary expectations were simply undreamed of, then perhaps it is also the case that the contraction in the range of critical forms was never quite so drastic, the sundering of critical writing from formal experimentation never quite so final. And if that is the case, then one might start to think of the history of literary criticism differently, less (to borrow Collini's terms) as 'a history of Precursors and Founding Parents' (though they will doubtless remain important) and more as a practice that has taken and continues to take a number of forms, such as reviews, introductions, and even conversations. In his

---

[12] Robbins, *Secular Vocations: Intellectuals, Professionalism, Culture* (London: Verso, 1993), 89.
[13] Robbins, 91.   [14] See Robbins 16–17, 75–7.

own amalgam of polemic, commonplace book, paean to almost universally despised 'academic writing', and dialogue, Eric Hayot at least asks what literary criticism might look like from something like this perspective:

> 'What if literary criticism were one of the major nonfictional genres of the twentieth century? What if we were to write a history of that genre, not as a story of schools of thought succeeding one another (New Criticism to New Historicism), but as a history of experiments in structure, rhetoric, and style?'[15]

In fact, it is not Hayot (or at least not simply Hayot) who asks these questions, but the idealistic persona of the dialogue phase of his eulogistic formal salmagundi. Every idealistic persona needs a sceptical interlocutor, and the sceptical interlocutor in this case seeks immediately to dampen any enthusiasm: ' "The only thing that's interesting about that is how completely obvious it would be if you said it about some other genre of writing." '[16] While it is tacitly granted that literary criticism *is* one of the major non-fictional genres of the twentieth century, it is held that actually coming up with a history of the genre of literary criticism could not itself be all that 'interesting'. It *is* interesting. But more than that, close attention to the different forms of criticism shows that, rather than fulfilling a single, predetermined function, different forms suggest different priorities, different conceptions of authority and the conduct of argument, and different constructions of the relationship between literary objects and discussion of them.

The questions asked by the idealistic persona in Hayot's dialogic defence of academic writing are, therefore, fundamental to *Critical Forms*. It is worthwhile, however, quickly to introduce four caveats in relation to the specific formulation of those questions. The first concerns literary criticism as a 'major non-fictional genre'. While it is true that I do not discuss any novels, poems, or plays as instances of literary criticism, nevertheless the non-fictionality of some writing in the forms that I do discuss is, to say the least, open to question. The second caveat (which has a relation to the first) is that *Critical Forms* is not exclusively focused on literary criticism produced by academics. At least in part for the reasons sketched above in my discussion of professional literary criticism, I take a broad purview, discussing criticism by academic literary critics, certainly, but also by practising poets, novelists, and playwrights, by journalists, and by that much contested hybrid creature, the poet-critic.[17] Third, however, there is a respect in which my

---

[15] Eric Hayot, 'Academic Writing, I Love You. Really, I Do', *CI*, 41 (2014), 53–77 (61).

[16] Hayot, 'Academic Writing', 61.

[17] See René Wellek, 'The Poet as Critic, the Critic as Poet, the Poet-Critic', in Frederick McDowell (ed.), *The Poet as Critic* (Evanston, IL: Northwestern University Press, 1967), 92–107; Lawrence Lipking, 'Poet-Critics', in *CHLC VII*, 439–67; Charles Bernstein, 'The Revenge of the Poet-Critic; or, the Parts Are Greater than the Sum of the Whole', in *My Way: Speeches and Poems* (Chicago: University of Chicago Press, 1999), 3–17.

scope is more limited than that implied by Hayot, since my focus is on form (his 'structure', perhaps), rather than with 'rhetoric, and style' as well—although, of course, any examination of form will necessitate some consideration of these features. As Michael Prince claims near the beginning of his *Philosophical Dialogue in the British Enlightenment*, '[g]enres become sites of competing interpretations because what is at stake in the definition of form is the power to establish normative frameworks for understanding complex phenomena'.[18] Not only, that is, are the works I investigate in this book attempts at understanding complex literary phenomena; their adoption and, in a number of cases, adaptation of specific forms also entail the attempt to establish frameworks for such understanding itself. Fourth and last, Hayot, rather in keeping with recent attempts to consider literary criticism as writing, envisages a history of literary criticism that explores writing from only the twentieth century (and perhaps, by extension, the twenty-first as well). I take a longer historical view, discussing work from around the middle of the eighteenth century to the twentieth century and beyond.

This book's historical scope and its concentration on form demand, I think, slightly fuller explanation. Let us take history first. As I have just mentioned, the earliest examples addressed in *Critical Forms* come from around the middle of the eighteenth century. The history of criticism in the mid- to late eighteenth century is the history of criticism we still inhabit.[19] This is substantially owing to the fact that it was at this period that many of the genres in which criticism continues to be practised emerged and were consolidated. It was, for instance, around the middle of the eighteenth century that the review started to gain a recognizable formal identity; that lectures on literature began concertedly to be published as lectures, advertising their prior delivery and, often, institutional imprimatur (the Oxford Professorship of Poetry, first occupied in 1708 by Joseph Trapp, is an important institution in this regard); and it was from the mid-eighteenth century that there was a remarkable flourishing of literary-critical letters, a phenomenon with an important relation to developments in the understanding of authorship, to a marked increase in the printing and circulation of literary works, and to the emergence of new readerships and new literary genres.

It should be granted that all of these forms—and the others that I examine in this book—have significant precedents prior to the eighteenth century, many of them stretching back to antiquity and consciously revived during and after the Renaissance. The anthology and dialogue are ancient genres, and prefaces, along

[18] Michael Prince, *Philosophical Dialogue in the British Enlightenment: Theology, Aesthetics and the Novel* (Cambridge: Cambridge University Press, 1996), 20.

[19] See, e.g., Simon Jarvis, 'Criticism, Taste, Aesthetics', in Thomas Keymer and Jon Mee (eds), *The Cambridge Companion to English Literature, 1740–1830* (Cambridge: Cambridge University Press, 2004), 24–42 (25) and Michael Gavin, *The Invention of English Criticism, 1650–1760* (Cambridge: Cambridge University Press, 2015), 1.

with other introductory paratexts, were an important feature of early printed book production.[20] The writers I examine are aware of much of this history and frequently invoke it in their own work. A significant strand in the rebirth of the dialogue in the eighteenth century, for instance, drew inspiration from Platonic and other Classical models (another significant strand invoked those models in order to eschew them), and the Classical and Renaissance subgenre of the dialogue of the dead has enjoyed (fittingly) a strange subterranean afterlife into the twentieth century and beyond. And, in order to be able to say that 'the biographical part of literature [...] is what I love most', Samuel Johnson had, of course, to be able to read some biographies before he wrote his own (he is indeed recommending Pierre Bayle's *Dictionnaire historique et critique* (first published in 1697) to Boswell).[21] Izaak Walton's lives of Donne (1640) and Herbert (1678), Aubrey's *Brief Lives* and their many memorable vignettes of literary figures, along with Sprat's 'An Account of the Life and Writings of Mr Abraham Cowley Written to Mr M. Clifford', which prefaced his 1668 edition of that poet's works—and which, in its combination of preface, biography, and letter is also a significant instance of generic multiplicity in literary-critical writing—are significant pre-eighteenth-century examples in English; earlier examples still may be gleaned, for instance, from the European continent, including Lionardo Bruni's and, especially, Giovanni Boccaccio's *Lives of Dante*, along with the numerous early biographies of Petrarch.[22] But in his *Lives of the Poets*, Johnson (as we will see in Chapter 7) developed a distinctive conception of the set of relations between a writer's life, a writer's work, and the life of the writer's works. Indeed, in recommending Bayle's *Dictionnaire* to lovers of the 'biographical part of literature', Johnson himself was operating with an older conception of both 'literature' and how biography might pertain to it—a conception he would do much to change. The relations between writing and life were theorized elsewhere as well and, in some respects, otherwise. For J. G. Herder, for instance, it was the work through which the writer lived on, and the task of biography was thus to attest to that still-animate life, 'the true

---

[20] Randall Anderson, 'The Rhetoric of Paratext in Early Printed Books', in *The Cambridge History of the Book in Britain*, 7 vols (Cambridge: Cambridge University Press, 1999–2019), iv. John Barnard and D. F. McKenzie (eds), *1557–1696* (2002), 636–44, and, for another national and linguistic context, see Bernard Weinberg, *Critical Prefaces of the French Renaissance* (Evanston, IL: Northwestern University Press, 1950), which collects prefaces and dedications to works in French from 1525 to 1611.
[21] James Boswell, *Life of Johnson*, ed. George Birkbeck Hill, rev. L. F. Powell, 6 vols (Oxford: Clarendon Press, 1934; repr. 1971), i. 425.
[22] Izaak Walton, *The Lives of John Donne, Sir Henry Wotton, Richard Hooker, George Herbert, and Robert Sanderson* (the collected edition of 1675) (London: Oxford University Press, 1927; repr. 1966), 8–89, 251–19; John Aubrey, *Brief Lives, with An Apparatus for the Lives of Our English Mathematical Writers*, ed. Kate Bennett, 2 vols (Oxford: Oxford University Press, 2015); Thomas Sprat, in *The Works of Mr Abraham Cowley* (London: printed for Henry Herringman, 1668), [no pagination]; Giovanni Boccaccio et al., *The Early Lives of Dante*, trans. Philip H. Wicksteed (London: Chatto and Windus, 1907); *The Three Crowns of Florence: Humanist Assessments of Dante, Petrarca and Boccaccio*, trans. and ed. David Thompson and Alan F. Nagel (New York: Harper & Row, 1972); William J. Kennedy, 'Petrarchan Poetics', in *CHLC III*, 119–26 (119–20).

metempsychosis and migration of the soul', rather, that is, than to the recoverable details of the personal life that is no more.[23] We will, as I say, examine life-writing further in Chapter 7—and the other forms I mention here in their respective chapters—but the point to emphasize here is that, while each of the forms of criticism I address does have a significant history prior to the mid-eighteenth century, and while periodizations are fated to be ragged, the eighteenth-century transformation of literary readerships and critical authority, the emergence of professional authors and critics, the slow development of the study of vernacular literatures in institutions of higher learning are, nevertheless, distinctive phenomena with which, crucially, we are still living, reading, and writing today. And, as at the middle of the eighteenth century, the adoption and adaptation of different forms for criticism continue to be vital ways in which these phenomena are negotiated.

There is, therefore, a history of significant continuity from the middle of the eighteenth century to today. A complementary way of understanding our current literary-critical situation would be to examine, not so much the continuities between the earlier period and our own, but rather the history that led up to what we might think of as the mid-eighteenth-century critical settlement. This is the approach of Michael Gavin's path-breaking *The Invention of English Criticism, 1650–1760*. Beginning from the recognition of the affinities between early and contemporary literary critics ('early literary critics stood at a crossroads similar to the one that confronts literary scholars today'), Gavin details how literary criticism as we know it came to be established against a background of expanding readership and authorship facilitated by dramatic changes in the dissemination and affordability of print, a situation comparable (albeit not 'too neatly') to 'the rise of digital media and online publishing'.[24] Operating on something like the celebrated Hegelian hypothesis that it is when a form of life has grown old that it may be properly understood, the suggestion is that the time is ripe for understanding the formation of literary criticism from which we may now be exiting. Furthermore, since the conditions prevailing at our exit are comparable with the conditions that prevailed at our entry into literary criticism as we know it, studying the past may give us some guidance concerning the future.

One thing that may happen to literary criticism in the context of its digital transformation, Gavin's book implies, is a return to the generic multiplicity that prevailed in literary criticism's early days. 'Early critical writing', Gavin remarks, 'appeared in a wide range of genres that often bear little resemblance to modern essays, so what counted as "discourse" was difficult to specify'.[25] The contrast here

---

[23] Johnson, *The Lives of the Most Eminent English Poets; with Critical Observations on their Works*, ed. Roger Lonsdale, 4 vols (Oxford: Oxford University Press, 2006); J. G. Herder, *Ueber Thomas Abbts Schriften*, first part ([Leipzig]: [Hartknoch], 1768), 8–9.
[24] Gavin, 1.
[25] Gavin, 2, 67, for exemplification in the work of John Dennis, Charles Gildon, and others.

is between a situation in which criticism appeared in a wide array of genres and a later situation (ours) in which the genres of criticism have been drastically reduced, in effect, to one—the essay. It is thus, for instance, that Jerome McGann can declare that the 'Enlightenment models' of the essay and treatise have 'dominated' literary criticism 'for almost two hundred years' or that other critics can cast the essay or article (this time spurning the treatise and other extended forms) as 'the natural unit for descriptive criticism ever since Dryden'—a writer, incidentally, whose essays were in large part actually prefaces and dialogues and prefaces-that-were-dialogues, and a 'natural' state of affairs that is in fact historical ('ever since Dryden').[26] Gavin dates the completion of the transformation in criticism and its accompanying generic reduction to 1760 at the latest. 'From an inchoate discourse that crossed the genres of conversational speech, stage performance, manuscript circulation, and print controversy,' he summarizes, 'criticism had become one of England's most prestigious forms of writing.'[27] Gavin does go on to allow that 'critical writing remained a social activity, whether printed or not, and conversation remained a legitimate, even central, genre of critical discourse' in the period after the middle of the eighteenth century.[28] In *Critical Forms*, I am interested in this ensuing period—not so much, that is, in the generic multiplicity out of which more stable and fewer critical forms emerged, but rather in the survival of different forms of criticism in the period of criticism's essayification and treatisification.

Such, then, are the historical parameters of this book. To summarize: something like the literary-critical situation in which we continue to find ourselves established itself in the mid-eighteenth century, but there has continued to be formal variety in critical practice despite the relative prominence of forms such as the essay and treatise in the subsequent centuries, and it is this formal variety that I wish to investigate.

Now, by way of considering a couple of examples, I want to focus in a bit more detail on what has been thought to be at stake in the form of criticism. In Oscar Wilde's 'The Critic as Artist; with Some Remarks Upon the Importance of Doing Nothing: A Dialogue', the figure of 'Gilbert'—whom we cannot perfectly identify with Wilde himself[29]—argues that criticism is itself an art and that, in particular, it 'works with materials, and puts them into a form that is at once new and delightful. What more can one say of poetry?' 'Indeed,' he goes on to declare,

[26] Jerome J. McGann, *The Point Is to Change It: Poetry and Criticism in the Continuing Present* (Tuscaloosa: University of Alabama Press, 2007), p. xii, and George Watson, *The Literary Critics: A Study of English Descriptive Criticism* (London: Penguin, 1986; first pub. 1973), 217.

[27] Gavin, 134.   [28] Gavin, 134.

[29] Lawrence Danson twice refers to Gilbert as 'Wilde's spokesman' (*Wilde's Intentions: The Artist in his Criticism* (Oxford: Clarendon Press, 1997; repr. 1998), 129, 140), though Henry Sussman remarks on Wilde's use in the dialogues of 'overtly fictional characters rather than a personal voice' ('Criticism as Art: Form in Oscar Wilde's Critical Writings', *Studies in Philology*, 70 (1973), 108–22 (110)).

warming to his theme, 'I would call criticism a creation within a creation'.[30] Gilbert's way of putting it—'I would call criticism a creation within a creation'— suggests that for him criticism is, so to speak, quintessentially creative. And criticism's creativity inheres, specifically, in its formal innovation. Gilbert goes so far as to assert that it is not art, which is allegedly repetitive and conventional, but rather criticism that creates new forms: 'For it is the critical faculty that invents fresh forms. The tendency of creation is to repeat itself' (p. 144). On the basis of this view of criticism, Gilbert goes on to argue that criticism, 'by transforming each art into literature, solves once for all the problem of Art's unity' (p. 161). Problem solved, Gilbert and his much less loquacious discussant, Ernest, break for a dinner of Chambertin and ortolans.

What is fundamental to Gilbert's enterprise is his insistence not merely on the creativity of criticism, but on the centrality of formal innovation to that creativity. Criticism takes materials and reforms them, thus making new forms in its turn. The problem that Gilbert thinks is solved by the re-forming of different materials in criticism—that is, the unity of art—was, of course, a major preoccupation for a number of nineteenth-century thinkers. For Gilbert, art is unified in literature because criticism, by virtue of the fact that it is creative, qualifies as literature. But the materials of criticism that Gilbert mentions are not themselves necessarily or primarily literary. Criticism can address itself to anything, and, while Gilbert depicts the critic transforming a good deal of literary dross—'Mr Lewis Morris's poems, M. Ohnet's novels, or the plays of Mr Henry Arthur Jones': 'Dullness is always an irresistible temptation to brilliancy' (p. 153) he remarks, surely thinking of Pope—the critic is as much at home in writing on paintings and sculpture as well. There are, of course, still more spheres, not directly cited by Gilbert, in which criticism could—and does—effect its re-formation of different materials, including gastronomy and oenology (those ortolans, that Chambertin), gardening, architecture, clothes, and sport, as well as the political, social, cultural, and linguistic concerns that criticism has historically involved.[31] 'Criticism remains the most miscellaneous, the most ill-defined of occupations,' remarks John Gross at the conclusion of his survey of English literary life from 1800 to the later twentieth century. 'At any given moment it is liable to start turning into something else: history or politics, psychology or ethics, autobiography or gossip.'[32] In Gross's view, criticism 'remains' miscellaneous and ill-defined: it was ever thus, despite

---

[30] Oscar Wilde, 'The Critic as Artist with Some Remarks on the Importance of Doing Nothing' (1891), in *The Complete Works of Oscar Wilde*, ed. Russell Jackson and Ian Small, 10 vols to date (Oxford, 2000–), iv: *Criticism: Historical Criticism, Intentions, The Soul of Man*, ed. Josephine M. Guy (2007), 123–206 (154). Further references to Wilde's works are to this volume of this edition and are given after quotations in the text.

[31] See, e.g., Terry Eagleton's insistence on the historical involvement of criticism with such concerns in *The Function of Criticism* (London: Verso, 2005; first pub. 1984), 124.

[32] John Gross, *The Rise and Fall of the Man of Letters: English Literary Life since 1800* (Harmondsworth: Penguin, 1973; first pub. 1969), 328.

the more than a tinge of regret with which Gross registers that fact. And, as Sianne Ngai has, with admirable candour, more recently declared: '[c]ertainly, there is little consensus even among criticism's most self-conscious practitioners about what criticism really is.'[33]

The attempt to define criticism, and, especially, the recognition usually following upon any such attempt that it is fraught with difficulty, will be usefully borne in mind throughout *Critical Forms*. As R. S. Crane argued in a seminal essay some years ago, a study of criticism that rejects an exclusive focus on 'the explicit content of what is said' (or, as Crane otherwise put it, on 'doctrines') will instead begin 'without prior commitments as to what criticism is or ought to be, its assumption being merely that criticism is any kind of argued writing about the literary arts that has seemed appropriate, at one time or another, to their natures'. Crane claimed, moreover, that merely doctrinal histories of criticism tend to produce 'an inadequate and external conception of the history of criticism', whereas studies of criticism with a more expansive focus on 'the three determinants of the internal character of any critical discourse'—namely, the particular critical problem that the critic wishes to resolve, the set of assumptions that enables the problem to be stated and an argument about its solution formulated, and 'some notion of the mode of argument best suited to my aims on this occasion'—are better calculated to 'throw light not simply on the dead opinions and pronouncements of dead critics but on the permanent and still living problems of analysis and reasoning which critics in all times and traditions have faced, and concerning which we ourselves might easily profit'.[34] I do not pretend that I adequately fulfil Crane's desiderata in this book, though I do adopt, at least, the focus on the modal and occasional reading of argument that he urges.

Insofar as literary criticism may be broadly identified, to continue with Crane's terms, as 'any kind of argued writing about the literary arts that has seemed appropriate, at one time or another, to their natures'—perhaps with the addition that the very question of the appropriateness of certain arguments to the nature of the literary arts and, indeed, of the nature of the literary arts themselves, have also been a part of literary criticism—then it is a kind of criticism distinct from the criticism of painting, say, or of gastronomy, because it shares its linguistic medium with its object. The re-formation of materials enacted by criticism (as described by Wilde in 'The Critic as Artist') in the case of the criticism of literature may then seem less stark, less dramatic—less creative—than is the case with respect to other, non-literary objects of criticism. Criticism of painting and sculpture, or of music, for instance, must be up to the task, at least according to Wilde's account, of somehow transmuting visual and sonic material into verbal form, whereas

[33] Sianne Ngai, *Our Aesthetic Categories: Zany, Cute, Interesting* (Cambridge, MA: Harvard University Press, 2016), 110.

[34] R. S. Crane, 'On Writing the History of Criticism in England 1650–1800', in *The Idea of the Humanities and Other Essays*, 2 vols (Chicago: University of Chicago Press, 1967), II, 157–75 (162–3, 174–5).

literature is already verbal. It is perhaps for this reason that literary criticism and its various forms so readily escape notice. But, though literary criticism shares its medium with literature, it need not simply share its form. While literary criticism does often imitate, adapt, and attune itself to the literary work it discusses—this is, for instance, one strand of the creative criticism I discussed above, insightfully documented by Mary Poovey[35]—it also differentiates itself from the literary work whose medium it shares. As Angela Leighton put it in the course of her discussion of the forms of Wilde's criticism, criticism 'need not guess intention or reproduce the formal properties of the work. Instead, it discovers in its own "form" the new meanings or relations of a work.'[36]

Wilde's Gilbert is hardly a modest character, and his project of rendering all art literary by means of criticism is, to say the least, ambitious. Comparable ambition for the genre of criticism, and comparable immodesty about his own genius for establishing it, is expressed by Walter Benjamin—ostensibly a quite different kind of critic from Wilde—when he sets out his hopes for his own literary-critical career in an important letter to his friend and mentor Gershom Scholem. Gilbert's vision of criticism rendering all art literary is predicated on the re-formation that critical writing performs on its materials. Benjamin's no less sweeping intervention aims to enthrone himself as the creator of criticism as a wholly new genre—if not *ex nihilo*, then raised on the rubble of the depreciated critical past. As Benjamin famously remarked in connection with Proust: 'It has rightly been said that all great works of literature establish a genre or dissolve one—they are, in other words, special cases.'[37] Unlike Gilbert, however, Benjamin's concern, like mine, is specifically with literary criticism. In the multilingual atmosphere in which much of Benjamin's writing subsists, Benjamin writes to Scholem in French and declares that he has set himself the goal of being regarded as the leading critic of German literature—a goal, although as yet unachieved, nevertheless within touching distance. Achievement of that goal, however, requires not only a final push from Benjamin, but the wholesale renovation of the genre of criticism itself: 'The difficulty,' Benjamin tells Scholem, 'is that, for more than fifty years, literary criticism in Germany has no longer been considered a serious genre. To make a reputation for oneself in criticism basically means: to create criticism as a genre. But serious progress has been made in this direction – by others, but above all by me.'[38] There are important historical, as well as the obvious personal, claims being made here. Benjamin dates the decline of the esteem in which the genre of

---

[35] See Poovey, e.g. 110, 127.

[36] Angela Leighton, *On Form: Poetry, Aestheticism, and the Legacy of a Word* (Oxford: Oxford University Press, 2007; repr. 2008), 11. I return to Leighton's account of form below.

[37] Walter Benjamin, 'On the Image of Proust' (1929; rev. 1934), trans. Harry Zohn, in *Walter Benjamin: Selected Writings*, ed. Michael W. Jennings, 4 vols (Cambridge, MA: Belknap Press, 1996–2003), II.i: *1927–1930* (1999; repr. 2005), 237–47 (237). Further references to Benjamin's works are given by volume and page number to this edition.

[38] 20 January 1930; *Walter Benjamin: Gesammelte Briefe*, ed. Christoph Gödde and Henri Lonitz, 6 vols (Frankfurt-am-Main: Suhrkamp, 1995–2000), iii: *1925–1930* (1997), 501–5 (502).

literary criticism has been held in Germany from around 1880 (a decline in esteem is not necessarily the same, it should be noted, as a decline in criticism itself). There may be several reasons why Benjamin sees 1880 as the date from which literary criticism has no longer been considered a 'serious genre' in Germany—it marks, perhaps, the final waning of the influence of the Romantic criticism that Benjamin had done so much to explicate, and also the rise, as elsewhere in Europe, of a more biographical, conversational mode of critical journalism, about which Benjamin was ambivalent—but whatever the reason, the loss of esteem for literary criticism requires a radical response. It is not simply, for Benjamin, that literary criticism can be saved by reinvigorating the old models; the lack of regard for criticism as a 'serious genre' necessitates nothing less than its wholesale creation as a genre.

The ambitious critical projects announced by both Wilde and Benjamin put a good deal of emphasis on the singularity of criticism's generic status. What I mean by this is that, in 'The Critic as Artist', the re-formation of the arts enacted by criticism is held to solve the problem of the unity of art: criticism is the unifying apex of all the arts. And while, for his part, Benjamin puts rather less emphasis on the unity of the genre of literary criticism than Wilde does, he nevertheless assumes that it is as one genre that literary criticism is to be renovated. But, if the reader has taken a glance at the contents page for this book, she or he will have noticed that more than one genre is addressed in it. The question of whether literary criticism is a genre in its own right or whether it takes various generic forms is a significant one, and answers to it have sometimes been quite decided. I discussed earlier the question in Eric Hayot's eulogy of academic writing: 'What if literary criticism were one of the major nonfictional genres of the twentieth century?' Others, however, have doubted whether literary criticism is a genre in this way at all. 'Criticism [...] is not a genre,' writes one commentator on the literary criticism of the period 1740 to 1830, 'nor even a name for a group of genres'; rather, 'criticism is an activity that can take place in almost any genre'.[39] 'Criticism', states another, '[...] was not just a particular genre of writing (the essay, say) but involved a wide repertoire of practices by writers, readers, and publishers as they navigated the shifting landscape of stage, manuscript, and print'.[40] The most forceful expression of the view that criticism is not a particular genre is advanced by Peter Uwe Hohendahl:

> The forms in which literary criticism has historically appeared—review, commentary, polemic, essay, dialogue, reportage, and finally also literary history—hardly permit its conceptualization as a single genre. Perhaps the history of the review could be written as the history of a particular genre—but not the history of criticism. The category 'criticism' is not even a generic term for a range of

---

[39] Jarvis, 25.   [40] Gavin, 117.

subgenres but rather—to introduce a preliminary definition—*public communication on literature* comprising both description and evaluation.[41]

The implication of Hohendahl's rejection of the generic history of criticism seems to be that such a history stands or falls on whether or not criticism can be identified as a single genre—and it cannot. But why must the viability of a consideration of literary criticism and its forms stand or fall on the singularity of that form? Criticism, as is widely acknowledged, has appeared in different genres—lots of them. The reasoning behind Hohendahl's refusal of the possibility of a study of criticism's genres is readily enough discerned—if literary criticism is not a single genre, then to claim that it may appear in many just multiplies the difficulties attendant on claiming that it is one—but the refusal to countenance at all a consideration of the forms that literary criticism has historically taken does not follow from this admission. An account of literary criticism and its forms need not be a merely taxonomic undertaking, involving the assignment of a finite number of fixed forms to fixed functions, but instead the elaboration of the formal resources and innovations of which literary criticism has historically availed itself in its fulfilment of different critical priorities and advancement of different critical claims.

Forms, indeed, are not fixed but constantly evolving, and individual works of criticism may conform to more than one form, or may, indeed, change form in the processes of composition and reception. One consequence of this latter fact is that some of the works discussed in this book have more than one generic affiliation, have shifted genre over time, or both. James Engell, now many years ago, insisted that coming to terms with the forms of criticism in their fluidity was indeed necessary to an adequate conception of the history of criticism:

> The range [of kinds of criticism] is fluid, and one might ask whether it makes sense to delineate types: the kinds in which criticism appears are varied enough in length, tone, and audience. But there is a reciprocal relation between form, length, style, and intended audience on one hand, and the critical discourse and its boundaries on the other. Until these issues are more widely delineated, the roles played by criticism in society, education, and culture will be confused and made targets for easy generalization.[42]

There is a fluid ranging to this passage itself, which suits its prospecting outlook. The rigorous-sounding delineation of 'types' envisaged at the beginning soon morphs into the rangier appeal for 'these issues' to be 'more widely delineated';

---

[41] Peter Uwe Hohendahl, 'Introduction', in Hohendahl (ed.), *A History of German Literary Criticism, 1730–1980* (Lincoln: University of Nebraska Press, 1988), 1–12 (2–3).

[42] James Engell, *Forming the Critical Mind: Dryden to Coleridge* (Cambridge, MA: Harvard University Press, 1989), 169–70.

the mutation of 'kinds' into 'types', then 'types' into 'form, length, style, and intended audience', and finally into 'issues' likewise evinces the liability of terminological distinctions to give way in this context. Which is by no means to claim that for Engell the project of delineating the kinds (or types) of criticism is anything less than vital to understanding criticism 'in society, education, and culture'—to understanding criticism, we might then say, at all. The purposes envisaged for criticism are (as Crane sought to emphasize) modal and occasional. Forms are suited to particular critical aims, certainly, but they also substantially shape criticism's range of possibilities as well.

It is high time to reflect a bit more directly on form itself. Indeed, recent years have witnessed a significant revival of interest in the category of form in literary studies. Angela Leighton's *On Form*, for example, traces the various, frequently conflicting senses of the term 'form' in a body of late-nineteenth- and twentieth-century writing. Leighton emphasizes that form is known by occasion and in its material instantiations, is braced against or held within its opposites, and 'is mobile, versatile'. The paradoxical nature of this situation has, of course, a certain analytical piquancy: 'It is as if there were something unfinished, even unformed, about form.'[43] These are conducive insights into form's dynamism, but Leighton's significance for my purposes lies above all in her consideration of the relation between form and criticism. Consideration of this relation is a thread running throughout Leighton's account and it receives perhaps its most sophisticated articulation in Leighton's appreciation of the theory of forms advanced by Henri Focillon in his *The Life of Forms in Art*. For Focillon, Leighton explains, form is not the mere container or outer garment of content, but rather, as Focillon puts it, 'the various interpretations of subject-matter that are so unstable and insecure.'[44] Form is always already an attempt to bring into view, to organize, to shape; 'the business of thinking, feeling, producing, interpreting, whether artist's or reader's' does not happen prior to form, but is the business of form itself. Form, therefore, is itself interpretative—or, to put this in a way still more suited to my purposes, is itself critical. The forms of criticism are not the outer husk of critical doctrines (to revert once again to Crane's terms) but are themselves critical in the first place. Leighton suggests that with 'luck and play' (a pairing she borrows from Theodor Adorno's 'The Essay as Form') 'it might be possible to catch at the notion of form, not in a philosophical nutshell, once and for all, but only along the way, in the part-gamble, part-guesswork which each singular, differently formed work inspires. The question of criticism's own form might thus become part of the story.'[45]

[43] Leighton, 2, 3. Compare the statement in Jonathan Kramnick and Anahid Nersessian, 'Form and Explanation', *CI* 43 (2017), 650–69, that 'form is an entity known by occasion, through encounters with its subsidiary phenomena' (p. 664).
[44] Leighton, 18; see Henri Focillon, *The Life of Forms in Art*, trans. by Charles B. Hogan and George Kubler (New York: Zone, 1989; repr. 1996), 35–6.
[45] Leighton, 29.

This is, of course, the whole story of *Critical Forms*, which does not principally tell a story about form, but one about criticism. Nevertheless, it is a story about criticism in which the determining activity of form is crucial. In Leighton's account, as also in many recent discussions of criticism that are attuned to its formal characteristics, it is the essay that is the emblematic form of criticism. The recent upsurge of interest in the essay as form is salutary, not least because it serves to furnish a consciousness, so to speak, to the deployment of a form that has come to dominate the humanities in general, both pedagogically and professionally. That said, for the reasons that I canvassed a little earlier when discussing the putative sway of the essay and treatise over literary-critical writing of the last three centuries, I do not add to recent appreciations of the essay in this book.[46] A basic aim of this book is to show that there are many critical forms, not all reducible without damage to the essay, however capaciously that form may itself be conceived. Different forms admit different features and pursue different critical desiderata, sometimes trying to achieve certainty, sometimes testing one subjectivity against others, sometimes exposing and probing their preconditions rather than downplaying or denying them.

I have tried in this Introduction to give a serviceable overview of why I think the study of literary criticism and form is worthwhile. I have also set out the historical parameters for *Critical Forms* and the rationale that informs those parameters. Most of the examples I discuss are Anglophone, though I do also comment on writings originally in French and German, and I draw on the work of scholars whose focus is criticism in other languages and from other cultures. In this respect, the claims I make concerning literary criticism in what follows pertain chiefly to criticism as it has been practised in Britain and the United States, and, although part of the aim of *Critical Forms* is to renew attention to and even the practice of different forms of literary-critical writing, the following discussion is by no means intended as dogmatic. I examine as critical forms in separate chapters prefaces, selections, reviews, lectures, dialogues, letters, and life-writing; though I do touch on them in the chapter on reviews, it may be felt that puffs and blurbs deserved a chapter of their own; and I have found space neither for marginal glosses and footnotes nor for editions, to name just two further forms of criticism. There is, that is to say, no pretence to exhaustiveness in what I have attempted.

I do not propose now to submit the reader to a chapter-by-chapter rundown. Suffice to say here that each of the following chapters serves to illustrate the ways in which literary criticism has availed itself of the resources of different forms, or, to put this another way, has been significantly shaped by the forms it has adopted.

---

[46] For recent discussions of the essay, see, e.g., Brian Dillon, *Essayism* (London: Fitzcarraldo Editions, 2017) and Thomas Karshan and Kathryn Murphy (eds), *On Essays: Montaigne to the Present* (Oxford: Oxford University Press, 2020).

I try to bring out the specifically sequential connections between chapters at the beginnings and endings of the chapters themselves. But I would also like to invoke here what Yohei Igarashi has pleasingly described as the '"subway system" view' of the relation between chapters in a monograph.[47] Each of the following chapters begins from a centre but heads out in different directions, and multiple different connections between the individual chapters are possible. Perhaps a word of explanation concerning the final chapter would, however, be helpful—hopefully without giving the game away or, indeed, putting too many potential readers off. As should by now be clear, this is a monograph about the variety of forms in which literary criticism has been practised. There is something of an anomaly lurking in that description, however, especially in the way 'monograph' (a near cousin of 'monologue', 'monomania', 'monolith', and the rest) glowers across at 'variety'. Surely the form of a treatment of the various forms in which literary criticism has been practised ought itself to be various. Of course, Samuel Johnson famously (and truly) said: 'You *may* abuse a tragedy, though you cannot write one. You may scold a carpenter who has made you a bad table, though you cannot make a table.'[48] While I do not take myself to be abusing or scolding anyone in *Critical Forms*, I nevertheless feel that a book such as this is not altogether licensed by Johnson's assertion, since, even if I cannot make a table, I do at least try to write literary criticism. The case for adopting a different form of writing at some point within a book such as this, however briefly, therefore seems to me persuasive. For what it is worth, the final chapter has amused, informed, annoyed, and mildly worried different readers of this book in typescript—including myself at different moments—in roughly equal measure.

I began this Introduction with an autobiographical reflection on an awkward moment in a job interview, which, I suggested, accounts for the genesis of the project of which this book is the result. That account of one of the minor misfortunes of my own life goes so far, but the inquiry conducted in this book has, of course, been shaped by much broader and, frankly, more significant intellectual, institutional, and historical forces and influences. Above all, I take the practice of literary criticism since the mid-eighteenth century that I study in this book to be more formally various than it is often assumed to be. Perhaps now is an especially good time to recover something of this history insofar as now is a time of acute change in literary criticism—the decline of the extended broadsheet review and also of the literary critical monograph, the rise of social media and other forms of online reviewing and commentary, and so on. I survey some of these tendencies in the final chapter; the wager of the book as a whole is that literary critics will gain from a renewed sense of the variety of the forms in which their work has been practised.

---

[47] Yohei Igarashi, *The Connected Condition: Romanticism and the Dream of Communication* (Stanford: Stanford University Press, 2020), 32.
[48] Boswell, i. 409.

1

Prefaces

Gathering together for publication the prefaces he had written over the years, Jorge Luis Borges reflected that the preface is an under-theorized genre, but, in view of its staleness and predictability, that, he claimed, hardly matters. 'As far as I know,' Borges disarmingly remarks,

> no one up to now has formulated a theory of the preface. This omission is no affliction, since everyone knows what the preface deals with. The preface is, in the sad majority of cases, replete with the oratory of the dinner table or with funerary panegyric, abounding with irresponsible hyperbole, which the incredulous reader accepts as conventions of the genre. There are other examples—let us recall the memorable study that Wordsworth prefixed to the second edition of his *Lyrical Ballads*—which formulate and present an aesthetic. The moving and laconic preface to the essays of Montaigne is not the least admirable page of his admirable book.[1]

The ease with which the (alleged) majority of prefaces succumb to the clichés of the dinner table or the graveside is all the more to be lamented in view of the achievement of the laudable examples of the preface that do exist. 'The preface, when the stars are propitious,' Borges goes on to declare, 'is not an inferior form of toast; it is a lateral kind of criticism.'[2]

Borges's formulation registers the ambivalence of the preface both as a form of criticism occupying a physical position in books actually adjacent to the text addressed and as a form somewhat aslant criticism itself. It is clearly, for Borges, a productive ambivalence, which is also intimated by the understanding of 'lateral' (available in Spanish as in English) as imaginative, creatively divergent, leftfield (as in the by-now somewhat hackneyed 'lateral thinking'). The incongruous pairing of the graveside and dinner table already suggests that there is something in

---

[1] Jorge LuisBorges, 'Prólogo de prólogos', in *Prólogos con un prólogo de prólogos* (Buenos Aires: Torres Agüero, 1975), 7–9 (8). For examples of attempts to formulate a theory of the preface, see: Jacques Derrida, *Dissemination*, trans. Barbara Johnson (London: Continuum, 2004; first pub. 1981), 1–66; Gérard Genette, *Paratexts: Thresholds of Interpretation*, trans. Jane E. Lewin (Cambridge: Cambridge University Press, 1997); Kevin Jackson, *Invisible Forms: A Guide to Literary Curiosities* (London: Picador, 1999), 104–23; and Uwe Wirth, 'Das Vorwort als performative, paratextuelle und parergonale Rahmung', in Jürgen Fohrmann (ed.), *Rhetorik: Figuration und Performanz* (Stuttgart: Metzler, 2004), 603–28.

[2] Borges, 'Prólogo', 8.

Critical Forms: Forms of Literary Criticism, 1750–2020. Ross Wilson, Oxford University Press. © Ross Wilson 2023.
DOI: 10.1093/oso/9780198881117.003.0002

the preface that does not quite conform to more professionalized modes of critical practice: neither graveside nor dinner table is the lectern or the journal. Half a century before Borges's 'Prólogo de prólogos', a certain 'B.D.' wrote in *The Athenæum* that 'the charm of a preface so often lies in the fact that it is here we meet the author in undress—in the cosy familiarity, as it were, of his study'.[3] The preface is above all a personal form, in which the writer thus appears at his 'most characteristic'.[4] Yet the author of what is itself a rather charming set of reflections on the preface situates the dressed-down writer neither by the graveside nor at the dinner table, as does Borges, nor 'in a comfortable parlor, greeting longing's desired object, sitting in an easy chair' or in a 'bower of jasmine', as does Søren Kierkegaard's 'Nicolaus Notabene'—but in his study.[5] Even if it is not itself work in a formal sense, the preface at least occurs in the room that takes its very name from a synonym for scholarship and learning. Indeed, 'B.D.' goes on to note that, '[a]s a further commendation of the preface, it may be recalled that this is often the only place in which a creative author will make his essays in criticism'— 'essays', that is, in the root sense of 'attempts', though the echo of the title of a work of criticism so routinely esteemed as Matthew Arnold's *Essays in Criticism* reinforces the impression that there is here more than a hint that the preface, its informality notwithstanding, is serious criticism. 'Even the professed critics', B.D. points out, 'often cast one of their gems in the form of a preface', offering Hazlitt's preface to his *Characters of Shakespeare's Plays* and Pater's to his *The Renaissance* as examples of such 'masterpieces in their own genre'.[6] Relaxation and work, creation and criticism, the layperson and the professional: despite the preface initially being associated with the former terms in these pairs, it comes to be situated on the threshold between them, belonging wholly to neither but retaining elements of both.

All of the imagined places of the preface (from graveside to bower of jasmine) are attempts metaphorically to characterize what Gérard Genette called 'the prefatorial *situation* of communication', and, indeed, they serve as useful reminders that the situation, the placement, of the preface in relation to the work it addresses is a crucial feature of the form.[7] The repeated suggestion that the place of the preface is not itself a workplace, but instead a sometimes ritualized, often domestic, convivial, and leisurely place, emphasizes the preface's marginality to the work it addresses, certainly, but more broadly to work in general as well. 'Books, too, begin like the week—with a day of rest in memory of their creation.

---

[3] 'B.D.', 'On Prefaces', *The Athenæum*, 31 October 1919, 1113–14.

[4] 'B.D.', 'On Prefaces', 1113.

[5] *Prefaces: Light Reading for People in Various Estates According to Time and Opportunity*, by Nicolaus Notabene, in [Søren Kierkegaard], *'Prefaces' and 'Writing Sampler'*, ed. and trans. Todd W. Nichol (Princeton: Princeton University Press, 1997), 1–67 (5–6).

[6] 'B.D.', 'On Prefaces', 1113–14.

[7] Genette, *Paratexts*, title of chapter 8, 161–95 (emphasis added). Further references are given after quotations in the text.

The preface is their Sunday.'[8] Thus Benjamin gave expression to a frequently encountered way of imagining the preface: 'May I be permitted to chat a little, by way of recreation, at the end of a somewhat toilsome and perhaps fruitless adventure?' asked Robert Browning at the beginning of the preface to his nothing if not arduous 1877 'transcription' of *The Agamemnon of Aeschylus*; 'a preface is more than an author can resist, for it is the reward of his labours,' claimed Robert Louis Stevenson in his first book, *An Inland Voyage*, a year later.[9] Benjamin's reflection on the preface belongs to a sequence of fragmentary notes he made in the late 1920s or very early 1930s that address, *inter alia*, the 'threshold before the realm of writing' (in the particular instance of the child's hand poised over the page), 'criticism in the form of stories', the sometimes antagonistic relation of writer to public, and the relation of thought to style ('Style is the rope that thought must vault over if it is to advance to the realm of writing'). In particular, Benjamin's reflection on the preface follows shortly after a note on the '[d]ialectics of happiness: a twofold will—the unprecedented, that which has never existed before, the pinnacle of bliss. Also: eternal repetition of the same situation, eternal restoration of the original, first happiness.'[10] Remarkably like happiness, the preface is dialectical, both memorializing the work of its creation by accounting for 'the original, first happiness' of its conception and initiating intention, while at the same time standing on the threshold, for the reader, of 'the unprecedented, that which has never existed before'. What the imagination of the preface as sabbath particularly invokes is the connection—or, rather, disconnection—of the preface with the labour of writing. The distinction between work and rest in Benjamin's aphorism is not, however, so absolute as it may at first appear. Though the preface marks the end of the author's work, it is the beginning of the reader's; Sunday may (in a secular temporal order) belong to the weekend, but it equally stands at the threshold of the working week. Recreation is one form of creation; leisure and work, the preface intimates, are never finally separable when it comes to reading.

Stevenson's and Browning's prefaces, along with those mentioned by 'B.D.' (Pater's, Hazlitt's) and by Borges (Wordsworth's, Montaigne's), are what Genette called autographic prefaces, the 'very common situation' in which the author of the preface is the author of the text it introduces (p. 178). To the autographic preface may be opposed the '*actorial* preface', in which a character from the prefaced text (if it has characters) is the 'alleged author' of the preface, and the '*allographic* preface', written by 'a wholly different (third) person' from the author of the text itself (p. 179). Genette furnishes a number of examples of each of these types

---

[8] Walter Benjamin, 'Notes (II)' (*c.*1928), trans. Rodney Livingstone, in *Walter Benjamin: Selected Writings*, ed. Michael W. Jennings, 4 vols (Cambridge, MA: Belknap Press, 1996–2003), II.i: *1927–1930* (1999; repr. 2005), 285–7.

[9] Robert Browning, *The Agamemnon of Aeschylus* (London: Smith, Elder, 1877), p. v; Robert Louis Stevenson, *An Inland Voyage* (London: Kegan Paul, 1878), p. v.

[10] Benjamin, 'Notes (II)', 287.

along with a useful tabulation of subcategories, including the 'fictive authorial' such as the preface of 'Laurence Templeton' to Walter Scott's *Ivanhoe* and the 'authentic allographic' (a fairly common type) such as Jean-Paul Sartre's preface to Nathalie Sarraute's *Portrait d'un inconnu* (p. 181). Yet, notwithstanding this useful differentiation of types, it is worth considering the degree to which the auto-graphic preface is uncomplicatedly autographic. As the examples mentioned above already suggest, the autographic author of a preface often seeks to establish a distinction from the author of the text, adopting a different posture in relation to the text and a different tone in which to address the reader, not least since the text itself may not contain any direct address to the reader at all. Introducing his *Thoughts and Things* with a text he titles 'Against Prefaces?', Leo Bersani, a psycho-analytic critic profoundly concerned with the self's legibility to itself and to others, suggests that the autographic preface is particularly fraught, since 'it is more difficult to get oneself right than to think we understand somebody else'. Introducing a text by 'somebody else' is easy, because the introducer has know-ledge only of that text, and not of the person who produced it; introducing a text I myself have written is hard, because not only do I know the text but I also know—that is, did experience and may now recollect—the complex process of the text's genesis, revision, and production, complicating factors that, so Bersani fears, can combine to make the autographic preface an impediment, rather than an aid, to reading. This is a problem for the autographic prefacer to overcome, but in doing so he or she may achieve a salutary estrangement of the self. 'I have become a lit-tle strange to myself', Bersani reports, 'and in so doing I have become my first critical reader', capable not merely of narrating the contents of the book (a mere pedagogical exercise and not really critical writing at all, according to Bersani) but also of elaborating a 'frictional rather than simply tautological relation' to it.

> Not being entirely sure of what I have done, I have become not the reader's friendly but superior facilitator, but rather an anticipatory (if obviously more privileged) version of all the first-time readers of this text. In already participat-ing in the critical distance of those readers, I have enacted a connectedness that, to make it all as starkly simple as possible, is the subject of this book.[11]

The enactment of the subject of the book in the preface that Bersani did manage to compose retains just a hint of tautology after all: the connectedness he has achieved suggests not distance from the book but continuity with its central focus. Yet the friction arises from the fact that the connectedness to which Bersani is laying claim is a connectedness with the reader, as yet unaware of what the book contains, a state in which Bersani comes to find himself ('Not being entirely

---

[11] Leo Bersani, *Thoughts and Things* (Chicago: University of Chicago Press, 2015), pp. vii–xv.

sure of what I have done'). Connection—to the text and to the reader—and distance—from the reader and from the text—are inextricable in the preface. The self of the autographic preface is never quite the author's self.

This may be one reason why not only the self-estrangement of autobiography, but the more radical self-fracturing of dialogue, have been a recourse of some notable prefaces. Peggy Kamuf's 'Introduction: Disavowals (A Foreword)' to her *Book of Addresses* (like Bersani's *Thoughts and Things*, a retrospective collection of essays produced many years into a critical career) titularly avoids the designation 'Preface' (there is an affinity here with Bersani's 'Against Prefaces?') and proceeds in dialogue form after the initiating putatively allographic question '—Aren't you going to write an introduction?' 'Perhaps I should write a foreword presenting these essays as though they were the work of someone else,' the apparent authorial voice muses, only for the 'Introduction' to conclude: 'But if you like, I'll write a foreword and confess everything in your place.—Oh, if only you could, that would indeed be wonderful.'[12]

Whoever 'you' is does not write such a 'foreword' to Kamuf's book, but, as noted above, the connection to and distance from the author's earlier self that the preface entails has indeed been negotiated through recourse to dialogue. Jean-Jacques Rousseau's dialogic preface to *La Nouvelle Héloïse*, having first been published separately, was appended to the second and subsequent editions (and to the English translation) of that work.[13] The 'Advertisement' explains that, although (so it is claimed) the dialogue had been intended as the work's preface all along, nevertheless Rousseau 'thought it proper to wait till the Book had taken its chance, before I discussed its inconveniences and advantages' (i, p. xiv). We shall meet again what we might call the second-edition preface (its English master is Charlotte Brontë); we shall also meet again, in the chapter on dialogues, the opening scenario of Rousseau's preface in which a participant in a dialogue vaunts his privileged access to a work in manuscript: 'There,' declares the 'Man of Letters' with whom Rousseau debates, 'take your Manuscript: I have read it quite through' (i, p. xv). The dialogue form allows Rousseau to anticipate sometimes sceptical reactions to what he has written, such as the charge that the letters making up the novel contain '[n]ot one strong delineation; not a single personage strikingly characterized' (p. xviii), with robust theoretical statement: 'true passion, full of itself, is rather diffusive than emphatical; it does not even think of persuasion, as it never supposes that its existence can be doubtful' (p. xix). But that form also allows Rousseau to estrange his authorship, to disperse the responsibility for his

---

[12] Peggy Kamuf, *Book of Addresses* (Stanford: Stanford University Press, 2005), 1, 21.

[13] References are to the near-contemporary English translation (*Eloisa; or, A Series of Original Letters Collected and Published by J. J. Rousseau*, 4th edn, 4 vols (Dublin: P. Wilson, 1766)) and are given after quotations in the text.

work, and to display potential objections to the final form of the work and the overcoming of those objections. The preface ends as follows:

N. […] If you print this work, tell the public what you have told me. Do more, write this conversation as a Preface: it contains all the information necessary for the reader.
R. You are in the right. It will do better than any thing I could say of my own accord. Though these kind of apologies seldom succeed.
N. True, where the author spares himself. But I have taken care to remove that objection here. Only I would advise you to transpose the parts. Pretend that I wanted to persuade you to publish, and that you objected. This will be more modest, and will have a better effect.
R. Would that be consistent with the character for which you praised me a while ago?
N. It would not. I spoke with a design to try you. Leave things as they are. (pp. xxxviii–xxxix)

The conclusion of Rousseau's preface to *La Nouvelle Héloïse* flaunts the factitious-ness of its form. *N.*, who is the interlocutor of *R.*, the thinly disguised representa-tive of Rousseau himself, issues a concluding instruction—'write this conversation as a Preface'—that might just as easily have been the other way around ('write this Preface as a conversation'), but his admission, 'I spoke with a design to try you', is apt. *N.* tries *R.*, of course, but *N.* is also trying the preface's readers, testing their patience on the threshold of the work and trying out on them certain tenets assumed in it. The preface prepares not only for the work, but for the kind of work that it is (it is described as being 'on the subject of romances') and, as such, is an important contribution to the theory of romance that was emerging in the latter part of the eighteenth century. That way of putting it, and the fact that Rousseau's preface was (as I mentioned above) first published separately from *La Nouvelle Héloïse* itself, may suggest that the preface need not be bound to the text that it addresses. The distinctive formal characteristics of the preface thus come to look somewhat tenuous. If the preface can float free of the text it introduces, becoming a free-standing essay or a chapter in a larger collection, then its defining formal characteristics are only provisional and temporary. The classic example here is James's prefaces to the New York edition of his novels and tales, which James him-self envisaged collectively as a guide to the profession of writer, a vision that R. P. Blackmur realized when he collected the prefaces as *The Art of Fiction*. Also worthy of mention are G. K. Chesterton's series of introductions to the Everyman Library editions of Dickens's writings, collected as *Appreciations and Criticisms of the Works of Charles Dickens* shortly after the completion of the initial Everyman Dickens in 1911, and Lionel Trilling's posthumous *Prefaces to 'The Experience of*

Literature', which had its origin in the 'commentaries' Trilling wrote for a grand anthology of key texts from the Western literary tradition, *The Experience of Literature*.[14]

The situation of the collection of prefaces and hence of the preface's transformation into a chapter or essay is acknowledged blithely enough by Genette, who notes that 'a preface may become a chapter in a collection of prefaces' (p. 173). That formulation contains a revealing, if tacit, acknowledgement that the preface remains a preface even once it is no longer situated before anything: it may become a chapter not in a collection of essays, say, but 'in a collection *of prefaces*'. To be sure, while all the examples I just adduced (James, Chesterton, Trilling) display their origins in prefaces, there are many examples of critical works that silently incorporate what had been prefaces as chapters. Even in that case, however, Michael Gorra has wanted to argue that the strength of such chapters—for example, Edward Said's introduction to Kipling's *Kim*, incorporated in *Culture and Imperialism*—is due to their origination in the form of the preface.[15] Genette's idea of the 'collection of prefaces' has, in any case, been radicalized in the persistent fantasy of the preface without any book at all—a fantasy that suggests that the formal character of the preface is not simply reducible to its dependency on and proximity to the text it addresses, but rather is dependent upon a distinctive attitude or posture towards criticism itself. At the end of his preface to prefaces—which already hinted at the kind of infinite regress in which he delighted—Borges conceived of a plan for a 'more original and better' book—a book he makes clear that he is not going to write. This book

> would consist of a series of prefaces to books that don't exist. It would abound in exemplary citations from these possible works. There are arguments that lend themselves less to laborious writing than to flights of fancy or to indulgent dialogues, such arguments would be the impalpable substance of these pages that will not be written.[16]

Two different kinds of non-entities are envisaged here—the book of prefaces that he is not going to write and the books that do not exist that those unwritten prefaces would preface—and moving between them involves the kind of ontological

---

[14] For information on the Everyman Dickens, see Isabella M. Cooper and Margaret A. McVety, *Dictionary Catalogue of the First 505 Volumes of Everyman's Library* (London: Dent, 1911), 15–20, 65, 96 (the only one of Dickens's works in this series not introduced by Chesterton was *The Uncommercial Traveller* (London: Dent, 1909), which was introduced by Ernest Rhys). See also Lionel Trilling, *The Experience of Literature: A Reader with Commentaries* (Garden City, NY: Doubleday, 1967) and *Prefaces to 'The Experience of Literature'* (Oxford: Oxford University Press, 1981).

[15] Gorra, 'Introductions: A Preface', *Sewanee Review*, 116 (2008), 124–7 (126).

[16] Borges, 'Prólogo', 9.

quickstep Borges particularly enjoys.[17] Borges's prospected non-prefaces to non-books are, nevertheless, revealing about the character of the preface. The preface is the form that accommodates 'flights of fancy' and 'indulgent dialogues' and is thus hospitable to particular kinds of argument. That the preface leans against another text, as it were (even where that text does not exist), that it is provisional upon the reader's further, future reading, that it cannot, for that reason, maintain a claim to finality or definition, do not disqualify it from criticism, but instead suit it to criticism understood as advancing knowledge and argument hypothetically, radically and proximally subject to the infinite and unpredictable tests of readers.

Yet, having stated that the preface may legitimately have a future apart from the text it prefaces, Genette later remarks that 'the preface, in its very message, postulates that its reader is poised for an imminent reading of the text (or, in the case of a postface, has just concluded a reading), without which its preparatory or retrospective comments would be largely meaningless and, naturally, useless' (p. 194). It is true that many prefaces do explicitly assume the reader's imminent reading of the text. Victor Hugo opens his 'Preface to *Cromwell*', for example, with insouciant confidence: 'The drama that you are about to read has no claim to the public's attention or good will'—a claim that introduces a distinction between 'you' and the implicitly inattentive and ill-willed 'public';[18] Zadie Smith takes this gesture further in her retrospective introduction to Hanif Kureishi's *The Buddha of Suburbia*, confidingly recollecting that, when she first encountered the book at school (where it was passed furtively from hand to hand, rather than being set for study in an English class) '[w]ord got around that there was a useful, masturbatory section depicting an orgy, somewhere around page 205', adding '(you can go look it up now if you like; I'll wait)'.[19] Yet Genette's statement that a preface is 'largely meaningless and, naturally, useless' once it comes adrift from an imminent reading of the text it addresses drastically countermands his earlier contention that a preface may undergo a transmutation into 'a chapter in a collection of essays', in which situation the reader is poised not 'for an imminent reading of the text' but for an imminent reading of the other texts in the collection.

The apparent contradiction between Genette's characterizations of the preface—as potential chapter, on the one hand, and as being wholly dependent on an imminent reading of the text it addresses, on the other—can be partially resolved by allowing that, wherever it appears, the preface betrays the assumption, first,

---

[17] As in Jorge Luis Borges, 'Pierre Menard, Author of the Quixote', in *Collected Fictions*, trans. Andrew Hurley (Harmondsworth: Penguin, 1998), 88–95.

[18] 'Preface to *Cromwell*', in *The Essential Victor Hugo*, trans. E. H. and A. M. Blackmore (Oxford: Oxford University Press, 2004), 16–53 (16).

[19] Zadie Smith, 'Introduction', in Hanif Kureishi, *The Buddha of Suburbia* (London: Faber and Faber, 2017; first pub. 1990), pp. v–xiii (v). The passage to which Smith is referring, incidentally, is on pp. 202–4 of the 2017 edition, though it is not quite as compelling as she suggests.

that it comes prior to a reading of the text it addresses and, second, that that reading is not a distant prospect or even one destined to remain unrealized. It is these features—the distinctive provisionality and particular temporality of the preface—rather than, say, its length that formally distinguish the preface. Thus many book-length critical works, not themselves made up of individual prefaces, announce their prefatory status: C. S. Lewis's *A Preface to 'Paradise Lost'* (1942) is a signal instance here, as are the Preface Books published by Longman since 1971 and intended, in the somewhat breathless formulation of the inaugural editor of the series, Maurice Hussey, as '[a] series of scholarly and critical studies of major writers intended for those needing modern and authoritative guidance through the characteristic difficulties of their work to reach an intelligent understanding and enjoyment of it'.[20]

Book-length prefaces of the kind described by Hussey, as well as introductions to paperback reprints (mentioned, as we saw in my own Introduction, in Collini's brief evocation of different kinds of criticism), do, however, present something of a challenge to a conception of the preface that stresses its provisionality, its adjacency to the work of writing, and its occasionally diffident anticipation of the test of readership. Indeed, the description of 'scholarly and critical studies of major writers intended for those needing modern and authoritative guidance' suggests a rather different set of prefatory functions: its performance of a more avowedly pedagogical function, its furnishing of a reader with information and guidance in how to use it, for instance. Prefaces certainly often aspire to the status of 'studies' (a suggestive term, incidentally, in the history of literary criticism, to which I return briefly in Chapter 4), and this has certainly been seen as the preface's particular function.[21] But, even in such situations, the preface is shaped by its presumption that its reader is not yet the reader of the text it addresses, and thus that its role is one of initiation and apology—for the text that it addresses, certainly, but equally for itself. A commonly imagined ur-scene for criticism is one person asking another 'What do you think of it?' or 'Did you like it?' with respect to an already encountered artwork. We will need to consider further how such a scene plays out when we turn to dialogues in Chapter 5, but it should already be clear from attention to the preface that this is not the only way that criticism proceeds, above all because the preface's reader is presumed not to have encountered the artwork being addressed and thus to be incapable of having formed an answer

---

[20] Lois Potter, *A Preface to Milton* (London: Longman, 1971), front matter. Potter's book was followed by James Winny's *A Preface to Donne* (also 1971) and Allan Grant's *A Preface to Coleridge* (1972), with subsequent titles following regularly throughout the 1970s and beyond, each adopting, with relatively minor variations, a standard pattern. A brief characterization of Maurice Hussey, incidentally, is given by Patrick Harrison, 'Downing after the War', in Ian McKillop and Richard Storer (eds), *F. R. Leavis: Essays and Documents* (London: Continuum, 2005), 244–63 (249, 255).

[21] See, e.g., Claude Gaugain, 'Les Préfaces dans le roman policier', in Phillipe Forest (ed.), *L'Art de la préface* (Nantes: Defaut, 2006), 187–99 (189). Cf. Forest, 'Marginalité de la préface autoriale', in ibid. 11–23, on historical transformations in the tone of the preface.

to 'What do you think of it?'. Nor, however, is it the case, as we shall see, that the preface simply aims to pre-empt critical conversation, announcing 'Think this!'.

My discussion of the preface as critical form has so far ranged quite freely across a number of examples in order to draw out some of the preface's formal features. I turn in what remains of this chapter to somewhat closer investigation of a series of case studies of different kinds of prefaces. The purposes of the preface are thus various, certainly, and each of the prefaces I examine exploits the prefatory situation to different ends, yet in each of the instances the question of criticism as initiating, rather than subject to prior initiation in the past experience of an artwork, and as anticipation, rather than reaction, is central.

*

In the elaboration of his fantasy of a collection of prefaces to unwritten books, Borges remarked that those prefaces would quote extensively from the non-existent books they would preface. We need not allow ourselves to be sucked again into Borges's vortex of textual non-entities here, other than to note that quotation is a favoured tactic of many prefacers. The prefacer may thus deploy the established critical procedure of quotation-plus-commentary, but may also thus give a sample of what is to come for the reader. In his preface to *The Plays of William Shakespeare* of 1765, however, Samuel Johnson derides the idea that quotation could ever give an accurate sense of Shakespeare's plays. Remarking that a character in the hands of other poets is 'too often an individual', whereas in Shakespeare's hands a character 'is commonly a species'—a significant contrast between the excessive yet fragmented ('too often') and the amply sufficient and evenly continuous ('commonly')—Johnson expands on this insight as follows:

> It is from this wide extension of design that so much instruction is derived. It is this which fills the plays of Shakespeare with practical axioms and domestic wisdom. It was said of Euripides that every verse was a precept; and it may be said of Shakespeare that from his works may be collected a system of civil and economical prudence. Yet his real power is not shown in the splendour of particular passages, but by the progress of his fable, and the tenor of his dialogue; and he that tries to recommend him by select quotations will succeed like the pedant in Hierocles, who, when he offered his house to sale, carried a brick in his pocket as a specimen.[22]

Johnson's aim here is to encourage a progressive, rather than piecemeal, reading of Shakespeare, not least by being distinctly lukewarm about what 'may be collected' from Shakespeare's works, while, paradoxically enough, introducing his

[22] *The Yale Edition of the Works of Samuel Johnson*, ed. Robert DeMaria, Jr et al., 23 vols (New Haven: Yale University Press, 1958–2019), vii: *Johnson on Shakespeare*, ed. Arthur Sherbo (1968), 62. Further references are given after quotations in the text.

own collection of them. Granted, Johnson does go on to acknowledge that, in the reading of Shakespeare, compulsion occasionally degrades into mere endurance 'in him of what we should in another loath or despise' (p. 91), and his emphasis on reading Shakespeare through is strikingly at odds with what we learn from Boswell was Johnson's own 'cursory mode of reading'.[23]

Johnson's own gift for the sentence—both grammatical and, as it were, judicial—makes him pre-eminently quotable, and his strictures on the practice of quoting from Shakespeare themselves rely on references to a body of apothegmatic wisdom that stops just short of direct quotation: though Johnson himself gives no source for the apparently commonplace view of Euripides, the joke about the pedant trying to sell his house is from Hierocles.[24] The deployment of the joke from Hierocles implicitly reiterates Johnson's basic aim in the preface—namely, the recommendation of Shakespeare, best undertaken without bricks in your pocket. Yet the ready recourse to the canonical estimation of Euripides, as well as the somewhat more recondite reference to Hierocles, show, despite his disavowals, that Johnson's pockets are bulging. Nevertheless, both playwright, as Johnson explicitly and repeatedly claims, and prefacer, as an examination of Johnson's own prefatory writing itself shows, are chiefly invested in the 'progress' and 'tenor' of what they write. Repeating slightly later his view that Shakespeare pleases not so much in particulars, but rather in the onward thrust of his drama, Johnson states, for example, that 'others please us by particular speeches, but he always makes us anxious for the event, and has perhaps excelled all but Homer in securing the first purpose of a writer, by exciting restless and unquenchable curiosity, and compelling him that reads his work to read it through' (p. 83). Exciting restlessness and curiosity is a necessary though delicate task of the preface-writer too: necessary, because readers should end the preface sufficiently excited and curious about the text on the threshold of which they have been made to wait; but delicate as well, because too much excitement might lead them to give over the preface without finishing it. It is for this reason that Johnson most concertedly mimics the onward thrust he praises in Shakespeare's drama towards the *end* of his preface, both because to do so earlier risks overheating the eager reader and because, nearing the end of the reading of one text, the reader may need propulsion into the reading of another. As readers draw to the close of Johnson's paratext (the preface), they encounter Johnson's explicit advice on how they should approach another

---

[23] Boswell, ii. 226, though compare Boswell's judgement that 'I always thought he did himself injustice in his account of what he had read' (i. 70).

[24] Sherbo (vii. 62 n. 2) gives the source of the statement about Euripides as Cicero, *Familiar Letters*, XVI.8: 'I look upon every verse that he wrote as an affidavit ["testimonia"]' (letter to Tiro, January 49?, in *Letters to Friends*, ed. and trans. D. R. Shackleton Bailey, 3 vols (Cambridge, MA: Harvard University Press, 2001), i. 88–9); and he gives the source for Hierocles as *Hieroclis Philosophi Alexandrini Commentarius in Aurea Carmina*, ed. Peter Needham (Cambridge, 1709), 462, where the joke, one of many about the pedant ('scholasticus'), does indeed appear.

paratext, the marginal notes to the plays themselves. Johnson precisely marginalizes those notes by re-emphasizing the importance of continuance in reading:

> Let him that is yet unacquainted with the powers of Shakespeare, and who desires to feel the highest pleasure that the drama can give, read every play from the first scene to the last, with utter negligence of all his commentators. When his fancy is on the wing, let it not stoop at correction or explanation. When his attention is strongly engaged, let it disdain alike to turn aside to the name of Theobald and of Pope. Let him read on through brightness and obscurity, through integrity and corruption; let him preserve his comprehension of the dialogue and his interest in the fable. And when the pleasures of novelty have ceased, let him attempt exactness, and read the commentators.   (p. 111)

The preface does not itself fall into the category of temporarily ignorable commentary to which the notes, according to Johnson, do belong. While, like the notes, the preface guides readers, unlike the notes, it does not interfere with their reading. The anaphoric crescendo of the interlocking and repeated words 'when' and 'let' acts to propel the reader into the works of Shakespeare themselves—works whose compulsive, onward thrust Johnson, as we have seen, praises in the preface. Johnson advocates here a sequential reading of the plays, beginning at the beginning and ending at the end (at which point, a sideways glance to the commentators such as Theobold and Pope may be in order). Both this concluding crescendo and the clearly sequential conduct of the reading envisaged by Johnson position the preface as an enabling impetus to the reading of Shakespeare itself. Remarking that it is not gratifying for the reader to find his opinion anticipated, Johnson nevertheless also states that '[s]ome initiation is however necessary' (p. 104). He is referring to the commentaries, but the remark is still more applicable to the preface itself, which, rather than anticipating the reader's judgement in the sense of assuming it beforehand, instead seeks to initiate her or him into a practice of which she or he will then be independently capable. 'The mind is refrigerated by interruption' (p. 111), but it is warmed by initiation.

*

Granted that one function of the preface is to anticipate and thus avert criticism, it may seem odd that Shakespeare required such protection—even in 1765, when neoclassical strictures still retained some currency. Johnson's assessment of Shakespeare was far from the effusive encomia bestowed upon him by 'his panegyrists',[25] though Johnson did still feel the need to ward off certain kinds of objection to Shakespeare—the charge that he is irregular when measured against

[25] Boswell, i. 497.

the dramatic unities being the chief among such neoclassically informed objec-tions, for instance (p. 79). It has also been claimed of prefaces that prefaced works 'tend to be those that history has placed at a remote distance without dealing them deathblows'.[26] That characterization was, admittedly, advanced with respect to a specific, mid-twentieth-century corpus of introductions to 'cheap editions of classic texts', and too-easy analogies between paperbacks produced for a burgeon-ing educational market in the middle of the twentieth century and editions of a major literary figure in the process of being established as England's national poet produced for an emerging middle-class readership in the second half of the eight-eenth ought probably to be avoided. What is more, if any writer seems safe from a deathblow, or even from a prevailing assumption of historical remoteness, either in 1765 or now, it is Shakespeare. Shakespeare is historically remote in 1765 but remains at the same time something that the common reader continues to pick up—and, given the growth in availability of editions around this time, does so all the more.

Johnson's preface, then, adopts a particular approach to the introduction of established works. When a preface instead introduces work that is new and unfamiliar—especially work that seeks to emphasize its novelty and unfamiliarity—then its role in forestalling anticipated criticisms is especially pertinent. Forestalling criticisms is not so much the obverse of criticism, though it is often cast that way, but is rather a form of criticism itself, since for criticisms to be anticipated the range of possible responses to a text need to be imagined and formulated—and for those anticipated criticisms to be *forestalled* they must themselves be criti-cized. This is certainly the case with Wordsworth's prefatory writings in the first and, especially, subsequent editions of *Lyrical Ballads*. Above all, Wordsworth stresses the importance of steady and first-hand acquaintance with writing—including, implicitly, his own—as a necessary condition for just judgement. In the advertisement to the first edition of *Lyrical Ballads*, the predecessor to the pref-aces of the later editions, for example, Wordsworth takes the opportunity to remind his reader that, short as this introductory text may be, long is the way and hard that leads to competence in reading: '[a]n accurate taste in poetry, and in all the other arts, Sir Joshua Reynolds has observed, is an acquired talent, which can only be produced by severe thought, and a long continued intercourse with the best models of composition.'[27] The rigour—or rather, to borrow Wordsworth's own term, severity—of this admonition, which in citing Reynolds displays its own intercourse with a notable model of composition, is softened by the explan-ation that follows:

[26] Gorra, 125–6.
[27] In *The Prose Works of William Wordsworth*, ed. W. J. B. Owen and Jane Worthington Smyser, 3 vols (Oxford: Oxford University Press, 1974), i., 116–17 (116). Further references are given after quotations in the text.

This is mentioned not with so ridiculous a purpose as to prevent the most inexperienced reader from judging for himself; but merely to temper the rashness of decision, and to suggest that if poetry be a subject on which much time has not been bestowed, the judgment may be erroneous, and that in many cases it necessarily will be so.   (pp. 116–17)

Like Johnson, Wordsworth does not want to appear to be telling his reader what to think, while at the same time he wishes to imply that some form of initiation for, at least, the 'inexperienced reader' is nevertheless necessary. A number of questions may at this point arise for any reader of the preface. Am I the 'inexperienced reader' or one of the 'many cases' whose judgement of poetry 'may be erroneous'? No, that is someone else, surely, since I *have* bestowed much time on poetry. So, the main beneficiary of Wordsworth's preface seems not, as he presents the case, to be any of its likely readers. Wordsworth's formulation here gives expression to, on the one hand, anxiety about an expanding group of inexperienced readers who might be carried away by sickly German tragedies and, on the other, exhilaration at the thought that such a readership might, at least potentially, not have been distorted by the mere fashion for poetic diction—a combination of anxiety and exhilaration that of course animated many Romantic considerations of what proper reading might consist in. Central to Wordsworth's performance of this balancing act between allowing autonomy to the reader's judgement and nevertheless schooling it is his attempt to forestall, not so much anticipated criticisms, in fact, but rather the profession of criticism as such: 'It is the honourable characteristic of Poetry that its materials are to be found in every subject which can interest the human mind. The evidence of this fact is to be sought, not in the writings of Critics, but in those of Poets themselves' (p. 116). The generality of this appeal to the writings of 'Poets themselves' and the brevity of the advertisement notwithstanding, Wordsworth manages, in a sequence of steps, to construct an ideal of the reader he envisages. Beginning with '[r]eaders accustomed to the gaudiness and inane phraseology of many modern writers', whom Wordsworth urges to 'ask themselves if [this book] contains a natural delineation of human passions, human characters, and human incidents', he goes on first to invoke '[r]eaders of superior judgment', then the reader 'more conversant [...] with our elder writers, and with those in modern times who have been the most successful in painting manners and passions', until, finally, near the close of the advertisement, there is the very particular situation of the reader who 'will soon discover' that 'the poem of the Thorn [...] is not supposed to be spoken in the author's own person' (p. 116). While the opening claim of the advertisement appeals to a reading of poetry unmediated by criticism, and its conclusion confidently predicts that the reader will 'soon' grasp who the speaker of 'The Thorn' is, Wordsworth nevertheless enjoins the reader to reflect, to cultivate 'superior judgment', and to engage in broad reading. And this he does while implicitly denying that he is engaged in criticism. The task of the advertisement is both to forestall the kinds of specific criticisms to be found in 'the writings of Critics' (such as strictures on the identity of the speaker of 'The Thorn' predicated on a misapprehension, for instance) and actively to prepare the reader for reading the poems. The advertisement is precisely ambivalent about criticism as such, shielding the *Lyrical Ballads* from it at the same time as schooling its readers in Wordsworth's own version of it.

This precise ambivalence towards criticism is a key affordance of the prefatorial situation—of, that is, the preface as form. The idealized situation of critical judgement is one in which an encounter with the object to be judged (in the case of poetry, an encounter that takes place through reading) comes first, prior to the formation of judgement, its comparison with the judgement of others, and discussion concerning it. The real situation of critical judgement is rarely like that, however. Instead of being initiated by the reading of a work (as in the ideal situation), it is often criticism that serves as an initiation into reading itself. To recognize this is not simply to disavow the ideal that criticism is secondary to the criticized work but to give an account of where the ambivalence towards criticism registered in the preface as form comes from.

It is such an ambivalence that is even more discernible on the larger canvass of the preface to the second edition of *Lyrical Ballads* in 1800. Wordsworth there famously recalls how '[s]everal of my Friends [...] have advised me to prefix a systematic defence of the theory, upon which the poems were written' (p. 120). It is worth noting, first, this acknowledgement of the role of his 'Friends' in the genesis of the preface. Prefaces frequently serve as a portal through which other voices are invited—or simply interpolated—into the emergent critical discourse concerning a text. With characteristic zest, Hugo, for example, puts in quotation marks a scurrilous version of the opposition to the case he is making in his 'Preface to *Cromwell*' ('"Aha!" cry the people who have "seen this coming" for some time, "now we've got you!"'); Henry James gives over a significant proportion of the preface to *The Portrait of a Lady* to a long quotation from Ivan Turgenev; and I discussed above instances of the preface in dialogue form (Rousseau, Kamuf).[28] Wordsworth, however, appears explicitly to reject the advice of the friends he mentions, giving two reasons for doing so: first, because he wishes to avoid giving the impression 'of having been principally influenced by the selfish and foolish hope of reasoning him [viz., the reader] into an approbation of these particular Poems', and, second, because in any case to do what the friends recommend would require 'a space wholly disproportionate to the nature of a preface' (p. 120). While sufficiently persuaded by the need to 'prefix' some kind of statement to his poems, it is significant that Wordsworth at the same time

---

[28] See Hugo, 24. James's preface is in *Literary Criticism: French Writers, Other European Writers, the Prefaces to the New York Edition*, ed. Leon Edel (New York: Library of America, 1984), 1072–3. Further references to this edition (abbreviated as *Prefaces*) are given after quotations in the text.

implicitly reproaches his friends for having suggested an inappropriate form—the preface—for the kind of critical undertaking they held to be the necessary accompaniment to his poetic experiments. In addition to outright refusal, a choice of different responses to the friends' request was certainly open to Wordsworth: to write the systematic defence they recommended, but not to do so in the form they suggested; or, to write in the form they suggested (one version of which Wordsworth had already adopted in the advertisement), but not to use it for the purpose they envisaged. 'I have therefore altogether declined to enter regularly upon this defence,' however, is his response (p. 120). The mention of the origin of the preface in his friends' suggestion again allows Wordsworth to intimate to the reader that she or he has got off lightly, thus recruiting the reader to his resistance against the need for a more thoroughgoing theoretical statement. Wordsworth's position is thus presented as distinctive and as tacitly occupying a particular critical stance that is all his own.

But is it that Wordsworth 'altogether' declines to do what his friends advised? And does his qualification that he will not enter upon the defence of his theory of poetry 'regularly' leave open the possibility that he will do so *irregularly*? First of all, the switch from advertisement to preface might be taken to suggest that, despite its critical importance, 'advertisement' was a suitable title for a short, blandly informative text, whereas, despite Wordsworth's sense that a preface could not accommodate the kind of full-scale critical defence that his friends advised, 'preface' suited a fuller, more freely discursive text. (In any case, it is worth noting that Wordsworth quite considerably augmented the preface in 1802 but did not seem to feel the need to change the title a second time.)[29] Second, Wordsworth remains sensible, he declares, 'that there would be some impropriety in abruptly obtruding upon the Public, without a few words of introduction, Poems so materially different from those, upon which general approbation is at present bestowed' (p. 120). Wordsworth's concern about the impropriety of obtruding unintroduced on the public is one version of a concern to maintain the rituals and standards of personal interaction among polite society and, as such, gives a telling indication of his imagined readership. But, aside from flattering the public (who bestow approbation) and abasing himself (for having produced poems that, without introduction, would be felt to be obtruding), there is something disingenuous about this rationale for prefixing a text to his poems after all. Even if we allow for the fact that the second edition of the *Lyrical Ballads* contains a large number of new poems not included in the first, it is not altogether the case that Wordsworth would, without the preface, be 'abruptly obtruding' these poems upon the public, since the public has already had two years to read most of them.

---

[29] For commentary on Wordsworth's additions to the Preface to *Lyrical Ballads* in 1802, see Theresa M. Kelley, *Wordsworth's Revisionary Aesthetics* (Cambridge: Cambridge University Press, 1988), 196–7.

Wordsworth does in fact offer in the preface a good many of the 'opinions' and 'arguments' he says he will *not* be advancing there. This often involves provision of the kind of account he says at the beginning he is not going to provide. Having said, for example, that 'to treat the subject with the clearness and coherence, of which I believe it susceptible, it would be necessary to give a full account of the present state of the public taste in this country, and to determine how far this is healthy or depraved', and that, moreover, he will not give such an account, he nevertheless gives at least a condensed version slightly later when he bemoans the effect on 'the discriminating powers of the mind' of the 'great national events which are daily taking place, and the encreasing accumulation of men in cities, where the uniformity of their occupations produces a craving for extraordinary incident which the rapid communication of intelligence hourly gratifies' (p. 128). As with his concern to maintain seemly habits of social intercourse, this complaint about national events, urbanization, the division of labour, the lust for incident, and their deleterious effects on the powers of the mind gives a good clue to Wordsworth's ideal readership. In recognizing the contemporary phenomena he outlines and the dangers that they pose, it is not *his* readers whose minds are affected by them, even as they are being persuaded that those dangers motivate the poems that Wordsworth has written. Wordsworth disavows the adumbration of the systematic defence to which he has been urged, but then does go on to offer at least partial aspects of it anyway. In the case of his opinions regarding the effect on the mind of the social, economic, and geopolitical context, his account is quite explicit.

Wordsworth's partial imitation of the polite formalities of social interaction is significant, then, in at least two respects. The argument of the preface, as is routinely acknowledged, seeks to overturn merely established habits of poetic composition (such as the observance of poetic diction) in favour of a more natural and immediate poetry. However, this is not to argue for the simple disintegration of social forms (such as polite introduction) to which the chaotic, enervating national circumstances are in any case tending. It is this balance that the preface seeks to strike and aims to do so through the exploitation of its formal situation.

The preface has frequent recourse to hypothetical constructions that register the tension between the statement of opinion and argument, on the one hand, and the disavowal of criticism, on the other. By means of hypotheses, Wordsworth's opinions and arguments are rendered explicitly contingent upon his readers, and, as already remarked, a great deal of what would otherwise belong to precisely the kind of systematic defence his friends envisaged does, in fact, find its way into the preface. Thus, for example, the steps leading up to Wordsworth's refusal of the distinction between 'the language of a large portion of every good poem' and 'the language of prose when prose is well written' are cast in hypothetical form:

> If in a Poem there should be found a series of lines, or even a single line, in
> which the language, though naturally arranged and according to the strict laws
> of metre, does not differ from that of prose, there is a numerous class of critics
> who, when they stumble upon these prosaisms as they call them, imagine that
> they have made a notable discovery, and exult over the Poet as over a man ignor-
> ant of his own profession. Now these men would establish a canon of criticism
> which the Reader will conclude he must utterly reject if he wishes to be pleased
> with these volumes.   (p. 132)

Critics who 'stumble' in the reading of a poem according with 'the strict laws of
metre' can hardly be accounted competent, let alone expert. This excoriation of
incompetent critics is, however, set in a passage couched hypothetically. The first
of its 'if' clauses introduces the description of what happens when critics discover
an alleged prosaism. The implication that critics are subject to a merely mechanical reflex—when they encounter a line of a particular character they respond in
an entirely predictable manner—has the effect of rendering the ascription of
imagination to them parodic. The second 'if' clause—the reader must reject the
critics' proscriptions 'if he wishes to be pleased with these volumes'—seems at
first to be just as mechanical, but its appeal to the reader's potential and hence
unpredictable response has quite the opposite implication. An independence of
response is ascribed to readers, which the dogmatism of critics would render
impossible for *them*. And it is notable that, as the chiastic 'let'/'when' structure of
Johnson's appeal for the freedom of the reader's imagination mounts to a crescendo towards the end of his preface to Shakespeare, so Wordsworth's interchange
of divergent hypothetical constructions likewise reaches its zenith near the close
of his preface to *Lyrical Ballads*, where Wordsworth, moreover, expresses his
awareness of the fact that his readers are about to put his claims to the test.

*

Johnson's and Wordsworth's gathering rhetorical momentums towards the ends
of their prefaces seek to conduct the reader into the prefaced works themselves,
not only because prefaces cannot but chart a trajectory towards the confirmation or
rejection of their hypotheses in the reading of the work being introduced, but also
because of the fear that prefaces might have the effect of putting the potential reader
off. Prefaces may school their readers out of, as well as into, the texts they introduce.

It is important to recall that neither Johnson nor, indeed, Wordsworth was
introducing works wholly unavailable to the reading public previously. The situation of Wordsworth's preface is quite particular: it introduces the second edition
of a previously published text. The situation of the second-edition preface allows
not only for the forestalling of criticism, of course, but for response to actual criticisms. Although not quite all of her prefaces were for second editions, there is a
distinctly reactive (a term I do not intend pejoratively) and belated cast to

Charlotte Brontë's writing in this form. For example, the draft preface to *The Professor* (probably written in late 1850, when Brontë was composing prefaces and notices to reissues of her sisters' works, and appearing with the posthumous publication of the novel in 1857) begins by adverting to the belatedness of that novel—a belatedness that, in fact, is twofold, since *The Professor* was written before those works of Brontë's that were in the event published before it and thus might, by rights, have appeared first. *The Professor* cannot, it transpires, even lay claim to primogeniture in this way, however: 'This little book was written before either "Jane Eyre" or "Shirley" and yet no indulgence can be solicited for it on the plea of a first attempt. A first attempt it certainly was not as the pen which wrote it had been previously worn down a good deal in a practice of some years.'[30] Brontë describes her intention that the hero of her book 'should work his way through life as I had seen real living men work theirs' and that this determination had led to surprising difficulties securing publication for *The Professor*: 'indeed until an author has tried to dispose of a M.S. of this kind he can never know what stores of romance and sensibility lie hidden in breasts he would not have suspected of casketing such treasures.' One would never suspect as much, because men of business (publishers included), owing to the 'calm and sober surface' they display to the world, are 'usually thought to prefer the real'. The preface concludes with the following inference from the fact of the book's difficult journey into print:

> Such being the case—the reader will comprehend that to have reached him in the form of a printed book—this brief narrative must have gone through some struggles—which indeed it has—and after all its worst struggle and strongest ordeal is yet to come—but it takes comfort—subdues fear—leans on the staff of a moderate expectation—and mutters under its breath—while lifting its eye to that of the Public,
> 'He that is low need fear no fall.'   (p. 4)

It is a brilliant ending to what remains a draft preface, aligning the fate of the manuscript (now novel) with the fate of the figure (now 'hero') at its centre. While acknowledging that the book must yet undergo its severest trial at the hands of the reader, the reminder of the trials that the book has already gone through serves as an intimation that it is capable of withstanding the reader's judgement. This combination of submission to the rigours of the reader's judgement with insistence on the book's ability to withstand them is evident in the subtle ingenuity of the preface's final sentence and the gloss it implies of its proverbial conclusion.

---

[30] *The Clarendon Edition of the Novels of the Brontës: Charlotte Brontë: 'The Professor'*, ed. Margaret Smith and Herbert Rosengarten (Oxford: Clarendon Press, 1987), 3. Further references to the Brontës' works will be to the relevant volume of the Clarendon edition (unless otherwise stated in the notes) and given after quotations in the text.

'He that is low need fear no fall': the preface mutters 'under' its breath, while 'lifting' its gaze; the book will stand, come what may, and the implication of the preface may be caught only by those with especially acute hearing capable of catching what it 'mutters' while it levels its gaze with them.[31]

In her preface to the second edition of *Jane Eyre*, having thanked in turn 'the Public, for the indulgent ear it has inclined to a plain tale with few pretensions', 'the Press, for the fair field its honest suffrage has opened to an obscure aspirant', and 'my Publishers, for the aid their tact their energy, their practical sense, and frank liberality have afforded an unknown and unrecommended Author', Brontë turns her attention

> to another class; a small one, so far as I know, but not, therefore, to be over-looked. I mean the timorous or carping few who doubt the tendency of such books as 'Jane Eyre': in whose eyes whatever is unusual is wrong; whose ears detect in each protest against bigotry—that parent of crime—an insult to piety, that regent of God on earth. I would suggest to such doubters certain obvious distinctions; I would remind them of certain simple truths.   (p. xxviii)

It is a resounding declamation, the prophetic character of which sets the tone for the rest of the preface. The simple truths are emphatically expressed in a series of aphorisms that suggest that Brontë would have made a good preacher in the revivalist mode that she would frequently have encountered: 'Conventionality is not morality. Self-righteousness is not religion. To attack the first is not to assail the last. To pluck the mask from the face of the Pharisee, is not to lift an impious hand to the Crown of Thorns' (p. xxix). Conventional, self-righteous, Pharisaical: the critics of the first edition of *Jane Eyre* (and Brontë is surely also thinking of the attacks by which the works of her sisters were also assailed) do not get off lightly. Brontë, perhaps partly deploying a more worldly tactic, also took the opportunity of the preface to the second edition to dedicate *Jane Eyre* to Thackeray, an already celebrated writer, whose *Vanity Fair* (which she can only just have read when composing the preface) she greatly admired.

Its considerable virtue of taking on the complacent moral conventions of the mid-Victorian critical establishment notwithstanding, Brontë came to be dissatis-fied with the preface to the second edition of *Jane Eyre*. Some dissatisfaction with aspects of her prefaces to subsequent editions of the works of her sisters, though not expressed by Brontë herself, is often hard to avoid, however. Those prefaces sometimes accommodate themselves too readily to criticisms stemming from the mere conventionality she had trenchantly repulsed in the preface to *Jane Eyre*. Reminiscent of Wordsworth's concern to avoid 'obtruding' on the public is

---

[31] Cf. Heather Glen's astute account of this preface in *Charlotte Brontë: The Imagination in History* (Oxford: Oxford University Press, 2002; repr. 2004), 33–4, 48.

Brontë's remark near the end of her 'Biographical Notice of Ellis and Acton Bell' that '[i]n externals, they were two unobtrusive women', a remark she expands with respect to Emily in particular (it is one of the peculiarities of the notice, incidentally, that Emily and Anne are granted their names, though Brontë preserves her own pseudonymous disguise), claiming that Emily was unfitted to the ways of the world, ill-equipped to defend herself or to pursue her own advantage. 'An interpreter ought always to have stood between her and the world,' she declares, with characteristic belatedness again.[32] The 'Biographical Notice' remains fittingly robust in response to those admonitions faced by the work of Anne and Emily, mobilizing, for instance, a distinction between criticism and other forms of response to their works that we will meet again when we examine Elizabeth Gaskell's account of Brontë herself in Chapter 7. 'The fixed conviction I held, and hold,' Brontë declares of Emily's work, 'of the worth of these poems has not indeed received the confirmation of much favourable criticism; but I must retain it notwithstanding'. And professional critics are hardly spared the sting of her biblically inflected satire: 'Too often do reviewers remind us of the mob of Astrologers, Chaldeans, and Soothsayers gathered before the "writing on the wall," and unable to read the characters or make known the interpretation' (p. 745). But it is here that, far from offering a robust defence of Anne Brontë's *The Tenant of Wildfell Hall* (at which she had shown herself adept in the case of her own *Jane Eyre*), she sided with the adverse, moralizing reaction to her sister's novel, pathologizing Anne's selection of subject and diagnosing the 'harm' done to her by witnessing the dissipation of their brother's talents.

Brontë's argument in her preface to the 1850 reissue of *Wuthering Heights* likewise gives significant ground to that novel's critics, though it does adopt a rather subtler stance than that which she had maintained with respect to *The Tenant of Wildfell Hall*. Brontë opens her 'Editor's Preface' (a designation that asserts a particular authority over her sister's text in a way she had not done previously) with the declaration that 'I have just read over "Wuthering Heights", and, for the first time, have obtained a glimpse of what are termed (and, perhaps, really are) its faults' (p. 748). Here again is the characteristically belated cast of Brontë's prefaces: it is only now, 'for the first time', that she is able to see the novel's faults, though this emphasis on the newness of her insight into the book's faults turns out to be at least a little disingenuous when we learn, later in the preface, that the initial 'auditor' of the book's 'manuscript' already 'complained that the mere hearing of certain vivid and fearful scenes banished sleep by night, and disturbed mental peace by day' (p. 749), a complaint that Emily simply failed, we are told, to comprehend. The passage from manuscript to book is, as we saw in the case of

---

[32] *The Letters of Charlotte Brontë: With a Selection of Letters by Family and Friends*, ed. Margaret Smith, 3 vols (Oxford: Clarendon Press, 1995–2004), ii. 742–7 (746). Further references are given after quotations in the text.

Brontë's preface to her own *The Professor*, a key concern of Brontë's prefaces, which are themselves, of course, an important marker of the textualization both of the works themselves and of the judgements on (and defences of) them. The mention of the manuscript here, and of its 'auditor', rather than reader, rests on a distinction between those who knew Emily, her environment, and her particularly significant relationship to that environment, and those—namely, readers— who do not. The novel's putative 'faults' are features of 'how it appears to other people—to strangers who knew nothing of the author' and who also know little of the quite specific 'characteristics of the outlying hills and hamlets of the West-Riding of Yorkshire' (p. 748)—of how it appears, that is, to everybody except the Brontës' acquaintance and those who know their quite particular West Yorkshire district. As we saw in Wordsworth's preface to *Lyrical Ballads*, readers and readerships are often invoked and shown to be either generally deficient or specifically ill-suited to the reading of the text at hand—the purpose of that invocation, however, being to enable readers of the preface to identify the deficient and ill-suited readership to which they do not belong. But that can hardly be the case here, since the deficiencies—not knowing the West Riding of Yorkshire or, indeed, Ellis Bell personally—are simply too widespread and not easily remediable. To be sure, it is part of Brontë's purpose to furnish the details of Emily's character and context in order to explain why she wrote as she did and thus, as she sees it, to expiate the faults of *Wuthering Heights*. Admitting the charge of rusticity, Brontë claims that '[n]or was it natural that it should be otherwise' (p. 748) owing to her sister's own upbringing and circumstances. Had circumstances been different, Brontë suggests, '[d]oubtless' (a word to which she twice has recourse) so had the book been different. Yet the emphasis on circumstances ultimately gives way to a somewhat contrary emphasis on Emily's 'seclusion' (p. 749). Though she 'knew' 'the people round', Brontë claims, '*with* them, she rarely exchanged a word'. The consequence of this, Brontë alleges, with somewhat obscure logic, was that her focus was exclusively on 'those terrible and tragic traits' of which 'the memory is sometimes compelled to receive the impress' (p. 749). Brontë goes on to emphasize the sombreness of Emily's imagination, though the underlying opposition is not so much one between a sombre and 'sunny' cast of mind, but rather between seclusion and nature, on the one hand, and, correspondingly, between society and artifice, on the other. Brontë detects 'a dry saturnine humour in the delineation of old Joseph' in *Wuthering Heights*, for example, but it is Heathcliff who is central to the book, and, despite the trace of artistic proficiency attested to by the term 'delineation', it is Heathcliff who reveals that it was nature that worked through Emily, rather than Emily herself creating anything. Heathcliff is 'a Ghoul–an Afreet', a description that, contrary to Brontë's intention to downplay the artistic ability of Emily herself and hence her entitlement to either praise or blame, suggests instead her kinship with figures such as Milton and Byron. The preface concludes with the following, virtuoso paragraph:

'Wuthering Heights' was hewn in a wild workshop, with simple tools, out of homely materials. The statuary found a granite block on a solitary moor: gazing thereon, he saw how from the crag might be elicited a head, savage, swart, sinister; a form moulded with at least one element of grandeur—power. He wrought with a rude chisel, and from no model but the vision of his meditations. With time and labour, the crag took human shape; and there it stands colossal, dark, and frowning, half statue, half rock: in the former sense, terrible and goblin-like; in the latter, almost beautiful, for its colouring is of mellow grey, and moorland moss clothes it; and heath, with its blooming bells and balmy fragrance, grows faithfully close to the giant's foot.   (p. 751)

Insofar as it is nature, *Wuthering Heights* is 'almost beautiful'; insofar as it is art, it is 'terrible and goblin-like'. Brontë does not defend the terrible and goblin-like as qualities that an artist may wish to achieve (the missing term here is, of course, the sublime: it is as if the sublime has reverted to the merely horrible), though she does, in conclusion, ascribe greater artistic agency to her sister than she had done a little earlier.[33] The beauty to which *Wuthering Heights* may lay claim also comes significantly to depend, not on the 'granite block', the 'crag'—the *cliff* in Heathcliff, perhaps—but rather on the 'moorland moss' and '*heath*, with its blooming bells and balmy fragrance' (emphasis added) that grows over it. Amber K. Regis has recently remarked that Currer Bell 'glimpses the statue in snatches' and persuasively argues for Shelley's 'Ozymandias', his great poem of a broken colossus partially obscured by desert sands, as a context both for *Wuthering Heights* itself and for Brontë's preface.[34] But a still closer echo, whether consciously deployed by Brontë or not, is Catherine's impassioned retort to Nelly's suggestion that she should separate herself from Heathcliff in chapter 9 of *Wuthering Heights* itself: 'My love for Linton is like the foliage in the woods. Time will change it, I'm well aware, as winter changes the trees. My love for Heathcliff resembles the eternal rocks beneath—a source of little visible delight, but necessary' (pp. 101–2). The temporalizing conclusion to Brontë's preface—the heath *still growing* around the giant's foot—is apt, because the book itself is subject to the changes wrought on it by each new reading—a reading on the threshold of which the reader of the preface stands poised. Brontë's extended metaphor of the block/statue, however, also visualizes a novel that itself reminds us that not all delight is visible. Brontë's own vision in the preface, even if its contextualization of Emily's work and its accession to certain strictures on the novel may be necessary, is partial and fleeting,

---

[33] On the horrible and the sublime, see Immanuel Kant, *Critique of Judgement*, trans. James Creed Meredith, rev. and ed. Nicholas Walker (Oxford: Oxford University Press, 2007), 76.

[34] Amber K. Regis, 'Interpreting Emily: Ekphrasis and Allusion in Charlotte Brontë's "Editor's Preface" to *Wuthering Heights*', *Brontë Studies*, 45 (2020), 168–82 (175, 178–9).

and, like the novel itself, contains glimpses of beauty. It is thus readers who must look more determinedly for themselves.

*

Brontë's prefaces, like all prefaces, stand both before and after the works they address. As we have seen, the belatedness of Brontë's prefaces is especially marked, not only by the biographical circumstance of her having survived her sisters, but by her own repeated emphases on how things might have been different. It is easy to see how prefaces appended to second and subsequent editions, and to reissues, might go hand-in-hand with the effort to make things different after all. Henry James revised the tales and novels for which he furnished his prefaces and, in doing so, elaborated a theory of the novel both out of them but also, so to speak, into them. James's major project in the prefaces to the New York edition was consciously and substantially to articulate a theory of the novel—or, at least, the Anglophone novel, of which he had said in his earlier 'The Art of Fiction' that '[o]nly a short time ago it might have been supposed that the English novel was not what the French call *discutable*. It had no air of having a theory, a conviction, a consciousness of itself behind it—of being the expression of an artistic faith, the result of choice and comparison.'[35] James's solution to this situation was to put a 'a theory, a conviction, a consciousness of itself' not behind the novel, but in front of it—in front, that is, of his own novels and tales. Already in the preface to *Roderick Hudson* (the first in the sequence), James casts the prefaces not as distinct introductions to discrete novels or collections of tales—or, at least, not only as that—but as 'the continuity of an artist's endeavour' (*Prefaces*, 1039–40). Though he did not live to see it, James envisaged the collection of the prefaces in a letter to W. D. Howells: 'They ought, collected together, none the less, to form a sort of comprehensive manual or *vademecum* for aspirants in our arduous profession.'[36]

The letter to Howells is certainly James in what R. P. Blackmur described as James's 'proud' attitude in relation to the prefaces.[37] Later commentators on the prefaces have, however, been keen to 'liberate' them, in Herschel Parker's phrase, from the structure envisaged for them by James and subsequently established by Blackmur.[38] Others have faulted James's vision and Blackmur's edition for separating the prefaces from their original occasions in James's novels and tales: John H. Pearson, for example, complained of Blackmur's edition that it 'severs the prefaces from the narratives they precede'.[39] Either way, Parker, Pearson, and a

---

[35] In Henry James, *Literary Criticism: Essays on Literature, American Writers, English Writers*, ed. Leon Edel (New York: Library of America, 1984), 44–65 (44).
[36] 17 August 1908; quoted in *The Art of the Novel: Critical Prefaces*, ed. R. P. Blackmur (New York: Scribner's Sons, 1947; first pub. 1934), 8.
[37] Blackmur, p. vii.
[38] Herschel Parker, 'Deconstructing the Art of the Novel and Liberating James's Prefaces', *HJR* 14 (1993), 284–307.
[39] Pearson, *The Prefaces of Henry James: Framing the Modern Reader* (University Park: Pennsylvania State University Press, 1997), 19, 20.

host of other commentators have sought to undermine the canonization of James's prefaces as a kind of *summa novelistica*.[40]

To view the reincorporation of James's prefaces with their corresponding texts as liberation, however, is questionable, since it might rather be thought that what James imagined and Blackmur wrought was precisely their liberation from bondage to the novels and tales that may have been their occasion but need not be their fate. We discussed earlier the fantasy of prefaces without books; needless to say, that is not the case with James's prefaces, but his conception of the purpose the prefaces were to serve, made plain in his explicit statements about them, does suggest that their function goes beyond introducing the tales and novels to which they are appended. In addition to the 'proud' mood that lies behind the envisioning of such a purpose, however, James also had, as Blackmur acknowledges, a more 'modest', or at least more nuanced, attitude to the prefaces. Announcing his intentions for them in a memorandum to his publisher Charles Scribner's Sons, he makes the following remarks:

> Lastly, I desire to furnish each book, whether consisting of a single fiction, or of several minor ones, with a freely colloquial and even, perhaps, as I may say, confidential preface or introduction, representing, in a manner, the history of the work or of the group, representing more particularly, perhaps, a frank critical talk about its subject, its origin, its place in the whole artistic chain, and embodying, in short, whatever of interest there may be to be said about it. I have never committed myself in print in any way, even so much as by three lines to a newspaper, on the subject of anything I have written, and I feel as if I should come to this part of the business with a certain freshness of appetite and effect. My hope would be, at any rate, that it might count as a feature of a certain importance in any such new and more honorable presentation of my writings.[41]

This memorandum enacts the process of James's conception of the prefaces, in which, as Simon During has remarked, the imperatives of professional, amateur, technical, and confessional criticism each play a part.[42] What is apparently a merely terminological vacillation—'confidential preface or introduction'—in fact

[40] Examples include: William R. Goetz, 'Criticism and Autobiography in James's Prefaces', *American Literature*, 51 (1979), 333–48; Laurence B. Holland, *The Expense of Vision: Essays on the Craft of Henry James* (Princeton: Princeton University Press, 1964; Baltimore: Johns Hopkins University Press, 1982), 155; David McWhirter, 'Introduction', in McWhirter (ed.), *Henry James's New York Edition: The Construction of Authorship* (Stanford: Stanford University Press, 1995), 1–19 (2); Paul B. Armstrong, 'Reading James's Prefaces and Reading James', in McWirther (ed.), 125–37; Ross Posnock, 'Breaking the Aura of Henry James', in McWirther (ed.), 23–38 (34); Eve Kosofsky Sedgwick, 'Shame and Performativity: Henry James's New York Prefaces', in McWirther (ed.), 206–39 (227); Vivienne Rundle, 'The Prefaces of Henry James and Joseph Conrad', *HJR* 16 (1995), 66–92.

[41] 30 July 1905; *The Letters of Henry James*, ed. Leon Edel, 4 vols (Cambridge, MA: Harvard University Press, 1974–1984), iv (1984), 367.

[42] Simon During, 'Henry James and Me', *Modern Language Notes*, 118 (2003), 1278–93 (1281, 1285).

betokens James's uncertainty of what it is precisely that the prefaces (which are not yet decidedly 'the Prefaces') are to be. We have seen what might usefully be envisaged as the outworking of this vacillation emerge in the precise ambivalence of Johnson's, Wordsworth's, and Brontë's prefaces: the consciousness the preface bears that it precedes reading and thus both seeks to determine and must await the judgement of the reader. Both of James's deployments of 'perhaps' in the above passage act as restraints on his more confident assertions about the nature of the prefaces, the first tempering the freedom and colloquialism of the prospected texts, the second, likewise, tempering the frankness with which the 'talk' of the prefaces is to be undertaken.

The combination of pride and modesty in James's prefaces is prevalent through-out them and essential to their distinctive critical cast. Genette concludes his account of the prefatory situation by cataloguing various 'dodges', especially 'the revealing frequency with which many preface-writers express a kind of reserva-tion, real or pretended, about the obligation to provide a preface', a reservation in response to which 'the most appropriate and most productive compromise con-sists of expressing the sense of unease in the preface itself, in the form of apolo-gies or protests' (p. 230). The form of apology or protest is thoroughly implicit in James's prefaces, certainly, and is integral to their character. But this unease of the preface—the form that, recall, has also been characterized as the form of ease, of rest from labour itself—is not accidental to it, nor a flaw in it, but rather affords expression to criticism as preparation and anticipation.

Not every reader of James's prefaces has appreciated their approach to literary criticism, however. It is unsurprising that one such reader was F. R. Leavis, who boldly declares his view of the prefaces at the beginning of his treatment of 'the later James': 'the James of the Prefaces [...] is so much *not* the James of the early books that he certainly shouldn't be taken as a critical authority upon them, at any rate where valuation is concerned. The interest of the Prefaces,' Leavis goes on, 'is that they come from the mind that conceived the late work—which is to say that, if they are not in any sense critically satisfying, they have distinct critical bearings'.[43] The importance to Leavis of the encounter with James-as-critic is registered by the prominence of signally Leavisian terms ('valuation', 'bearings') in this account. That 'if' with which Leavis nearly concludes ('if they are not in any sense critically satisfying') is, however, quite a big one, not least because crit-ical satisfaction, in the senses of achieved fulfilment and agreement, is precisely eschewed in the preface form in favour of critical hypotheses radically subject to trial by reader. Nevertheless, a few pages further on, Leavis characterizes the artistic practice of the later James and summarizes his verdict on the prefaces:

---

[43] F. R. Leavis, *The Great Tradition: George Eliot, Henry James, Joseph Conrad* (Harmondsworth: Penguin, 1977; first pub. 1948), 178.

This inveterate indirectness of the later James, this aim of presenting, of leaving presented, the essential thing by working round and behind so that it shapes itself in the space left amidst a context of hints and apprehensions, is undoubtedly a vice in the Prefaces; it accounts for their unsatisfactoriness. It appears there, in criticism, as an inability to state—an inability to tackle his theme, or to get anything out clearly and finally.[44]

Leavis's 'there, in criticism' is piquant, since that is where he, Leavis, is himself at work. One of the virtues of Leavis's criticism is the ability he athletically displays to 'tackle his theme' and to make sure that whatever is got out is got out clearly and finally, and these priorities are certainly observable in the above passage: Leavis's vigorous deictics contrast starkly with the anxious, shadowy, and ultimately (according to Leavis) vicious 'hints and apprehensions' that are alleged to characterize James's criticism in the prefaces. Commenting on this passage of Leavis's, Oliver Herford remarks that one may certainly object to Leavis's 'too narrow view of James's "theme" in the Prefaces' before he (Herford) astutely acknowledges that Leavis is nevertheless attempting to describe something that is significant about the prefaces: 'in particular,' Herford notes, 'the writer's *concentration* can only be made visible by means of its opposite, a register of the distracting sensory phenomena which gather around it and break in upon it'.[45] Working round and behind is a persistent feature of the preface. And though finality is a virtue of criticism in Leavis's view, its appropriateness to texts that are instead initial is moot at best. Of course, a critic with a sometimes-salutary intolerance for the provisional like Leavis may go on to object that the preface is thus an unsuitable form for criticism. But so to argue is to deny to criticism the ability to initiate as well as to respond and to seek to place criticism above the multiple tests that the preface must forever face.

Instances of the indirect approach abound in James's prefaces. Whereas James confidently recalls the circumstances of the composition of *The Princess Casamassima* and, especially, *The Awkward Age* ('I recall with perfect ease the idea in which "The Awkward Age" had its origin' (*Prefaces*, 1120)), in the preface that stands between them he declares that 'I profess a certain vagueness of remembrance in respect to the origin and growth of "The Tragic Muse"' (*Prefaces*, 1103). A natural consequence of the vicissitudes of memory, maybe, but also strikingly akin to the confession of 'the full license for sketchiness and vagueness and dimness taken indeed by my picture' with which the preface to *The Princess Casamassima* in fact concludes (*Prefaces*, 1102). More tellingly still, the great

---

[44] Leavis, 183.
[45] Oliver Herford, *Henry James's Style of Retrospect: Late Personal Writings, 1890–1915* (Oxford: Oxford University Press, 2016), 189.

critical set pieces of the prefaces,[46] where James most fully exercises the painterly and theatrical aspects of his imagination, are frequently followed by apologies for and qualifications of them, introduced by phrases such as 'all of which is to say' and 'at any rate'—the latter already met at the conclusion of his memorandum to Scribner's, for instance, where James's descriptions of what are to become the prefaces settle on a characteristically self-revising 'at any rate', signalling the retreat to the general hope that these texts are to be 'important'.

This kind of move signalled in this kind of way is key to the prefaces as they negotiate their different roles. To keep for the moment with the preface to *The Princess Casamassima*, for example, James attempts to draw the lesson from the many impressions by which he was 'assault[ed]' while walking the streets of London during the period of the novel's composition:

> There was a moment at any rate when they offered me no image more vivid than that of some individual sensitive nature or fine mind, some small obscure intelligent creature whose education should have been almost wholly derived from them, capable of profiting by all the civilisation, all the accumulations to which they testify, yet condemned to see these things only from outside—in mere quickened consideration, mere wistfulness and envy and despair.   (*Prefaces*, 1087)

Slightly later, James returns to his consideration of the character central to *The Princess Casamassima*, Hyacinth Robinson, and declares:

> I had had for a long time well before me, at any rate, my small obscure but ardent observer of the 'London world', saw him roam and wonder and yearn, saw all the unanswered questions and baffled passions that might ferment in him—
> (*Prefaces*, 1087)

And reverting to Hyacinth a little further on again:

> I remember at any rate feeling myself all in possession of little Hyacinth's consistency, as I have called it, down at Dover during certain weeks that were none too remotely precedent to the autumn of 1885 and the appearance, in the 'Atlantic Monthly' again, of the first chapters of the story.   (*Prefaces*, 1100)

The phrase 'at any rate' serves as a marker of the shifts of accent that characterize James's prefaces. In particular, the prefaces frequently fall into a rhythm of critical

---

[46] On 'a famous set piece in the Prefaces', namely, the 'house of fiction' in the preface to *The Portrait of a Lady*, see Dorothy J. Hale, 'Henry James and the Invention of Novel Theory', in Jonathan Freedman (ed.), *The Cambridge Companion to Henry James* (Cambridge: Cambridge University Press, 1998), 79–101 (83).

set piece followed by apparent apology, of elaborated authorial statement followed by self-revising summary. Both in James's hands as well as in the linguistic record more broadly, 'at any rate' paradoxically announces the at once general and limited significance of the statements it introduces. Something of this oscillation between minimum and maximum is registered in the *OED*'s explanation of 'at any rate' as both 'at all events' and 'at least'.[47] Where 'at all events' registers what will happen in every case and thereby registers a maximum, 'at least' names a minimum, which may, in the event, be exceeded. The moment early in *The Princess Casamassima* (book I, chapter 5) when Millicent Henning declares that she does not care whether or not Hyacinth is clever is, as it happens, one of the examples cited by the *OED* for the use of 'at any rate' in this sense: 'He had at any rate a mind sufficiently enriched to see what she meant', which is, incidentally, an important revision of the first edition—'and Hyacinth was at any rate quick-witted enough to see what she meant by that'—elevating to a discrete sentence what had been a glossing subclause and tellingly seeking to emphasize Hyacinth's mental enrichment (the relations between mental and material riches being a leading concern of the novel).[48] The exact resonance of the phrase, moreover, depends on the quality for which a minimum or maximum is being stated: the resonance of the 'at any rate' in the passage from Leavis I quoted above, for instance—'at any rate where valuation is concerned'—is a decided judgement rather than subtle self-qualification, because, for Leavis at least, there is little else to criticism but valuation.

Where Leavis's 'at any rate' is expansive, James's most characteristic deployments of this term tend to come when he wishes to return to a theme from which he has digressed or when he is offering some relief from a comparatively abstract discussion. The example of James's account of his arrival at the character of Hyacinth Robinson in the process of the composition of *The Princess Casamassima*—'There was a moment at any rate when they offered me no image more vivid than that of some individual sensitive nature or fine mind'—shows that 'at any rate' here culminates a movement that began with James declaring he was presenting the reader with '[t]he simplest account of the origin of "The Princess Casamassima"' that he could think of. That declaration precedes a phenomenologically detailed, finely interwoven, and figuratively fertile account of how '[p]ossible stories, presentable figures, rise from the thick jungle as the observer moves, fluttering up like startled game' (*Prefaces*, 1086). Other occurrences likewise bring into view the larger movements otherwise only dimly discernible in the prefaces. After his sweeping statement in the preface to *The Tragic Muse*

---

[47] See 'rate, *n.1*', P. 3. *at any rate*. *OED Online* <www.oed.com/view/Entry/158412> (accessed 19 April 2023).
[48] See, for the variant, Henry James, *The Princess Casamassima*, ed. Adrian Poole (Cambridge: Cambridge University Press, 2019), 689.

that the recognition of the importance of art has become 'more than a custom, [it] has become on occasion almost a fury' James returns to his own practice of composition and rereading: 'The more I turn my pieces over, at any rate, the more I now see I must have found in them, and I remember how, once well in presence of my three typical examples, my fear of too ample a canvas quite dropped' (*Prefaces*, 1106–7).

Were 'at any rate' the unfailing marker of James's attempts simply to restrain his theoretical ambitions, that would, however, be less formally significant than it is. Such restraint, in fact, rarely lasts long: 'The more I turn my pieces over, at any rate,' is the beginning of the long paragraph in which James goes on to describe the capacious class of 'large loose baggy monsters'—a description that surely owes something of its appeal to its own adjectival corpulence, discernible in those three terms, unseparated by commas—to which *The Newcomes*, *Les Trois Mousquetaires*, and (as James calls it) *Peace and War* all belong. Another striking example is to be found at the opening of the second paragraph of the preface to *The Spoils of Poynton*, etc. The long first paragraph to that preface begins in storytelling mode and, in particular, with the Dickensian moment of Christmas Eve: 'It was years ago, I remember, one Christmas Eve when I was dining with friends' (*Prefaces*, 1138). The storytelling opening soon gives way to the recuperative reflection on the origins of composition that is fundamental to the preface, itself a culmination for the author but the origin, over again, for the reader. '[A] lady beside me', James recollects, 'made in the course of talk one of those allusions that I have always found myself recognising on the spot as "germs"' (*Prefaces*, 1138). The specific situation—Christmas Eve, the (unnamed) lady beside James, the flow of dinner-party conversation—is quickly made to exemplify the general point concerning the immediate recognizability (to James) of the 'germs' of composition. The second paragraph, with its 'at any rate', puts us back around the dinner table on that Christmas Eve and hence returns us to the story whose initiation quickly gave way to critical extrapolation:

> So it was, at any rate, that when my amiable friend, on the Christmas Eve, before the table that glowed safe and fair through the brown London night, spoke of such an odd matter as that a good lady in the north, always well looked on, was at daggers drawn with her only son, ever hitherto exemplary, over the ownership of the valuable furniture of a fine old house just accruing to the young man by his father's death, I instantly became aware, with my 'sense for the subject', of the prick of inoculation; the whole of the *virus*, as I have called it, being infused by that single touch.   (*Prefaces*, 1139–40)

The combination of the paragraph break and the summative 'So it was, at any rate [...]' returns us to the situation with which the preface began while also serving as a phenomenology—a pathology, even—of the moment the 'germ' takes hold. The opening sentence of the preface's second paragraph looks both fore and aft: its presentation of the recollection of the moment of inspiration is, of course, also the anticipation of the narrative of *The Spoils of Poynton* itself. It is revealing, that is to say, that the 'only son' of the 'lady in the north' was 'ever hitherto exemplary', because, while his filial exemplarity may now be compromised, he becomes precisely thereby the exemplar for the story that James will compose. Moreover, while James's 'at any rate' here certainly returns the reader to the initiating situation, that situation is again quickly exploited, metaphorically and conceptually, for the critical point that James wishes to draw out. James is conscious of the demands his recollective and critical set pieces may place on his reader, but the apologetic consolidations of basic tenets announced by 'at any rate' in turn serve as the basis for repeated, renewed articulations of just such set pieces.

James's prefaces, then, mount through extensive trails of metaphorical reasoning to the peaks of critical declamation, before descending from their proudest eminences—and then ascending them again. His apologetic tone often accompanies the most critically assertive moments in the prefaces. James is aware that his explanations might do little in the way of explaining, as he acknowledges in the preface to *Lady Barbarina*:

> If it be asked then [...] why they [*The Wings of the Dove* and *The Golden Bowl*] deviate from that natural harmony, why the author resorts to the greater extravagance when the less would serve, the answer is simply that the course taken has been, on reflexion, the course of the greater amusement. That is an explanation adequate, I admit, only when itself a little explained—but I shall have due occasion to explain it.   (*Prefaces*, 1209)

Such self-admonishing summary abbreviations abound in the prefaces. James is constantly rereading and self-revising in the prefaces, even as they stand before the great effort of rereading and revision that is the New York Edition itself. As John Carlos Rowe put it: 'James's Prefaces constitute a unique work in the history of modern literature: the explicit exploration of what it means for an "author" to become a "reader".'[49] There is in the prefaces no concealment or denial of revision, but rather its repeated and explicit performance.

It is, crucially, at just those moments of ambitious critical declamation and theoretical speculation that James most frequently assumes the at once apologetic and assertive tone characteristic of the prefaces, as he does in a celebrated moment from the first of the prefaces, that to *Roderick Hudson*:

---

[49]   John Carlos Rowe, *The Theoretical Dimensions of Henry James* (London: Methuen, 1984), 234.

Really, universally, relations stop nowhere, and the exquisite problem of the artist is eternally but to draw, by a geometry of his own, the circle within which they shall happily appear to do so. He is in the perpetual predicament that the continuity of things is the whole matter, for him, of comedy and tragedy; that this continuity is never, by the space of an instant or an inch, broken, and that, to do anything at all, he has at once intensely to consult and intensely to ignore it. All of which will perhaps pass but for a supersubtle way of pointing the plain moral that a young embroiderer of the canvas of life soon began to work in terror, fairly, of the vast expanse of that surface, of the boundless number of its distinct perforations for the needle, and of the tendency inherent in his many-coloured flowers and figures to cover and consume as many as possible of the little holes.   (*Prefaces*, 1041)

It is little noted that this famous set piece is immediately followed by an apology for it. That apology is itself, however, a qualified one. For James to write, '[a]ll of which will perhaps pass but for a supersubtle way of pointing the plain moral', and so on, is perhaps not entirely free of falsity in its modesty. Subtlety is a Jamesian value and in evidence to a superlative degree here. And, as soon as the need for a halt to the description of relations has been announced, relations reassert themselves, as if uncontrollably: the rare usage, already by this date, of 'pointing a moral'—a phrase, nevertheless, that recurs repeatedly in James's critical writing—suggests the ensuing metaphor of needlepoint. Relations stop nowhere indeed, and it is the critic's, as much as the artist's, job to call a halt to them—and then to set them going again. Michael Wood deploys James's 'really, universally relations stop nowhere' as a kind of tag for '[t]he great gift to us of Empson's open sense of ambiguity', which Wood characterizes as 'the challenge of unexplored verbal territory, of discoveries to be made, and especially discoveries of what is already there, of worlds we thought we knew'. The perhaps unexpected resolution of 'unexplored verbal territory' into 'worlds' rather than 'words' is extremely adept, reminiscent of James's (as of Empson's) sense that worlds are made, at least in part, from words.[50] James's prefaces, like many we have considered in this chapter, are 'discoveries of what is already there', a phrase apt to the specific character of the preface as form, even if it is a strange way of conceiving of discoveries, since discoveries, in order to be discoveries, can hardly be of what is *not* already there. It is precisely the equivocation between the past ('worlds we thought we knew') and the prospective, future-oriented character of discovery that is characteristic of the preface.

Famous as it has become as an article of novel theory, the above passage from the preface to *Roderick Hudson* and, crucially, its apology—and, even more crucially, the resurgence of the critical, metaphorical elaboration for which that

[50] Michael Wood, *On Empson* (Princeton: Princeton University Press, 2017), 46.

apology is proffered—imply a great deal about the preface as form and, especially here, the kind of relations that obtain between the preface and what it prefaces. Prefaces are related to what they preface, and often to such an extent that they share family traits—particular quirks of expression, as well as large, commonly held attitudes—with their relations. Note, for instance, the repetition of 'arches' in the preface to *The Portrait of a Lady*, a text that dedicates much of its energy to considering the genesis of the novel's central character, who is named, of course, Isabel Archer (*Prefaces*, 1080); note as well the quite explicit play on the central drama and title of 'Paste', when James articulates the relation of his tale to its mirrored model in Maupassant's 'La Parure', stating that 'a new setting for my pearls—and as different as possible from the other—had of course withal to be found' (*Prefaces*, 1243); and, likewise again, the 'concerted play on the word "point" that breaks out at the beginning of the preface' to *The Spoils of Poynton* observed by Herford, who also notes the significance of James's residence in East Sussex—Point Hill—during the composition of this work.[51] The prefaces are formed, often intimately, by their relations with the texts that they address, and yet their inherited traits are as much their own, harnessed to their own critical concerns and imperatives. In the preface to *The Golden Bowl*, prefatory material, said James, addressing Coburn's photographs for the New York Edition, 'should exactly be *not* competitive and obvious, should on the contrary plead its case with some shyness' (*Prefaces*, 1327). James's prefaces plead their case with 'some'—a nicely indefinite quantity, especially when set against 'exactly' in the preceding clause—'shyness'. They are nothing less than the attempt to furnish a theory of the novel at the head of the authorially sanctioned canon of his own works, though the claim they make on the reader is presented tentatively, subject, potentially, to the kinds of judgement that James, whose rereading of his own work is the paradoxical condition for the attempt to install himself as first reader of it, frequently passes on them himself.

*

It may seem evidence of the ultimate inadequacy ('unsatisfactoriness', Leavis had said) of James's prefaces that, while reprinted in most later editions of his work, they find themselves in such places supplemented with introductions of the kind frequently found in paperback reprints. This situation is hardly unique to James, of course. It is perhaps unsurprising that a late-twentieth-century edition of *Orlando*, for instance, includes Virginia Woolf's own parodic 'Preface', as well as a 'Biographical Preface' by Frank Kermode and an 'Introduction' by Rachel Bowlby that is fully aware of the challenges the text poses to the production of the kind of introductory paratext the modern editor is enjoined to supply. 'What is *Orlando*'s editor to do? She—but there is every doubt of her sex—finds herself in the

---

[51] Herford, 198–9.

hopeless situation of dealing with a book which is already a parody of the kinds of scholarly enterprise which the introduction might try to emulate'—a formulation that gives expression, once again, to the temporal disjointedness of the introduction, which in this case finds the model to which it might aspire already parodied in the text it presumes to introduce.[52]

The key conundrum of the preface, as we have seen throughout this chapter, is encapsulated in the (appropriately hackneyed) critical phrase, 'always already': for the preface's addressees, reading the text lies before them, a situation to which the prefacer must respond by conducting readers into their reading, but from her or his position of having always already completed her or his own reading. In the case of the autographic preface (to adopt Genette's terms again), this is handled by taking a further step back in the process of the production of the text—to its origins, to what James famously called the 'germ'. The reader is presented with the germ, and her or his reading can thus germinate along with it as the text unfolds. But the distinction between the responses of autographic and allographic prefacers to this conundrum is not as sharp as one might perhaps be tempted to assume it would be. Allographic prefacers also frequently situate the text they are introducing in some form of origin, often the origin of their own identity as writers, and it is that situation to which I turn now in conclusion.

The 2000 Vintage edition of Richard Wright's seminal novel *Native Son* is printed with two introductions. Wright's own 'How "Bigger" Was Born' was written at around the same time as the novel itself, part of it appearing initially as a free-standing essay in the *Saturday Review of Literature* three months after the novel's own initial publication, before being included in its entirety in later editions of the novel, sometimes as an afterword, but more regularly as an introduction— which is how it appears, immediately before the text of the novel itself, in the Vintage edition, published in 2000, with which I am concerned here.[53] Wright opens his account by declaring that 'I am not so pretentious as to imagine that it is possible for me to account completely for my own book, *Native Son*'—a formulation that of course leaves open the possibility of *partially* accounting for it— going on to draw particular attention to the 'sources' of the book, 'the material that went into it, and my own years' long changing attitude toward that material' (p. 1). Wright focuses in particular on the special character of the writer's imagination, which he characterizes as 'a kind of community medium of exchange: what he has read, felt, thought, seen, and remembered is translated into

---

[52] Rachel Bowlby, 'Introduction', in Virginia Woolf, *Orlando: A Biography* (1928), ed. Bowlby (Oxford: Oxford University Press, 1992; repr. 2000), p. xii.

[53] Richard Wright, 'How "Bigger" Was Born', *The Saturday Review of Literature*, 1 June 1940, 3–4, 17–20; 'Introduction: How "Bigger" Was Born', in *Native Son* (London: Vintage, 2000), 1–30. References are to the Vintage edition and given after quotations in the text. Information on the publication date (1 March 1940) of *Native Son* is taken from Wright, *Early Works* (New York: Library of America, 1991), 893.

extensions as impersonal as a worn dollar bill' (p. 1). And, as much as the writer's imagination is extended outwards and circulated in this way, it is not the writer who, so to speak, originally mints that dollar bill, but rather the writer who occupies—or Wright, at least, himself occupied—a dual position in which conception and reflection are paired: 'Always, as I wrote, I was both reader and writer, both the conceiver of the action and the appreciator of it' (p. 27). Wright means this metaphorically—writing is conception; reading, appreciation—but in the writing of 'How "Bigger" Was Born', the metaphor is literalized as Wright indeed becomes his own reader. He affirms that 'any honest reader knows as much about the rest of what is in the book as I do; that is, if, as he reads, he is willing to let his emotions and imagination become as influenced by the materials as I did' (p. 29). In accounting for the sources of *Native Son*, Wright, therefore, seeks to put the reader in something like his position as writer—which is now the position of reader, as he reads what he has done. Wright closes his essay with a deliberately audacious move, situating his work in relation to a lineage of American writing, not in order to establish his continuity with it, but rather to imply instead that, were James, Hawthorne, and Poe (the reverse chronological order seems significant) alive today, then they would not so much write in a certain way, but would be satisfied by the kind of story that he, Wright, has written:

> we do have in the Negro the embodiment of a past tragic enough to appease the hunger of even a James; and we have in the oppression of the Negro a shadow athwart our national life dense and heavy enough to satisfy even the gloomy broodings of a Hawthorne. And if Poe were alive, he would not have to invent horror; horror would invent him.   (p. 31)

The progenitors of American fiction are rendered passive—appeased, satisfied, invented—in the present historical moment, of which Wright had starkly declared in opening this concluding paragraph: 'I feel that I'm lucky to be alive to write novels today, when the whole world is caught in the pangs of war and change' (p. 30).

Wright's conclusion of 'How "Bigger" Was Born' with this implicit account of his own relation to earlier writers is significant in its own terms, but it also provides an instructive paradigm with which to consider the second (but in fact placed first in the book) introduction with which the 2000 Vintage *Native Son* is furnished—namely, the 'Introduction' by Caryl Phillips. Phillips opens by relating the role of *Native Son*, not in Wright's, but in his, Phillips's, formation as a writer. It is, of course, not uncommon for the allographic prefacer to relate how the book under discussion played a significant role in her or his own life, especially when her or his life is that of a writer (which, in some senses, it of course always is), but Phillips's development of this common trope is especially notable for a number of reasons. 'The year was 1978,' he opens. 'I was a twenty year old, denim-clad, backpacker who had just made his way across the United States by Greyhound bus.

In common with others of my generation, I was living cheaply, moving erratically from one place to the next, and I was hungry for experience' (p. ix).[54] Phillips goes on to make clear that he had traversed the whole of the continental United States, arriving at its western edge, where he bought a copy of Wright's *Native Son* '[o]ne Californian afternoon'. Phillips's remark that all this took place 'ten days or so' before his return to Oxford, 'where I had one more year of studying before being set loose upon the world, hopefully clutching a bachelor's degree in English', both establishes a literary critical and academic context for Phillips's reading of Wright, though one that is held firmly in the background: where, after all, could be further from Oxford than California? Phillips, as he also emphasizes, was a representative of his generation, another important detail that helps both to explain what he confesses was his ignorance of Wright and his work (nearly forty years after it was published) as well as the continuing relevance of Wright to the late 1970s—a period of resurgent, often politically organized and legislated racism both in the United Kingdom and in the United States.

But this is not the only element of Phillips's past that he evokes in his account of his discovery of *Native Son*. Phillips had related the anecdote of the Californian bookshop purchase and of his reading of *Native Son* on the shores of the Pacific once before, in the 'Introduction', not to Wright's novel, but to his own first collection of essays, *The European Tribe* (1987).[55] Phillips quotes that account again here. Most simply, he does so to avoid self-plagiarism, but there is more to his self-recollection than that. The backward glancing of Phillips's 'Introduction'—to one ur-scene in 1978, then to a second in 1987—seeks to establish the role of Wright's *Native Son*, which has become established as Wright's own inaugural work, in the inauguration of Phillips's writing career, in which *The European Tribe*, of course, has its own privileged place. 'If I had to point to any one moment that seemed crucial in my desire to be a writer,' Phillips had remarked there, as he quotes it again here, 'it was then, as the pacific surf began to wash up around the deck chair'. Far from being a simple concession to the conventions of properly acknowledging already published work (though it is that too), the passage from the 'Introduction' of *The European Tribe* supplies evidence of the successful issue of Phillips's resolution and, hence, crucially, of Wright's effective influence.

Phillips mentions Wright's other work (specifically, *Uncle Tom's Children* and *Black Boy*) in his 'Introduction' to *Native Son*, but also discusses James Baldwin's

---

[54] It is worth remarking that Phillips's 'Introduction' is paginated with Roman numerals, indicating its marginal position in relation to the main body of the book, whereas Wright's is paginated with Arabic numerals.

[55] Caryl Phillips, 'Introduction', in *The European Tribe* (London: Faber and Faber, 1987), 1–9. The passage Phillips quotes in his 'Introduction' to *Native Son* is on p. 7, before which he gives details of British and American racism in the late 1970s (pp. 1–2, 6). It is notable, incidentally, that *The European Tribe* is itself a book with multiple beginnings: in addition to the 'Introduction', it has a 'Foreword' and a 'Preface', both also written by Phillips himself.

critique of the novel in his essay 'Everybody's Protest Novel' (1949) and Wright's 'How "Bigger" Was Born', which, as noted above, immediately follows Phillips's 'Introduction' as another introduction to the novel. Phillips offers a fairly modest defence of Wright from Baldwin's critique, implicitly conceding Baldwin's strictures on the 'structural or ideological weaknesses of the novel', while averring that 'these cannot diminish the remarkable spell which *Native Son* has managed to cast over successive generations of readers' (p. xiii). Wright's own attempt to account for the novel (albeit one, as we have seen, that was published before Baldwin's critique) is, though, given notably shorter shrift. The only section of 'How "Bigger" Was Born' that Phillips discusses is, revealingly, a heavy-handed passage on 'Bigger's tensity and the German variety' and 'Bigger's longing for self-identification and the Russian principle of self-determination' (quoted p. xvii). Phillips only cursorily sets up this quotation, commenting immediately after it: 'Mercifully, the text of *Native Son* remains unencumbered by such pedantry.' Phillips's sensitivity to 'pedantry' is in keeping with Johnson's, Wordsworth's, and James's sense that pedantry is the besetting sin of the preface and hence with a perennial anxiety of the preface form: the sense that it unwarrantably interferes with or forestalls the reader's entry into the text and is therefore pedantic *as such*. In its ponderousness, the passage Phillips quotes is uncharacteristic of Wright's candid and direct essay, a fact that reinforces the idea that the preface-writer is especially on the lookout for pedantry, whether her or his own or someone else's. The effect of this criticism of 'How "Bigger" Was Born' close to the end of Phillips's own 'Introduction', moreover, is of the kind of displacement of an earlier writer that Wright himself intimates with respect to James, Hawthorne, and Poe. It is the displacement of the writer as her or his own reader, or the writer who is first the reader of her or his own text. Wright's reaction to his own text is cast as inferior to Phillips's reaction to it—a reaction that is, in Phillips's case, the inauguration of a writing career, rather than a recuperative, recollective accounting of it, as 'How "Bigger" Was Born' is taken to be. Yet Phillips's account of his own writing career is, as we have seen, itself a recollection—of reading Wright in 1978 and of writing about that reading in 1987. It is doubtless significant that Phillips points out he has 'never returned to the Californian beach where, over twenty years ago, Richard Wright's *Native Son* fuelled my ambition to be a writer' (p. xvii). But, while no return is made to this scene of origin, many visits are made to places significant to Wright's life, career, and, perhaps notably, his death. Phillips 'sought out Wright's final resting-place in Pere-Lachaise [*sic*] Cemetery where his ashes are interred' but 'the final irony, of course,' Phillips concludes his 'Introduction' by informing us,

> is that I now live in Greenwich Village, only a few short blocks from Charles Street where, back in the mid-forties, the great American writer Richard Wright endured much difficulty and unspeakable humiliation trying to live and write as

a free man in the country of his birth. With chin held high, Richard Wright chose to leave for France; this 'native son' was not going to allow the United States to turn him into a 'Bigger Thomas'.   (p. xvii–xviii)

The historical changes, insufficient and incomplete though without doubt they are, that have occurred since the 1940s, and even since the 1970s, that make it possible for a black man nurturing Wright's and Phillips's hope—'to live and write as a free man'—are crucially at play in this conclusion, of course. Phillips fulfils a wish as man and writer that Wright could not, including, as we saw in Phillips's brisk treatment of 'How "Bigger" Was Born', the wish to account for *Native Son* and what its reading may enable. The preface-writer is the exemplary reader of the text she or he introduces to the extent of assuming the role, if not the identity, of the person who first produced it and, as such, who first read it.

2

Selections

T. S. Eliot, a preface-writer much in demand in the middle of the twentieth century, wrote the following in his 'Note of Introduction' to a special reissue of the poet David Jones's *In Parenthesis*:

> A work of literary art which uses the language in a new way or for a new purpose, does not call for many words from the introducer. All that one can say amounts only to pointing towards the book, and affirming its importance and permanence as a work of art. The aim of the introducer should be to arouse the curiosity of a possible new reader. To attempt to explain, in such a note as this, is futile.[1]

Eliot disavows one of the uses—explanation—to which 'such a note as this' might be put. All, in fact, that an introducer can do is point mutely towards the book, an act that itself, so it is claimed, would constitute affirmation of the book's importance and permanence. And Eliot's 'can' ('All that one can say') surely implies, as it were, an 'ought': the introducer ought to fall silent and merely indicate works of linguistic inventiveness.

The idea that the best thing for criticism to do would be to fall silent before the works upon which it might comment and *thereby* merely indicate their importance and permanence had a significant hold in twentieth-century literary criticism. The New Critical condemnation of the heresy of paraphrase, for one prominent example, culminates, as Frances Ferguson has put it, in 'a manifesto for direct quotation' that arises from 'the impulse to make criticism seem as if it were always reverting to the mere rehearsal of the exact words of the text'.[2] The implication that criticism only *appears* to be the rehearsal of the text ('seem as if...') suggests the difficulty that criticism will have in making the rehearsal of texts more than merely its appearance. The idea, moreover, that this involves a 'reversion' hints not only at the priority ascribed to literary texts as the basis of criticism, but at a mythic past in which criticism was pure and transparent,

---

[1] In *The Complete Prose of T. S. Eliot: The Critical Edition*, ed. Ronald Schuchard et al., 8 vols (Baltimore: Johns Hopkins University Press, 2014–19), viii: *Still and Still Moving, 1954–1965*, ed. Jewel Spears Brooker and Ronald Schuchard (2019), 479–81 (479) (first pub. in David Jones, *In Parenthesis* (London: Faber & Faber, 1961), pp. vii–viii). On Eliot's 'recurring idea' that a writer 'can point to good literature and then be silent', see Jim McCue, letters to the Editor, *TLS* 8 May 2009, 6, and James H. Dee's response, letters to the Editor, *TLS* 29 May 2009, 6.
[2] Frances Ferguson, 'Now It's Personal: D. A. Miller and Too-Close Reading', *CI* 41 (2015), 521–40 (532).

Critical Forms: Forms of Literary Criticism, 1750–2020. Ross Wilson, Oxford University Press. © Ross Wilson 2023.
DOI: 10.1093/oso/9780198881117.003.0003

unclouded by commentary, theory, and interpretation. In their pair of frequently reissued anthologies, *Understanding Poetry* (1938) and *Understanding Fiction* (1943), the first of which in particular had a powerful influence over the teaching of English literature in North America for many years, Cleanth Brooks and Robert Penn Warren did indeed attempt to revert to the selection and presentation of the exact words of texts. Yet those anthologies also contained considerable guidance for interpretation, and, reflecting on Brooks's reading of Robert Herrick's 'Corinna's Going A-Maying' in *The Well-Wrought Urn*, Ferguson observes that, while Brooks may have fulfilled his desire to avoid 'maul[ing] and distort[ing]' the poem in his discussion, 'he has not eschewed translation or statements of meaning' while he has 'largely abandon[ed] the desire merely to quote'.[3] *Understanding Poetry* and *Understanding Fiction* themselves were likewise composed not just of selections of poems and short fictions, but of numerous paratexts—from the explicitly directive texts entitled 'Letter to the Teacher' that preface both anthologies, to the interpretative glosses by which each selection is followed. The indictment of paraphrase and the attempt to cultivate an appearance of critical mutism are thus qualified the minute we notice that the texts presented in selections come with numerous critical paratexts, which, it may readily be assumed, is where all the critical action happens.[4]

The problem of the relation between the anthology predicated on the mere presentation of texts and the paratexts that accrue to those texts did not simply arise with the New Criticism, of course. The anthology is a classical form in origin, but it also played a pivotal role in the burgeoning of print, the emergence of national literatures, and the development of professional literary criticism during the eighteenth century and into the nineteenth.[5] Throughout the anthology's history, the relation between the apparently silent presentation of texts and their discursive adumbration has been crucial. The student of anthologies is thus bound to spend a considerable amount of time examining the paratexts of anthologies 'where the editor becomes a writer' because anthologists' silences are of necessity harder to interpret than the explanations and rationales they supply in the paratexts to their selections.[6] Yet, while that may be so, it is salutary to remember as well that 'extratextual passages and critical culs-de-sac (introductions, headnotes, footnotes, endnotes, digressions, essays, glossaries, addenda, errata)' that seek to furnish explicit rationales for selections can often have a rather uneasy relationship with the texts they supposedly explain, tending to

---

[3] Ferguson, 532.

[4] Cf. Helen Thaventhiran's account of paraphrase as critical practice in *Radical Empiricists: Five Modernist Close Readers* (Oxford: Oxford University Press, 2015), 125–51.

[5] See, e.g., chapter 2 on anthologies in Multigraph Collective, *Interacting with Print: Elements of Reading in the Era of Print Saturation* (Chicago: University of Chicago Press, 2017), 33–48 (esp. 35–6).

[6] Leah Price, *The Anthology and the Rise of the Novel: From Richardson to George Eliot* (Cambridge: Cambridge University Press, 2000), 11–12.

obscure as well as to clarify.[7] The deliberate abstention from critical discourse, along the lines suggested by Eliot and explicitly avowed by the New Critics, has therefore remained a strong impulse in many anthologies. Although there are not one, but two, introductory paratexts in Christopher Ricks's *The Oxford Book of English Verse* (1999)—'Preface: The Oxford Book' as well as 'Introduction: Of English Verse'—Ricks writes in his 'Introduction' that '[p]oems in an anthology are best left to do what poems are particularly good at: speaking for themselves'. Yet Ricks nevertheless allows that 'criticism, provided that it knows its place, has its place'.[8] That place, the implication is, is in prefaces, introductions, notes (where they are present), and other such paratextual apparatuses. Criticism, on such a view, is all in the paratexts of anthologies—where the anthologist becomes writer and thus becomes critic—in contrast to the texts of others that make up the anthology and with respect to which the anthologist is merely a sampler.

This chapter is certainly concerned with the paratexts of selections and their discursive presentation of the (often suppositious) methodologies of selection that have been adopted in the anthologies they address. But its main concern is with the practice of selection itself. Leah Price advances a distinction between 'verbal judgments' and 'editorial acts'—the former evident in the discursive paratexts with which selections are furnished and crucially amenable to the resources of 'close reading', the latter registered only in the silence of the anthologist and thus hard to grasp with the tools available to literary criticism and its history. It is a somewhat stark distinction, and one to which Price's masterful study does not finally adhere, not least because 'editorial acts' of the kinds performed by anthologists themselves involve several kinds of 'verbal judgment': which texts to include, where to place them in relation to other texts, which to include whole and which to excerpt, and so on. What anthologists produce in their selections, even when that production is not explicitly explicated or justified in paratextual discourse, is distinctly amenable to close reading as a textual product bearing the traces of editorial activity. What is more, their own silence (as Ricks's comment above already intimates) does not always pass without comment by anthologists themselves. In the preface to the first edition of his *The Oxford Book of English Verse* (1900), for example, Arthur Quiller-Couch confessed that it was with some regret that he had forgone notes when explanation of a recondite word or passage might have been in order, but that he had done so 'with more equanimity when the temptation was to criticize or "appreciate". For the function of the anthologist includes criticizing in silence.'[9] It is, of course, no accident that the anthology and criticism—at least when criticism is implicitly understood to take place *out loud*—have often

---

[7] Nick Groom, *The Making of Percy's 'Reliques'* (Oxford: Clarendon Press, 1999), 216.
[8] Christopher Ricks (ed.), *The Oxford Book of English Verse* (Oxford: Oxford University Press, 1999), p. xli.
[9] Arthur Quiller-Couch (ed.), *The Oxford Book of English Verse* (Oxford: Oxford University Press, 1900), pp. vii–viii.

been presented as being inimical to one another (this is how, for just one example, Laura Riding and Robert Graves presented the relation between anthologies and criticism in their polemic *A Pamphlet against Anthologies*). As Price has suggested, 'a lack of interest in more crudely parasitic operations like excerpting, abridging, compiling' is one correlation of literary critics' primary interest in 'uncovering subtle intertextual maneuvers', however much literary criticism may itself be dependent on anthologies, as well as on the very process of selecting text for quotation. Perhaps more substantially, Price also notes that the role of the anthologist cuts across the various divisions of labour according to which the field of literature is usually divided—'writer and reader, writer and critic, writer and publisher, writer and censor', the anthologist at different moments switching from one side of these binaries to the other. Anthologies contain the anthologist's writing, but also 'a trace of reading'—a trace that is silently registered not in the anthologist's prefaces or other paratexts but in the exclusions and inclusions, placements, and orderings that go to make up the anthology itself.[10] Quiller-Couch's insight that the anthologist criticizes in silence is thus crucial to this chapter. Criticism takes its place in the anthology, and not just in its paratexts. Anthologizing acts are critical acts just as much as verbal judgements are critical judgements. The anthology is a critical form, furthermore, because, in selection, the formalizing processes of inclusion and exclusion are paradigmatic—and those are processes, moreover, that are fundamental (often controversially) to *criticism* in its root sense as well.[11]

Yet the view of criticism as a process of inclusion and, especially, exclusion has been controverted from many directions in recent years. In his widely influential call for the abandonment of close reading, for example, Franco Moretti aims to disabuse literary scholars of the superstition of selection:

> [T]he trouble with close reading (in all of its incarnations, from the new criticism to deconstruction) is that it necessarily depends on an extremely small canon. This may have become an unconscious and invisible premiss by now, but it is an iron one nonetheless: you invest so much in individual texts *only* if you think that very few of them really matter. Otherwise, it doesn't make sense. And if you want to look beyond the canon (and of course, world literature will do so: it would be absurd if it didn't!) close reading will not do it. It's not designed to do it, it's designed to do the opposite. At bottom, it's a theological exercise—very solemn treatment of very few texts taken very seriously—whereas what we really need is a little pact with the devil: we know how to read texts, now let's learn how *not* to read them.[12]

[10] Price, 2.

[11] See 'critic, *adj.*', *OED Online* <https://www.oed.com/view/Entry/44589> (accessed 28 March 2022), for the derivation of 'critic' and its cognates from κριτός, 'separated, chosen', and κρίνειν, 'to decide, judge'.

[12] Franco Moretti, 'Conjectures on World Literature', *New Left Review* (January–February 2000), 54–68 (57).

For Moretti, selection produces the bible of a critical church. Indeed, there is evidence that that is precisely how some anthologies have functioned or have wished to function. In her invaluable study of anthologies and their role in the formation of poetic taste, Anne Ferry remarks that in settling on the title *The Oxford Book of English Verse*, for example, Quiller-Couch sought to benefit from the 'slightest suggestion of sanctity'—Oxford University Press being the publisher of *the* Book—which 'would have helped to free the venture from the taint of commercialism'.[13] Quiller-Couch's preface to that volume is certainly also cast in his characteristically homiletic style, and the sweep of valedictory poems with which the first edition draws to a close (Alice Meynell's 'The Lady of the Lambs', Dora Sigerson's 'Ireland', and Margaret L. Woods's 'Genius Loci') concludes with the moralizing remonstrance of R. D. Blackmore's 'Dominus Illuminatio Mea' that 'even the purest delight'—such as that to be found in poetry—'may pall, | [...] But the glory of the Lord is all in all'.[14]

Such biblical ambitions were not confined to Quiller-Couch's *Oxford Book*, of course. In his history of *The Norton Anthology of English Literature*, Sean Shesgreen seeks to bring to light the 'stratagems [by which] it has managed to canonize itself as the bible of English literature'—one such stratagem having been the use of Bible paper to render the Norton light and portable without any reduction in content.[15] The idea that a selection of texts functions—or aims to function—as a sacred text is a potentially promising one, in part because the actual Bible is itself a selection of texts, the product of many inclusions and probably many more exclusions, of tendentious arrangements and connections.[16] One might also ask a touch heretically (taking a cue from Moretti) whether all of the texts gathered in the Bible are equally sacred, or, at least, demand equally to be read. The stories of Adam and Eve, Abraham, Moses and the Ten Commandments, Noah and the Flood, naturally—yes, and Job, Jonah, David and Goliath, Samson and Delilah, Daniel in the lions' den, and the Song of Songs, since it is both short and (for the Bible) racy—but surely you can skip Numbers and Deuteronomy and only read the Psalms that are routinely deployed at funerals? And if you have read Romans and the bit about faith, hope, and charity in 1 Corinthians, you need not plough through *all* of the epistles? By analogy, once you have accepted that you can pick and choose from among the vast corpus of potential literature, surely there is no need to read any selection of literary texts *through*?

---

[13] Anne Ferry, *Tradition and the Individual Poem: An Inquiry into Anthologies* (Stanford: Stanford University Press, 2001), 21.

[14] Quiller-Couch, 862.

[15] Sean Shesgreen, 'Canonizing the Canonizer: A Short History of *The Norton Anthology of English Literature*', *CI* 35 (2009), 293–318 (296, 297).

[16] Though note, here, John Guillory's important argument that the analogy between ecclesiastical and literary canons is ultimately unsustainable. See Guillory, 'Canon', in Frank Lentricchia and Thomas McLaughlin (eds), *Critical Terms for Literary Study*, 2nd edn (Chicago: University of Chicago Press, 1995), 233–49.

At the opposite pole of Moretti's rejection of selection as such is the sense—familiar from the significance granted to the names of God in the Hebrew Bible and to the sayings of Jesus in certain Christian liturgical practices—that the site of real holiness is particular *words*, rather than texts, however rigorously selected. Somewhat monomaniacally pursuing the thought that anthologies are made up of poems only one stanza of which, or even one line of which, is really worthwhile, Paul Chowder—the hapless protagonist of Nicholson Baker's novel *The Anthologist*—argues that what we need is more, not less, selection:

> But then, if you stare for a while at one of the single lines—stare into its rippling depths where the infant turtles swim—you realize that there's usually one particular word in that line that slays you. That word is so shockingly great. Maybe it's the word 'sometime.' 'They flee from me that—sometime—did me seek.' The little two-step shuffle there in the midst of the naked dancing feet of the monosyllables. Or maybe it's the word 'quiet.' 'Give me my scallop-shell of quiet.' Do you hear the way 'scallop' is folded and absorbed into the word 'quiet'?
>
> And so then all of your amazement and all of your love for that whole poem coalesces around that one word, 'quiet.' [...] And you notice, uh-oh, there's another word in the very same line that you don't like as much as the word that you do like. 'Give.' Hm. 'Give.' You've never liked 'give' all that much. It's a bad word, frankly. Give.
>
> And so you think, maybe I should have made an anthology of individual words taken from poems. Like this:
>
> sometime
>
> — Thomas Wyatt
>
> Or:
>
> quiet
>
> — Sir Walter Ralegh
>
> And of course that's not going to work. That's just a bunch of disembodied words plucked from great poems. And that's when you realize you're not an anthologist.[17]

That's not going to work because Chowder's publisher won't have it, but the moment you decide to make an anthology of single words might actually just be the moment you realize you are, in fact, an anthologist in the strictest sense, one whose commitment to selection is so strong that it gives (uh-oh. 'Gives'. Hm.)

---

[17] Nicholson Baker, *The Anthologist* (London: Simon & Schuster, 2009), 46–7. On the idea of an anthology of single lines (if not single words), compare R. S. Gwynn's poem 'Approaching a Significant Birthday, He Peruses *The Norton Anthology of Poetry*', in *No Word of Farewell: Poems 1970–2000* (Ashland, OR: Story Line Press, 2001), 42–3, which is composed entirely of single lines taken from different poems in *The Norton Anthology of Poetry*. I am grateful to Deborah Bowman for drawing my attention to Gwynn's poem.

no quarter. But another reason the anthology of great words is not going to work is that even Chowder's account of the focus on the single, shockingly great word cannot quite escape the force field of the whole poem or even the whole authorship: 'all of your amazement and all of your love *for that whole poem* coalesces around that one word'; 'a bunch of disembodied words plucked *from great poems*'; and finally, of course, it is not just anyone's 'sometime' and 'quiet' that Chowder wants to anthologize but Wyatt's and Raleigh's.

*

Unsurprisingly, we leave Chowder at the end of *The Anthologist* still working on his own anthology, having both catalogued a great number of his anthologistic models and rivals and having produced one of the most insightful characterizations of the difficulties of anthologizing we have. Chowder lists many of the leading poetry anthologies of the twentieth century, and it is notable that major anthologists, likewise, tend to reserve a special place in their discursive paratexts for acknowledgement of predecessor anthologists—acknowledgement, however, that is careful to point out that other anthologies have been consulted only after their selection was completed.[18] Anthologies, as Ferry has shown, both compete commercially and for cultural prestige with other anthologies, and belong to a tradition of selection in which they then themselves intervene by repeating some selections, deleting others, and expanding in other directions the field from which selection may be made. The period from the middle of the eighteenth century—when numerous anthologies not only sought to satisfy the demand of a burgeoning readership but also sought to establish and shape that readership, to inculcate particular habits of reading, and to determine what would and would not count as literature—to the end of the nineteenth—when Quiller-Couch's *Oxford Book* consolidated the lyricizing tradition of Palgrave's *Golden Treasury* but also prepared the way beyond it—saw the anthology emerge not only as a vital literary form, rather than mere vessel, but also as a decisive site of literary-critical practice.

Standing in some ways as the culmination of the eighteenth-century anthologistic tradition, Isaac D'Israeli's *Curiosities of Literature* offers a good way into thinking about selection as a form of criticism. D'Israeli himself ventures multiple descriptions of the form of the *Curiosities* within its opening pages: it is a 'Miscellany'; an 'inventory of knowledge'; an 'essay'; a 'LITERARY MANUAL'; a 'repository'.[19] It is, to use D'Israeli's own terms, a curious text, but one that is, so

---

[18] See, e.g., Quiller-Couch, p. ix, and William Stanley Braithwaite, *The Book of Elizabethan Verse*, 2nd edn (Boston: Herbert B. Turner & Co., 1907; first pub. 1906) [no pagination].

[19] Isaac D'Israeli, *Curiosities of Literature: Consisting of Anecdotes, Characters, Sketches, and Observations, Literary, Critical, and Historical*, 3rd edn (London: John Murray, 1791), pp. vi, ix, xi, xii. Further references to this edition are given after quotations in the text. For more on the form of D'Israeli's *Curiosities*, see April London, 'Isaac D'Israeli and Literary History: Opinion, Anecdote, and Secret History in the Early Nineteenth Century', *Poetics Today*, 26 (2005), 351–86 (esp. 358).

he claims, critical throughout. But what does it mean to claim that it is critical *throughout*? After all, there is a separate—albeit the first—section dedicated to 'Literature and Criticism', while other topics have their own sections in their turn. The *Curiosities*, that would suggest, are only partially critical. But, if we attend carefully to the work's title, we see that, in addition to literature itself being a rather unsettled category, such that the items labelled 'curiosities of literature' in the main title are adjectivally qualified as literary—doubly literary, then?—those items are also critical and historical as well. While those three determiners— literary, critical, and historical—may be taken to advert to the book's different sections, they do not perfectly map onto those sections, since D'Israeli chooses to entitle them 'Literature and Criticism' (as we have seen), 'Historical Anecdotes', and, teasingly, 'Miscellanea'. D'Israeli's claim is, then, that it is the whole book that is at once and indistinguishably literary, critical, and historical. This is made especially clear in D'Israeli's *The Illustrator Illustrated*, his defence of the *Curiosities* against Bolton Corney's attack. D'Israeli writes: 'On the principle of demonstrating important truths, or elucidating interesting topics by a reasonable number of apposite facts, a work of research might become *at once* ethical and critical, philosophical and historical.'[20]

D'Israeli's *Curiosities of Literature* is animated throughout by a conviction of the centrality of selection to the exercise of critical judgement. The article on 'Criticism', which borrows extensively from the seventeenth-century French scholar Pierre-Daniel Huet, gives at its conclusion a prospect for future criticism, now that earlier forms of criticism have been superseded thanks to technological advances:

> Now that the best authors are no more scarce, but multiplied without end by the invention of printing, verbal criticism, the chief merit of which is to catch syllables, deserves no longer our esteem. Critics of this kind may, not unaptly, be compared to weeders; they eradicate the worthless plants, and leave to more skilful cultivators the art of gathering and distinguishing the more valuable ones.   (p. 27)

Tracing the metaphor of the anthologist as picker of flowers from Montaigne via Vicesimus Knox to A. P. Wavell's *Other Men's Flowers* (1944), Ferry has commented that '[t]he humility professed in these simply described acts of gathering and binding is called in question because the sentence disregards the gardener who originally planted the flowers [...] while the maker of the posie [...] is

---

[20] D'Israeli, *The Illustrator Illustrated* (London: Edward Moxon, 1838), 6. For further commentary on the above passage in D'Israeli's '1838 self-vindication', see London, 352, and, for a broader defence of D'Israeli's characteristic practice against the many attacks upon it, see Ina Ferris's valuable essay 'Antiquarian Authorship: D'Israeli's Miscellany of Literary Curiosity and the Question of Secondary Genres', *Studies in Romanticism*, 45 (2006), 523–42.

granted full powers to pick and choose the flowers and to arrange them in a new design.'[21] Certainly, D'Israeli's depiction of 'skilful cultivators' as opposed to an earlier generation of verbal critics who were mere 'weeders' is not especially modest. But, more importantly, his distinction between the two kinds of critic is not quite as secure as he would like it to be. Weeding, just like the skilful cultivation that D'Israeli wants us to think he is practising, involves distinguishing one plant from another according to the comparative value ascribed to them. This attempt to indicate the path that criticism should take in the age of the mechanical reproducibility of texts is freighted by an anxiety (however unconscious) that the generative activity of skilful cultivation may not be that distinct from—may in fact depend upon—the merely negative activity of controlling unwanted growths. As Price and others have emphasized, the anthology cuts across established divisions in the field of literature—divisions that, at the time D'Israeli wrote, were becoming more firmly established—to both liberating and destabilizing effect.

Throughout the *Curiosities* D'Israeli is preoccupied with the mode of production that a book like his has involved and the kind of labour expended upon it. Selection requires skill, as the article on 'Criticism' claims, but it also requires other qualities as well. For one thing, it is not always the result of methodical research, but of serendipitous discovery. In an article equivocally titled 'Poets, Philosophers, and Artists Made By Accident' (the article may address that subset of poets, and so on, who were made by accident, or the title may be taken to aver that poets, and so on, are, *tout court*, made by accident), D'Israeli declares that '[a]ccident has frequently occasioned the most eminent geniuses to display their powers' (p. 75). What this entails is that no less an attribute than genius is only ever displayed intermittently, a conviction clearly echoed later in the *Curiosities*: 'Faultless *mediocrity* Industry can preserve in one continued degree; but *excellence* is only to be attained, by human faculties, by starts' (p. 206). This conception of genius and excellence is crucial to D'Israeli, since intermittence is characteristic of the form of the *Curiosities* themselves: certain themes are intermittently taken up and explored, and D'Israeli's comments *in propria persona* are themselves only intermittent. But such features, so the claim is, need not disqualify the *Curiosities* from being esteemed excellent—far from it, in fact. In addition to underwriting any potential claim of D'Israeli's own to excellence, the emphasis on the intermittent and accidental character of excellent literature seeks likewise to establish selection as the form most appropriate to literature's criticism.

While skilful cultivation may be reliant upon ruthlessly weeding out what does not belong in any literary garland, the judgement that D'Israeli exercises is

---

[21] Ferry, *Tradition*, 220, 275 n. 1. For the earlier history of this way of thinking about anthologies, see Theodore Tregear, 'Anthologizing Shakespeare, 1593–1603' (unpublished doctoral thesis, University of Cambridge, Trinity College, 2019), in *Apollo—University of Cambridge Repository* <https://doi.org/10.17863/CAM.40256> (accessed 23 December 2020) (esp. 9–12).

nevertheless tempered with mercy. This can be seen in his allowance, quoted above, that 'human faculties' are capable of attaining genius only 'by starts', and he had earlier, under the heading 'Severe Criticism', offered the following reflections on both literary and critical labours:

> An unmerciful Critic observes, that there are few books to which an Author can prefix his name, without trespassing upon his veracity: for there is not one work which is the labour of a single person.
>
> When a poet was reproached for his Plagiarisms, (which he probably called Classical Imitations) he defended himself in this manner—That a painter was not less a painter, nor an architect less an architect, because the one purchases his colours, and the other his building materials. 'It is all pouring out of one bottle into another,' exclaimed Sterne.—Unhappy Authors! Unrelenting Critics!   (p. 145)

Transferred to an unnamed poet and painter, this defence may of course serve for D'Israeli himself. The sequence of borrowings in evidence in this very passage is especially vertiginous: the apothegm, 'It is all pouring out of one bottle into another', though in quotation marks and explicitly attributed to Sterne, inaccurately recollects what Sterne's Tristram in fact poses as a question at the beginning of the fifth volume of *Tristram Shandy*, Tristram's implication being that it would be better to cease modelling the making of books on apothecary: 'Shall we forever make new books, as apothecaries make new mixtures, by pouring only out of one vessel into another?'[22] But Sterne had himself borrowed this bemoaning of borrowing from Robert Burton's *The Anatomy of Melancholy*, where—rather more akin, actually, to D'Israeli's casting of this sentiment—the analogy is more neutrally deployed: 'As Apothecaries we make new mixtures every day, poure out of one Vessel into another [...].'[23]

The tonal vagaries of the literature-as-apothecary apothegm are revealing because they attest to an anxiety about, but also willingness to defend, the process of making books from materials ready to hand. One source of that anxiety, of course, arises from a doubt about whether existing works are really materials for the poet in the way that paint or stone is for the painter or architect. That analogy uncomfortably straddles the distinction between form and matter: selections from existing literature (whether viewed as 'Plagiarisms' or 'Classical Imitations')

---

[22] Laurence Sterne, *The Life and Opinions of Tristram Shandy, Gentleman*, ed. Melvyn New and Joan New (London: Penguin, 2003), 309.

[23] Robert Burton, *The Anatomy of Melancholy*, ed. Thomas C. Faulkner et al., 6 vols (Oxford: Clarendon Press, 1989–2000), i (1989), 9. As Melvyn and Joan New note in their edition of *Tristram Shandy*, James A. Work had already remarked on Sterne's borrowing from Burton in his edition, *The Life and Opinions of Tristram Shandy, Gentleman* (New York: Odyssey, 1940). See *Tristram Shandy*, ed. Melvyn New and Joan New, 672–3. Work, as the News note, was following John Ferriar, *Illustrations of Sterne, with Other Essays and Verses* (London: printed for Cadell and Davies, 1798), in which Ferriar—perhaps guilelessly, perhaps rather knowingly—describes as 'very singular' Sterne's 'evident copy' (p. 66). Christopher Tilmouth first brought the D'Israeli–Sterne–Burton sequence of debts to my attention.

are more like sections of a painting or fragments of a building—a bucolic back-ground here, a salvaged cornice there—than they are like unworked colours or stones. D'Israeli is suggesting that such forms can, as it were, be rematerialized, rendering them available for formation into something new. And this, of course, is central to D'Israeli's own practice in a way that has significant consequences for his role as (merciful) critic. It is frequently hard to decide in reading D'Israeli's articles if they are D'Israeli's. Sometimes, as in the case of Sterne, he quotes a source quite explicitly. Sometimes he more broadly acknowledges an authority—frequently another collector of anecdote and ana, such as Huet or Gilles Ménage; sometimes, he thanks an anonymous 'friend'; sometimes, he cannot remember where he initially found something, though he says that there is indeed a source; and, sometimes, he makes no such acknowledgement. An instructive comparison between Ménage and D'Israeli suggests itself here. The *Menagiana, ou Les Bons Mots et remarques critiques, historiques, morals, et d'érudition de Monsieur Ménage* was *recueillies par ses amis*—collected by his friends—whereas, for D'Israeli, the relationship between scholar and friends is inverted: *Curiosities* is not a collection by his friends of his *bons mots*, but a collection by him of the *bons mots* of his friends.[24] This has consequences for the cultivation of critical authority, such that Ménage's authority is established by being collected, while D'Israeli's is dependent upon collecting. The act of collection is critical, involving distinction and rec-ommendation, such that we are asked to trust those recommendations on the authority of the collector. But that act at the same time entails a tempering of critical authority, since what is being advanced is not so much a principled discourse containing explicit judgements, but rather a series of examples that the reader ('the reader' being essentially a composite and undifferentiated mass itself) is invited to consider. Both enacting and inviting judgement, the anthologist is more exemplary of the composite reading public than the unmerciful critic, and hence the ambivalence—even invisibility—of whose authorship is crucial to her or his role.[25]

*

I mentioned briefly above Riding and Graves's sense that the anthology and criticism are inimical.[26] Riding and Graves identified what they called the 'true' anthology in three forms, none of which is exactly, by their own admission,

---

[24] The *Ménagiana* were first published at Paris in 1693, but in a letter to John Wilson Croker of 28 January 1829 D'Israeli specifies the edition prepared by Bernard de la Monnoye in 1715 as the one he uses (the context is D'Israeli's recollection of his youthful view that Boswell's *Life of Johnson* would outlast the *Ménagiana*). See James Ogden, *Isaac D'Israeli* (Oxford: Oxford University Press, 1969), 134–5, where the letter is quoted.

[25] Compare Price's comments on the anthologist's abdication of editorial responsibility and conse-quent exemplification of 'the undifferentiated passivity of the reading public' (pp. 68–9).

[26] *A Pamphlet against Anthologies* (1928), in Laura Riding and Robert Graves, *'A Survey of Modernist Poetry' and 'A Pamphlet against Anthologies'*, ed. Charles Mundye and Patrick McGuinness (Manchester: Carcanet, 2002), 151–256 (164).

unproblematic: the anthology expressing private taste; the 'rescue-anthology'; and their signally ambivalent category of the critical anthology. Given their claim that 'an anthology implies a work of pure collection and display', it would seem that it is the 'rescue-anthology', which presents 'historical material in the raw', that is the truest instance of the 'true anthology'. As we have already seen in the case of D'Israeli, however, the raw and pure turn out to be cooked and to bear the taint of prior working, even (indeed, especially) where the claim of authorship is made to rest on the practices of the collection and display of available materials. The idea of 'rescue', moreover, may seem precisely adverse to criticism, which must jettison, as well as retain and recover. But the historical anthology itself, of course, has sought to do much more than rescue. Historical anthologists have rarely rescued everything that they might have pulled from the ashes of the past and so must, therefore, justify what they have chosen to gather together.

Published at a significant point in the evolution of the anthology, Charles Lamb's *Specimens of English Dramatic Poets* (1808) is an important instance not merely of rescue but of the critical recuperation of passion over wit, tragedy over comedy, antique moral sense over contemporary manners. While it is true, that is, that admirers of Lamb's critical achievement in his *Specimens* have tended to emphasize the critical acuity of his direct and discriminating notes, it is nevertheless clear that the critical ambitions of Lamb's anthology are vested as much in its effort of literary-historical rescue itself as in his commentary. In excusing himself in his preface from providing 'biographical notices' in the manner of eighteenth-century collections, Lamb remarks that '[t]he few notes which are interspersed will be found to be chiefly critical', a remark that may itself have suggested to readers that those notes are the privileged site of criticism in the selection. Yet Lamb's articulation of his design, not in composing his notes, but in making the selections, repeatedly gives expression to a distinctly critical intention: 'I have expunged without ceremony all that which the writers had better never have written'; '[t]he kind of extracts which I have sought after have been, not so much passages of wit and humour, though the old plays are rich in such, as scenes of passion, sometimes of the deepest quality, interesting situations, serious descriptions, that which is more nearly allied to poetry than to wit, and to tragic rather than to comic poetry'; '[m]y leading design has been, to illustrate what may be called the moral sense of our ancestors'.[27] And it is not just the selection of texts that fulfils a critical design, but, Lamb makes clear, their arrangement as well. Mentioning a final object in making his selections, Lamb explains his motivation

---

[27] Charles Lamb, *Specimens of English Dramatic Poets, who Lived about the Time of Shakespeare. With Notes*, 2nd edn, 2 vols (London: Edward Moxon, 1835; repr. Cambridge: Cambridge University Press, 2013), i, p. vi. Further references are given after quotations in the text. For an illuminating account of the 'strict structure and interpretive framework' that Lamb imposes on his selections, see Felicity James, 'Charles Lamb', in Peter Holland and Adrian Poole (eds), *Great Shakespeareans*, 18 vols (London: Continuum, 2010–13), iv: Adrian Poole (ed.), *Lamb, Hazlitt, Keats* (2010), 10–63 (41, 49, 50).

not just for selecting certain texts—in this case, 'the most admired scenes in Fletcher and Massinger, in the estimation of the world the only dramatic poets of that age who are entitled to be considered after Shakespeare' (i, p. vii)—but for juxtaposing them 'in the same volume' with others—namely, selections from Marlowe, Haywood, Tourneur, Webster, Ford, and so on. Lamb's purpose in bringing together the already admired Fletcher and Massinger with less regularly heralded figures is, explicitly, to correct the world's estimation of the dramatists who lived about the time of Shakespeare: 'To show what we have slighted, while beyond all proportion we have cried up one or two favourite names' (i, p. vii). The opening selection, from *Gorboduc, a Tragedy*, by Thomas Sackville and others, may not seem especially propitious with respect to this stated desideratum—'The style of this old play is stiff and cumbersome,' Lamb remarks in his note, 'like the dresses of its times. There may be flesh and blood underneath, but we cannot get at it' (i. 6)—and, even where the play's capacity to illustrate the morality of its time is concerned, Lamb is hardly emphatic: 'Sir Philip Sidney has praised it for its morality. One of its authors might easily have furnished that' (i. 6), he remarks, nonchalantly. Instead, Lamb gives the reader a post-hoc interpretative steer—'The chief beauty of the extract is of a secret nature. Marcella obscurely intimates that the murdered prince Porrex and she had been lovers'—which certainly would suggest that there may be flesh and blood underneath the stiff and cumbersome outer garments of a play like this.[28] It is in any case not until the second volume that excerpts are included from either Fletcher or Massinger, by which time Lamb has included specimens not just from such (now) routinely recognized playwrights as Marlowe and Jonson, Ford and Webster, but also a selection from the work of figures such as Peele, Tailor, Brewer, Cook, Rowley, and Sackville.

The example of Lamb's *Specimens* should lead us to be wary of any attempt (such as Riding and Graves's) to distinguish between the presentation of 'pure', 'raw' historical material and the anthology as criticism. The *Specimens* cannot be disaggregated into distinct anthologistic and critical elements, identifying the first with the volumes' arrangement and the second with its notes. As Lamb himself makes clear, his critical intentions are fulfilled by the practice of selection itself.

The historical significance of Lamb's *Specimens* arises in part from the expression it gives to the early nineteenth-century espousal of an earlier poetic sensibility explicitly opposed to what are cast (and in some cases, indeed, confected) as established artistic priorities (wit, comedy, fashionable manners). Lamb's focus on drama specifically is also significant given the process of what has been described as the lyricization of poetry (if not of literature generally) that took effect during the nineteenth century—a process that in many ways reached its apogee in

---

[28] Lamb is probably thinking of the passage in which Marcella recalls Porrex 'Shining in armour bright before the tilt, | And with thy mistress' sleeve tied on thy helm, | [...] Which never now these eyes may see again' (quoted in Lamb, i. 4–5).

another anthology, Francis Turner Palgrave's *The Golden Treasury*.[29] The process of anthologistic lyricization had an early critic in the prolific American anthologizer William Stanley Braithwaite, who was at pains in the preface to his *The Book of Elizabeth Verse* (1906) to mark his distinction from previous anthologists: 'With very few exceptions,' Braithwaite declared there, 'I have been particular to give each poem without omission of stanzas or lines; especially has this been so in cases where longer verses have been "fashioned" by former editors to give the lyric form and quality, and depleted of fine lines and single stanzas which will be met with here as new to many readers'.[30] Nevertheless, drama in particular was felt to present particular difficulties to the anthologist long into the twentieth century, after other consequences of the prioritization of the lyric were recognized and (at least in part) overcome. In her *The New Oxford Book of English Verse* (1972), for instance, Helen Gardner sought to counteract the prioritization of lyric and consequent 'neglect of the tradition of satiric, political, epistolary, and didactic verse in English' that Quiller-Couch had inherited from Palgrave, while nevertheless maintaining the exclusion of dramatic verse (it was not until Christopher Ricks's *The Oxford Book of English Verse*, published in 1999, a century after Quiller-Couch had established this particular franchise, that drama was accorded a place in it).[31] Yet Lamb's *Specimens* of course has an ambivalent, rather than simply divergent, relation to the tradition of lyricization on the cusp of which it stands. Just because it selects from dramatic works does not mean it is guiltless (if it may be put like that) of lyricization, since it includes only relatively short extracts of the plays it includes, in which not action, but rather, as Lamb had asserted, passion is the main concern.

However the matter of lyricization ultimately stands with Lamb, for Palgrave, half a century later, poetry is lyric. Contemporary descriptions of Palgrave's critical powers, moreover, cast them in a distinctly lyric vein. In his entry on Palgrave for the old *Dictionary of National Biography*, J. W. Mackail, himself the compiler of an important selection of epigrams from the *Greek Anthology* and thus not altogether personally disinterested in his attempt to identify the making of anthologies with the practice of criticism, remarks of Palgrave's 'now little known' *The Passionate Pilgrim*, his collection of autobiographical reflections published under the pseudonym 'Henry J. Thurstan' in 1858, that it is 'the *Dichtung und Wahrheit* of a

---

[29] For a useful and succinct account of lyricization, see Virginia Jackson, *Dickinson's Misery: A Theory of Lyric Reading* (Princeton: Princeton University Press, 2005), 7–8. On Palgrave and lyricization in particular, see Christopher Clausen, 'The Palgrave Version', *Georgia Review*, 34 (1980), 273–89 (esp. 274–5, 279), and Christopher Ricks's even-handed defence in 'The Making of *The Golden Treasury*', in Francis Turner Palgrave, *The Golden Treasury*, ed. Ricks (London: Penguin, 1991), 437–50 (449). References to *The Golden Treasury* are to Ricks's edition and are given after quotations in the text.

[30] Braithwaite, *Elizabethan Verse*, p. xvii. In practice, very few of Braithwaite's selections stretch over more than a couple of pages.

[31] Helen Gardner (ed.), *The New Oxford Book of English Verse, 1250-1950* (Oxford: Oxford University Press, 1972), p. v.

highly cultured and sensitive mind'.[32] Since *Dichtung und Wahrheit* was itself the *Dichtung und Wahrheit* of perhaps Europe's most highly cultured and sensitive mind, this is quite a claim—but the historical and aesthetic tenets on which it rests are clear. Mackail tempers his praise a little when he notes that *The Passionate Pilgrim* 'is only marred by a slight overloading of quotation'. Even this blemish, however, is excused when Mackail puts it down, revealingly, not to 'ostentation of learning, but the natural overflow of unusual knowledge and a power of critical appreciation which was in excess of his own creative faculty'.[33] The Wordsworthian stamp of this praise ('natural overflow of unusual knowledge') dilutes Mackail's continued emphasis on the distinction between critical and creative faculties, concluding his encomium on Palgrave as follows: 'Palgrave was one of those men whose distinction and influence consist less in creative power than in that appreciation of the best things which is the highest kind of criticism, and in the habit of living, in all matters of both art and life, at the highest standard'.[34] The Wordsworthian quality of Mackail's praise for Palgrave is joined by the Arnoldian tenor of this estimation ('appreciation of the best things', and so on), and it is fitting to recall here, along with the transfer of Wordsworthian qualities of creation to Palgrave's powers of criticism, Arnold's own alliance of criticism and creation. Arnold had himself, in 'The Literary Influence of Academies', remarked of Palgrave that he was 'certainly endowed with a very fine critical tact: his *Golden Treasury* abundantly proves it'.[35] Palgrave was not only a critic, then, but a 'very fine' one, practising not just any kind of criticism, but the 'highest' kind.

Mackail's attempt to uphold the distinction between criticism and creation, while describing the former in terms often applied to the latter, has developed in later readers of *The Golden Treasury* into a less qualified estimation of the creative quality of what Palgrave did. Ricks emphasizes what Palgrave created in *The Golden Treasury*, even if that creation is different from other more conventionally recognizable literary works: 'Palgrave decided *to create* his own anthology of the best songs and lyrical poems in the English language'; '*The Golden Treasury* [...] made such sacrifices as were called for if the anthology were to appeal to, and *bring into being*, the most stable mid-Victorian readership for poetry'.[36] And Arnold himself, of course, while acknowledging the priority of the 'creative' over the 'critical power', had in 'The Function of Criticism at the Present Time' argued that the creative power may in fact be exercised in criticizing (as also in

---

[32] 'J. W. Mackail on Palgrave', in Palgrave, *Golden Treasury*, ed. Ricks, 455–8 (456). See also J. W. Mackail (ed.), *Select Epigrams from the Greek Anthology* (London: Longman, 1890).
[33] Mackail, 'Palgrave', 456.   [34] Mackail, 'Palgrave', 458.
[35] In *The Complete Prose Works of Matthew Arnold*, ed. R. H Super, 11 vols (Ann Arbor: University of Michigan Press, 1960–74), iii: *Lectures and Essays on Criticism* (1962), 232–57 (252).
[36] Ricks, 'Making of *The Golden Treasury*', 438, 442 (emphases added).

'well-doing' and 'learning'), and that, moreover, truly great creative work is 'nourished by a great critical effort providing the true materials for it'.[37]

The title page of *The Golden Treasury* states that the 'best songs and lyrical poems in the English language' that it contains were 'selected and arranged with notes' by Palgrave. While this certainly documents Palgrave's contribution of 'notes', the emphasis is on the twin achievements of selection and arrangement. The remarks of both Mackail and Arnold clearly imply that it was his selection of texts—his 'appreciation' (Mackail) or 'tact' (Arnold)—rather than his paratextual commentaries in which his critical accomplishments are most evident. Indeed, Arnold's praise for Palgrave in 'The Literary Influence of Academies' comes just before he blames him for shoddy criticism in one of his notes (which he in fact describes as 'a freak or a violence').[38] It is the selection, for Arnold at least, rather than the commentary that is the basis of Palgrave's claim to critical fame. 'I hope you liked the arrangement and my notes &c.', Palgrave had himself written to Alexander Grant. 'In this sort of paste-and-scissors authorship these trifles are all one can call one's own.'[39] Though this description of his labours may, as both Ferry and Ricks suggest, be disingenuous, it is also revealing that it is not just those elements of *The Golden Treasury* that he actually wrote ('and my notes &c.') that Palgrave claims as his own, but rather 'the arrangement' as well. The disingenuousness shows itself all the more fully in that it is arrangement (paste) and selection (scissors) that Palgrave takes as constituting nothing less than 'authorship'.[40]

Anthologists are understandably keen to lend some sort of significant order to what could easily appear either chaotic or subject to an arbitrarily imposed schema. With his eye on the latter peril, William Stanley Braithwaite rather floridly declares in the preface to his *The Book of Elizabethan Verse* (1906) (the first of 'a series of four volumes designed to cover the entire range of British poetry from the publication of *Tottel's Miscellany*, 1557, to the end of the Victorian epoch', only three of which in fact appeared) that, rather than adopt a strict scheme of organization, he 'preferred instead, to come out of a prodigal and fragrant field with an armful of flowers with perfumes and colours arranged by kind, indifferently, to give something of Nature's variety'.[41] Braithwaite's schemes of organization, like those of other significant anthologists, are rather more artful than that would suggest. The placement of opening and, perhaps specifically, closing poems has been a site charged with significance for many anthologists, for instance. We touched above on Quiller-Couch's hortatory and beatifying conclusion to the first

---

[37] In Arnold, *Complete Prose*, iii. 258–85 (260, 262).   [38] Arnold, *Complete Prose*, iii. 253.
[39] 22 February 1862; Gwenllian F. Palgrave, *Francis Turner Palgrave: His Journals and Memories of his Life* (London: Longmans, Green, and Co., 1899), 71.
[40] Cf. Anne Ferry, 'Palgrave's "Symphony"', *VP* 27 (1999), 145–62 (148).
[41] Braithwaite, *Elizabethan Verse*, p. xvii. The quotation in the parenthesis is from Braithwaite's preface to *The Book of Georgian Verse* (New York: Brentano's, 1909; London: Grant Richards, 1909), p. xiii.

iteration of *The Oxford Book of English Verse* above; Helen Gardner's *New Oxford Book* comparably builds to a climax with Dylan Thomas's 'A Refusal to Mourn the Death, by Fire, of a Child in London', 'Do not go gentle into that good night', and 'Fern Hill', before offering excerpts from Louis McNeice's 'A Fanfare for the Makers' as an 'Epilogue'. Gardner had drawn attention in her preface to her inclusion of poems paying tribute to other poets (p. vii) and hence to the commentary on poetry internal to the history of English verse itself. McNeice's tribute to those 'who compose | A book of words or deeds' returns to this focus. Indeed, the poem opens by invoking 'A cloud of witnesses', who may surely be identified with the poets that have gone before this final poem in Gardner's anthology, but also, perhaps a little more speculatively, with the more undetermined and indefinite readership before which the anthology itself now stands. This kind of recollection of the anthologist's priorities is likewise in evidence at the conclusion of the most recent iteration of the *Oxford Book*—namely, Ricks's. Justifying his inclusion of Seamus Heaney—the only poet included who was younger than himself—in his introduction, Ricks described Heaney as a 'truly open poet',[42] whose devotion to openness is avowed at the very close of the anthology itself, in the final lines of the final poem, 'The Pitchfork', which invoke 'an other side | Where perfection—or nearness to it—is imagined | Not in the aiming but the opening hand'. The opening rather than aiming hand is the anthologist's, refusing the indication of any particular critical direction while opening a field for the imagination of perfection or nearness to it—for, that is, the exercise of a version of critical judgement.

In the suggestiveness of the openings and closings to their anthologies, Quiller-Couch, Gardner, and Ricks all follow Palgrave. Openings and closings are especially charged in selections of what are, for the most part, short poems, since there are so many of them. Moreover, even setting aside the many cuts that Palgrave, for instance, made to individual poems, it is of course between endings and beginnings that the anthologist wields her or his scissors, dabs her or his paste— and thus ambivalently asserts authorship on the basis of a kind of activist readership. In the echoes, repetitions, and anticipations that Palgrave arranged in *The Golden Treasury* there is an insistence on variance, on the ambivalence of any settled conclusion, on the subjection, even, of greatness to time and tide—and, above all, on the centrality of minutely attentive and unencumbered critical comparison. *The Golden Treasury* opens, as has often been noted, with Thomas Nashe's frolicsome 'Spring' (the title is Palgrave's, not Nashe's) rather than with a recognizable anthology piece by a celebrated writer like Shakespeare, who must wait for his first appearance in the anthology not only until after Nashe but also after William Drummond of Hawthornden has had his turn (pp. 11–14).[43]

---

[42] Ricks (ed.), *Oxford Book of English Verse*, p. xxxiv.
[43] Shakespeare was promoted to second and third place in subsequent editions, albeit as represented by brief songs extracted from the plays.

Likewise, as Ferry has remarked, the placement of Keats's 'On First Looking into Chapman's Homer', with its description of the experience of encountering a text, at the head of book IV initially seems out of keeping with the emphasis on natural cycles in the opening poems of the three preceding books—an apparent incongruence that Ferry persuasively argues encourages a more precise and fuller reading of the poem's literary-history-in-miniature (from Homer to Chapman to Keats—and thence to Palgrave's reader).[44] Palgrave's desire to charge beginnings of the books of his anthology is matched by a comparable impulse with respect to endings. What is in fact only the penultimate poem of the anthology, Wordsworth's 'Intimations' ode, would surely, in the grandiloquence of its extended exploration of the great process of coming and ceasing to be, have provided a fitting conclusion. Yet the anthology has elsewhere its setting—in Shelley's much briefer, more whimsically melancholic 'Music, when soft voices die', in keeping with the volume's attitude with respect to great themes and the pretensions of human achievement in general.

The qualification of endings—the glossing of last words with last, last words—occurs not just at the end of *The Golden Treasury*, in fact, but throughout.[45] The culmination of book I with Drummond's 'Saint John the Baptist', which is followed by the opening of book II with Milton's 'On the Morning of Christ's Nativity', is only the most obvious example of an ending that is recast as an anticipation. Other cases of the significant qualification of endings tend to a quite different effect, however. The concluding couplet of Shakespeare's Sonnet 30, '—But if the while I think on thee, dear Friend, | All losses are restored, and sorrows end', is at once final and uplifting, yet the opening two lines of the poem that (in 1861) immediately followed it—'Like as the waves make towards the pebbled shore | So do our minutes hasten to their end'—are not. Palgrave has arranged things here, within a larger sequence of poems that are themselves concerned with looking backward, so that, through the word 'end', the opening of the following poem looks back to the close of the preceding one in order to unsettle its resolute and happy conclusion by reminding us that we are not yet, actually, at the end, though we are racing, alas, towards it.

*

The Golden Treasury itself has had a longer life than its conclusion envisages for the mortal individuals that make up its readers.[46] 'No Victorian anthology has had a longer life or a wider influence', remarked Kathleen Tillotson; 'more truly

---

[44] Ferry, 'Palgrave's "Symphony"', 154–6.

[45] I owe 'last, last words' to Christina G. Rossetti ('The Prince's Progress', l. 374) via Eric Griffiths, 'The Disappointment of Christina G. Rossetti', *Essays in Criticism*, 47 (1997), 107–42 (107).

[46] For an informative account of the afterlives of *The Golden Treasury*, see Bartholomew Brinkman, *Poetic Modernism in the Culture of Mass Print* (Baltimore: Johns Hopkins University Press, 2017), 45–70.

educational than anything else that came out of an Education Department'.[47] Anne Stevenson, in her appreciation of *The Golden Treasury*, likewise stresses the public and educational value of anthologies as such, which are, 'even at their crudest, show cases providing the bewildered nonspecialist at least with a starting point'.[48] Braithwaite's prospected four-volume selection of British literature like- wise aimed to fulfil a pedagogical function, which he emphasized by acknowledg- ing the assistance of 'professors of English in many of our leading universities';[49] the ongoing rival enterprises of the Norton, Longman, and Oxford anthologies situate themselves even more explicitly, not just as selections from the history of literature, but as curricula; longer ago and elsewhere than the Anglosphere, Theodor Echtermeyer's 1836 *Auswahl deutscher Gedichte für die untern und mittlern Classen gelehrter Schulen*, a franchise that has seen 'Echtermeyers' continuously revised and updated up to the present day, explicitly announced its intended scholastic audience in its title.[50]

The trouble is that Stevenson's 'bewildered nonspecialist', having found her or his starting point, may be subject to the unhelpful but true advice that, in order most easily to get to where she or he wants to go, she or he should not start from there. Palgrave has found eloquent and persuasive admirers in Tillotson, Ferry, Ricks, and many others, but the role that *The Golden Treasury* played in forming a certain lineage and curriculum of English poetry has not always found favour. Though Palgrave made no secret of the fact that *The Golden Treasury* was a treas- ury of the 'best songs and lyrical poems in the English language', that part of his title soon disappeared from view and, with it, the reminder that Palgrave's focus was on a particular kind of poem as potentially (at least) distinct from poetry as such. Any selection is of course open to expressions of regret concerning what is not in it, and even of censure concerning what is, but Palgrave is only the last in a line of anthologists who failed to include any writing by anyone not stale (it was established as a criterion that no living writer should be included in *The Golden Treasury*), pale, and male, despite women poets having themselves been the sub- ject of four anthologies in Britain and America in 1848 alone—twelve years before the idea for *The Golden Treasury* was conceived.[51] While detailing Palgrave's attempt to associate lyric 'with heroic virtues and manly values in a way that

---

[47] Kathleen Tillotson, 'Palgrave's *Golden Treasury* and Tennyson: Another Source', *Tennyson Research Bulletin*, 5 (1988), 49–54 (52).
[48] Anne Stevenson, 'Why Palgrave Lives', *VP* 37 (1999), 211–14 (211).
[49] Braithwaite (ed.), *Elizabethan Verse*, p. xv.
[50] See, again, Shesgreen, who discusses the challenge posed to Norton by Oxford and Longman (pp. 306–9); on Echtermeyers, see Multigraph Collective, *Interacting with Print*, 35–6.
[51] For an informative contextualization of Palgrave's (non-)selection of women poets, see Linda H. Peterson, 'Anthologizing Women: Women Poets in Early Victorian Collections of Lyric', *VP* 37 (1999), 193–209. On the 1848 anthologies of women poets, see Paula Bernat Bennett, *Poets in the Public Sphere: The Emancipatory Project of American Women's Poetry* (Princeton: Princeton University Press, 2003), 17–39, and Jackson, *Dickinson's Misery*, 209–10.

earlier Victorian anthologies did not', Linda H. Peterson has argued that, in addition to his desire to masculinize lyric, another influence on Palgrave's near-exclusion of female poets from *The Golden Treasury* was the emergence through a series of earlier nineteenth-century anthologies of a tradition of women's poetry as distinguishable from men's.[52] Though she comments on earlier anthologies like Alexander Dyce's *British Poetesses: Selected and Chronologically Arranged* (1825 and complete with sexist preface), it is with Anne Katherine Ellwood's *Memoirs of the Literary Ladies of England* (1842) and Jane Williams's *Literary Women of England* (1850) that gender comes to displace genre as the principle for selection, and 'a particular interest of women in women' is assumed, inaugurating 'a shift from literature written by women to women's literature, from lyrics written by women to women's poetry'.[53] Peterson acknowledges the 'recuperative effort' of Williams's 1850 anthology but goes on to emphasize that the distinct lineage of women's writing that such anthologies are seen to have established was 'not always for the benefit of women writers'.[54] What gives rise to Peterson's concern is not only, or even chiefly, the suggestion that the emergence of a distinct tradition of women's poetry in the nineteenth century made it all the easier for an anthologizer like Palgrave to mark off women's poetry as belonging to a separate literary sphere, but rather that the emergence of that tradition gave rise to a tacit, scarcely evidenced, and yet powerful identification of writing *by* women with writing *about* women.

The relations between *by* and *about* are frequently vexed. Leah Price rightly contends that '[a]nthologies are more than a referendum', and I have spent most of this chapter concerned with what Price calls the anthology as 'a genre in its own right', which determines 'not simply who gets published or what gets read, but who reads, and how'.[55] More than a referendum they may be, though that itself does not disqualify anthologies from being at least a referendum in part, and their role in determining who gets published or what gets read, especially in a cultural field that is cut across by relations of social, political, and economic power, is vital to them. The anthology is undeniably a key site for the establishment and contestation of literary traditions. As Amiri Baraka wrote in his introduction to the anthology he edited with Amina Baraka, *Confirmation: An Anthology of African American Women* (1983), the fact that black women, for example, are 'usually and notoriously' absent from American letters 'alone would justify the publication of *Confirmation*—to "confirm" that a whole body of American Literature has been consistently ignored or hidden'.[56] The decades separating *Confirmation* and the earlier *Black Fire: An Anthology of Afro-American Writing* (1968) (which Baraka

---

[52] Peterson, 'Anthologizing Women', 200–2 (200).
[53] Peterson, 'Anthologizing Women', 204.   [54] Peterson, 'Anthologizing Women', 205.
[55] Price, 3.
[56] Amiri Baraka and Amina Baraka (eds), *Confirmation: An Anthology of African American Women* (New York: William Morrow, 1983), 16.

(as LeRoi Jones) had edited with Larry Neal and of which *Confirmation* is a continuation) from James Weldon Johnson's *The Book of American Negro Poetry* (1922) and Alain Locke's *The New Negro* (1925) mark more than the passage of time, of course: Baraka, Neal, and later black American writers criticize what they see as the accommodation to white, bourgeois canons of judgement in those anthologies and the literary movements they attempt to represent. In the introduction to his anthology, for instance, James Weldon Johnson averred that '[t]he final measure of the greatness of all peoples is the amount and standard of the literature and art they have produced. The world does not know that a people is great until that people produces great literature and art.'[57] It is certainly a questionable claim, not only in its invocation of the hackneyed notion of popular and aesthetic 'greatness', but in its readiness to concede that a people must prove itself in this (or any other) way. Nevertheless, Johnson boldly claims not only a place in an already established field of American literary culture, but also that it is the American Negro people (to adopt his terms) who have fulfilled in a distinctively American manner the criterion he establishes: 'the Negro [...] [is] the creator of the only things artistic that have yet sprung from American soil and been universally acknowledged as distinctive American products.'[58] The task of Johnson's anthology is thus to gather the main literary accomplishments of black Americans, but it is also part of his endeavour to elaborate a living tradition for writers and readers who have been denied one. 'I feel confident that the reader will find not only an earnest for the future,' he remarks at the conclusion of his preface, 'but actual achievement.'[59] Indeed, many of the poems Johnson selects, especially those of the younger poets gathered towards the end of the volume, strike this prospective note, rather than the valedictory note that is discernible at the conclusions to many other anthologies: Frank Horne's 'Immortality', Helene Johnson's 'Invocation', and, in last place, Lucy Ariel Williams's 'Northboun'', despite the intervening of Waring Churney's despondently Keatsian 'Finis', are all earnest for the future at the very end of the collection.

Johnson's combination of proof of achievement and prospects for the future is radicalized in *The New Negro*, 'Dr Locke's interpretive anthology' (as it is described by Robert Hayden).[60] Yet, here, the question of the relation between *by* and *about* is explicitly posed in a way that would become all the more urgent for figures like Baraka, their criticisms of the Harlem Renaissance with which *The New Negro* is closely associated notwithstanding. Locke writes in his 1925 'Foreword':

---

[57] James Weldon Johnson (ed.), *The Book of American Negro Poetry*, rev. edn (New York: Harcourt, Brace, 1931; first pub. 1922), 9.

[58] Johnson (ed.), *American Negro Poetry*, 10.   [59] Johnson (ed.), *American Negro Poetry*, 47.

[60] Robert Hayden, 'Preface to the Atheneum Edition', in Alain Locke (ed.), *The New Negro* (New York: Boni, 1925; repr. New York: Atheneum, 1975), pp. ix–xiv (p. ix).

Of all the voluminous literature on the Negro, so much is mere external view and commentary that we may warrantably say that nine-tenths of it is about the Negro rather than of him, so that it is the Negro problem rather than the Negro that is known and mooted in the general mind. We turn therefore in the other direction to the elements of truest social portraiture, and discover in the artistic self-expression of the Negro to-day a new figure on the national canvas and a new force in the foreground of affairs.[61]

Moreover, where Johnson, only three years before Locke's *The New Negro*, had sought to balance the imperatives of retrospect and prospect, for Locke, the emphasis is firmly on the latter: 'we speak of the offerings of this book embodying these ripening forces as culled from the first fruits of the Negro Renaissance,' Locke declares in his 'Foreword', going on to argue in his eponymous essay 'The New Negro' that, owing to 'renewed self-respect and self-dependence', 'the life of the Negro community is bound to enter a new dynamic phase, the buoyancy from within compensating for whatever pressure there may be of conditions without'. Perhaps the posture struck by *The New Negro* is best described, then, by saying that it seeks to do justice to the old in an innovative form, while maintaining a generally prospecting outlook.

Though generic multiplicity had been a key feature of earlier anthologies and commonplace books since the Renaissance (the example of D'Israeli, discussed above, is worth recollecting here), *The New Negro* makes it an explicit principle of composition. Essays—a number of which (such as Walter White's 'The Paradox of Color' and W. E. B. Du Bois's 'The Negro Mind Reaches Out') invoke the conventions of fiction or autobiography—short stories, verse, drama, and transcriptions (both musical and verbal) of spirituals are interspersed with verse (Helene Johnson's 'The Road', for instance, strikes the prospective note of the whole anthology, 'Rise to one brimming golden, spilling cry!', as the first element of the final section, 'The New Scene'), drawings, images of African sculpture, and 'Negro-Americana: Title Pages from the Schomburg Collection'. Though convicting the Harlem Renaissance of multiple failings—above all, what was alleged to be its mere recruitment to a dominant culture without changing it and consequent failure to address 'black people [...] their needs, sufferings and aspirations'—later anthologists such as Baraka and Neal take over the formal diversity of *The New Negro* and radicalize its insistence on the anthology as a site of self-representation and interpretation. 'We are they whom you seek,' declares Jones (Baraka) at the end of his foreword to *Black Fire*, apostrophizing the poets gathered there. 'Look in. Find yr self. [...] We are presenting. Your various selves. We are presenting, from God, a tone, your own. Go on. Now.'[62]

---

[61] Locke (ed.), *New Negro*, p. xv.
[62] LeRoi Jones and Larry Neal (eds), *Black Fire* (New York: William Morrow, 1968), p. xviii.

While the absence of particular social groups from adequate representation in literary culture (such as the black women whose writing is collected in *Confirmation*, for example) and doing something about it is one—laudable—thing, to maintain that everyone who has previously been excluded has something in common over and above being excluded may be another. To present a distinctly black 'voice' or 'tone' is certainly the aim of *Black Fire*, as much as it had been of *The Book of American Negro Poetry* and *The New Negro*, yet even in Jones's (Baraka's) exhortation there remains the acknowledgement that 'We are presenting. Your *various* selves' (emphasis added). Toni Morrison has spoken eloquently of the historical irony of white racial blindness: black people have been violently subjected to racialization for half a millennium, but it is at just the point when they articulate a racial consciousness for themselves that race is dismissed by white readers and critics as an empty category.[63] The exact significance of the question of literary representativeness for the anthology as form—for its rationale, such as it espouses one, and for the manner of reading it invites—is usefully rehearsed in a debate between Juliana Spahr (who, with Claudia Rankine, edited *American Women Poets of the Twentieth Century*) and Stephanie Young, on the one hand, and, on the other, the critic Jennifer Ashton. As is sometimes the way in debates, there is right on both sides of this one. Writing in 2006, Ashton takes issue with a clutch of early twenty-first century anthologies of 'innovative' poetry by women. Her chief contention is that, since the publication of the anthologies of women's writing of the 1970s and 1980s, there has been a shift in focus 'from producing conditions of fairness for women's writing to producing accounts of what makes women's writing different from men's'.[64] The emphasis in recent anthologies of *particular kinds* of writing by women—which are no longer, that is, just anthologies of writing of *different kinds* by women—Ashton argues, is that the writings themselves, rather than the writers alone, are taken to be 'distinctively gendered [...] because they have been produced by women's bodies. It is as if', she remarks, 'the woman poet's formal innovation were something akin to a mollusk's secretion of its shell'.[65] Form, that is, has gone from 'a choice made by the artist' to 'something the artist's own body caused her to make'.[66] Following Simone de Beauvoir and Toril Moi, Ashton holds instead that (in Moi's words) 'no specific form of subjectivity is ever a necessary consequence of having a particular body'; thus by extension no particular literary form necessarily follows from any particular bodily form.[67]

---

[63] See, e.g., Toni Morrison, 'Unspeakable Things Unspoken: The Afro-American Presence in American Literature', The Tanner Lectures on Human Values, 7 October 1988, University of Michigan <https://tannerlectures.utah.edu/_resources/documents/a-to-z/m/morrison90.pdf> (accessed 21 March 2023), 126. I discuss Morrison's lectures in Chapter 4.

[64] Jennifer Ashton, 'Our Bodies, Our Poems', *American Literary History*, 19 (2007), 210–31 (225).

[65] Ashton, 'Our Bodies', 225.   [66] Ashton, 'Our Bodies', 224.

[67] Moi, *What is a Woman?* (New York: Oxford University Press, 1999), 114; quoted in Ashton, 'Our Bodies', 230.

Spahr and Young's initial response to Ashton is to contend that Ashton has been far too sanguine about the supposed 'success' of anthologies of women's poetry. Through recourse to some damning statistics, they are able to show that women were, in 2007, still relatively excluded from major anthologies, from literary prizes, and so on (a comparable case may doubtless be made today). The anthology organized according to the situation of the writers that appear in it, Spahr and Young are thus able to claim, is still justified by the ignored or hidden status of the writers it gathers (just as Baraka had argued in his introduction to *Confirmation* in 1983).[68] Ashton appears happy at least in principle to acknowledge this necessity, while pointing out that the numbers issue is really beside her point: '[t]he effort to redress numerical imbalances does depend on thinking that poets are gendered (there's no other way we could notice the discrimination in the first place) but it doesn't require us to think that their poems are gendered.'[69] The shift from thinking that it is not just writers of poems but poems themselves that are gendered is where, for Ashton, the trouble begins, because it is difficult to see how it must follow that writers in a given situation (in the instance that Ashton is considering, the situation of being female) will, as a necessary consequence of that situation, write in a given way.

Yet there is evident in Ashton's argument—especially in its reliance on Toril Moi's claim that 'no specific form of subjectivity is ever a necessary consequence of having a particular body'—a distinct tinge of idealism. While Moi's assertion may be true, it need not entail that no specific form of subjectivity is *sometimes* a *contingent* consequence of having a particular body, especially when having a particular body has had specifiable social, political, economic, educational, and cultural consequences, none of which is 'necessary', but all of which are no less real for that. In addition, it is worthwhile to revisit Ashton's apparent acceptance in principle of the need to redress numerical imbalances and thus to achieve conditions of fairness for women poets. At certain points in her argument, that is, it seems instead that a rather stronger argument against women-only anthologies is in fact being advanced. In her response to Spahr and Young, Ashton reports that another (imaginary) instance of the situation-based anthology had been put to her by an editor: what about an anthology of Chicago poets? Such a thing need not necessarily entail essentialism about writing in Chicago, in which case, why should an anthology of writing by women entail any such essentialism? The answer one might have expected Ashton to give would surely be along the following lines: it is true that there is nothing necessarily essentializing about an anthology of Chicago poets, and perhaps if people living in Chicago have been excluded from anthologies published in, say, New York and San Francisco and London, then an

---

[68] Juliana Spahr and Stephanie Young, 'Numbers Trouble', *Chicago Review*, 53 (2007), 88–111.

[69] Jennifer Ashton, 'The Numbers Trouble with "Numbers Trouble"', *Chicago Review*, 53 (2007), 112–20.

anthology of writers of Chicago would redress a historic wrong. For Ashton, a corrective anthology of this kind, however, would have to forgo any specific and unifying claims about the poems contained in it, because such claims can be predicated only on the assumption that being from Chicago necessarily entails a particular kind of writing.[70] Neither Ashton nor the editor who formulated the thought experiment in the first place, however, really emphasizes an imagined scenario in which Chicagoans have been systematically and historically discriminated against; rather, Ashton wants to consider what a plausible 'organizing principle' for an anthology of Chicago poets would be—a principle that she understands as being exclusively literary-aesthetic, as distinct from social or political. She draws the conclusion that this imaginary anthology would only have such a principle if the writers collected in it shared a common aesthetic, communicated ideas amongst themselves, and thus constituted an intellectual and artistic community—in which case, even were their mutual influence and collaboration facilitated by their physical proximity in a particular city, their being from Chicago would be merely nominal and hence contingent: it would have made no difference had they been from New York, or Stoke-on-Trent, or anywhere. Otherwise, she asks, 'what would rationalize our interest in reading the poems collectively?'[71] This is a question underpinned by a strong sense that the collection of texts in an anthology prompts a kind of collective reading of them—a reading that in advance sees the texts as related on the basis of a set of common principles. Likewise, the demand for a rationalization of our interest in such collective reading necessarily assumes that that interest requires an advance rationalization—and one, moreover, predicated on clearly discernible intellectual and artistic commonalities amongst the anthologized texts themselves, or alternatively (and, for Ashton, unpersuasively) on an essence supposed to be transferred by osmosis from their authors to those texts. Ashton's formulation of the foundation of her argument is, I think, helpful here: '[t]he point, in other words, is that the moment you're in the business of celebrating a poem for the situation in which it was produced *at the same time* that you're celebrating its form as such, you've basically got a machine built for nothing but the business of essentializing.'[72] But what if those things were not necessarily celebrated 'at the same time'? What if you broke the chain binding women to innovation—or binding anyone to any feature of any literary text, for that matter? There need then in general be no *prior* rationale for reading the texts of an anthology *collectively*—for reading them in a way that takes each text included in the collection as necessarily having a particular, critically significant relation to all the other texts in the collection. No such reading rationale may obtain, that is, even if a rationale for producing anthologies

---

[70] Ashton, 'Trouble', 119–20.   [71] Ashton, 'Trouble', 120.
[72] Ashton, 'Trouble', 120 (emphasis added).

of the work of writers who have been discriminated against for reasons having nothing to do with writing (or reason) does still obtain.

The argument between Ashton, Spahr, and Young illuminates the often-unstated principles of anthologization but also brings into sharp focus the contentiousness of both numbers—how many poets and how much of each of them should get included in an anthology?—and reasons—on what grounds are they included? Ashton's demand for a rationale for collective reading can look like one version of a common enough complaint against anthologies: that they lack a discernible and defensible literary principle of selection and rely instead either on extra-literary criteria or on the anthologizer's private taste. Disagreement about rationales and numbers in the composition of anthologies is the central disagreement in the caustic but nevertheless revealing exchanges between Rita Dove and Helen Vendler, provoked by the latter's hostile review of Dove's *The Penguin Book of Twentieth-Century American Poetry*, and expressly concerned with rival approaches to the roles of taste and criticism, and how they might inform the 'agenda' of an anthology, or, indeed, whether anthologies ought to have an agenda at all.[73] Vendler avers that there are too many poets (a hundred and seventy-five) in Dove's selection and that the anthology exhibits no principle of selection (despite in fact suggesting that it does: namely, to be 'accessible'). Vendler's own catalogue of the 'most significant names and texts' of twentieth-century American poetry is itself revealing: 'T. S. Eliot, Robert Frost, William Carlos Williams, Wallace Stevens, Marianne Moore, Hart Crane, Robert Lowell, John Berryman, Elizabeth Bishop (and some would include Ezra Pound).' The initial *ex cathedra* confidence of this list of poets is muted somewhat by the parenthetical nod, not so much to Pound himself, but to the 'some' who 'would include' him. Though the list that might expand to include Pound is known, according to Vendler, 'worldwide', the 'some' who compose it does not include anything like the indefinite readership of the world and certainly does not include Rita Dove, the editor of the anthology, herself. Unless we accept that the number of those who count as 'some' is small, this parenthesis has the potential to open onto a field that might quickly race well past ten—perhaps even to 175.

Far from being so much pseudo-statistical cavilling, this focus on numbers is significant, because it gives expression to a stark difference in how the basis of selection is seen. In responding to Vendler's review, Dove cheerfully accepts Vendler's charge that her anthology does not evince a principle of selection—does not, as Dove puts it, advance a particular 'agenda'—though she then immediately announces what she does call her 'criterion': that is, to 'choose significant poems

---

[73] Rita Dove (ed.), *The Penguin Anthology of Twentieth-Century American Poetry* (New York: Penguin, 2011); reviewed by Helen Vendler, 'Are These the Poems to Remember?', *New York Review of Books*, 24 November 2011 <https://www.nybooks.com/articles/2011/11/24/are-these-poems-remember/> (accessed 1 February 2021).

of literary merit'.[74] Dove emphasizes throughout her response that 'by no means all of [her selections are] in adherence to [her] own aesthetic taste buds', a way of putting it that somewhat depreciates aesthetic taste by aligning it with the mere gustatory taste from which it is usually held to be distinct, while nevertheless retaining a category of poetic 'significan[ce]' and 'literary merit'. The effect of this tacit opposition of poetic significance and literary merit, on the one hand, with a metaphorically physicalized aesthetic taste, on the other, is to distinguish the former from merely subjective estimation and hence lend it a degree, at least, of objective validation. This is an important ground on which Dove replies to Vendler's charges. Rebutting Vendler's suggestion that Dove necessarily admires the Black Arts poems that she anthologizes, for instance, Dove asks: 'Shouldn't a literary theorist of Vendler's stature be aware that a good anthologist is capable of reading beyond and against mere personal taste?' It is a good (and not merely rhetorical) question. For one thing, it casts Vendler's assessment of Dove's anthology as a failure of literary theoretical acumen, not to be expected from someone of Vendler's standing. For another, it rests on an important distinction between reading and judging that is implicitly held to be pivotal to the kind of advanced literary theory of which Vendler is (temporarily) failing to be an exemplar ('reading *beyond and against* mere personal taste'). Vendler's own concession to taste is, likewise, at most partial, and the intention of it is clearly to undermine what claims to objectivity are implicit in Dove's selection: '[i]t is popular to say (and it is in part true) that in literary matters tastes differ, and that every critic can be wrong. But there is a certain objectivity bestowed by the mere passage of time, and its sifting of wheat from chaff.' Vendler certainly assumes, however, that Dove's anthology is an accurate and exclusive expression of the latter's taste. (The locution 'a certain objectivity', like the 'some' who would select Pound for the first team of American poets, allows Vendler, as is perhaps the reviewer's prerogative, a degree of latitude that does not, though, seem altogether in keeping with objectivity or the highly selective canon of American poets she adduces.)

'Taste is the judgement that an individual makes of a thing according to its fitness in his private scheme of life. Criticism is the judgement that an individual makes of a thing according to its fitness to itself, its excellence as compared with things like itself, regardless of its application to his private scheme of life. With taste, a poem is good because it is liked; with criticism, it is good because it is good'.[75] So wrote Riding and Graves in their *A Pamphlet against Anthologies* in 1928. As we have just been seeing, the parameters of taste and criticism, of the subjective predilections of the anthologist and the putative bases for their claims to objectivity, are crucially at issue in the framing and reception of anthologies.

---

[74] Dove, 'Defending an Anthology' (letter to the Editors), *New York Review of Books*, 22 December 2011 <https://www.nybooks.com/articles/2011/12/22/defending-anthology/> (accessed 1 February 2021).
[75] Riding and Graves, p. 170.

Yet the distinctions between taste and criticism that anthologists, in their paratextual discourses, and the critics of anthologists, in their polemics, seek to maintain often turn out to be less firmly established than they are made to appear. We might respond to Dove that, to be able to read against and beyond taste, one would have to know where taste stops and mere reading begins (as well as to accept that 'taste' just names what one likes, rather than the faculty by which one measures liking and disliking). And we might respond to Vendler that time does not simply pass in literary matters, without its course being at least in part determined by the interaction of many different tastes and the effect of many different anthologies. Even Riding and Graves tellingly cannot avoid allowing that taste and criticism are both forms of 'judgement'. The critical authority of the anthologist is at once paramount in establishing which texts are to be judged in the first place while at the same time that authority is shared with the reader of whom the anthologist is (only) an emblem.

3
Reviews

We certainly encountered some scorn for the anthology in the previous chapter, but, of all the forms of criticism examined in this book, the most commonly despised is the review. First, it is not really criticism. Second, it is not really a form. Or so it has often been alleged. Here, for instance, is a selection of twentieth-century regrets, fears, and complaints about the review. 'There was a time', Anthony Burgess declared in 1966, possibly channelling Wordsworth, 'when reviewing was a branch of criticism; but nowadays criticism is only a branch of reviewing'.[1] Once, that is, reviews were capacious and candid; now they are short and cagey. Thirty years before Burgess, George Orwell had blamed the fact that the novel 'is being shouted out of existence' on 'the disgusting tripe that is written by the blurb-reviewers. The hack review', he asserted, 'is in fact a sort of commercial necessity, like the blurb on the dust-jacket, of which it is merely an extension'.[2] Orwell's categorization of the review as a 'commercial necessity' and his meta-phorical description of it as a type of food (however repulsive) emphasize the role of the review in regulating, but above all encouraging, the consumption of litera-ture. The food metaphor in particular is remarkably tenacious. Writing in 1959, Elizabeth Hardwick at least thought reviews more immediately palatable than tripe—but neither more nutritious nor less sickening in the end: 'A book is born into a puddle of treacle; the brine of hostile criticism is only a memory'; 'the soupiest encomiums' (more messy food) 'are siphoned into harmless blurb quotes', declared Wilfrid Sheed in his inaugural column in the *New York Times*, which he used to expose the skulduggery and desperation of the reviewer's trade; 'book reviewing is at a low ebb', announced Jay Parini in 1999.[3]

But, as if these concerns about the quality of book reviewing were not enough, they are trumped by the fear that the review may become extinct altogether, at least in venues frequented by a non-specialist readership. Steve Wasserman,

---

[1] Anthony Burgess, 'Bagehot on Books' (review of *The Collected Works of Walter Bagehot*, ed. Norman St John-Stevas, i, ii), *The Spectator*, 7 January 1966, 15.

[2] George Orwell, 'In Defence of the Novel' (1936), in *The Collected Essays, Journalism, and Letters of George Orwell*, ed. Sonia Orwell and Ian Angus, 4 vols (London: Penguin, 1970), i: *An Age Like This 1920–1940*, 281–3 (281–2).

[3] Elizabeth Hardwick, 'The Decline of Book Reviewing', in *The Collected Essays of Elizabeth Hardwick*, ed. Darryl Pinckney (New York: New York Review Books, 2017), 59–68 (59) (first pub. in *Harper's* (October 1959), 138–43); Wilfrid Sheed, 'The Good Word: The Politics of Reviewing', *New York Times*, 7 February 1971, 15–16; Jay Parini, 'The Disappearing Art of Reviewing Books', *Chronicle of Higher Education*, 23 July 1999, 4–5.

Critical Forms: Forms of Literary Criticism, 1750–2020. Ross Wilson, Oxford University Press. © Ross Wilson 2023.
DOI: 10.1093/oso/9780198881117.003.0004

long-time editor of the *Los Angeles Times Book Review*, for example, notes that fears for journalistic book coverage are hardly new, but that the pace of decline has nevertheless quickened exponentially, such that '[j]obs, book sections, and pages are vanishing at a rate rivaled only by the degree to which entire species are being rendered extinct in the Amazonian rain forest'.[4] The conflagration threatening book reviews—at least those written by professional critics in traditional media such as newspapers—is confirmed by Phillipa K. Chong's recent cultural sociology of book reviewing.[5] There is in Wasserman's curiously disproportionate comparison of the decline of book review sections in broadsheet newspapers to the decline of 'the Amazonian rain forest' (the latter imperils life on earth; the former does not) a hint at one real source of trouble for the contemporary professional book review: not *the* Amazon, but Amazon.[6] Chong quotes one anonymous professional critic's complaint:

> The Amazon.com reviewers, it's like they're reviewing a product. It's like they bought a pair of Nikes and they are going on and saying, 'Oh, my Nikes feel just great, they fit perfectly and I love them.' Then they go on and review a book and say, 'Oh, this book was too long, I got really sleepy halfway through,' and just stuff like that.[7]

Though Chong later points out that the majority of reviews on Amazon are positive, the sense that Amazon reviewing redounds to the benefit of consumer goods ('Oh, my Nikes feel just great') and the detriment of works of literature ('Oh, this book was too long') represents another important stage in the fraught relationship between mass culture and high art. The anonymous critic's repeated 'they go on' refers, of course, to going online or onto the Amazon website, but it also carries the pejorative sense of *going on* about something, especially something of which the writer knows little (books), or which is unlikely to interest anyone else (her or his shoes). It is not easy to adjudicate this particular expression of antagonism, at least in its own terms, since the defence of pertinent and alert reviewing is made to seem dependent on the mere disparagement of ordinary readers, while the defence of the latter seems to entail the celebration of corporations such as Amazon and Nike.

There are certainly distinctive features to reviewing in the digital era (Chong's 'uncertain times'). But the association of the review with commercial imperatives; its situation with respect to professional and academic criticism, on the one hand,

---

[4] Steve Wasserman, 'Goodbye to All That', *Columbia Journalism Review*, 46 (2007) <https://archives.cjr.org/cover_story/goodbye_to_all_that_1.php> (accessed 23 February 2020) (2 of 21).

[5] Phillipa K. Chong, *Inside the Critics' Circle: Book Reviewing in Uncertain Times* (Princeton: Princeton University Press, 2020), 2, 125–6.

[6] See Chong, 121–2, 127, 139, for discussion.   [7] Chong, 121.

and to new and expanding media, on the other; contemporaneity and tradition; the proper place and conduct of evaluation: all of these concerns with respect to the review have a significant pedigree, cropping up repeatedly at different historical moments in the history of the form, and it is the major concern of this chapter to investigate them. One further illustration of the perennial nature of many of the questions that have come to be asked of reviewing practice is the matter of anonymity, which in turn has a significant connection to the relation between professional and amateur criticism and to the proper conduct of evaluation. While speculation about the identity of reviewers in early reviews such as the *Monthly* and *Critical* may have been minimal, not least owing to the relative obscurity of many reviewers, anonymity was also exploited in order to secure charitable reviews that maintained the appearance of disinterestedness (or, at least, the lack of the appearance of interestedness). The eighteenth century boasts numerous instances of self-reviewing—though, again, this is hardly a practice that has died out.[8] Perhaps inevitably, therefore, the anonymity of reviewers came to be seen in the latter part of the eighteenth century as the source of the failings of established reviews. Attacks on anonymity were frequent in the mid- to late-eighteenth-century periodical press, and a number of polemicizing new reviews based their claims to novelty—and hence to critical rigour—on the eschewal of anonymity.[9] Yet, in practice, the determination to forgo anonymity was often itself effectively forgone—individual reviews, for instance, were often signed with misleading initials, all but impossible to decode; most of the complaints against anonymity were also signed with pseudonyms, which, however hard they tried ('Honestus', 'Anti-Zoilus'), could scarcely escape the irony of their own evasion of accurate naming. Thus the question of anonymity was always liable to return, as it did in the nineteenth century, and again in the twentieth—in, for example, the pages of the *TLS*, where it was rehearsed with just as much fervour on both sides as had been in evidence two centuries before.[10]

As I mentioned above, far from being exclusively a matter of the identification and administration of reviews, the question of anonymity focused (and, indeed, continues to focus) concerns to do with professional standing and critical authority,

---

[8] See John Mullan, *Anonymity: A Secret History of English Literature* (London: Faber and Faber, 2007), 182–6. For a useful catalogue of self-reviews stretching into the twenty-first century, see the responses to Dan Chiasson's appeal on Twitter for information on this topic (@dchiasso, 3 January 2020).

[9] See Antonia Forster, 'Introduction', in *Index to Book Reviews in England 1775–1800* (London: British Library, 1997), pp. xiii–xliii (pp. xvii, xxiv) for details.

[10] For the nineteenth century, see Oscar Maurer, Jr, 'Anonymity vs. Signature in Victorian Reviewing', *Studies in English*, 27 (1948), 1–27; Dallas Liddle, 'Salesmen, Sportsmen, Mentors: Anonymity and Mid-Victorian Theories of Journalism', *Victorian Studies*, 41 (1997), 31–68; and, especially for the kinds of working practice anonymity made possible, Joanne Shattock, 'Spreading it Thinly: Some Victorian Reviewers at Work', *Victorian Periodicals Newsletter*, 9 (1976), 84–7. For the *TLS*, see Derwent May, *Critical Times: The History of the Times Literary Supplement* (London: HarperCollins, 2001), 11–12, 414–20, and John Gross (the editor who dropped anonymity), 'Naming Names', *TLS* 7 June 1974, 610.

the reliability of evaluation, and, in some instances, the imbrication of reviewing with commercial interests. The fact that significant shifts in the approach to anonymity in reviewing recur, for instance, in the eighteenth and twentieth centuries underscores the abiding nature of many of the questions freighting the review. Yet it is equally important to note that there have been changes in the practices of reviewing and in the persons (so to speak) of reviewers. Both the longue durée and the innovations have come increasingly to light thanks to the scholarly effort to resituate reviewing practices in their original contexts of publication, instead of taking reviews as merely a source among many other, equally undifferentiated sources, of literary opinion. Both Leah Price and Marilyn Butler have, for instance, criticized the tendency of the Routledge 'Critical Heritage' series to flatten generic differences, assigning different forms such as reviews, letters, diaries, lectures, and journal articles to a uniform 'heritage'.[11] This tendency is, however, nothing new: the review has long been subject to scholarly reclamation predicated on generic erasure. A number of mid-nineteenth-century reviewers, for instance, gave titles to their collections of republished reviews designed, as Joanne Shattock has put it, 'to counter the haste and hand-to-mouth circumstances of original publication': Shattock cites Leslie Stephen's *Hours in a Library* (1874) and *Studies of a Biographer* (1898), along with John Morley's *Studies in Literature* (1891), as examples, and indeed, retitling reviews as the more circumspect and scholarly 'studies' was a particular tactic adopted for many collections of reviews in this period.[12] The gathering of reviews under dignifying titles, of course, continues, but the effect of Shattock's salutary reminder is to raise the question of the differences between reviews and 'studies', and, in turn, of the particular kind of criticism that the review specifically may afford.

Likewise issuing a reminder that the accommodation of reviews to what have become standard critical expectations involves a narrowing in the range of what may count as criticism, Butler has stated that '[m]odern critics of early critics generally look out for evaluative judgments [...], and condemn reviews as unsophisticated if, instead, they summarize a book's contents or, worse, quote at length: the last practice is known as "padding"'.[13] The enclosure of the description of quotation, 'padding', in its own quotation marks is a deft touch—and again, as with tripe, treacle, and soup, the implication (though, importantly, explicitly disowned by Butler) is that the well-padded review is soft, homogeneous, and easy. As well as highlighting the methodological challenges that face the student of

---

[11] Leah Price, *The Anthology and the Rise of the Novel: From Richardson to George Eliot* (Cambridge: Cambridge University Press, 2000), 12, and Marilyn Butler, 'Culture's Medium: The Role of the Review', in Stuart Curran (ed.), *The Cambridge Companion to British Romanticism* (Cambridge: Cambridge University Press, 1993), 120–47 (147).

[12] Joanne Shattock, 'The Culture of Criticism', in Shattock (ed.), *The Cambridge Companion to English Literature 1830–1914* (Cambridge: Cambridge University Press, 2010), 71–90 (86–7).

[13] Butler, 126.

reviews, one consequence of the insights of Shattock, Butler, and others is to have brought the review to light as a distinctive form of critical writing, with its own historical development that is not straightforwardly subsumable within a unitary literary-critical heritage.

If 'modern critics' are on the lookout for 'evaluative judgments', then they are the unselfconscious inheritors of an early nineteenth-century polemic about earlier reviews. The foundation of the *Edinburgh Review* in 1802 was often heralded—not least by the *Edinburgh*'s founding editors themselves—as a crucial turning point in the history of the review, which would establish, allegedly for the first time, criticism as evaluative, disinterested, and rigorous. Walter Scott decried the 'dawdling, maudlin sort of applause' meted out by the 'mawkish' 'common Reviews [...] to everything that reached even mediocrity' (it is doubtless little accident that the repeated *aw*-sounds of Scott's description are liable to provoke a y*aw*n). In keeping with the culinary metaphor that implicitly attests to the role of the review in regulating literary consumption, Scott sharply contrasted this tedious practice with that of '[t]he Edinburgh folks', who 'squeezed into their sauce plenty of acid, and were popular from novelty as well as from merit'.[14]

Perhaps inevitably, there is at least a tinge of history as told by the winners to this view. In his still valuable study of reviewing before the founding of the *Edinburgh*, Derek Roper found Scott's assessment preferable to later accounts of the faults of the eighteenth-century reviews, but notes, first, that Scott exaggerates, and, second and more substantially, that 'uncritical leniency, where it exists, seems at least no worse a fault than indiscriminate severity'.[15] It was not simply that earlier periodicals like the *Monthly Review*, founded in 1749, contained writing by timid or incompetent critics; on the contrary, a kind of principled reticence with regard to criticism (understood above all as the expression of negative opinion) was often consciously embraced. Ralph Griffiths, founding editor of the *Monthly*, announced in an early number that its articles were 'to enter no farther into the province of criticism, than just so far as may be indispensably necessary to give some idea of such books as come under our consideration'.[16] The tenor of this statement is unmistakably one of restraint—'enter no farther', 'just so far as', 'indispensably necessary'—and yet the capacious vagueness of the implied instruction to reviewers to 'give some idea' of the books they are reviewing might at least suggest that sometimes it would be necessary to stray into the province of criticism after all since the provision of an idea (even an 'idea' in this colloquial,

---

[14] To George Ellis, 18 November 1808; *Letters of Walter Scott*, ed. H. J. C. Grierson (1932–7), ii. 128; quoted in Derek Roper, *Reviewing before the 'Edinburgh': 1788–1802* (London: Methuen, 1978), 32.

[15] Roper, 32. See also Antonia Forster, 'Book Reviewing', in John Barnard et al. (eds), *Cambridge History of the Book in Britain*, 7 vols (Cambridge: Cambridge University Press, 1999–2019), v: Michael F. Suarez, SJ, and Michael L. Turner (eds), *1695–1830* (2009), 631–48 (639–40).

[16] *Monthly Review*, 1, 2 (1750), 260; quoted in Roper, 20, where it is aptly described as an 'elastic criterion'.

philosophically modest sense) is surely one function of criticism. Consideration ('such books as come under our consideration') also potentially connotes assessment, comparison, and evaluation. Earlier periodicals like the *Monthly* (as well as the *Critical* and, slightly later, the *Analytical*) were, then, in part characterized by what Jonathan Brody Kramnick has called their 'temperance', but, as Kramnick also makes plain in his seminal account of the emergence of literary criticism as a discipline, this did not entail the mere abdication of criticism but rather a distinctive view and practice of it: '[a] great weight fell on the *mediation* of expertise and laity,' writes Kramnick, 'whereby criticism chooses certain works to write about and to offer the public as worth reading'.[17] We examined the practices of choice and offering (to adopt Kramnick's terms) as criticism in the previous chapter, where it was shown that the silence of the anthologist served to cut across the divisions of labour (above all, the division between reader and critic) by which the literary field is structured. The review, under the abiding influence of the *Edinburgh*, may have become a quintessentially chatty, even shouty form, and, unlike the anthology, it was always essentially writing about, rather than presentation, of texts. But what Kramnick shows is that the practices of editorial selection and extensive excerption in earlier reviews was crucial to their '*expert mediation of the literary*'.[18] Both the reviewer's presentation of text and her or his discursive elaboration of it—akin to the anthologist's selections and paratexts—constituted her or his critical practice.

The transition from the kind of reviewing practised by earlier reviews like the *Monthly* to later reviews like the *Edinburgh* thus looks rather more nuanced than it does from the perspective of the revisionary history advanced by the editors and admirers of the latter. For one thing, there is a good measure of mere historical accident in the shift from extensive excerption to discursive elaboration in reviews, as William St Clair has shown: tighter legal restrictions on both anthologization and excerption were introduced in the early nineteenth century.[19] But, as we have also been seeing, mediation of texts, rather than the espousal of evaluative judgement with respect to them, did not necessarily entail a wholesale dereliction of criticism, as even Griffiths's cautious prospectus for the *Monthly* ends up making clear. But it is also simply the case that decided reviews written by writers cultivating an identifiable position as a reviewer did get written before the foundation of the *Edinburgh*. A signal instance here is Mary Wollstonecraft's career as reviewer for Joseph Johnson's *Analytical Review*.[20] Even in her first review for the

---

[17] Jonathan Kramnick, 'Literary Criticism among the Disciplines', *Eighteenth-Century Studies*, 35 (2002), 343–60 (355).

[18] Kramnick, 'Literary Criticism', 355.

[19] William St Clair, *The Reading Nation in the Romantic Period* (Cambridge: Cambridge University Press, 2004), 186–8.

[20] On Wollstonecraft as reviewer, see Ralph M. Wardle, 'Mary Wollstonecraft, Analytical Reviewer', *PMLA* 62 (1947), 1000–9; Mitzi Myers, 'Sensibility and the "Walk of Reason": Mary Wollstonecraft's Literary Reviews as Cultural Critique', in Syndy Conger McMillen (ed.), *Sensibility in Transformation:*

Analytical—a notice of around 200 words of *Edward and Harriet, or the Happy Recovery* 'By a Lady'—Wollstonecraft dispatches the unhappy novel under review in two sentences and an illustrative example: 'The Happy Recovery is an heterogeneous mass of folly, affectation, and improbability. Metaphors and vulgarisms abound. The countess,' (Wollstonecraft does not explain who this character is) ' "wrapt up in the sable and all-encircling mantle of despair, is seized with a violent puking of blood" '.[21] She then gives over the rest of the review to a first articulation of how this kind of thing in general should be dealt with and, more important still, to a statement of the dangers of an excessively licensed imagination: 'the imagination, suffered to stray beyond the utmost verge of probability, where no vestige of nature appears, soon shuts out reason, and the dormant faculties languish for want of cultivation' (p. 19). Perhaps justifying the brevity with which she has treated *Edward and Harriet*, Wollstonecraft remarks that '[a]n analysis of novels will seldom be expected, nor can the *cant* of sensibility be tried by any criterion of reason; ridicule should direct its shafts against this fair game' (p. 19), both giving fair warning that not everything discussed in the *Analytical* is necessarily a fit subject for analysis and taking aim in what will become a characteristic fashion at one of the buzzwords (in this case, 'fair') of the sentimental novels that she consistently censures.

The theoretical claim concerning the relation of imagination and reason, coupled with the justification for the abandonment of analysis (the *Analytical's* title is clearly in her mind here) and embrace of ridicule, the latter thus established as the fallback position of the reviewer, combine in this early review to make explicit the bases on which Wollstonecraft practises. In fact, it is only a month further into her *Analytical* reviewing career that Wollstonecraft takes on, at much greater length, *Emmeline, the Orphan of the Castle*, by Charlotte Smith—a more considerable figure, certainly, than the anonymous author of *Edward and Harriet*. Wollstonecraft concludes her account of *Emmeline* with (measured) praise for Smith's 'poetical talents': 'Indeed some of the descriptions are so interesting and beautiful that we would give a specimen, if they could be separated from the woven web without injuring them, and if we had not already exceeded the bounds prescribed' (p. 27), though this way of putting it makes clear that Smith's praiseworthy descriptions are nevertheless inextricable from the rest of her (less praiseworthy) work and, deploying the reviewer's tactic of the reminder that her space is limited, hints, moreover, that 'specimens' of those descriptions are in any

Creative Resistance to Sentiment from the Augustans to the Romantics (Rutherford, NJ: Fairleigh Dickinson University Press, 1990), 120–44; and Mitzi Myers, 'Mary Wollstonecraft's Literary Reviews', in Claudia L. Johnson (ed.), *The Cambridge Companion to Mary Wollstonecraft* (Cambridge: Cambridge University Press, 2002), 82–98 (82).
[21] *Analytical Review*, 1 (June 1788), 207–8; in *The Works of Mary Wollstonecraft*, ed. Janet Todd and Marilyn Butler, 7 vols (London: Pickering, 1989), vii. 19. Further references to this edition are given after quotations in the text.

case not good enough to displace any of Wollstonecraft's strictures on the novel in general. Wollstonecraft deploys another of the reviewer's conventions at the start of the review, emphasizing the mismatch between the great length of the work and the narrow space she has in which to give an analysis of it (p. 22). Her response to this particular formal constraint of the review—namely, its limited length—is to omit the attempt to subject the novel to discursive analysis, taking over and lampooning the idiolect of the novel itself instead, pointing up the subtle but ultimately decisive differences between sentimental and rational descriptions. In a note, for instance, she complains that '[w]e do not understand what the author means, when she talks of a *mind originally elegant*' (p. 22). Wollstonecraft is thinking of the passage in which Smith describes the character of Mrs Stafford, friend and confidante of the eponymous heroine: 'She had read a great deal; and her mind, originally elegant and refined, was highly cultivated, and embellished with all the knowledge that could be acquired from the best authors in the modern languages.'[22] It is telling that Wollstonecraft picks on this passage, since it concerns the cultivation and embellishment of the mind *through reading*, which is what both the reader of Smith's novel and the reader of Wollstonecraft's review of Smith's novel, as well as Mrs Stafford, are doing. Smith's suggestion that reading is good for the mind is a significant one, of course, in the (still at this date) contested genre of the novel—and perhaps it might even contain the invitation to include Smith herself among 'the best authors in the modern languages'. Whether that invitation is taken up or not may of course significantly depend upon the judgement of a reviewer like Wollstonecraft. The effect of her cool admission of incomprehension at the idea of a '*mind originally elegant*', moreover, suggests that elegance is no original property of the mind, but may only be acquired—perhaps through the mind's encounter with the writings of the best authors. At the very least, Wollstonecraft's incomprehension, far from undermining the reviewer's own authority, sensitizes her reader to other half-thought-through and sentimental conventions. An interview between Emmeline and her paramour, Wollstonecraft remarks, 'of course produced vows of love on one side, and sighs and tears on the other'; 'Emmeline begs Mrs Stafford, in a whisper, for heaven's sake to hasten home' (in fact, Mrs Stafford does not do this—but Wollstonecraft has again taken over here the role of sentimental writer in order to expose it to ridicule); other characters 'harass the timid fair one' (Emmeline is, in fact, repeatedly characterized as 'timid' throughout the novel):[23] by the time that Wollstonecraft returns to the locution she has already openly criticized—Emmeline is a 'lovely person' with a 'pure and *elegant* mind' (p. 23; Wollstonecraft's emphasis)—what looks like a summary of the plot of *Emmeline* has become analysis by means of mockery.

---

[22] Charlotte Smith, *Emmeline, the Orphan of the Castle*, 4 vols (London: printed for T. Cadell, 1788), i. 106.
[23] See, e.g., Smith, *Emmeline*, iii. 199, iv. 5.

Wollstonecraft turns most decisively against the language of the novel when, having stated that in the sentimental novel '*adventures* are sought for and created, when duties are neglected, and content despised' (p. 26; Wollstonecraft's emphasis), she opens the following paragraph—the review's penultimate one—as follows: 'We will *venture* to ask any young girl if Lady Adelina's theatrical contrition did not catch her attention, while Mrs Stafford's rational resignation escaped her notice?' (p. 27; emphasis added). The ventures of enquiring reason are preferred to the adventures of sentimental imagination. The danger of contamination by the work under review is warded off by marking mimicry as mockery. Critical distance is preserved even as it is collapsed for critical ends.

*

By any account, Wollstonecraft was a major reviewer in the period before the foundation of the *Edinburgh*, and her example demonstrates that the recourse to critical acidity (so to speak) was not inaugurated by the latter periodical. But neither is it the case that the *Edinburgh*'s claims to novelty were simply spurious. More recent discussion of the foundation of the *Edinburgh*, while cognizant of the significance of Roper's qualifications of the *Edinburgh*'s own triumphalist self-presentation, have nevertheless cast it as a 'media landmark'.[24] Samuel Badcock, one of Ralph Griffiths's employees on the *Monthly*, excoriated the practice of the rival pre-*Edinburgh* periodical, the *Critical Review*, casting its reviewers as mere intermediaries: 'I would call them Transcribers, not Critics.' But Badcock was candid enough also to inform Griffiths of what, by 1782 (thirty-three years into the *Monthly*'s existence), had come to seem the *Monthly*'s own limitations in criticism as well:

> Your poetical Department is very generally disliked. It consists of mere general Observations. There is nothing pointed, acute, or discriminating. [Criticism] requires cool Judgement, Acuteness, and Taste. The Mind should be quick to espy and delicate to feel. [...] The Critic is not barely to *hit off* a good Thought. He is to produce a Chain of good ones. He must compare—He must argue; he must *pursue* Argument.[25]

By the last decades of the eighteenth century the critical restraint of the *Monthly* seemed to some blunt, slow, and obtuse. Though Badcock's frank asseveration— 'Your poetical Department is very generally disliked'—might itself qualify as a 'mere general Observation[ ]', the desire to which he gives expression is

---

[24] Jon Klancher, *Transfiguring the Arts and Sciences: Knowledge and Cultural Institutions in the Romantic Age* (Cambridge: Cambridge University Press, 2013), 77–8. See also Massimiliano Demata and Duncan Wu (eds), *British Romanticism and the 'Edinburgh Review': Bicentenary Essays* (Houndmills: Palgrave Macmillan, 2002).

[25] Oxford, Bodleian Library, MS Adds. C.90, fo. 100ᵛ; quoted in Roper, 44.

nevertheless for a mode of reviewing that would be more consistent—key here is the opposition of sportively hitting off one good thought and diligently producing a whole series of them—and tenacious, a quality modelled in miniature by Badcock's mounting repetition: 'He must argue; he must pursue Argument.'

We can get some sense of the characteristics of an *Edinburgh* review by comparing how the same work—in this case, Robert Southey's poem *Thalaba the Destroyer*—was reviewed in both the *Edinburgh* and the *Monthly*. This comparison is perhaps especially revealing, since the reviewer in both instances was the same person, namely, Francis Jeffrey, one of the *Edinburgh*'s founders, himself. In Jeffrey's review of *Thalaba* for the *Edinburgh*, published in the very first issue of that journal, he freely and sweepingly animadverts on the '*sect* of poets, that has established itself in this country within these ten or twelve years' to which Southey belongs. But Jeffrey does not limit his aim even to this already broad target, encompassing, rather, poetry as such, the perils of the adoption of simplicity as an artistic principle, exemplary life-lessons that may be derivable from the pretensions of poets, and decided (and outrageously tendentious) social and ethical proclamation: 'If it be natural for a poor man to murder and rob, in order to make himself comfortable, it is no less natural for a rich man to gourmandize and domineer, in order to have full use of his riches. Wealth is just as valid an excuse for the one class of vices, as indigence is for the other.'[26]

Jeffrey's review of *Thalaba* in the *Monthly*, likewise, is by no means uniformly positive, yet its concern is neither explicitly to undermine the whole project of the Lake Poets nor to assert Jeffrey's own poetical doxa. The opening of the review in the *Monthly*—'It is not easy either to class or to appreciate this singular performance. It has many faults and many striking beauties. It is irregular and splendid, improbable and interesting, and at once extravagant and elaborate'—takes care, first of all, to announce the reviewer's difficulties in arriving at a judgement of this work, balancing both the poem's merits and demerits, and, if anything, emphasizing the former: its beauties are accorded an adjective ('striking') whereas its faults are not.[27] Above all, the description of the work as 'singular' establishes the leitmotif of this review in contrast to the *Edinburgh*'s emphasis not so much on *Thalaba* as on its author, Southey, as an instance of an ultimately deplorable tendency in recent poetry. Nowhere is this distinction more marked than in the contrasting summaries given in the concluding paragraphs of the two reviews: where the *Monthly* judges that 'this work contains more ample and decisive proofs of the author's genius and capacity for poetical impressions, than any of his former publications' and resumes its balanced view that it will both 'please' and 'offend' in

---

[26] [Francis Jeffrey], 'Art. VIII. *Thalaba, the Destroyer*: A Metrical Romance. By Robert Southey', *Edinburgh Review*, 1 (October 1802), 63–83 (63, 65, 70, 72). Further references are given after quotations in the text.

[27] [Francis Jeffrey], 'Art. II. *Thalaba the Destroyer*; a Metrical Romance. By Robert Southey', *Monthly Review*, 39 (November 1802), 240–51 (240). Further references are given after quotations in the text.

more or less equal measure (p. 251), the *Edinburgh*'s final paragraph begins by invoking '[a]ll the productions of this author', which 'bear very distinctly the impression of an amiable mind, a cultivated fancy, and a perverted taste' (p. 83)— the third term, tellingly, tipping the balance definitively against the writer. And, where the *Monthly* confines itself to Southey alone, even to *Thalaba* in particular, the *Edinburgh*, in concluding, again takes him as 'a faithful disciple' 'of that new school of poetry [...] to the glory of which he has sacrificed greater talents and acquisitions, than can be boasted of by any of his associates' (p. 83). To be informed that your talents and acquisitions are greater than those of your friends is a particularly exquisite pleasure; to be informed that you have wasted them, rather less so.

It is easy to see the attraction of the approach Jeffrey took in the *Edinburgh*. Readers are rarely asked to consider one side, then the other, but rather know where they stand from the outset; and they are told not just how to judge a recent poem, but how to judge poetry and art in general, the dangers of hubris, and the nature of poverty and wealth as well. In the review of *Thalaba*, Jeffrey was of course only beginning to hone his *Edinburgh* voice; by the time he came to write his review of Wordsworth's *The Excursion* twelve years later, he had even less compunction about condemnation: 'This will never do', that review—and, indeed, the number in which it appears—notoriously opens; 'The case of Mr Wordsworth, we perceive' ('we believe', 'we conceive', 'we perceive' are the characteristic markers of Jeffrey's most forthright judgements) 'is now manifestly hopeless; and we give him up as altogether incurable, and beyond the power of criticism'.[28] What this announcement of the critical abandonment of Wordsworth does show is that Jeffrey conceived of his reviews as offering guidance not only to readers, but to writers as well—something he needs must continue even once Wordsworth has been given up for lost: 'We cannot indeed altogether omit taking precautions now and then against the spreading of the malady' (p. 2).

It is perhaps hardly a surprise that the targets of Jeffrey's criticisms became circumspect at best about the kind of critical reviewing that he pioneered. What can easily be dismissed as merely a hurt reaction to biting criticism did, however, sit within the broader intellectual context of a philosophical reconsideration of the relation between literary writing and its critical reception in the Romantic period. The critique of the review as such was not merely reactive. In Germany, writers such as Schlegel and Novalis developed an aesthetics privileging works that appeared to forestall the need for review or, rather, that furnished their own auto-review. Continuous, for instance, with Wordsworth's sense that the taste for his poetry did not exist before he created it, Schlegel declared of Goethe's *Wilhelm*

[28] [Francis Jeffrey], 'Art I. The Excursion, being a portion of the Recluse, a Poem. By William Wordsworth', *Edinburgh Review*, 47 (November 1814), 1–30 (1, 2). Further references are given after quotations in the text.

Meister that 'it is one of those books that judge themselves' and Novalis, speaking more generally, claimed that '[m]any books need no review, only an announcement; they already contain their own review'.[29] Novalis's statement in particular may just seem like a simple reversion to an earlier model of reviewing as an extension of publishers' catalogues (books need 'only an announcement'), but, in fact, he, like Schlegel, emphasized the latent self-assessment that 'many books' contain. For Schlegel and Novalis, as Benjamin put it, criticism is, then, 'far less the judgment of a work than the method of its consummation'.[30]

A similar sense that judgement is external to and interferes with the proper consummation of the work itself is discernible in Samuel Taylor Coleridge's comments on the review. Though he himself hardly refrained from reviewing, Coleridge nevertheless complained in the 'Introductory Essay' to his early periodical, *The Watchman*, of the flattery, on the one hand, and calumny, on the other, served up in the reviews of the time; and fifteen years later, he would intone in his lecture 'On the Principles of Criticism' of 1811, that '[r]eviews are pernicious because the writers [of reviews] decide without any reference to fixed principles, because they are filled with personalities; and, above all, because they teach people rather to judge than to read; they encourage superficiality, and a disposition to adopt the sentiments dictated under the word We, than to form opinions of our own'.[31] The implication is that the rise of the review has gone hand in hand with the fall of the writer: 'In elder times writers were looked up to almost as intermediate beings, between angels and men. Some time afterwards they were thought venerable teachers; from thence they descended to instructive friends; and now they are deemed rather culprits than benefactors.'[32] Coleridge's friend (and Jeffrey's target in his *Edinburgh* review of *Thalaba*), Robert Southey, haughtily dismissed reviewing as 'the ungentle craft' on several occasions.[33] Byron's first major poem, *English Bards and Scotch Reviewers*, was a Popean riposte to 'self-constituted' judges of poetry, and, late in his career, Byron quoted Southey's estimation of reviewing in order to excoriate the radical-turned-Laureate for having 'Become as base a critic as ere crawl'd – | Fed, paid, and pamper'd by the very men

[29] See Walter Benjamin, 'The Concept of Criticism in German Romanticism' (1920), trans. David Lachtermann, Howard Eiland, and Ian Balfour, in *Walter Benjamin: Selected Writings*, ed. Michael W. Jennings, 4 vols (Cambridge, MA: Belknap Press, 1996–2003), i. *1913–1926* (1996), 116–200 (149–50).

[30] Benjamin, 'Concept of Criticism', 151.

[31] Coleridge, 'Introductory Essay' (1 March 1796), in *The Watchman*, ed. Lewis Patton (Princeton: Princeton University Press, 1970), 15, and *Coleridge's Lectures on Shakespeare*, ed. Adam Roberts (Edinburgh: Edinburgh University Press, 2016), 6. See for further commentary Nicholas Mason, '"The Quack Has Become God": Puffery, Print, and the "Death" of Literature in Romantic-Era Britain', *Nineteenth-Century Literature*, 60 (2005), 1–31 (2).

[32] Coleridge, 'On the Principles of Criticism', in Roberts (ed.), ibid.

[33] Letter to Mary Hays, 7 March 1807, in *The Collected Letters of Robert Southey*, part III (1804–9) <https://romantic-circles.org/editions/southey_letters/Part_Three/HTML/letterEEd.26.1283.html> (accessed 29 December 2020); *The Remains of Henry Kirke White [...], With an Account of his Life*, by Robert Southey, 2 vols (Cambridge: printed for Vernor and others; Nottingham: printed for Dunn and Tupman, 1807), i. 23; and *The Works of William Cowper*, ed. Southey, 15 vols (London: Baldwin & Cradock, 1835–7), i (1835), 77.

l,By whom his muse and morals had been maul'd.'[34] Keats affected somewhat unconvincing though nevertheless considered insouciance about reviews, though Shelley would famously go on to blame one for killing him.[35]

The early nineteenth-century reaction to reviews on the part of Coleridge, Southey, Byron, Keats, and Shelley may, with its class antagonism, accusations of perfidy and, indeed, of manslaughter, seem to lack the philosophical sophistication of Novalis's and Schlegel's conception of the self-fulfilling consummation (and hence redundancy) of reviews. Later in the nineteenth century, in any case, a subsequent generation of reviewers and editors would take stock of the putative innovations of reviews like the *Edinburgh*, reflecting significantly on the characteristics of the review as form and their relation to contemporary reading habits.[36] Walter Bagehot's review of retrospective collections of writings by the *Edinburgh*'s founders, for instance, afforded him the opportunity to consider the epochal status of the kind of writing if not exactly pioneered by the *Edinburgh*, then at least cultivated by it:

> In this transition from ancient writing to modern, the review-like essay and the essay-like review fill a large space. Their small bulk, their slight pretension to systematic completeness, their avowal, it might be said, of necessary incompleteness, the facility of changing the subject, of selecting points to attack, of exposing only the best corner for defence, are great temptations. Still greater is the advantage of 'our limits.' A real reviewer always spends his first and best pages on the parts of a subject on which he wishes to write, the easy comfortable parts which he knows. The formidable difficulties which he acknowledges, you foresee by a strange fatality that he will only reach two pages before the end; to his great grief there is no opportunity for discussing them. As a young gentleman, at the India House examination, wrote 'Time up' on nine unfinished papers in succession, so you may occasionally read a whole review, in every article of which the principal difficulty of each successive question is about to be reached at the conclusion. Nor can any one deny that this is the suitable skill, the judicious custom, of the craft.[37]

---

[34] Byron, *The Vision of Judgment*, 98. 780–2; *Lord Byron: The Complete Poetical Works*, ed. Jerome J. McGann, 7 vols (Oxford: Oxford University Press, 1980–93), vi, ed. McGann and Barry Waller (1991), 309–45 (343).

[35] I discuss Keats's letter to George and Georgiana Keats of 8 October 1818 in Chapter 7; see Shelley's Preface to *Adonais*, in *Shelley's Poetry and Prose*, 2nd edn, ed. Donald H. Reiman and Neil Fraistat (New York: Norton, 2002), 410.

[36] See Joanne Shattock, 'Contexts and Conditions of Criticism 1830–1914', in *CHLC VI*, 21–45 (esp. 32–5) for details.

[37] Bagehot, 'The First Edinburgh Reviewers' (1855), in *The Collected Works of Walter Bagehot*, ed. Norman St John-Stevas, 15 vols (London: The Economist, 1965–86), i (1965, repr. 1986), 309–41 (312) (first pub. in *National Review*, October 1855). Further references are given after quotations in the text. On Bagehot's characterization of 'the review-like essay and the essay-like review', see also Terry Eagleton, *The Function of Criticism* (London: Verso, 2005; first pub. 1984), 49–50; Joanne Shattock, *Politics and Reviewers: The 'Edinburgh' and the 'Quarterly' in the Early Victorian Age* (London: Leicester University Press, 1989), 111–18; and Shattock 'The Culture of Criticism', 77–8.

The subtle play on the 'avowal, it might be said, of necessary incompleteness' in reviews, hints both that avowals in reviews are made not, as it were, avowedly, but rather conditionally ('it might be said'), and that there is a paradoxically systematic aspect about the *necessity* of their incompleteness. Following his articulation of 'the review-like essay and the essay-like review', Bagehot expatiates in a sequence of large yet measured steps on the relation between the generic characteristics of the review and 'our times', which are thus continuous with the time in which the *Edinburgh* was founded at the beginning of the century, notwithstanding the significant developments that have taken place since. The focus of the review as it has come to be practised since the foundation of the *Edinburgh* is, indeed, on the literature of 'our times'. 'Comments on ancient writings are scarcely so common as formerly; no great part of our literary talent is devoted to the illustration of ancient masters,' Bagehot observes, 'but what seems at first sight less dignified, annotation on modern writings was never so frequent' (p. 309). Bagehot's delicate equivocation concerning the contemporary situation is revealed in the cautionary note struck by 'at first sight', on the one hand, and, on the other, in the contrast between 'ancient masters' and 'modern writings', the latter tellingly not ascribed to any sort of productive agency (such as 'masters') at all. Bagehot goes on as follows:

> In truth review-writing but exemplifies the casual character of modern literature. Everything about it is temporary and fragmentary. Look at a railway stall; you see books of every colour, blue, yellow, crimson, 'ring-streaked, speckled, and spotted,' on every subject, in every style, of every opinion with every conceivable difference, celestial or sublunary, maleficent, beneficent—but all small. People take their literature in morsels, as they take sandwiches on a journey. The volumes at least, you can see clearly, are not intended to be everlasting. It may be all very well for a pure essence like poetry to be immortal in a perishable world; it has no feeling; but paper cannot endure it, paste cannot bear it, string has no heart for it. The race has made up its mind to be fugitive, as well as minute.
>
> (p. 310)

The quotation is from Genesis 30:39 (with 'ring-streaked' for the Authorized Version's 'ring-straked'), and it is notable that a quotation from The Book should be used to illustrate this description of little, colourful books, indifferently 'maleficent, beneficent' and 'not intended to be everlasting'. There is thus a stark contrast between such books and the Bible, but the quotation also lends a certain appeal to the scene that Bagehot depicts, as if the multitude of modern books partakes of the fecundity and variety of Jacob's flocks.

The attempt to cast the ephemerality of modern writing as pleasingly bountiful and various was anticipated by Leigh Hunt in his essay on periodical literature for his journal *The Examiner* in 1808, six years after the *Edinburgh*'s foundation.

The distinctly transitory materiality of periodical publications was, Hunt sought playfully to suggest, in fact an advantage over 'the majesty of a quarto or all the gaiety of a beau duodecimo'. Books are burdensome and take up space, whereas periodical writings have various uses once they have been read: 'how many pleasant modes are there of getting rid of a periodical essay? It may assist your meditation by lighting your pipe, it may give steadiness to your candle, it may curl the tresses of your daughter or your sister, or lastly, if you are not rich enough to possess an urn or a cloth-holder, it may save you a world of opodeldoc by wrapping the handle of your tea-kettle. These are advantages.'[38] Likewise, Bagehot saw the ephemerality of 'review-writing' as in keeping with the age's fast pace (the railway) and easy consumption (sandwiches), but he subverts the Romantic assumption that poetry's claim to permanence goes hand-in-hand with its status as the province of feeling—on the contrary, the fact that poetry is 'a pure essence' renders it unfeeling, whereas the mere materiality of review-writing renders it acutely susceptible to the thousand natural shocks that flesh is heir to: 'paper cannot endure it, paste cannot bear it, string has no heart for it', he declaims, nimbly evoking the heartstrings in that culminating phrase, provoking pity for the review so that no one will demand it endure against its nature.

Bagehot, it must be recalled, wrote nearly fifty years after Hunt and, significantly, from a political position that prioritized stability above all else—in contrast to the critique of establishment and the associated advocacy for reform for which Hunt suffered imprisonment.[39] Bagehot's was also a moment that, despite being importantly continuous with that of the *Edinburgh*, was at the same time distinguishing itself from it by the rise of professionalized, scholarly criticism, as well as by the cursory review notice required by the daily and weekly press. Bagehot's retrospective of the kind of writing fostered by the *Edinburgh* thus partakes of this moment—of its confidence in increasingly professionalized criticism and of its anxiety about the audience for such criticism in light of the growth of shorter and more rapid journalistic forms. This combination of factors is echoed in Bagehot's lukewarm assessment of the collection of Jeffrey's writings that he is reviewing, which extends in decidedly more muted tones his mock-heroic appeal on behalf of review-writing. Noting the sheer number of Jeffrey's reviews and making clear his relatively low estimation of Jeffrey's gifts as a critic (an estimation of Jeffrey that he shared with Leslie Stephen, David Masson, John Morley, and others, as detailed by Shattock), Bagehot remarks that '[s]ome things, a few things, are for

---

[38] Leigh Hunt, 'On Periodical Essays', in *The Selected Writings of Leigh Hunt*, ed. Greg Kucich and Jeffrey N. Cox, 6 vols (London: Pickering and Chatto, 2003), i: *Periodical Essays, 1805-14*, 35–57 (35) (first pub. as 'The Literary and Philosophical Examiner No. 1', in *The Examiner*, I (10 January 1808)). Compare Frank Kermode's remark that '[m]ost reviews […] claim houseroom only for as long as the paper they are printed on—a day or a week, at most a month' (*The Uses of Error* (London: Collins, 1990), p. ix).

[39] See, e.g., Walter Bagehot, 'The Morality of the Coup d'État' (1852), in *The Collected Works of Walter Bagehot*, iv. 35–44 (36).

eternity; some, and a good many, are for time. We do not expect the everlastingness of the Pyramids from the vibratory grandeur of a Tyburnian mansion' ('The First Edinburgh Reviewers', p. 329). The pronouncement of such a judgement in (let it be recalled) a review is hardly neutral. The apodictic certainty of Bagehot's rendering unto eternity that which is eternity's and rendering unto time that which is time's has the effect of reinforcing the distinction between Jeffrey's reviews and Bagehot's review of Jeffrey. Bagehot's 'The First Edinburgh Reviewers' was posthumously placed by Richard Holt Hutton as the first of Bagehot's *Literary Studies*, out of chronological sequence with the rest of the essays that follow it in that collection. Bagehot's reviews, recast as 'studies', are pyramidal; Jeffrey's, Tyburnian.

*

Bagehot implicitly rebuked the very idea of a collection of Jeffrey's writings. Bagehot—and certainly his posthumous collector, Hutton—thus distinguished between reviews that deserved collection and, thereby, elevation to a different generic status, and those that did not. Such collection-and-elevation entails the effacement of the temporal, even ephemeral nature of reviews, as they take their place in a now established literary history subject to 'studies' conducted by profes-sionalized students. What is involved here, then, is not just the retrospective collation of a writer's ephemeral work for the sake of testimony or convenience but an attempt to negotiate the distinction between generalist and professional authorship that itself maps on to particular forms of critical writing.

In her introduction to a collection of periodical reviews that sought not to efface but rather to emphasize the temporal and provisional character of review-ing, Isobel Armstrong argued that, because reviewers have 'to get to grips with a new work for the first time [...] the theories and generalisations about poetry which emerge from this process of assimilation, definition and interpretation have a peculiar immediacy lacking in the abstract treatises on poetry' (she lists John Henry Newman's 'Poetry, with Reference to Aristotle's *Poetics*' (1829), E. S. Dallas's *Poetics: An Essay on Poetry* (1852), and George Henry Lewes's *Principles of Success in Literature* (1865) as examples of the latter). Periodical criti-cism has a 'necessary concern with the actual', Armstrong goes on to declare, with a notably Hegelian resonance, and thus 'displays the immense variety of emphasis with which an idea can be interpreted'.[40] Occasionally, reviews do attend to what is not strictly actual in this sense, discussing either new editions of old works or (the more interesting case) a work that 'is neither old nor new [...] when it must be admitted that the work lacks, on the one hand, the assurance of age and, on the other, a current and pressing fame', as Elizabeth Hardwick, the subtlest guide to this literary twilight zone, formulates the matter in the opening of her account of

---

[40] Isobel Armstrong, 'Introduction', in Armstrong (ed.), *Victorian Scrutinies: Reviews of Poetry 1830–1870* (London: Athlone, 1972), 1–68 (3).

'The Neglected Novels of Christina Stead'.[41] Armstrong's claim, however, is that the actual is the special province of the review, which must do without the assurance of age and is in large part responsible for determining how current and pressing fame may in the first place become. It is important to note that Armstrong's concern is not to establish a crude opposition between theory and practice, but rather to document their implication—the emergence, that is, of 'theories and generalisations' out of 'the actual'. Yet the explicit distinction between immediacy and abstraction, and between works informed by reference to established poetic principle written by authors such as Newman, Dallas, and Lewes, on the one hand, and periodical reviews written by W. J. Fox, Frederick Lushington, John Morley, and other, similarly journalistic, writers, on the other hand, remains. The sublation of the variety of interpretation into settled critical orthodoxy is a process not, the implication is, without loss. Though Armstrong certainly does not, other writers have been more than willing to assert that academic criticism is ill-suited to the evaluation of new work. It was George Saintsbury's blurb for Ian Hay's novel *A Safety Match* that moved Orwell to rail against the errors of judgement that inevitably follow when 'professors of literature [...] are so unwise as to write about contemporary books'.[42]

Like Armstrong, the prolific reviewer (rather than academic) Alfred Kazin looked back on the periodical culture of the nineteenth century from the standpoint of a hundred years later and paid tribute to Anton Chekhov as a writer for magazines, describing how in general a 'magazine is always a date, an "issue", a moment; it is created out of an exacting sense of time and it is about time. The spirit of occasion, the tone of conversation, the modesty of the passing moment, are what most belong to it.'[43] Armstrong's collection of reviews is a work of literary-historical scholarship, an early instance of the attempt to resituate criticism in its original occasions of production and publication that I associated above with Shattock, Butler, and others. Yet it nevertheless registers a tension between journalistic and (proto-)academic criticism that has often characterized discussion of reviews; Kazin's characterization of the magazine as occasional, conversational, modest, and ephemeral draws an implicit contrast with the long preparation and aspiration to permanence of different forms of writing. Adorno declared in the mid-1950s that 'academia and the feuilleton have always mistrusted one another', an uncharacteristically eternizing statement and one that has, moreover, come to require qualification in the light of attempts within academia

---

[41] Hardwick, *Collected Essays*, 44–50 (44) (first pub. in *The New Republic*, 1 August 1955, 17–19).

[42] Orwell, *Collected Essays*, i. 262. Saintsbury is quoted on the jacket-blurb for Ian Hay, *A Safety Match* (Edinburgh: William Blackwood, 1911) as follows: 'Let me congratulate you on "A Safety Match". I have read nothing so good for a long time.'

[43] Alfred Kazin, 'Writing for Magazines', in *Contemporaries* (London: Secker and Warburg, 1973), 471–4 (474).

to take the measure of the origins of some significant criticism in the feuilleton.[44] Granted, George Watson, writing twenty years after Adorno and addressing the Anglophone context, still felt able to abominate William Hazlitt as 'the father of our Sunday journalism', before then going on to declare admiringly of Edmund Wilson that his 'talents as a critic are, in the noblest sense, journalistic'—an expression of approval for Wilson, however, that David Bromwich would then censure as typical academic condescension.[45] The fact that writers holding academic positions (Armstrong, Adorno, Watson, Bromwich) variously praise journalistic criticism, blame journalistic criticism, and blame the blaming of journalistic criticism should indicate to us that, whatever mistrust obtains in the relationship between academia and the feuilleton, it is not simply directed by one side towards the other and vice versa. The fact that Wilson himself also held a series of (albeit temporary) academic appointments, while a figure like Saintsbury (the target of Orwell's scorn for 'professors of literature') had begun his literary career as a journalist, should do likewise.

*

One of Wilson's most valuable reflections on the career of reviewer was, in fact, originally framed in response to the bestowal of a certain kind of academic plaudit. Describing to students at Princeton how to exploit the medium of the review for the purpose of sustained and autonomous literary projects of the kind more usually associated with academic careers and the specialisms on which, at the time of his remarks, they were coming increasingly to be based, Wilson gave the following advice:

> To write what you are interested in writing and to succeed in getting editors to pay for it, is a feat that may require pretty close calculation and a good deal of ingenuity. You have to learn to load solid matter into notices of ephemeral happenings; you have to develop a resourcefulness at pursuing a line of thought through pieces on miscellaneous and more or less fortuitous subjects; and you have to acquire a technique of slipping over on the routine of editors the deeper independent work which their over-anxious intentness on the fashions of the month or the week have conditioned them automatically to reject, as the machines that make motor parts automatically reject outsizes.[46]

---

[44] Theodor W. Adorno, 'On the Crisis of Literary Criticism' (1952/3), in *Notes to Literature*, trans. Shierry Weber Nicholsen, 2 vols (New York: Columbia University Press, 1992), ii. 305–8 (306).

[45] George Watson, *The Literary Critics: A Study of English Descriptive Criticism* (London: Penguin, 1986; first pub. 1973), 125 (on Hazlitt) and 204 (on Wilson). Cf. David Bromwich, 'Wilson's Modernism', in Lewis M. Dabney (ed.), *Edmund Wilson: Centennial Reflections* (Princeton: Princeton University Press, 1997), 39–52 (40).

[46] Wilson, 'Thoughts on Being Bibliographed' (1943), in *Literary Essays and Reviews of the 1930s & 40s*, ed. Lewis M. Dabney (New York: Library of America, 2007), 557–69 (562). Further references are given after quotations in the text.

Wilson views editors on analogy with machines, which the guileful writer must learn to manipulate effectively. The qualities required to construct a career out of reviewing—'pretty close calculation and a good deal of ingenuity'—are desirable qualities in reviews themselves, and, indeed, Wilson's description of how to get one over on a rigidly pre-programmed editor sounds in general like a description of how to negotiate between the generic conventions of the review as form and the need for successful writing to be more than merely conventional.

Reviewing as a career thus rests on the intelligent manipulation of established forms, as do reviews themselves. The image of reviews as immediate reactions to the actual out of which abstract theorization eventually emerges in established and permanent forms (such as the treatise) thus requires qualification at this point. Instead of simply being swept along in the stream of the actual, the review is itself a form, underlying which are conventions, formulae, and abstract theoretical principles, whose exploitation and subversion are, moreover, a part of its formal character. Such formulae prove most telling when they are made explicit in order to be subverted. Wilson, for instance, offers ratings for the books or writers under review—first rate, second rate, fourth rate (curiously enough, there seems to be no third rate)—and does so with sufficient regularity to suggest that this comparative evaluation (stratification, even) is a fundamental task of literary criticism. A collection of poems by Angelica Balabanoff, for instance, is 'hardly a first-rate work of literature'; Somerset Maugham is a 'second-rate' artist in general (pp. 549, 725). The strong sense that it is impossible to move up to being first rate if you are 'a second-rate man' is no guarantee, however, against demotion from the higher ranks. In a review of 1944, Wilson comments that the novelist Louis Bromfield 'used to be spoken of as one of the younger writers of promise', but '[b]y the time he had brought out *Twenty-four Hours*, it was more or less generally said of him that he was definitely second-rate' (p. 595). But that is not where Bromfield comes to rest: 'he has gradually made his way into the fourth rank, where his place is now secure' (p. 595)—the third tier in Wilson's literary hierarchy, recall, being wholly unpopulated.

Yet the conventional rating of literary works—which achieves its apogee in the ubiquitous lists of best books and bestsellers to which Wilson's ratings appear to come troublingly close—is often subverted or qualified by Wilson. This is even the case in Wilson's excoriation of Bromfield. Warming to his theme, Wilson's firm conviction that Bromfield was 'definitely second-rate' is nevertheless a conviction that is only 'more or less generally' admitted. Wilson goes on to allege, in the kind of humorous barb to which he was given, that Bromfield, though securely of the fourth rank, does not actually betray the characteristics of the novelists of that rank: '[m]ost novelists of Mr. Bromfield's rank have some hobby about which they become interesting', and Bromfield has not attained even to this lacklustre benchmark of the mediocre novelist's craft. Likewise, Wilson elsewhere suggests that an anthology of tales of horror 'by really first-rate modern writers' might be assembled, which Wilson, however, then fleshes out by giving details of works that do not clearly seem to belong to this class, such as 'a couple of stories of Kipling's— say, *At the End of the Passage* and *Mrs Bathurst*—as examples of borderline cases of the genuinely imaginative story which is nevertheless not first-rate' (pp. 612–13). Works that are not first rate can, therefore, be 'genuinely imaginative'. Comparably, reviewing Leonid Leonov's *Road to the Ocean*, Wilson concludes that, on the evidence of this book, Leonov is not a first-rate artist, but is nevertheless 'talented', has 'some serious idea of what literature ought to be', and has produced 'a real social novel that would stand up with Malraux or Dos Passos' (p. 675). Wilson also describes Jean-Paul Sartre as 'a writer of undeniably exceptional gifts', who nevertheless, according to Wilson's doubly hedged assessment, '*somehow* does not *seem* quite first-rate' (p. 785; emphasis added). Genuine imagination; talent; having a serious idea of literature; producing a social novel comparable with the best of the kind; boasting exceptional gifts: none of this, however, necessarily adds up to what emerges, not as a numerable quantity, but as the ineffable quality of being 'first-rate'. The apparent rigidity of Wilson's classificatory system is always tempered by the expression of agnosticism as to whether it in fact applies to the case under discussion, the conventions of reviewing being flexibly deployed as foils for the reviewer's more fully articulated judgements.

Notable works therefore emerge as those that disable the review's conventions— without which, however, they could not be marked out as notable. The review is a form made to be broken—but a form all the more for that reason. Reviewing Katherine Anne Porter's *The Leaning Tower and Other Stories* a few months after his evisceration of Bromfield in 1944, Wilson gave one of his most explicit accounts of what he takes the review's generic conventions to be—before announcing that they do not apply in the present case:

> Miss Katherine Anne Porter has published a new book of stories, her third: *The Leaning Tower and Other Stories*. To the reviewer, Miss Porter is baffling because one cannot take hold of her work in any of the obvious ways. She makes none of the melodramatic or ironic points that are the stock in trade of ordinary short story writers; she falls into none of the usual patterns and she does not show anyone's influence. She does not exploit her personality either inside or outside her work, and her writing itself makes a surface so smooth that the critic has little opportunity to point out peculiarities of color or weave. If he is tempted to say that the effect is pale, he is prevented by the realization that Miss Porter writes English of a purity and precision almost unique in contemporary American fiction. If he tries to demur that some given piece fails to mount with the accelerating pace or arrive at the final intensity that he is in the habit of expecting in short stories, he is deterred by a nibbling suspicion that he may not have grasped its meaning and have it hit him with a sudden impact some minutes after he has closed the book. (p. 647)

This opening passage of Wilson's review of Porter's collection—especially the transition from the assertive 'She makes none of...' and 'She does not...' applied to Porter, to the qualified 'If he is tempted to say...' and 'If he tries to demur that...' applied to the putative reviewer—reveals both what the conventions of the review are and that this actual reviewer has at least been 'tempted' to deploy them. Wilson's confession of the critical temptations he faced—and withstood—in reviewing Porter's collection both manages to give 'a nibbling suspicion' of just those criticisms of Porter's collection that are ultimately to be rejected and at the same time displays the process of the critic's arrival at second, sounder thoughts. The unavailability to this review of the form's conventions is dictated, it is implied, by the innovative refusal of generic convention evinced by the work it is considering.

The suspension of the review's conventions is not always the result (as it was in Porter's case) of praiseworthy literary innovation, however. It is necessary at this point to return to the hapless Louis Bromfield one last time in order to witness Wilson's reflections on the frustration of the reviewer's usual procedures by bad, rather than good, writing. Wilson begins a short coda to his demolition of Bromfield's recent work by remarking, wearily, that 'I have been trying to describe this production in the manner appropriate to it—that is, as far as possible, in the language of the ladies who admire Louis Bromfield and who write enthusiastic reviews in the *Times* and the *Herald Tribune*' (p. 600). To prove his point—which is tinged with sexism, not least since Wilson's protestation that he has been attempting the style of Bromfield's lady-admirers is entirely disingenuous— Wilson appends to the version of the review collected in *Classics and Commercials* the concluding paragraph of Mary Ross's review of Bromfield in the *Herald Tribune*, in which she praises Bromfield's 'simply told and unassuming story' as 'an appealing novel which it is hard to lay down, and I think it will be hard to forget' (p. 600)—a judgement that had already failed to age well by the time Wilson selected his assessment for inclusion in *Classics and Commercials* in 1950. Mary Ross's review is, of course, conventional to the point of cliché in its praise of Bromfield—there is no troubling of the standard lexicon of praise or of the reviewer's routine procedures here—but Wilson confesses to his inability to come to grips with Bromfield at all: 'the truth is that the book reviewer is baffled when he attempts to give an account of a work which already turned its back on litera- ture and embarrasses him on every page by stretching out its arms to Hollywood' (p. 600). Wilson uses the same terms ('baffled') as he had in reviewing Porter ('baffling'), but here the bafflement is a wholly negative consequence of Bromfield's writing. The crucial difference is that the attempted application of the established conventions of a review in Porter's case results in more mature consideration as to why those conventions do not apply. Porter's writing is in the process of establish- ing new conventions and thus requires new procedures in response on the part of the review. Needless to say, this is risky for the reviewer. At the end of his opening summation, Wilson remarks of Porter's stories that '[t]here is no place for general reflections', but that she has at the same time 'managed to say something about the values involved in the experience'. The conundrum for the reviewer is in attempting to explain what is said, an attempt Wilson says he will undertake 'though I am afraid I shall land in ineptitude' (p. 647). And indeed, having attempted to make good on his promise to suggest what it is that Porter says about the 'values involved in the experience' (p. 647) of her characters and thus to uncover the role in Porter's stories of 'a conception of a natural human spirit', Wilson gives up on the attempt and declares, in a vein we encountered at the beginning of Chapter 2 in Eliot's insistence on the silence of an innovative book's introducer, that 'I am spoiling Miss Porter's stories by attempting to find a formula for them when I ought simply to be telling you to read them' (p. 649). It is not that the formula Wilson has attempted to find is to be wholly discarded, but rather that it can never substitute for reading itself, in relation to which it is neither complete nor definitive, but rather partial and heuristic—but it is, at least, that.

Wilson's reviews of Bromfield and Porter display the frustration of the review's conventions, though the source of frustration in the former's case is his inadequacy to convention and, in the latter's, her supersession of it. What these reviews bring out is that the review has clearly identifiable generic conventions— but only generically conventional objects of review, so Wilson is implying, actually serve to activate those conventions. It is as if, in reviewing Bromfield, Wilson harbours a suspicion of the refusal or, rather, failure to conform to established models, finding in the abandonment of convention a mere emptiness. And it is as if, in reviewing Porter, the transition in the history of aesthetics from the evaluation of artworks on the basis of their conformity to established models, to the evaluation of artworks with reference to the subject's experience of them, is played out in Wilson's own experience of reading Porter's short stories. Major positions in the history of aesthetic response are thus traceable in the seeming minutiae of the reviews of works by (now) largely forgotten writers. As well as disabling the distinction between the mere modesty and occasionality of reviewing, on the one hand, and abstract theorization, on the other, what this testifies to is that the assessment and assimilation of new work does not come to settle once and for all into abstract theorization reposited in treatises, but that different occasions again and again entail different consequences for theorization.

*

It is worth revisiting in conclusion the relationship between academia and the feuilleton that we have met in this discussion of the formal characteristics of the review. It is worth doing so not only because this relationship or a predecessor version of it has been central in attempts to consider the history of the review (this chapter being no exception) but rather in order to offer some reflections on how it may have developed since the time of a figure like Wilson—who, it is worth recalling, was at least in part an academic, however much of a journalist subject to the condescension of academics he may also have been.

Adorno's sense of the opposition between academia and the 'feuilleton', a continental term that has never quite established itself in the Anglosphere, may itself have arisen in response to a distinctly German opposition between *Literaturwissenschaft* and *Literarturkritik*—a distinction that does not quite map onto that between scholarship and criticism as that distinction is understood in Anglophone discourse. Writing around the same time as Adorno, and drawing on a roughly comparable experience of exile and of formation in German and Anglophone literary cultures, René Wellek explained *Literaturkritik* as 'day-by-day reviewing' but then went on to worry that any straightforward identification of *Literaturkritik* with 'daily book reviewing' would be 'dangerous because it leaves evaluation to the journalist and isolates "Literaturwissenschaft" as a discipline removed from contemporary literature and released from the task of discrimination and evaluation'.[47] Some years later, Peter Uwe Hohendahl advanced the claim that the profession of freelance critic existed in Germany in a way that it did not in the United States, his evidence being (in 1982) that the majority of reviewers for the *New York Review of Books* were academics.[48] And one consequence of the mid-1970s deanonymization of reviews in the *TLS* was to reveal that its reviewers were increasingly academics—a situation resented by some correspondents since it meant (as they saw it) that salaried academics were taking bread out of the mouths of writers who lived solely by writing.[49] Introducing in 2001 one of his collections of reviews, *Pleasing Myself: Beowulf to Philip Roth*, whose subtitle echoes and extends the shorthand description of the once-standard university English curriculum from Beowulf to Virginia Woolf, Frank Kermode remarked that '[i]t is almost true to say that this middle ground between the barbarous jargons and swollen books of the modern academy and the quick satisfactions of the newspaper review is nowadays cultivated only by a few journals like these [namely, the *London Review of Books*, the *New York Review of Books*, and the *New Republic*], and it is just as well for our intellectual well-being that they should exist'.[50]

However matters stand in different national or linguistic literary cultures, the alleged economic discomfort caused to some reviewers by the academization of

---

[47] René Wellek, *Concepts of Criticism*, ed. Stephen G. Nichols, Jr (New Haven: Yale University Press, 1963; repr. 1969), 3, 35–6

[48] Peter Uwe Hohendahl, *The Institution of Criticism* (Ithaca, NY: Cornell University Press, 1982), 13–16.

[49] See May, 425.

[50] Kermode, *Pleasing Myself: From Beowulf to Philip Roth* (London: Allen Lane, 2001), p. vii. Kermode makes similar remarks in, for example, the introduction to *Uses of Error*, p. ix—though the word limits seem to have shrunk between this earlier collection ('the six or eight thousand words sometimes allows by such journals as *The New York Review of Books* and *The London Review of Books*') and *Pleasing Myself*.

reviewing serves as a vital reminder that the 'freelance' writer depends on what are sometimes large and ruthless media corporations, just as the academic depends on the institution of the university. Whether the academic, by virtue of her or his institutional and professional status, is any less free than the freelance writer is questionable, to say the least.[51] On the other hand, few would dispute that academic freedom has itself come to be more and more subjected to the laws of supply and demand, and to managerial oversight. Neither the review nor the academic essay or book ever belonged to a pristine sphere of freedom—at the very least because academics and reviewers have frequently crossed over onto what is fantasized as the other's territory. 'Not disembodied freedom, but diverse embodiednesses and incomplete servitudes have to become the common sense view of intellectual work.'[52] And, as this chapter has shown, diverse embodiedness and incomplete servitude to conventional expectations have been the markers not only of the practice of reviewing but of the form of the review as well.

---

[51] The thirty years and many changes to university administration since its publication notwithstanding, I am drawing here on Bruce Robbins, *Secular Vocations: Intellectuals, Professionalism, Culture* (London: Verso, 1993), esp. pp. 9–10, 16–18, 75–7.

[52] Robbins, 10.

4

Lectures

One concern of the previous chapter was with the way that reviews have frequently been repackaged as 'studies' or 'essays'. My aim was thus in part to draw attention to what is at stake with respect to the cultivation of professional esteem and the entitlement to a place in posterity as a consequence of such a repackaging. As such, I was addressing what I called in the Introduction the invisibility of critical forms and was attempting to restore one of them (the review) to greater visibility, along with considering its specific conventions and the kind of criticism they foster.

This chapter is concerned with lectures, whose formal characteristics are likewise often effaced as they are assimilated to the history of literary criticism. A great deal of literary criticism and scholarship, especially but not only literary criticism and scholarship written by those literary critics who are required to give lectures in universities, had its origins in lectures: to a certain extent, this book is no exception. But where a metaphor of vision may be apt in the case of reviews (their 'invisibility'), it is less so in the case of lectures, since what is at issue in their accommodation to the history of literary criticism is rather their inaudibility. The oral performance of lectures, that is, is transmuted into the visible medium of text. The ease and frequency with which the origins of literary critical works in lectures are effaced may indeed be especially owing to the fact that lectures are often already texts. In his wryly insightful chapter on the lecture in his *Forms of Talk*, Erving Goffman, for example, acknowledges that a lecture is often 'merely aloud reading from a typed text'—or, before the invention of the typewriter, from a handwritten one.[1]

I want to turn a bit more concertedly to Goffman's valuable account in a moment, but first it is worth acknowledging that not all lectures in the history of literary criticism began life as texts, even if that was the form in which they came to be transmitted to posterity: the example of Coleridge's often extemporized and only subsequently textualized lectures is significant here, for instance. But even those lectures that have both their ends and origins in written script frequently retain traces of their passage through (so to speak) the lecture form. Such traces of the event of the lecture can be highly significant to the critical concerns and claims of lectures that have come down to us as texts. Gertrude Stein's

---

[1] Erving Goffman, *Forms of Talk* (Oxford: Oxford University Press, 1981), 161. Further references are given after quotations in the text.

Critical Forms: Forms of Literary Criticism, 1750–2020. Ross Wilson, Oxford University Press. © Ross Wilson 2023.
DOI: 10.1093/oso/9780198881117.003.0005

extraordinary *Lectures in America*, delivered in 1934 and published the following year, are a signal instance of published lectures whose status as both text and spoken event is crucial to the arguments they develop. For instance, in the third of the six lectures, 'Plays', Stein offers the following observation and, in doing so, poses a question:

> Plays are either read or heard or seen.
>
> And there then comes the question which comes first and which is first, reading or hearing or seeing a play.
>
> I ask you.[2]

Lectures are like plays in being read or heard or seen, and like plays they prompt the (subtly different) questions of which comes first and which is first.[3] The question is put to Stein's (both listening and reading) audience, but with the gnomic caveat, advanced slightly later, that 'in asking a question one is not answering but one is as one may say deciding about knowing' (p. 102). The matter of which comes first—reading or hearing—might seem to be settled at the opening of the following, retrospective lecture, 'The Gradual Making of *The Making of America*', in which Stein reflects on the composition of one of her own texts and where she informs her audience that 'I am going to read what I have written to read because in a general way it is easier even if it is not better and in a general way it is better than to say what has not been written. Any way that is one way to feel about it' (p. 135). The lecture was a text that was read out and is now a text again. But Stein's text, with its looping repetitions ('to read...to read', 'in a general way...in a general way', 'any way...one way') and seemingly live-action revisions ('it is easier even if it is not better...it is better'), is not a very textual text, as it were, not one in which the fluid, sometimes hesitant, self-revising character of speaking has been written out or written over, but is rather a text that bears the traces of speaking within it. Yet it is important to recall that this text is not merely or primarily a transcript of oral performance, since, as Stein tells us, that oral performance is already the reading-out of a written text. The poet Eileen Myles's recollection of encountering Stein's hesitations and repetitions—'I thought, wait a second. *Is that a stutter, is that a typo?* No, that's her taking her time. Pacing herself.'—usefully registers the difficulty of deciding whether such features are oral (stutter) or textual (typo), refusing to decide between these options and emphasizing instead their temporalizing effect, not just, however, of 'taking her time' but of giving it as

[2] Gertrude Stein, *Lectures in America* (London: Virago Press, 1988; first pub. 1935), 95. Further references are given after quotations in the text.
[3] See Steven Meyer, 'Gertrude Stein', in *CHLC VII*, 93–121, which also discusses Stein's lecturing prior to *Lectures in America*.

well.[4] Stein, in a gesture that we may recognize from a number of the autographic preface-writers we encountered in Chapter 1, casts herself, moreover, as her own first reader ('I am going to read what I have written to read') and, crucially, as her own listener: 'I always as I admit seem to be talking but talking can be a way of listening' (p. 135). The authority of speaker and the different modes of passivity of listener and reader, the passage from oneself to another, the differences between words in the mind, in text, and in the air are all at issue throughout *Lectures in America*, where their critical importance is not merely announced but performed. 'Every one's own history of English literature is their own until they tell it some-body else as I am now telling mine', Stein declares near the start of the opening lecture 'What is English Literature' (a title without a question mark since the question mark is 'complete entirely completely uninteresting' (p. 214)). This is a process of telling that affects what is told because '[o]ne of the things that is a very interesting thing to know is how you are feeling inside you to the words that are coming out to be outside of you' (p. 209). The unfolding self-reflection of such statements again places the emphasis on the process of transmission from Stein to her audience. The text of *Lectures in America* is not simple simulation of oral delivery, not only because such simulation would in turn be complicated by the fact that what had been orally delivered was first textual, but because the occur-rence of enunciation is a central focus of her discussion.[5] Stein's repeated cajolings—'But slowly you will see what I mean. If not why not'; 'Oh yes you do see. You do see that' (pp. 24, 34)—are a register of the fact that coming to see what people mean is as much a process of attending, of hearing them out, as it is, in fact, of *seeing* what they mean. The text on the page is at once a record of and script for the word in the air, in the ear, and in the mind.

The hesitations, revisions, and stutters of Stein's lectures evoke the performance of an actual lecturer. In his account of what he calls the 'noise' that is an inevitable consequence of the 'layered composite structure—electronic, physical, biological, and so forth' that is the 'communication system' deployed in the delivery of a lec-ture, Goffman offers his own sketch of some of the things that an actually living lecturer does in the act of lecturing:

> A speaker must breathe, fidget a little, scratch occasionally, and may feel cause to cough, brush back his hair, straighten her skirt, sniffle, take a drink of water, finger her pearls, clean his glasses, burp, shift from one foot to another, sway, manneristically button and unbutton a jacket, turn the pages and square them off, and so forth—not to mention tripping over the carpet or appearing not to be entirely zipped up.   (p. 183)

[4] Erica Schwiegershausen, 'Eileen Myles on the Book that Made Writing like Talking', *The Cut*, 29 August 2017 <https://www.thecut.com/2017/08/eileen-myles-on-lectures-in-america-by-gertrude-stein.html> (accessed 14 January 2022).

[5] See Jan Mieszkowski, *Crises of the Sentence* (Chicago: University of Chicago Press, 2019), 240–1.

In addition to such 'bodily faults' (among which Goffman appears to include the need to breathe), Goffman goes on to list 'minor peculiarities of human sound equipment' that may still more directly affect how words are said and heard. Goffman makes plain that such 'faults' and 'peculiarities' are distractions from the conveyance of the text of a lecture and, as such, are to be ignored. Yet he goes on to acknowledge that 'what is noise from the perspective of the text as such can be the music of the interaction—the very source of the auditors' satisfaction in the occasion, the very difference between reading a lecture at home and attending one' (p. 186). And the reason one might not only expose oneself to such 'noise' but in fact experience it as 'music' is because it is the product of access to a speaker, 'a much more exclusive claim than ordinarily can be made by a readership' (p. 187).

But texts (as we have seen with Stein) can have their noises too. In addition to wondering whether it is true, as Goffman seems to hold, that a lecturer *must* fidget and scratch, or whether turning the pages of a lecture script is only something that the lecturer *may* feel the need to do, we may notice that Goffman's own account is strikingly performative. It is not merely a list of what goes missing when lectures are turned (back) into text; it is a performative evocation of just that. The quixotic list in general; the image of a nasally irritated, gaseous, somewhat unsteady, mildly *déshabillé* scholarly eminence (the paralipsis 'not to mention...' that introduces the suggestion that the lecturer's attire may not be properly arranged adds to its mildly titivating character); the burlesque of mannerism; even the very uncertainty as to what a lecturer *must* or only *may* do: all of this goes some way to re-creating the effect of witnessing first hand the human, and distinctively physical, idiosyncrasies displayed by someone whose role as lecturer necessarily entails some pretension, at least, to intellectual authority, as well as some way towards evoking the element of unpredictability in the delivery of a lecture by even the most scripted and experienced lecturer. As Goffman makes clear in introducing *Forms of Talk*, 'glances, looks, and postural shifts carry all kinds of implication and meaning', as do, when words are spoken, 'tone of voice, manner of uptake, restarts, and the variously positioned pauses' (pp. 1–2).

The difference between speaker and writer has, of course, been a concern for a long time: 'a speaker can directly perceive the circumstances of his recipients and a writer cannot', Goffman observers (p. 179), a fact that Socrates famously held against writing in Plato's *Phaedrus*.[6] Goffman's way of putting this difference is, however, especially notable. First, the designation of the members of a speaker's audience as 'his recipients' emphasizes their passivity in relation to the lecturer, which might then lead us to wonder what consequence, if any, the lecturer's ability to perceive their circumstances might in fact have. And is it really the audience's circumstances, specifically—as distinct from their *actions*, such as

---

[6] Trans. Alexander Nehamas and Paul Woodruff, in *Plato: Complete Works*, ed. John M. Cooper (Indianapolis: Hackett, 1997), 506–56 (551–3 (274e–276b)).

fidgeting, yawning, furiously taking notes, despairingly stopping taking notes, shifting in their seats, sneaking out halfway through, stomping out halfway through—that can in any case have an effect on what the speaker says or how she or her says it? Goffman's way of putting the lecturer's perception of the audience—'*directly* perceive'—holds open the possibility that a writer may *indirectly* perceive her or his readers' circumstances, such as by means of inference from the lecturer's own circumstances as a reader.

Given his insistence that what the lecture involves is not a dialogue of the type that Socrates would have preferred to the polished orations of a Sophist like Phaedrus, but much rather, in fact, the conveyance of a pre-prepared script, Goffman emphasizes nevertheless that there is something else, other than the text, to which the lecturer gives his auditors access: himself (and notwithstanding Goffman's envisaging of the quirks of both male and female lecturers, his lecturer is ultimately imagined as male). As Goffman explains:

> What a lecturer brings to hearers [...] is added access to himself and a commitment to the particular occasion at hand. He exposes himself to the audience. He addresses the occasion. In both ways he gives himself up to the situation. And this ritual work is done under cover of conveying his text. No one need feel that ritual has become an end in itself.   (p. 191)

It is tempting to titter at Goffman's claim that the lecturer 'exposes himself to the audience', especially when we recall his earlier suggestion that lecturers may occasionally appear 'not to be entirely zipped up'. There is a serious point here, though, because the sense in Goffman's account that there is something exposing and hence at least potentially embarrassing about the situation of the lecture is significant to the interpretation of the form of the lecture that he is seeking to develop. Cover for this 'ritual' exposure is provided by the conveyance of the text of the lecture itself—which one may have presumed, however, was the lecture's 'end in itself'. On the contrary, according to Goffman, conveyance of the text of the lecture serves to inoculate the audience from the unwelcome sense ('No one need feel...') that the text is just a pretext for access in the person of the lecturer to an institutionally anointed authority, intellectual pioneer, crowd-pleasing chancer—or uneasy combination of all three.

What 'access' means here is, therefore, clearly important, albeit unexplained by Goffman. In his history of communication, John Durham Peters attempts to describe what the stakes might be of embodied co-presence in a situation of communication:

> The quest for presence might not give better access to the other's soul, per se, but it does to their body. And the bodies of friends and kin matter deeply. The face, voice, and skin have a contagious charisma. There is nothing so electric or

unmanageable as touch: we feast our eyes on each other, kiss, shake hands, and embrace. Whether any of these gestures is a token of affection or constitutes harassment is a matter of interpretation subject to all the same problems as any signifying act.[7]

The segue from 'the other' to 'friends and kin' might give us pause even before (Durham Peters's cautions notwithstanding) we get to shaking hands, kissing, and embracing. Admittedly, Durham Peters is not addressing the lecture or any other situation of pedagogical communication here, yet the way in which considerations of bodily co-presence often come tacitly to assume that the bodies of others are the bodies of friends and kin is telling. In an era where the supposedly erotic nature of the teaching relation, once hymned by George Steiner and others, has become increasingly suspect (which is not, however, to suggest that it was ever anything else), an account of bodily presence that comes to rest on the possibility of touching cannot really account for what is distinctive about the live lecture.[8] And even 'contagious charisma', which does not seem to be predicated on touch, necessarily, rather lost its appeal in the course of the COVID-19 pandemic, although it must at the same time be acknowledged that one effect of the pandemic was to dent the sheen of the managerially vaunted pedagogical utopias that are apparently promised by lecture-capture and video-conferencing.

Goffman's account of 'access' remains under-elaborated and Durham Peters's is unsustainable, at least as an account of the kind of access that the lecture, specifically, yields. This is not to say that the matter of 'access', which we might provisionally understand as something like the representative role of the lecturer, is insignificant, especially when we consider specifically the invitation- or prize-lecture of the kind in which Goffman's own consideration of the lecture had its origins. Henry Louis Gates Jr's 2002 Jefferson lecture, for example, appears to open with familiar gestures of addressing the occasion—'Tonight marks the thirtieth anniversary of the Jefferson Lectures', 'I stand here as a fellow countryman of Thomas Jefferson's, in several senses'—before craving the audience's indulgence: 'Bear with me as I try to recreate imaginatively a curious scenario indeed.'[9] The 'curious scenario' is the literary inquisition in Boston's Old Colony House on 8 October 1772 of the poet Phillis Wheatley by the grandees (many of them slave-owners) of colonial-era Boston. Gates gives the names and brief biographies of 'the gentlemen assembled in this room [...] perhaps gathered in a semicircle', slightly later describing the scene as 'the makeshift seminar room' and remarking

[7] John Durham Peters, *Speaking into the Air: A History of the Idea of Communication* (Chicago: University of Chicago Press, 1999), 264.

[8] George Steiner, *Lessons of the Masters* (Cambridge, MA: Harvard University Press, 2003), *passim*.

[9] Quotations are from Henry Louis Gates, Jr, 'Mister Jefferson and the Trials of Phillis Wheatley', 23 March 2002 <https://www.neh.gov/about/awards/jefferson-lecture/henry-louis-gates-jr-biography> (accessed 19 January 2022), no pagination.

on '[w]hat an astounding collection of people were gathered in the room that morning—relations and rivals, friends, and foes [...] this group, a self-constituted judge and jury', before even mentioning the name, Phillis Wheatley, who was the subject of this inquisition. Gates, as he asked for forbearance to do, thus imaginatively re-creates the scenario of Wheatley's first literary-critical examination, going on to detail the later, comparably sceptical, reception of her work on the part of a number of black critics. Yet this imaginative re-creation of a scenario—the evocation of a literary as well as a political elite, of the room in which they met, and of how they were arrayed within it around the focus of their investigation—takes place after Gates's own drawing of attention to the real scenario of his own lecture, and hence his place in one tradition stretching back to Jefferson and in another that includes the most significant American literary critics of the previous three decades. 'I stand here', Gates is also implying, as the countryman of Phillis Wheatley and as representative of her—the re-creator of her literary-critical inquisition at several hands throughout American history and, crucially, as the advocate and defender that she lacked on the occasion of that fateful interview in 1772. 'We have no transcript of the exchanges that occurred between Miss Wheatley and her eighteen examiners', Gates notes, remarking that we must then imagine what questions were asked of her—though the transcript we do have of his own lecture also demands the imagination of his re-creation of a scene, not now, significantly, of Wheatley's inquisition, but of her defence before another audience by another, later, participant in 'an African American literary tradition'. Access can be extorted and one-sided, as it was in the case of Wheatley's submission to that first literary-critical trial, or restitutive and revisionary, as it is in the case of Gates's subtle charging of the conventional gestures towards the scenario of a prestigious lecture with more than the usual historical significance.

Gates's performance of Wheatley's literary-critical recuperation suggests that the lecture scenario can be put to specific political and literary ends. As Gates mentioned, we do not have a transcript of Wheatley's interview, although we do have the script of his lecture. While it is perhaps unremarkable that a Jefferson lecture or a lecture in a comparably esteemed series should have been delivered from a script, it is nevertheless a curiosity that literary critics and scholars tend to continue to read their lectures and papers (according to the text-to-reading-aloud model outlined by Goffman and assumed by Stein), where lecturers in otherwise adjacent displines in the arts and humanities ad lib instead in relation to PowerPoint slides or some other form of visible presentation, such as a paper handout. Why this disciplinary difference? In his astute consideration of the everyday activity of literary criticism, Jonathan Kramnick seeks to demonstrate that literary-critical arguments are dependent on their specific verbal performance. 'The truth of whatever is before the reading is not simply there for the critic to discover; it requires the active coaxing and commingling of the critic's words for it to take shape.'[10] This does not mean that such arguments may not be summarized, though the summary remains epistemically (as well as, like all summaries, temporally) secondary to the critical performance itself. Kramnick's is a significant claim for the argument that I am pursuing throughout this book. Literary criticism is not detachable from the particular features of its performance in any given case and hence the forms in which it is conducted can never be merely accidental to the judgements and arguments ventured in them. Kramnick's emphasis on performance has, moreover, a particular bearing for how literary critics present their work orally. 'My strong hunch', Kramnick declares, 'is that the priority of the performance over the paraphrase is why literary humanists still read talks rather than extemporize over PowerPoint as our colleagues in analytic philosophy and most of the social sciences do.'[11] The hunch is certainly correct—but then it surely entails the further question of why 'literary humanists' bother with the oral presentation of their work at all. The performance so insightfully illuminated by Kramnick is more specifically, that is, a *textual*, rather than merely a verbal, one.

Many fairly mundane answers might be given in response to the question why literary critics do not dispense with oral communication of their work altogether. (Even if the question is more acute for literary humanists than it is for people working in other disciplines because the former write texts that they read out and the latter tend not to, the answers I am about to suggest to the question of why literary humanists bother with aloud-reading of their work may nevertheless apply to other discplines as well.) The lecture is a well-established teaching method, dispensing with which would involve more pedagogical rethinking than anyone could bear; the lecture is also the site of considerable sunk costs, in the form of lecture theatres, related technology, and infrastructure, to the extent that writing them off would be difficult to countenance; the conference paper is as much an opportunity (the alibi, even) for modes of unanticipated and informal exchange of the kind it is difficult to imagine happening without it; the keynote lecture and suchlike are major markers of professional esteem, important for purposes of promotion, the signalling of professional status, the gratification of ego, and so on. These may or may not be particularly convincing reasons for reading written work out loud, and some have certainly called for the abandonment of the lecture format altogether, the locus classicus of this appeal being Virginia Woolf's plaintive 'Why?', in which she opines that 'the human voice is an instrument of varied power; it can enchant and it can soothe; it can rage and it can despair; but when it lectures it almost always bores'. 'Why not abolish prigs and prophets?' she asks, 'Why not invent human intercourse? Why not try?'[12]

---

[10] Kramnick, 'Criticism and Truth', *CI* 47 (2021), 218–40 (231).
[11] Kramnick, 'Criticism and Truth', 231 n. 32.
[12] Virginia Woolf, 'Why?' (first pub. 1942) in *Collected Essays*, 4 vols (London: Hogarth Press, 1966), ii. 278–83 (281).

That Woolf was herself a frequent lecturer may arouse the suspicion that it is other people's lectures that are boring, priggish, and (falsely) prophetic. The possibly confected example of a tedious lecture that she elaborates at the beginning of 'Why?' is, in any case, on the history of the French Revolution, not on literature. And, needless to say, there are certainly contrary voices to Woolf's, which present the lecture as animate and its textual mediation as dead. Mary Cappello, for instance, has described the lecture as 'knowledge's dramatic form', which 'lives on the stage and not on this page', its chief significance being 'not the what but the how'.[13]

Cappello's evocation of the distinction between what and how is comparable to Kraminck's emphasis on literary-critical writing as 'know-how' and the idea that literary criticism takes a dramatic form is likewise promising for thinking about the potential affinity of the lecture with criticism.[14] As Eric Griffiths put it in his only book of criticism that is not a collection of lectures, 'the heart of literary criticism' is 'imaginative voicing which turns readers into an audience'.[15] The term 'audience' has a particular meaning here that it does not necessarily always have: throughout this book and, indeed, even in this chapter, for instance, I have used 'audience' to indicate the recipients, intended or otherwise, for a text—in other words, the readership of a text. But in Griffiths's definition of literary criticism 'audience' carries a specific sense, derivable from its etymology, of listening, and hence the implication that an audience does not just receive words as they appear on a page but attends to them as they are heard in the ear (whether the outer or the inner one). But 'audience' in the context of thinking about lectures carries the further connotation of a group of individuals listening at the same time to the same speech. Audiences in this sense, Goffman remarks, 'hear in a way special to them' (p. 137): they are entitled to scrutinize the speaker more directly than would perhaps be acceptable in conversation; with some rare exceptions, any action to be undertaken by the audience is only recommended, rather than immediately required, and even then, for performance in the future; audiences may appreciate the speaker's remarks, but do not offer a reply (at least while the lecture itself is ongoing) (p. 138). Furthermore, as William Empson speculated in *Some Versions of Pastoral* (1935), the 'mutual influence' in an audience 'of its members' judgements, even though expressed by the most obscure means or only imagined from their presence, is so strong as to produce a sort of sensibility held in common, and from their variety it may be wider, more sensible, than that of any of its members'. As Empson goes on to claim (now, incidentally, taking his speculation to be a 'fact'), it is for this reason that the audience of the theatre is 'more really public' than the readership of novels.[16]

[13]   Mary Cappello, *Lecture* (Oakland, CA: Transit, 2020), 13, 112.
[14]   Kramnick, 'Criticism and Truth', 231 (on 'know-how').
[15]   Eric Griffiths, *The Printed Voice of Victorian Poetry*, 2nd edn (Oxford: Oxford University Press, 2018; first pub. 1989), 36.
[16]   Empson, *Some Versions of Pastoral* (London: Penguin, 1995; first pub. 1935), 59–60.

These remarks on audience—taken not, now, as a synonym for readership, but as something quite distinct, as characterized both by listening and by the more or less occult mutual influence of audience members on one another—are consequential for the consideration not just of the lecture, but (bearing Griffiths's definition in mind) of literary criticism, and of the relation between the lecture and literary criticism. The transformation of readers of lectures back into their audience involves not only the imaginative audition of the text being read, but the situation of that text in the context of an imagined gathering of other recipients. The textual transmission of literary-critical lectures, and hence their bequest to the history of literary criticism, not only contains a record of imaginative voicing but demands it as well. The traces of voicing, the transformation of audience into readers and back into audience, and the performance of literary criticism in script are thus the central concerns of this chapter—as they are of literary criticism as such.

*

I turn now to pursue these considerations by examining a series of examples drawn from the middle of the eighteenth century to the early twenty-first century. At the end of his monumental *A History of Criticism and Literary Taste in Europe*, George Saintsbury appended a usefully opinionated account of the history of the Oxford Professorship of Poetry (it would be uncharitable to remark that his assessments might have been coloured by the fact that he was never elected to this particular chair himself). Giving a brisk overview of the career of each of the chair's holders, Saintsbury identifies Robert Lowth as the major early figure (among a crowd of distinctly minor ones) coming before what Saintsbury jauntily calls 'the rally' of the nineteenth century.[17] In this section, I examine Lowth's lectures before turning in the next section to those Saintsbury identified as the best of the nineteenth-century 'rally'—namely, John Keble's. The lectures that Lowth delivered in Oxford from 1741 were not the *Lectures on the Sacred Poetry of the Hebrews*, published some forty-six years later in a translation by George Gregory, but rather his 'prælectiones' *De Sacra Poesi Hebræorum*, first published in 1753.[18] The journey of Lowth's lectures from Latin given before an audience of 'Academici' (which is rendered in the English translation as the more worldly 'Gentlemen'), to their publication by the Clarendon Press, and, finally, to their translation into English some forty years after they were delivered, is, needless to say, a long one. What the Anglophone reader of Lowth's *Lectures on the Sacred Poetry of the Hebrews* reads is thus far removed in time, and is the product of many phases of transmission, from what the audience accustomed to being taught in Latin heard.

---

[17] George Saintsbury, 'Appendix I. The Oxford Chair of Poetry', in *A History of Criticism and Literary Taste in Europe*, 3 vols (Edinburgh: Blackwood, 1900–4), iii: *Modern Criticism* (1904), 615–29 (618–20).
[18] Lowth, *De Sacra Poesi Hebræorum* (Oxford: Clarendon Press, 1753). Further references to this edition (abbreviated as *De Sacra*) are given after quotations in the text.

We can be under no illusion that Lowth's *Lectures* are anything other than a printed text, rather than the transcript of an oral performance. But neither is that to say that the evocation of their oral and aural situation is wholly deleted from them. It is perhaps noteworthy that, on the title page of Lowth's *Lectures* in Gregory's translation, it is Gregory who is marked out as the writer ('Author of Essays Historical and Moral'), whereas Lowth is described instead as the holder of two positions, both requiring public speaking of different but related sorts: 'Late Prælector of Poetry in the University of Oxford, and Now Lord Bishop of London'.[19] In addition, despite the mediation of Gregory's translation and the opportunities for revision that it would have afforded, not to mention the gap in time between Lowth's delivery of his lectures and their publication in their original Latin (nine years, from 1744 to 1753), Lowth's work continues to display its origins in a particular time, place, and manner of expression (Lowth in fact remarks on the changes that he did make to the text—as well as those he did not—in his preface to the second edition (*Sacred Poetry*, i, pp. xix–xx)). This includes the opening, mildly defensive, remarks of Lecture I on the timing of the beginning of the course of lectures, to which Gregory appends a detailed note regarding the University Statute and its stipulations with respect to when the lectures are to be delivered (*Sacred Poetry*, i. 1–2). Lowth goes on to describe the 'particular department of science', namely, poetry, 'which you have constantly distinguished by your presence and attention', and 'which has hitherto received in this place all the embellishments of grace and elegance, of which it is naturally susceptible' (*Sacred Poetry*, i. 4), before then arguing for the supremacy of poetry over both philosophy and history. Having elaborated on the merits and effects of Homer, Lowth rouses his audience near the middle of Lecture I in the following manner:

> And who so thoughtless, or so callous, as not to feel incredible pleasure in that most agreeable occupation [viz., 'the perusal of Homer']; who is not moved, astonished, enraptured by the inspiration of that most sublime genius? Who so inanimate as not to see, not to feel inscribed, or as it were imprinted upon his heart, the most excellent maxims concerning human life and manners? From Philosophy a few cold precepts can be deduced; in History some dull and spiritless examples of manners may be found: here we have the energetic voice of Virtue herself, here we behold her animated form. (*Sacred Poetry*, i. 12)

The assertion of poetry's superiority to philosophy and history—advanced in much less assertive terms prior to this point—is swept in on the roll and swell of

---

[19] Lowth, *Lectures on the Sacred Poetry of the Hebrews*, trans. George Gregory, 2 vols (London: printed for J. Johnson, 1787), i, title page. Further references to this edition (abbreviated as *Sacred Poetry*) are given after quotations in the text. George Gregory, *Essays Historical and Moral*, was published, also by Joseph Johnson, in 1785 (the date is given, incorrectly, as 1783 in 'Gregory, George' by L. C. Sanders, rev. Philip Carter, *ODNB* <https://doi.org/10.1093/ref:odnb/11463>).

questions that precede it. The distinction between poetry, on the one hand, and philosophy and history, on the other, is no less than the distinction between life and death itself: 'Who so inanimate as not to see...?'; 'here we behold her animated form.' Poetry, crucially, has its own living representative on the rostrum. Lowth is not just describing the inspiration effected by Homer's poetry but performing it. The anaphora in '*here* we have the energetic voice of Virtue herself, *here* we behold her animated form' builds to the suggestion that the energetic voice and animated form of the lecturer are themselves the effects of Homer's poetry he is describing. It is worth remarking, indeed, that in 'energetic' and 'animated' Gregory varies Lowth's Latin adjective, which had been 'vivas', living or animated, in both instances, though he retains a repetition with 'here...here' (Lowth having had just the one 'hic'): 'vivas hic Virtutis voces audimus, vivam effigem cernimus' (*De Sacra*, i. 5). It is as if the absent presence of the lecturer is made up for in the translation by verbal variation, on the one hand, and a reiterative emphasis on presence, on the other. Even in text, the lecturer acts as medium, and animated form is here before us.

Along with the panegyric on the powers of Homer's poetry and the display of its effects that the above passage evinces, there is at least a hint of blasphemy—if only against the pagan Homer—in Lowth's implicit assumption of 'the voice of Virtue' that speaks through the poet. But Lowth goes further than this potential assumption of the powers of the semi-divine Homer by speaking of Homer's pagan texts in terms derived from sacred ones. As we have seen, on reading Homer, he asks, 'Who so inanimate as not to see, not to feel inscribed, or as it were imprinted upon his heart, the most excellent maxims concerning human life and manners?' The formulation up to which Lowth builds here is taken fairly directly from the Epistle to the Hebrews, 'For this is the covenant that I will make with the house of Israel after those days, saith the Lord; I will put my laws into their mind, and write them in their hearts' (Hebrews 8:10), a formulation that the writer of Hebrews has in turn borrowed from Jeremiah 31:33 (which the translators of the Authorized Version curiously manage to make into something approaching a rhyming couplet: 'I will put my law in their inward parts, and write it in their hearts'). If an insistent emphasis on voice and presence (the 'animated form') emerges from Lowth's account of Homer and the effects of his poetry, Lowth's manner of envisaging the ethical import of Homer's poetry instead reaches for an image derived not from speaking but from writing. Crucially, however, that writing is described, both in the Bible and in Lowth, as an internalized, mystical writing explicitly juxtaposed to the external writing that everyone can see: the Hebrew Law in the Bible and the 'cold precepts' of philosophy and 'dull and spiritless examples' of history in Lowth. The three attempts to describe what is, for Lowth, surely impossible for any reader of Homer—'not to see, not to feel inscribed, or as it were imprinted upon his heart'—do not constitute three equally good ways of envisaging how Homer's maxims are received by his readers, but effect instead a real-time revising of the initial, inapposite suggestion that the reception of Homer—who was, let us remember, traditionally held to be blind—is itself ultimately a matter of seeing anything. The most important writing, according to the Christian preacher and Professor of Poetry, happens not on the page but on the heart.

*

Though Lowth's lectures involve little in the way of explicit self-presentation apart from more or less conventional apology in opening the series, the role of lecturer as representative of what he is discussing is nevertheless discernible in his lectures. This is, as I suggested in opening this chapter, not merely accidental, but rather a trace of the performance of imaginative voicing that is at the heart of literary criticism. In the years separating the original delivery of Lowth's lectures from those of John Keble, beginning in 1832 and ending in 1841 a century after Lowth's inauguration, the person of critic had come to be more germane to the practice of criticism, not least thanks to the affective and contemplative turn of much Romantic literary criticism (Keble dedicated his lectures, incidentally, to Wordsworth). It was also a period whose literary and political (and literary-political) upheavals had provoked a number of intergenerational conflicts, not least concerning whether age necessarily confers wisdom and authority, which were directly germane to the pedagogical situation of the lecture, especially to lectures of an established kind like those of the Oxford Professor of Poetry. Literary criticism had increasingly become more than a matter of either wisdom or authority, at least as traditionally, scholastically conceived. Keble's lectures opened with a reflection on the suitability of a discussion of poetry from someone of what he took to be his advanced age and stage (Keble had attained the age of 40 when he gave the first of his lectures in 1832): 'that keen pleasure which beguiles the young to the study of the poets becomes daily weaker and, as old age draws nigh, feebler,' he declares. Surely hoping to provoke a positive retort in his youthful audience, Keble then asks: 'Who would tolerate a criticism of poetry from one whose own fount of inspiration has dried up and who has lost the sense of the Muses' charm?'[20] Predictably, Keble goes on to set against his account of the diminishing pleasure in poetry that comes with age, an avowal of his own continuing delight in it—'I still feel, and to an eminent degree, the marvellous charm of these studies' (*Lectures*, i. 12)—before cautioning that, 'in my judgement, it is true that, especially in the present day, it is the bridle rather than the spur which he needs who speaks to others about poetry' (*Lectures*, i. 12).

---

[20] John Keble, 'Inaugural Oration, or, Lecture I', in *Keble's Lectures on Poetry 1832–1841*, trans. Edward Kershaw Francis, 2 vols (Oxford: Clarendon Press, 1912), i. 12; cf. Keble, *Praelectiones Academicae: Oxonii Habitae Annis MDCCCXXXII–MDCCCXLI*, 2 vols (Oxford: Parker, 1844), i. 2. Further references to these editions (abbreviated as *Lectures* and *Prælectiones* respectively) are given after quotations in the text.

This is the real focus of Keble's opening oration—not so much the conventional rehearsal of his own lack of qualification for the office to which he has been elected, as rather the reining-in of the pretensions of criticism as currently practised. 'Far, far too familiarly (I do not hesitate to say) are we—both young and old—accustomed to handle and criticize the achievements and works of great poets; too rashly and irreverently do we burst into these sanctuaries' (*Lectures*, i. 12). Edward Kershaw Francis, Keble's translator, has pulled quite sharply on the reins in his translation from the Latin here—'achievements and works of great poets' is surely a tame equivalent for 'magnorum vatum monumenta ac reliquias' (*Prælectiones*, i. 2)—though he will have found a warrant for such restraint in the conclusion to Keble's quite lengthy consideration of the continuing appropriateness of Latin to the lectures to be given by the Oxford Professor of Poetry: any English translation of those lectures should be done, Keble remarks, 'with extreme modesty, sensibly, and with due restraint': 'ita tamen ut summa quæque religione, sobrie atque severe, agantur', where the original's 'religione' gives a stronger sense than the translation's 'modesty' of the ritual aura attaching to the delivery and transmission of lectures (*Lectures*, i. 18; *Prælectiones*, i. 8). These are important considerations because Keble is addressing a contemporary controversy—'[t]here are many at present, I am fully aware, who confess themselves at a loss to understand why, within these walls, we may only speak in Latin', a formulation that conjures images of being dumb-founded ('who confess themselves at a loss') and of restrictions on speech arising from having to do it in a taxing and institutionally mandated way ('within these walls, we may only speak in Latin') (*Lectures*, i. 18). But Keble's reflections on the use of Latin for the Oxford Poetry lectures are also important because in his strictures on contemporary criticism he takes aim specifically at the 'rush of writing' that those 'all claiming the name and authority of critics' produce: 'nothing can be imagined more troublesomely insistent than their publications: some weekly, others more modestly once a month, those who are most self-restrained not less than four times a year' (*Lectures*, i. 17). Complaints against the rise of the periodical press and the perceived subsumption of literary criticism within it were becoming commonplace by this point in the nineteenth century, but Keble is here mobilizing the lecture specifically as a site of critical discussion against the review (relations between critical forms are not always cordial). The requirement to present lectures in Latin acts precisely as the bridle that Keble had claimed was necessary for anyone 'who speaks to others about poetry': he admits that, thanks to the requirement to lecture in Latin, he 'is in some degree hampered and restricted, the edge of my fancy is blunted, and my whole spirit more quickly fatigued and exhausted' (*Lectures*, i. 16), and yet these are prices worth paying in order to avoid the distinctly writerly extravagances he alleges against contemporary criticism. The pen and the printing-press are out of control; the tongue, properly governed by the institutional statutes laid down concerning the Oxford Professorship of Poetry, may pronounce on the nature of poetry.

Keble's lectures are persistently interested in the capacities of the voice, and it is in keeping with this interest that the comparison between Homer's presentations of Diomed and Achilles in Keble's eighth lecture, for example, reaches its culmination with 'the most splendid instance' of Achilles' glory—namely, the fact that 'Achilles standing unarmed intimidates [the Trojan advance] by his mere voice and aspect' (*Lectures*, i. 127). Keble first quotes the description of Diomed from book XVI of the *Iliad*:

> Then Pallas breathed in Tydeus' son, to render whom supreme
> To all the Greeks, at all his parts, she cast a hotter beam
> On his high mind, his body filled with much superior might,
> And made his complete armour cast a far more complete light,
> (*Lectures*, i. 127)[21]

commenting that '[o]ne would say, assuredly, that nothing finer could be conceived' before immediately admitting that 'we must change our opinion [...] when we are confronted' with the description of Achilles in book XVIII—confronted, that is, rather as the Trojan advance is by the Greek hero himself. The hint of a comparison between the Trojans confronted with Achilles and the reader confronted with Homer's description of the same—a hint that we owe to Francis's translation, since there is no real basis for it in Keble's Latin, though what Francis is doing is compensating for the absence of the presence of the lecturer—is significant because it accords to Homer something of the majesty attributed to the voice of Achilles:

> And as a voice is heard
> With emulous affection, when any town is sphered
> With siege of such a foe as kills men's minds, and for the town
> Makes sound his trumpet: so the voice from Thetis' issue thrown
> Won emulously th' ears of all. His brazen voice once heard,
> The minds of all were startled so they yielded[.]
> (*Lectures*, i. 128)

Almost as if to dispel any sense that it is he who is confronting his audience with these lines, and, with it, any sense that it is the voice of the lecturer that has such

---

[21] Francis quotes from George Chapman's translation of the *Iliad* whereas Keble had quoted from the Greek.

power, Keble is moved to reflect, rather as he had done in his opening lecture, on the rights and wrongs of literary criticism as such:

> I confess, gentlemen, that when I ponder over these lines I feel unable to repress a certain feeling that literary critics, as they are called, act a little profanely when they make it a kind of business, without delicacy or scruple, to canvass, and, so to speak, pull about and dissect such poetic beauties as these. The result is that such men's minds grow callous, and the more they understand about the composition of these artistic beauties, the less they are affected by them.
>
> (*Lectures*, i. 129)

Conventional disavowal of the presumptions of criticism this may be, but, by adopting the confessional mode, Keble gains recognition for his modesty, even though it is not he who pulls about and dissects such poetic beauties, but 'literary critics, as they are called' ('Critici, qui vocantur' (*Prælectiones*, i. 110)), men with callous minds. Francis perhaps falters slightly, therefore, when, after Keble has advanced his justification for proceeding to examine the comparison between Diomed and Achilles at length anyway, he translates Keble's intention as venturing 'to compare these two passages, relating the one to Diomed, the other to Achilles, rather more critically', despite the fact that Keble's promise to compare them 'argutius paullo' (*Prælectiones*, i. 111), a little more shrewdly, is aimed precisely at setting him apart from the Critici.

Keble's lectures highlight a number of what I have identified as key issues in the literary-critical lecture and its transmission to the history of literary criticism: the relations between voice and pen, especially when the latter is wielded by an undifferentiated mass of 'critics'; the transmission of a ritualized, even sacred, situation to a textual tradition; and, again, the representative capacities of the lecturer and how these may or may not be retained in lectures in their published form. As we have seen, Keble opened his lectures with a consideration of the appropriateness of Latin to them and he returns throughout the lectures to the state of literary criticism at the present time, as well as, moreover, its legitimacy when faced with the achievements of an artist like Homer.

*

I drew attention above to the semi-autobiographical opening of Keble's lectures, and especially to its framing in terms of the relation between youth and age, which must be seen in the light of the Romantic poetry and criticism that influenced Keble. Having traversed a century in the history of the Oxford Professorship of Poetry, from Lowth to Keble, I want to turn back at this point to a Romantic poet and lecturer, whose lectures complicate still further the issue of the transmission of orality to the textual history of literary criticism. Although, as we have seen, Lowth's *Prælectiones* certainly went through many transitions to become

Lectures, the process by which they did so seems straightforward when compared to the process through which the records of Coleridge's lectures have come down to us. Coleridge's lectures have been extensively discussed by a number of recent scholars, and one reason they have attracted such scholarly attention is their somewhat fraught editorial condition and historical transmission.[22] The texts that are commonly received as the texts of Coleridge's lectures, that is, are more or less nothing of the sort—not least because of the simple but, as we shall see, consequential fact that Coleridge, unlike many of the lecturers considered in this chapter, did not write scripts for his lectures; rather, the texts of Coleridge's lectures are an accretion of the evidence to be gleaned from his own advertisements and prospectuses for his courses, from journalistic reviews, from the notes and attempted transcriptions of his listeners, from reported anecdote and conversation, from reminiscence and memoir, and from editorial intervention, the latter itself informed by a mixture of scholarship, reasonable assumptions about readability, and fantasy.

The question of the oral origins, which were not directly subtended by a text of Coleridge's, and subsequent textual transmission of Coleridge's lectures is especially pertinent because, again, the relation between speech and text is a crucial concern of them. In 'On the Principles of Criticism' and his lecture on *Love's Labour's Lost*, two of Coleridge's 1811 lectures, for instance, the matter of imaginative voicing that turns a reader into an audience is vital to the articulation of Coleridge's argument. This is even—or perhaps especially—the case at moments that might otherwise be dismissed as the traces of the conventional gestures of a lecturer warming himself up. 'On the Principles of Criticism' was the first of Coleridge's 1811 lectures on literature, and its opening paragraph appears at first sight to be a quintessential exercise in throat-clearing:

> I cannot avoid the acknowledgement of the difficulty of the task I have undertaken; yet I have undertaken it voluntarily, and I shall discharge it to the best of my abilities, requesting those who hear me to allow for deficiencies, and to bear in mind the wide extent of my subject; *inopem me copia fecit*. What I most rely upon is your sympathy; and, as I proceed, I trust that I shall interest you:

---

[22] See Jon Klancher, 'Transmission Failure', in David Perkins (ed.), *Theoretical Issues in Literary History*, Harvard English Studies, 16 (Cambridge, MA: Harvard University Press, 1991), 173–95; David Hadley, 'Public Lectures and Private Societies: Expounding Literature and the Arts in Romantic London', in Donald Schoonmaker and John A. Alford (eds), *English Romanticism: Preludes and Postludes: Essays in Honor of Edwin Graves Wilson* (East Lansing, MI: Colleagues Press, 1993), 43–57; Peter J. Manning, 'Manufacturing the Romantic Image: Hazlitt and Coleridge Lecturing', in James Chandler and Kevin Gilmartin (eds), *Romantic Metropolis: The Urban Scene of British Culture, 1780–1840* (Cambridge: Cambridge University Press, 2005), 227–45; Sarah Zimmerman, 'Coleridge the Lecturer, A Disappearing Act', in Alexander Dick and Angela Esterhammer (eds), *Sphere of Action: Speech and Performance in Romantic Culture* (Toronto: University of Toronto Press, 2009), 46–72, and *The Romantic Literary Lecture in Britain* (Oxford: Oxford University Press, 2019).

sympathy and interest are to a lecturer like the sun, the spring and the showers to nature—absolutely necessary to the production of blossoms and fruit.[23]

To say that this 'paragraph' is 'throat-clearing' already suggests a number of important issues in the reading of lectures. Does it make sense to think of a lecturer speaking in paragraphs, or is the paragraph only really a feature of written text? Is throat-clearing more forgivable when there is an actual throat involved? We should also note from the above passage that appealing, as Coleridge does, for the 'sympathy and interest' of an audience is very different from appealing to a readership for the same indulgence. The difference is evident in the fact that the responsibility for the production of the 'blossoms and fruit' that Coleridge hopes his discourse will yield is partly assigned to the lecture audience, who, therefore, cannot be sure that any such products will be forthcoming; a reader, at least, is holding a book of texts—'blossoms and fruit'—waiting to be devoured in her or his hand. In addition, while there is perhaps always something disingenuous about the statement that 'I cannot avoid the acknowledgement…', the declaration of voluntary engagement on a difficult task has a different force when uttered before an audience in contrast to that which it has when addressed to a readership: again, the reader has the completed texts in her or his hand, whereas all the listener has is the declaration of intention.

Coleridge is keen, in these early moments of the first lecture in his series, to manage his audience's expectations—both, that is, their expectations of himself and those of their own critical abilities. He goes on, for example, to anatomize the obstacles that stand in the way of 'a sound Judgment of the comparative merit of poems'. Among '[a]ccidental' obstacles, which arise 'from particular circumstances of the age and people amongst which we live', Coleridge includes '[t]he passion of public speaking, which encourages a too great desire to be understood at first blush' (p. 5), a point he expands upon in his lecture 'On Dramatic Poetry', delivered a week later on Monday, 25 November 1811, where he contrasts the objects of authors writing in the first decades of the nineteenth century with those of authors writing during the 'reigns of Elizabeth and James': 'At the present, the chief object of an author is to be intelligible at the first view; then, it was to make the reader think—not to make him understand at once, but to show him rather that he did not understand, or to make him to review, and re-meditate till he had placed himself on a par with the writer' (p. 32). This statement has a considerable bearing on the relation between spoken-and-heard lecture and written-and-read text. Coleridge is admonishing his listeners to recall that one effect of public speaking is the expectation that understanding will be instantaneous—an

---

[23] Samuel Taylor Coleridge, *Coleridge's Lectures on Shakespeare*, ed. Adam Roberts (Edinburgh: Edinburgh University Press, 2016), 4. Further references to this edition are given after quotations in the text.

expectation that is itself an impediment to understanding. That admonition would have a particular force in the context of an orally delivered, extemporized lecture, since a member of the audience cannot, like a reader, go back over a difficult passage or return to it after the whole argument has been unfolded.

But we must not rush to infer a simple preference for reading the written word over hearing the spoken one—at least, that is to say, there is no preference here for what Coleridge characterizes as the dominant forms of the written word at the time that he is speaking. As we saw in the preceding chapter, Coleridge excoriated the degrading and proliferating nature of much contemporary writing, character-ized above all, for him, by '[t]he prevalence of Reviews, Magazines, Selections and so on'—an antagonism that, as we have seen, Keble would likewise go on to rehearse—'these with Newspapers and *Novels*, constituting nine-tenths of the reading of nine-tenths of the reading Public from their habits as Readers' (p. 5). Before going on to cite one of his favourite authorities, Jeremy Taylor, Coleridge complains that there nowadays seem to be few barriers to writing: 'for in these times, if a man fail as a shoe maker, and can read and write correctly—*for spelling is not necessary*—he becomes an author' (p. 6). Leaving to one side the interesting question as to why it is here that shoemaking is the emblematically illiterate trade, and likewise merely noting the good measure of personal professional anxiety in Coleridge's sense that anyone can be an author when it so often proved difficult for him to be one, what is especially noteworthy in this complaint is that Coleridge fixes on '*spelling*' as the marker of a proper author. To be sure, this is a signal instance of the age-old grumble that standards are slipping, which can be seen by the disgraceful fact that even celebrated literary figures cannot spell any more. No member of Coleridge's audience would have had any proof, of course, that he himself could spell, not least since, in English at least, what a word sounds like is such a treacherous guide to how it is written.[24] We might note, then, that the impeccable spelling in the edition of Coleridge's lectures from which I am quot-ing in this chapter is not *Coleridge's*, but rather that of his editor, Adam Roberts. Something similar pertains to the italics in which, for just one example, the state-ment about spelling is set. This textual feature may attempt to record an emphasis of Coleridge's; it may be the trace of what one of his audience members, whose notes have come down to us, considered to be important—perhaps because *she or he* was obsessed with a perceived decline in standards of orthography owing to the alleged infiltration of literature by the semi-literate; or it may, again, be Roberts's clarifying intervention.

---

[24] Though note here the recollection of Coleridge's lecturing by the painter Charles Robert Leslie: 'His pronunciation was remarkably correct: in some respects pedantically so. He gave the full sound of the *l* in *talk*, and *should* and *would*'(Tom Taylor (ed.), *Autobiographical Recollections by the Late Charles Robert Leslie*, 2 vols (London: John Murray, 1860), i. 47; quoted by Roberts, 'Introduction', in *Coleridge's Lectures*, 7–8).

This may all seem to add up to quite a trivial point, as if I have caught Coleridge winning the spelling bee by a slight (sorry: sleight) of hand. But, in fact, it indicates that Coleridge's authority on certain matters throughout his lectures has no verifiable—which, in this case, means written—guarantee, but rests rather on whether or not his own presence and performance, as well as his reputation, commanded confidence. The subtle but decisive differences between speech and text—or, to put it another way, between the lecture we read and the one that we, as inhabitants of this globe two centuries after Coleridge delivered his lectures, could not have attended—do not entail a total severance of the written from the spoken lecture. As Sarah Zimmerman has noted, Romantic literary lectures were interwoven with texts, such as advertisements and prospectuses, on the one hand, and notes and reviews, on the other—and of course also with the texts that such lectures addressed, many of which were visible to Coleridge's audience, strewn across the table in front of him. Coleridge mentions the prospectus for his course of lectures at a couple of points in 'On the Principles of Criticism', saying first that 'the Prospectus has promised for me that I should discuss [the obstacles to sound Judgment concerning the comparative merit of poems] under the name of false criticism, especially in poetry' (p. 5). This makes it rather seem as if the prospectus for his own lectures was imposed upon him, or that it has a kind of volition of its own, when in fact it is *his* prospectus. Coleridge may be taken to be hinting here that text is inconveniently binding, imposing a requirement on the otherwise fluid, in-the-moment, situation of the lecture. Towards the end of the lecture 'On the Principles of Criticism', though, by which time Coleridge has yet really to address any actual poetry, the prospectus comes to his aid as a warrant to the effect that so-far-unfulfilled tasks will indeed be addressed at some undetermined point in the future course of his lectures. Like the electoral manifesto of a political party—binding statement of intention or wish-list subject to change, as occasion dictates—the prospectus can both be an inconvenient reminder of Coleridge's promises and a useful catalogue of good, if as yet unfulfilled, intentions.

Coleridge's lectures have often been mined for elements of his theories of literature and language—and with good reason, since they are where he articulates some of the most important premises informing his thinking. Attending to the specific occasionality of the lectures as, in Coleridge's case, extemporized spoken performances, however, helps us to realize the emergence of his view of language in its very articulation. In his lecture ostensibly on *Love's Labours Lost* but in fact extensively on the nature of language, Coleridge is recorded as making the following at once cryptic and revealing statement:

> It is known that all deviations from ordinary language (by which I mean, such language as is used, by a man speaking without emotion, to express anything simply; not that I am quite correct in using the last phrase, because all language

arises out of passion);—the only difference is in the *figure* that is employed, old or new;—thus, we say, the tops of trees, or the heads of mountains, which expressions, with innumerable others in common use, are figurative, and originally used in a state of emotion; but they are now worn out. Passion is the true parent of every word in existence in every language.   (p. 49)

What makes this passage hard to follow is precisely its build-up of clarifications and corrections—its deviations, in other words. Coleridge goes on to reinforce the point he is trying to make about the grounds for justifying deviations from ordinary language, telling us that 'all deviations from ordinary language must be justified by some passion which renders it natural'—a passion of which we can perhaps see a trace in the strikingly direct statement that '[p]assion is the true parent of every word in existence in every language'. The question again arises, as it did implicitly with Lowth and would explicitly with Keble, as to the passion with which Coleridge's words are invested—the answer to which may be discernible in the increasing passion with which he comes, as the lecture progresses, to make his declarations on the nature of language: 'The word is not to convey merely what a certain thing *is*, but the very passion and all the circumstances which are conceived as constituting the perception of the thing by the person who used the word' (p. 50). Moments from the end of the lecture—by which point his audience may have been pondering a complaint to the effect that it had not been as advertised, Coleridge having discussed not quite a score of lines from *Love's Labours Lost*—he declares: 'I trust that what I have thus said in the ardour of my feelings will not be entirely lost,'—he trusts, that is, that his love's labours will not be lost—'but will awaken in my audience those sympathies without which it is vain to proceed in my criticisms of Shakespeare' (p. 56).

Coleridge speaks in the ardour of his feelings in order to awaken in his audience those sympathies without which his criticisms of Shakespeare are, so he says, vain; whether those sympathies are thus awoken in his *readers*, who do not hear him speak, is another matter, freighted by the sometimes vexed transmission of his lectures to textual posterity and by the success with which his readers are able to turn themselves into the audience that Coleridge once had by means of the imaginative voicing of his imaginative voicings.

*

From Lowth's lectures beginning in 1741 to Keble's ending a century later and with Coleridge's from the 1810s in between, the preceding two sections have traversed a period that saw important developments in the history of the literary-critical lecture, as it saw important developments in the history of literature as well. In his *The Printed Voice of Victorian Poetry*, Eric Griffiths placed the relation between text, voice, and the imagination of voice at the centre of the developments in English literary history in this period, singling out in particular the influence of Wordsworth on 'the discovery of the most characteristic and fertile of nineteenth-century poetic forms: the dramatic monologue'.[25] Griffiths characterizes Wordsworth's early writing especially as 'dramatic in the deeper and more elusive sense that it makes even the most lyrical utterance, utterance that might be thought to spring from the fullness of an "I", dramatically self-conscious, watched by a "he"'.[26] A 'he' (or 'she' or 'they') may now, thanks to advances in recording technology, indeed watch what an 'I' utters, but it was not always so, as Griffiths remarks:

> It is an essential accident in the history of literature that machines for recording speech were not invented until the second half of the nineteenth century— essential, for the possibilities of misunderstanding which arise in the absence of such machines give substantial life to those disputes of value which provoke misunderstanding, and make what might be mere technicalities of notation the very air of cultural exchange.[27]

The transformation of distinctly textual 'technicalities of notation' into the 'air of cultural exchange', with its connotations of living, oral communication, is noteworthy, as is the vital suggestion that misunderstanding is not something simply to be eradicated. Griffiths's attempt accurately to describe Wordsworth's distinctive contribution to nineteenth-century (and, indeed, later) literary history is part of a wider attempt to describe the ways in which all writing is 'dramatic' in the sense that Griffiths intimates here—and that attempt may help us think about the nature of the lecture as well, not least, as we shall see shortly, Griffiths's own. Central to Griffiths's account of the dramatic nature of all writing is a careful discrimination of drama from theatre. This is not motivated by anything like an antitheatrical prejudice, but rather from an insight into both the incapacities and the demands of print. Since '[p]rint does not give conclusive evidence of a voice', argues Griffiths, '[a]ll writing is dramatic, though not all writing is theatrical. "Dramatic" in the sense that writing is an act of supplication to an imagined voice.'[28] And, while we may—'must', writes Griffiths—'elicit accent from writing', 'this literary critical activity is not trying to provide the kind of data which would enable an actor to do an accurate impersonation of a writer, but rather to bring us to understanding and pleasure in a printed voice which remains in print even as we hear it'.[29]

---

[25] Griffiths, *Printed Voice*, 70.   [26] Griffiths, *Printed Voice*, 70.
[27] Griffiths, *Printed Voice*, 16. For reflections on the potential impact of recording equipment on university lecturing around the period of the increased availability and affordability of such equipment, see Max Horkheimer, 'Fragen des Hochschulunterrichts' (1952), in *Gesammelte Schriften*, ed. Alfred Schmidt and Gunzelin Schmid Noerr, 19 vols (Frankfurt-am-Main: Fischer, 1985–96), viii: *Vorträge und Aufzeichnungen, 1949–1973* (1985), 391–408.
[28] Griffiths, *Printed Voice*, 12.   [29] Griffiths, *Printed Voice*, 89.

Freya Johnston attempts the 'literary critical activity' described by Griffiths in her 'Introduction' to *If Not Critical*, her collection of Griffiths's unpublished lectures. Those lectures themselves attempted 'to bring us to understanding and pleasure in a printed voice'—'they demonstrated criticism in action', as Johnston puts it—as well as being, in their printed form, ' "evidence of a voice" and,' as Johnston crucially adds, 'of its absence'.[30] Johnston remarks poignantly of Griffiths that '[h]earing his critical and creative voice in print is now the only way to hear it in something like full flow', before going on to evoke Griffiths's distinctive vocal performance in his lectures, 'marinated as they were in cigarettes, watered-down whisky, coffee, and milk'.[31] Unlikely as that is to catch on as a recipe for a marinade, the connections between Johnston's account of Griffiths's 'public voice'—'fast, sardonic, protesting, and exact'—and his writing—'scornful, rude, and slangy'—are clear.[32] Johnston's particular emphasis is on the speed of Griffiths's speaking, if not necessarily of his writing. It is worth taking the time to attend to this account:

> Eric Griffiths never gathered up his unpublished work for revision into published form, but the task of editing it has been made a lot easier than it might have been by the fact that he usually typed out every single word of what he was going to say. The lectures were delivered fast, 'so conceptual gaps do not become obvious', as he once said (very quickly) on his way to an auditorium. The speed at which they were given is obvious from how long they are: on average, around 8,500 words; nearly all the sentences and many of the quotations in them are pretty long, too.[33]

In keeping with the muted poignancy of Johnston's 'Introduction', there is a sense here that Griffiths, who by modern standards published relatively little, might have readily published more, since 'he usually typed out every single word of what he was going to say' and thus was in possession of a sizeable raft of exhaustively prepared typescripts. Johnston relays Griffiths's facetious remark that the speed of delivery of his lectures was ' "so conceptual gaps do not become obvious" '—a speed of delivery facilitated by careful and exhaustive preparation, which in turn facilitated the concealment of lapses in careful and exhaustive preparation. Certain things would have been obvious in Griffiths's delivery of his lectures—such as that he was delivering them fast—that remain obvious in their written form: '[t]he speed at which they were given is obvious from how long they are.' Certain other things are not obvious in writing that would have been in speaking, such as 'the crafty lulls and rushes built into his delivery', which were dependent on a particular delivery (Griffiths's) but at which we may guess, in part

---

[30] Freya Johnston, 'Introduction', in Eric Griffiths, *If Not Critical*, ed. Johnston (Oxford: Oxford University Press, 2018), 1–7 (1).
[31] Johnston, 'Introduction', 1.   [32] Johnston, 'Introduction', 1, 5.
[33] Johnston, 'Introduction', 5.

from the anecdotal information with which Johnston provides us, and in part from the fact that considerations of timing ('lulls and rushes') are themselves the topics of many of the lectures. Still more things, at least potentially, become obvious in print that were not obvious in delivery—such as those 'conceptual gaps'. As we have already seen, in *The Printed Voice of Victorian Poetry*, Griffiths ventured another characterization of what lies at 'the heart of literary criticism', namely, 'imaginative voicing which turns readers into an audience', a point he would also make in similar terms in an unpublished lecture from which Johnston quotes: 'The most practical form which criticism can take is performance, reading aloud, whether theatrically or not, for when we read aloud we put ourselves in the world of those whose beliefs may be other than our own, if only for the time the reading lasts.'[34] But, in reading lectures, as in reading plays, audiences have been turned into readers—who must turn themselves into audiences again, since that is (for Griffiths, at least) the central operation of literary criticism. In his lecture on *Hamlet*, for example, Griffiths remarks (with a sideswipe at Tom Stoppard for writing plays that 'kick[ ] around large ethical and metaphysical issues') that '[i]t is more remarkable to write a play in which "debate" occurs not through ruminative prosings but through event and interaction, in which thought *occurs* to and between people. This is what happens in *Hamlet*, thinking *happens*.'[35] Griffiths's work in general evinces little patience for 'ruminative prosings', and, although, as we have seen, his lectures fundamentally involved the speedy delivery of large swathes of text, they also functioned as event and interaction.[36] Griffiths declares slightly earlier that '[m]y claim is that Shakespeare's material as an artist *is* interaction, interaction of two kinds—between the figures on the stage, and between the figures on the stage and the audience'[37]—a claim that modesty may have prevented Griffiths explicitly extending from playwright to lecturer, but that, *mutatis mutandis*, may nevertheless be so extended. At the very least, Griffiths was acutely alive to the overlaps between writing for the theatre and writing for the lecture-hall, and the pedagogical opportunities (though he would never have put it that way) they presented. Having remarked on certain matters in the history of French pronunciation, for instance, he goes on to make the following observation:

If you could see the script from which I am now speaking, you would not see in that script an indication of my accent or other tricks of my voice, or the fact that

---

[34] Griffiths, *Printed Voice*, 36, and unpublished lecture, 'Practical Criticism 8: "A girl can't go on laughing all the time"', quoted in Johnston, 'Introduction', 3.
[35] Griffiths, 'A Rehearsal of Hamlet', in *If Not Critical*, 86–111 (108).
[36] See Johnston, 'Introduction', *passim*; Jonathan Bate, 'Reckless Eric' (review of *If Not Critical*), *TLS* 22 August 2018, 3–4; and John Mullan, 'Beastliness' (review of *If Not Critical* and *The Printed Voice*), *LRB* 23 May 2019 <https://www.lrb.co.uk/the-paper/v41/n10/john-mullan/beastliness> (accessed 14 January 2021).
[37] Griffiths, 'A Rehearsal of Hamlet', in *If Not Critical*, 107.

I suddenly shouted the word 'shouted', though there could have been a stage direction to that effect, but in fact there isn't.[38]

Despite what must have been the rather arch bravura of its delivery, it is, in script, actually quite an affecting moment. We *can* see the script, but only because this script, from which Griffiths will not speak again, has been published in what is, at least in part, a valedictory volume. The cost of access to the script is the impossibility of access to the voice. It is also a rather beguiling moment in a number of ways. Griffiths does not describe himself as reading from the script, but rather as 'speaking' from it, a minor enough difference in itself, perhaps, but one that gains in significance when we recall the importance of the relations between writing and speech, reading and hearing, across Griffiths's critical enterprise. It is true, certainly, that there are here no indications of the 'tricks of my voice'. As Griffiths acknowledges, we may have a sense of elements of the vocal performance of this script, when, for example, we read that he shouted 'shouted', although in that case we do not know whether that was the first or second 'shouted', or both ('the fact that I shouted the word "shouted"'), or when he describes the 'coarse jokes' Racine's contemporaries made about the playwright's 'refayned protagonists', a spelling that surely indicates a mock-refined pronunciation in delivery. This may just be a misspelling, the editor's oversight, or a printer's devil, but it may likewise be an instance of what Goffman calls 'keyings', the 'paralinguistic markers' (hard, he asserts, to identify, and harder still to transcribe) by which speakers signal their relative detachment from certain passages of speech, delivered under the guise of 'sarcasm, irony, "words from another's mouth," and the like' (Goffman, 174). The difficulty of identifying and transcribing such features is perhaps evident in Goffman's recourse to metaphors in accounting for them—and metaphors, moreover, borrowed from the eye and put into the mouth: 'a competent lecturer will be able to read a remark with a twinkle in his voice, or stand off from an utterance by slightly raising his vocal eyebrows' (p. 175). Again, such features of the (at least) competent delivery of lectures form an important part of the experience of a lecture's audience, for, according to Goffman, it is thanks to the sense that 'these vocally tinted lines' (more visual metaphors) 'could not be delivered this way in print' that hearers further intimate that 'they have preferential access to the mind of the author, that live listening provides the kind of contact that reading doesn't' (p. 175).

Such markers may not be amenable to being 'delivered this way in print', but maybe there are other ways. It is worth emphasizing here that, while it is not always the case that works of literary criticism having their origins in lectures are advertised as such, many are, and they frequently, as we have been seeing, retain

---

[38] Eric Griffiths, 'French as a Literary Medium', in *If Not Critical*, 131–53 (144).

aspects of their spoken performance: repetitions, phonetic spellings, expressions of thanks to organizers and others, remarks on the specific circumstances and timing of delivery, intermittent addresses to the audience, and so on. And it is also often the case that printed lectures are situated within a responsive textual field of review, recollection, and anecdote. The congeries of responses to Coleridge's lectures, for instance, have been vital to the textual editing, and hence transmission to literary critical posterity, of them; more recent instances are less editorially formalized, but the point that I wish to stress here is that they are no less significant for the reasons I have been canvassing concerning the connections between reading, audition, and imagination that are indelible from the activity of literary criticism itself.

It is this context that frequently preserves the happy accidents, as well as the 'paralinguistic markers', that may befall a lecturer, and, as such, may hint at things more than they had meant to mean. The tricks, for example, of anyone's voice may be its distinctive and more or less virtuosic capacities, exercised for the edification and pleasure of an audience, but they may also be tricks played by the voice on the person whose voice it is. Although there is no basis for it in the text that has been transmitted to us, Griffiths's editor Johnston, for instance, recalls hearing Griffiths refer in his lecture on 'The Disappointment of Christina G. Rossetti' to 'the elephants of criticism', rather than 'the elements of criticism'—'such a happy infelicity', as Johnston remarks, 'as to make even Eric pause before resuming the usual verbal canter'.[39] Elephants, though they sometimes do, are rarely imagined cantering; they are, proverbially, ignored when they are in the room—as, so Griffiths often wanted to argue, are the most finally unavoidable elements of criticism. Paul de Man—a very different kind of literary critic from Griffiths, with a different sense of the relation between print and voice—despite many years' lecturing in English in the United States, could not pronounce the distinction between 'tread' and 'thread' on which his lecture about Shelley's 'The Triumph of Life' was (as Marc Redfield quippingly puts it) 'hanging'. Toni Morrison's coinage 'testosteronic', to describe one of the many false directions that we will have to rue 'during longer more comfortable lives', failed her in speaking her Jefferson lecture to her own amusement as well as that of her audience.[40] Morrison's text is (fittingly) portentous in its consideration of the longer human lives we are told to expect set against the mess that continues to be made of human society and,

---

[39] Johnston, 'Introduction', 5.
[40] See Marc Redfield, 'Appendix 1: Courses Taught by Paul de Man during the Yale Years', in *Legacies of Paul de Man*, ed. Redfield (New York: Fordham University Press, 2007), 179–83 (181); Toni Morrison, 'The Future of Time: Literature and Diminished Expectations', 25th Jefferson Lecture in the Humanities, 25 March 1996 <https://neh.dspacedirect.org/bitstream/handle/11215/3774/LIB39_002-public.pdf?sequence=1&isAllowed=y> (accessed 22 March 2022), 5; and Jacqueline Trescott, 'Toni Morrison, Reading Ahead', *Washington Post*, 26 March 1996 <https://www.washingtonpost.com/archive/lifestyle/1996/03/26/toni-morrison-reading-ahead/baa0c80f-3769-47a7-9fda-551ec79fc89d/> (accessed 22 March 2022).

as such, returns repeatedly to the question, 'What will we think during these longer more comfortable lives?', but the happy accident of her stumble over 'testosteronic' itself enacts the inadequacy of our super-sophisticated methods of control and also intimates the bleak, unintended comedy of taking 'our cue to solving social inequities from computer games […] winning points or votes for how many of the vulnerable and unlucky we eliminated'.[41]

Our knowledge of the performance (and revealing vagaries) of lecturing frequently comes from recollections like Redfield's of de Man's lectures and reviews like Jacqueline Trescott's of Morrison's Jefferson lecture, even when, as in both of these cases, the lectures in question were delivered long after the invention of viable recording technologies. It is a curious feature of Trescott's write-up of Morrison's lecture that she quotes a substantial passage of the latter—'I am not ferreting out signs of tentative hope, obstinate optimism in contemporary fiction; I believe I am detecting an informed vision based on harrowing experience that nevertheless gestures toward a redemptive future. And I notice the milieu from which this vision rises. It is race inflected, gendered, colonialized, displaced, hunted'—before declaring: 'And then she smiled, and stopped.' It would have been a resonant ending, to be sure—but it is not the ending in the published text of the Jefferson lecture. In that text, Morrison goes on to develop an image of literature as, revealingly, at once sonically exacting and sharp-sighted—'Literature, sensitive as a tuning fork, is an unblinking witness to the light and shade of the world we live in'—before castigating 'the world of commentary' (by which she means, not specifically literary commentary, but more broadly the world in which acceptable opinion circulates) as backward-looking, reactionary, and timid. The text's ending is an expression of hope: 'Time does have a future. Longer than its past and infinitely more hospitable—to the human race.' That conclusion perhaps deserves a smile, but whether or not it was the conclusion that Morrison spoke, we cannot finally know. However, it is the case that elements of Trescott's account do appear to recruit Morrison's argument to the bleak, backward-looking prospect that Morrison in fact worked through and beyond. Trescott's account appeared in the *Washington Post*, a major organ of 'commentary' in Morrison's specific sense, and in it Trescott was keen to emphasize 'the direness of the message' communicated in Morrison's lecture, 'underscored by [her] clear, lithe voice, which has breaths of unbelievability and exasperation that she releases like bubbles you can't really catch'. The pairing of 'unbelievability and exasperation' is almost the exact opposite of the concluding reflections as they appear in the text: 'not only is history not dead, but […] it is about to take its first unfettered breath. Not soon, perhaps not in thirty years or fifty, because such a breath, such a massive intake, will take time. But it will be there. If that is so, then we should heed the meditations of literature.' Belief and inspiration, for which (as Trescott does acknowledge) she draws sustenance from literature, are the concluding notes of Morrison's lecture.

As I remarked above, the evidence we have for Morrison's Jefferson lecture is its published text and Trescott's account of its delivery. The availability of the former does not necessarily invalidate the latter, even where it disagrees with it, because we cannot know for sure whether the text includes sections that were not in the event delivered or whether Trescott's account happens to be partial for whatever reason. Certainly, the invocation of the present moment in relation to an indeterminable (or at least undetermined) future, the thematization of breath, and emphasis on the lecture's central theme of the insufficiently acknowledged significance of literature make the text's ending a good ending for the performance of a lecture. It is not necessary to pursue this (in any case) unsolvable conundrum any further, but I do want to conclude this chapter by examining Morrison's lecturing a little more fully. In his essay on 'Footing', Goffman remarks that, '[f]or the effective conduct of talk, speaker and hearer had best be in a position to *watch* each other. The fact that telephoning can be practicable without the visual channel,' he goes on to argue, 'and that written transcriptions of talk also seem effective, is not to be taken as a sign that, indeed, conveying words is the only thing that is crucial, but that reconstruction and transformation are very powerful processes' (p. 130). Indeed, Morrison's lectures can be read, heard, or watched—some of them both read and heard (in the case of her Nobel lecture); some both read and watched (in the case of her Ingersoll Lecture on Immortality); some, only read; and a few, only watched—and it is notable that her lectures exist in different states that variably indicate their origins in delivered lectures: perhaps her most celebrated critical work, *Playing in the Dark: Whiteness and the Literary Imagination*, given as the William E. Massey, Sr Lectures in American Studies at Harvard University in 1992 and published by the university's press later that year, makes no explicit acknowledgement in its published form of its origin in lectures, whereas her Jefferson lecture and 'Unspeakable Things Unspoken' clearly advertise their origins as lectures in the available texts.[42] We have seen in a number of

---

[42] Toni Morrison, 'Nobel Lecture', 7 December 1993, audio recording <https://www.nobelprize.org/mediaplayer/?id=1502> (accessed 22 March 2022), and text <https://www.nobelprize.org/prizes/literature/1993/morrison/lecture/?_ga=2.30313530.46266796.1647959409-500863312.1647959409> (accessed 22 March 2022); *Goodness and the Literary Imagination: Harvard's 95th Ingersoll Lecture with Essays on Morrison's Moral and Religious Vision*, ed. Davíd Carrasco et al. (Charlottesville: University of Virginia Press, 2019), and *Goodness: Altruism and the Literary Imagination* (2012 Ingersoll Lecture on Immortality), online video recording, YouTube, 14 December 2012 <https://www.youtube.com/watch?v=PJmVpYZnKTU> (accessed 22 March 2022); *Playing in the Dark: Whiteness and the Literary Imagination* (New York: Vintage, 1993; first pub. Cambridge, MA: Harvard University Press, 1992); 'The Future of Time'; and 'Unspeakable Things Unspoken: The Afro-American Presence in American Literature', The Tanner Lectures on Human Values, delivered at the University of Michigan, 7 October 1988, <https://tannerlectures.utah.edu/_resources/documents/a-to-z/m/morrison90.pdf> (first pub. in *Michigan Quarterly Review*, 28 (1989), 1–34).

places in this book that the formal specificity of critical writing is frequently effaced in the processes of revision, publication, and canonization, and that its recovery from under such effacement may lead to fresh critical perspectives and a more nuanced understanding of the stakes of literary critical work. That project has frequently had to rely on paratexts, anecdotes, contemporary reports, and non-literary media—and that is all the more the case with the late-twentieth-century lecture, which has available to it more means for recording and dissemination than were available at earlier points in the history of human communication. In the specific case of Morrison as lecturer, as we saw with her Jefferson lecture, the process of reconstruction and transformation (to redeploy Goffman's terms) effected by a journalistic report had at least the potential to be a 'very powerful' process. Morrison's lectures—the form in which almost all of her substantial body of critical work has its origins—are themselves directly concerned with the processes of reconstruction and transformation, above all of a literary tradition that has silenced or suppressed its black contributors, along with its own presuppositions. Perhaps the most transformative achievement of Morrison's criticism in this regard has been the sustained examination of the literary construction and normalization of whiteness, which has in turn involved the dethronement of whiteness as a norm from which other 'races' are supposed to diverge, a move that has thus enabled the investigation of 'the impact of racism on those who perpetuate it'.[43] Giving voice, uncovering hidden presences, discerning who and what speaks through, beneath, and around texts have thus all been fundamental to Morrison's criticism—and all performed in her art of lecturing. In reflecting, for instance, on the very inauguration of her own writing career—namely, the opening phrase of her first novel, *The Bluest Eye* (1970)—Morrison remarks in 'Unspeakable Things Unspoken' that ' "Quiet as it's kept," is also a figure of speech that is written, in this instance, but clearly chosen for how speakerly it is, how it speaks and bespeaks a particular world and its ambience' (p. 147). The immediate aim of that phrase was the achievement of 'the intimacy between the reader and the page' (p. 148) via the evocation of spoken language. The imagination of what it means to say certain words is likewise crucial at pivotal points of her lectures. We saw in the case of the coinage of 'testosteronic' that the voice may be an unreliable agent of terminological innovation, but the drama, for instance, of the appropriation of 'miscegenation' and 'savage', words with deep histories of racist associations, at a vital moment in a lecture tellingly (a word I use advisedly) titled 'Unspeakable Things Unspoken' is indicative of Morrison's deliberate deployment of the force of speech and, particularly, of the force that inheres in certain people speaking certain things. Addressing 'the present turbulence' in contemporary

---

[43] Morrison, *Playing in the Dark*, 11. For a useful account of the intellectual background to this project, see Hanna Wallinger, 'Toni Morrison's Literary Criticism', in Justine Tally (ed.), *The Cambridge Companion to Toni Morrison* (Cambridge: Cambridge University Press, 2007), 115–24 (120–1).

discussions of canonicity, Morrison remarks that the debate 'seems not to be about the flexibility of a canon, its range among and between Western countries, but about its miscegenation. The word is informative here and I do mean its use' (p. 129). And, commenting on 'the radical upheaval in canon building that took place at the inauguration of classical studies and Greek', she declares, again deliberately thematizing the (or, rather, her) usage of the word, that it 'was not merely radical, it must have been (may I say it?) savage' (p. 130). By the start of her all but unrivalled lecturing career, Morrison was certainly an authority to whom, in Goffman's terms, an audience would desire access—and one to whose demeanour, vocal timbres, and rapport, they often paid close, devoted attention.[44] Yet that '(may I say it?)' has a special force of its own. Morrison was not averse to the comic potential in blurting out what must not be said—'What brought her joy?' she was asked after her Norton lectures at Harvard, '*Sex.* I'm sorry—I meant to say "my writing"'—but equally the force of the appropriation and redirection of 'miscegenation' and 'savage', an appropriation and redirection whose verbal performance is explicitly emphasized in her lecture, against a tradition that used them to quite opposite ends, is an essential bequest, not just of her literary criticism, but of the specific form of that literary criticism in the performed word, in the presence on the podium, and in the career-long occupation of a position of discursive authority too long denied to her forebears.

[44] See Wallinger, 114–15, for details of Morrison's institutional standing at the time of the most prestigious of her various lecture series.

5

Dialogues

The previous chapter was concerned with how the lecture both relies on and examines the centrality to literary criticism of the imagination of voice. It is tempting to think of the lecture as a thoroughly monologic (or, perhaps better, univocal) form, because, in many ways, it is. The lecturer mounts the podium and addresses the audience, the members of which remain silent. Sometimes, of course, members of an audience speak back, both in regulated and predictable ways, such as by means of invited questions or administratively mandated feedback, and in irregular and unpredictable ways, such as protest and exclamation. But, in addition to these forms of audience participation, we also examined the involvement in the transmission of the lecture to literary-critical history of audiences, translators, and editors. The univocality of the lecture is qualified both by the numerous, often fraught mechanisms of its transmission, as well as by the necessity to it of what Eric Griffiths called the sense of 'an "I", dramatically self-conscious, watched by a "he" '—and heard by a 'he', a 'she', and a 'they'.

If the lecture is not as univocal as it may appear to be, the dialogue (which is the focus of this chapter) has often been convicted of a failure to be as multiply discursive as it might initially seem.[1] One response to monologue in the guise of dialogue would be to cease to participate and thus to expose the appearance of dialogue as, indeed, appearance only. The refusal of dialogue has, in fact, been cast as an essential recourse of proper critical judgement. The refusal to be swayed by fashionable chatter constitutes a key principle, for example, of Kant's *Critique of Judgement*, the seminal text in the history of modern philosophical aesthetics, which, by means of its consideration of the exchange of aesthetic judgements, seeks to model the management of disagreement, the role of authority and experience, and the rights of the uninitiated in a discursive public sphere. Refusing to engage in dialogue is essential to its proper functioning:

> If anyone does not think a building, view, or poem beautiful, then, *in the first place* he refuses, so far as his inmost conviction goes, to allow approval to be wrung from him by a hundred voices all lauding it to the skies. Of course he may affect to be pleased with it, so as not to be considered as wanting in taste.

---

[1] See, e.g., Gilles Deleuze and Félix Guattari, *What is Philosophy?* (1991), trans. Hugh Tomlinson and Graham Burchell (New York: Columbia University Press, 1994), 29. I thank Sam Warren-Miell for drawing my attention to this text.

Critical Forms: Forms of Literary Criticism, 1750–2020. Ross Wilson, Oxford University Press. © Ross Wilson 2023.
DOI: 10.1093/oso/9780198881117.003.0006

He may even begin to harbour doubts as to whether he has formed his taste upon an acquaintance with a sufficient number of objects of a particular kind [...] The judgement of others, where unfavourable to ours, may, no doubt, rightly make us suspicious in respect of our own, but convince us that it is wrong it never can.[2]

Kant acknowledges that the 'hundred voices' extolling the merits of the building, view, or poem may give the judge who judges otherwise pause—and, according to Kant, that is potentially salutary, because it makes the judge acquaint himself with more and different things. Even so, when it comes to other kinds of persuasion— specifically, the invocation of supposed rules for beauty established by eminent critics—the judge's retreat into his own silent judgement is more drastic still, doubtless because 'a proof *a priori* according to definite rules is still less capable of determining the judgement as to beauty':

> If anyone reads me his poem, or brings me to a play, which, all said and done, fails to commend itself to my taste, then let him adduce *Batteux* or *Lessing*, or still older and more famous critics of taste, with all the host of rules laid down by them, as a proof of the beauty of his poem; let certain passages particularly dis-pleasing to me accord completely with the rules of beauty, (as set out by these critics and universally recognised): I stop my ears: I do not want to hear any reasons or any arguing about the matter.   (p. 114)

It is notable that these two examples of aesthetic contrarianism involve the failure to find beautiful something that is widely held to be so, instead of the insistence that something widely held *not* to be beautiful *is*. While Kant does earlier imagine a scenario in which a young poet stands by his view that his own poem is estim-able despite the general derision with which it is greeted, it is nevertheless the case that the two examples above suggest Kant chiefly considers the judgement of taste as a subjectively grounded redoubt against the widespread celebration of reputed beauties; and, as such, these examples bear an important relation to the view that Kant's account of judgements of taste does not allow for the possibility of negative judgements of taste—for, that is, the judgement that something is ugly, rather than beautiful.[3] It is also worth noting that, when Kant is warding off the arguments of other theorists, rather than mere general opinion, he switches from the third to the first person: disenfranchising Batteux, Lessing, and others older

---

[2] Immanuel Kant, *Critique of Judgement*, trans. James Creed Meredith, rev. and ed. Nicholas Walker (Oxford: Oxford University Press, 2007), 114. Further references are given after quotations in the text.

[3] For useful overviews of this controversy (and robust avowals of the position that Kant's aesthetics can account for ugliness), see Christian Wenzel, 'Kant Finds Nothing Ugly?', *British Journal of Aesthetics*, 39 (1999), 416–22, and *An Introduction to Kant's Aesthetics: Core Concepts and Problems* (Oxford: Blackwell, 2005), 128–33.

or more famous (he means Aristotle above all) is personal if you aim to be a critic of taste yourself. Kant's account seeks above all to effect a transition from the discursive—dialogical, even—formation of critical judgements, to their formation solely within the subject, independent of any potentially coercive debate or discussion. The subjective judge of taste must deliver his judgement and block his ears. Critical dialogue is a misleading distraction, in which the discussant is prey to the persuasive arts of eloquent opponents able to cite venerable authorities, to advocate the current fashion, or both. To such persuasions, the judge of taste must be deaf.

The prospects for critical dialogue may thus appear bleak. Yet we should recall here that Kant admits that the 'hundred voices' contradicting our opinion may at least give us pause, and still more significant is the attempt, later in the *Critique of Judgement*, to draw a distinction between disputing (the Latin-derived *Disputieren* may assume a certain air of philosophical pretension) and arguing (the more homely, robust *Streiten*). Whereas the aim of disputing is to secure agreement by means of proofs, arguing, according to Kant, can avail itself of no such method. In that case, there is the potentially unending exchange of views, attempts to give reasons for them, and the hope that the encounter with unfavourable opinions might in general generate a useful suspicion about one's own views.

This chapter examines dialogue as a critical form and, thereby, explores the contest over authority, the cultivation of critical insight, and the often-tendentious rehearsal of sometimes conflicting critical opinion. More particularly, in keeping with one of the central preoccupations of the previous chapter, it focuses on the roles of text and of silence in an ostensibly spoken genre, focusing in particular on who, in dialogue, has access to texts on which the authority of critical judgement is often made to rest.

*

Allan Ramsay's *A Dialogue on Taste*, published in 1755 and issued in a second edition in 1762, stands near the beginning of the period addressed in this book but also at a significant moment in the historical development of the dialogue form. Ramsay's depiction of the conflict between free judgement (in the person of Colonel Freeman) and established fashion (Lord Modish), along with the distinction between end-determined disputation and more open-ended argumentation, are, as they would be for Kant, central to *A Dialogue on Taste*. Colonel Freeman is the driving force of Ramsay's *Dialogue*, monopolizing the discourse to the extent, for instance, that at one point he recollects himself and apologizes 'to the Ladies' for having fallen into what he fears is 'a Professorial kind of discourse' (they understandably resent the implication that they would not understand such a discourse).[4] He opens his discourse on the nature of taste by maintaining his

---

[4] [Allan Ramsay], *A Dialogue on Taste*, 2nd edn (London, 1762), 26–7. Further references to this edition appear after quotations in the text.

preference for *Hudibras* over Virgil—a preference that, along with his apparently comparable claim that he prefers 'Canary to Champaign', Modish takes as evidence that Freeman is, in a delightful phrase, 'an absolute Goth' (pp. 2–4).[5] In his defence, Freeman goes on to develop a stark distinction (which bears some similarities with that articulated by Jackson and Graves which we encountered in Chapter 3) between 'reason and judgement', on the one hand, and 'taste, or feeling', on the other:

> Whatever has a rule or standard to which it may be referred, and is capable of comparison, is not the object of taste, but of reason and judgment. On the other hand, the proper objects of taste, or feeling, are such as are relative to the person only who is actuated by them, who is the sole judge whether those feelings be agreeable, or otherwise; and being informed of this simple fact from himself, no farther consequence can be drawn from it, neither does it admit of any dispute.
>
> (pp. 9–10)

Freeman, warming to his theme, goes on to insist that matters of mere taste do not—or should not—admit of discussion. When someone declares that he prefers venison with currant sauce rather than gravy, he may reason no further than the declaration of his preference and, indeed, 'he must have the like patience to hear me, in my turn, declare that gravy sauce is far before currant; and this without making any reply, if he has a grain of sense' (p. 10).

Hudibras versus Virgil; canary wine versus champagne; currant sauce versus gravy: the focus here hardly seems to be on matters of literary criticism exclusively, and it is certainly true that Ramsay (like Kant) adduces a wide range of examples of things that are subject to taste. Yet poetry, in *A Dialogue on Taste*, does admit of judgement, instead of, like wines and sauces, being merely submitted to taste. It might already be objected to Freeman's vision of the sequence of unarguable declarations, curtly enough made but patiently heard, that any declaration of a contrary opinion offered after, say, a declared preference for currant sauce is already what Freeman says should not be advanced in such a situation— namely, a 'reply'. When it comes to literature, despite Freeman's initially expressed preference for *Hudibras* over Virgil—which Michael Prince judiciously ascribes to Freeman's adoption of 'an antic disposition'[6]—it is not simply a case of the non-discursive, and hence somewhat sterile, expression of private inclinations. For, according to Freeman, and following the definition of 'one of the most sagacious of the ancients', an art is '*a system of rules acquired by study, and reduced to practice,*

---

[5] The pagination skips p. 3, and thus pp. 2 and 4 are in fact consecutive.
[6] Michael Prince, *Philosophical Dialogue in the British Enlightenment: Theology, Aesthetics, and the Novel* (Cambridge: Cambridge University Press, 1996), 193.

for some useful purpose' (p. 55). Thus the arts are all referable to a standard. In the cases of painting and poetry in particular

> there is not only a standard, but one so level to the common sense of mankind, that the most ignorant are acquainted with it; and, if it is unknown or mistaken by any, it is by the half-learned, who from their own conceit, or a respect for the authority of coxcombs, have tried to undervalue common sense, in order to sub-stitute something which they thought better, in its stead.   (p. 56)

Modish concedes that there are rules for poetry and painting, but he is not con-vinced by Freeman's assertion that they are 'so universally known as you would have us believe' (p. 56). In response to this expression of doubt, Freeman proposes an experiment that would, he claims, prove his point:

> Your Lordship has only to hide yourself behind the screen in your drawing-room, and order Mrs Hannah to bring in one of your tenant's daughters, and I will venture to lay a wager that she shall be struck with your picture by La Tour, and no less with the view of your seat by Lambert, and shall, fifty to one, express her approbation by saying, they are *vastly natural*.   (p. 57)

He concludes his account of this proposed experiment by claiming that what is applicable to paintings is transferable to poetry:

> The general standard of poetry is exactly the same, and equally obvious with that of painting; and any experiment you make in that art upon a farmer's daughter, will be found to have a like event. It is only middling poetry which the illiterate do not understand and admire; when it arrives at a supreme degree of excellence it is adapted to the lowest class; and though other poets might have their par-tisans amongst the critics, there is no question, but Homer was the delight of every cook-maid in Greece.   (p. 58)

Freeman insists, notably, that social classes and aesthetic classes are discrepant: Greek cook-maids and British farmers' daughters alike 'understand and admire' Homer; it is only critics who are 'partisans' for 'middling poetry'. The implication is that low and high unite, reaching across a merely 'middling' morass in which 'other poets' and 'critics' come indistinguishably together; taste, therefore, is the preserve of an allied class of masters and servants, set against an emergent profes-sional and partisan middle class, which would claim taste as its own preserve.

We must nevertheless note a number of oddities about Freeman's account of this proposed experiment. Why does Modish conceal himself when the farmer's daughter is brought in to give her view of his painting? In the episode in Plato's

Meno (which is surely Ramsay's model here) in which Socrates quizzes a slave in Meno's household about the mathematical properties of squares, neither Socrates nor Meno thinks to conceal himself from the slave.[7] Crucially, Socrates and Meno are asking the slave about an epistemological matter, whereas Modish's quizzing of the farmer's daughter concerns a matter of aesthetic judgement, the object of which, moreover, he owns. The distinction of rank, the gulf in wealth and hence the ability to purchase objects amenable to fashionable judgement, and the privileges of ownership are all thus at play in this scene of *A Dialogue on Taste* in a way that they are not in the *Meno*, despite the fact, of course, that ownership is hardly beside the question in the *Meno*, since the slave himself is owned by Meno in a way that the farmer's daughter in *A Dialogue on Taste* is not (quite). As we have already seen in Freeman's declaration of the delight Greek cook-maids took in Homer, Ramsay is certainly interested in the role that wealth and social standing play in the formation of fashion and the expression of taste: 'It is the nature of all fashions', he claims, '(I except only those of a religious kind) to take their rise from the sovereign will and pleasure of the rich and powerful' (p. 34). But Modish's concealment behind the screen in his drawing room has a still more fundamental bearing on the argument concerning the relation of taste and judgement, especially concerning the allegedly non-discursive character of the former in contrast to the discursive character of the latter, that *A Dialogue on Taste* seeks to articulate. Contrasting with Socrates' open and repeated questioning of the slave, Modish, hidden behind the screen, does not explicitly prompt the responses of the farmer's daughter at all. Freeman comes to acknowledge that taste and judgement are, in the end, remarkably similar in operation: the 'reflective and compound operation of the mind' by which comparison of an artwork to a standard of art is undertaken 'is indeed so quick and instantaneous, that it often passes for a simple feeling or sentiment' (p. 58). With neither time nor necessity for the intervention of dialogue, even between the soul and itself, judgement often 'passes for' taste. Where Socrates' questions lead the slave to a realization of the knowledge that inheres within him, Modish's covert observation of his tenant's daughter allows her to express a view that she has acquired by the kind of experience supposedly basic to any member of the human race. In Platonic dialogue, dialogue conduces to the discovery of knowledge that transcends experience; in anti-Platonic dialogue, it is experience that speaks.

*

Modish's self-concealment in Ramsay's *A Dialogue on Taste* is more than just a faintly comic episode; it plays a vital role in the development of the dialogue's argument, specifically by rendering dialogue or even the potential for dialogue between Modish and the farmer's daughter impossible. As I suggested above, who

---

[7] Plato, *Meno*, trans. G. M. A. Grube, in *Plato: Complete Works*, ed. John M. Cooper, (Indianapolis: Hackett, 1997), 870–97 (881–6 (82–86^b)).

speaks, and when—and who stays silent, and when—are key elements in the cultivation of critical authority in dialogue, influenced by gender, social rank, and age, as well as (as we shall see) by relative fame and obscurity, depth of learning, and access to textual sources. The interplay of speech and silence, and turn-taking between them, is pivotal even in an extended set of dialogues like Johann Peter Eckermann's *Conversations with Goethe*, in which the identities of master and pupil, sage and scribe, inspired artist and mere amenuensis seem so obvious but turn out to be so complex.[8] Eckermann's *Conversations*, along with other records of conversations, ana, and dicta such as Hazlitt's *Conversations of James Northcote, Esq., RA* (1830) (which, though conversations with a painter, are frequently concerned with literary matters), Marguerite Gardiner, Lady Blessington's *Conversations with Lord Byron* (1834), Coleridge's *Table Talk* (1835), and the notes on his poems that Wordsworth dictated to Isabella Fenwick (1843), to cite just a handful of examples from this burgeoning genre, are the inheritors of a tradition of transcribed conversation that stretches back to antiquity and has a (perhaps unlikely) post-antique exemplar in Martin Luther's *Table Talk*. In addition, by virtue of their participation in an emerging celebrity culture and expressionist aesthetic, which both put significant weight on categories such as genius, inspiration, and intention, such records of conversation anticipate the rise of the literary interview.[9] The literary interview both promises to explain the sources of a writer's writing, while also frequently reasserting the ineffability of those sources in the still silent recesses of the writer's personality: in response to Leopoldina Pallotta della Torre's questions about her childhood in colonial-era Vietnam, for example, Marguerite Duras oscillates between avowing that 'I sometimes think the whole of my writing originates from there—between the paddy fields, the forests and the solitude', before then declaring that 'I have overwhelming memories, memories so strong that they can never be evoked by writing', and finally asserting that it was precisely 'to make the silence speak—that silence under which I'd been crushed' that she 'took to writing'.[10]

Silence is thus a precious and difficult resource in the cultivation of literary expression and critical authority. If we return, for instance, to Eckermann's opening descriptions of Goethe's house and person, and, especially, of his 'most friendly words' and of Goethe's manner of speaking 'slowly and easily, so that one just imagines an elderly monarch', we can recognize that these descriptions set the scene for the ensuing conversations without actually relating much, if anything, of what Goethe in fact said. But they also, significantly, establish Eckermann as a

---

[8] For a discussion of the *Conversations with Goethe* and Eckermann's role in the formation of Goethe's posthumous reputation, see Avital Ronell, *Dictations: On Haunted Writing* (Lincoln: University of Nebraska Press, 1993; first pub. 1986), esp. 65–191.

[9] For a useful account of this history, see Rebecca Roach, *Literature and the Rise of the Interview* (Oxford: Oxford University Press, 2018), esp. 2–3 for the prehistory of the literary interview.

[10] *Marguerite Duras: Suspended Passion*, trans. Chris Turner (London: Seagull Books, 2016), 13, 17.

CRITICAL FORMS

(or even the) privileged participant in the dialogues, since it is he who decides what of Goethe's conversation we get to read. In fact, the first thing quoted by Eckermann directly is Goethe's initially somewhat bewildering claim that he has already spent plenty of time with Eckermann that day: 'I have just come from you,' Goethe says; 'I have been reading your work the whole morning; it needs no recommendation; it recommends itself'.[11] Few could resist the temptation of relaying Goethe's praise for their work, and Eckermann is most certainly not among them. But what is especially important here is the fact that the conversation had actually begun with a text—and a text of Eckermann's, rather than Goethe's—which Goethe treats as a synecdoche of Eckermann himself (or of which Eckermann, in fact, is himself a synecdoche). It is a text, too, to which only the participants in the conversations have access, even if we assume that it is the manuscript of one of the works of Eckermann's that will be published, and it is, moreover, the introduction of another text to which the participants of the dialogue have privileged access that cements the friendship: Goethe brings to his second meeting with Eckermann 'two thick books' containing the 'little reviews' he wrote in 1772 and 1773, and which he asks Eckermann to read with a view to whether they would be worth publishing in a future edition of his works (p. 42). The relationship between Goethe and Eckermann is, therefore, substantially based on texts, and not on texts to which any reader of their conversations may have the same degree of access, but in texts to which they have privileged access and to which others have access thanks to Eckermann's subsequent editorial endeavours. The development of the friendship and literary collaboration attested to in the *Conversations with Goethe* is itself, that is, the background to the appearance of a number of Goethe's texts—namely, the ones he wishes Eckermann to examine—as well as Eckermann's too.

Needless to say, the texts that persons in dialogues read aloud from, refer to, and bring along to their meetings are not just any dramatic prop. Rather, the presence of text in dialogue is a vital aspect of criticism's own historical negotiation of what Michael Gavin has called 'the textualization of judgment'.[12] Gavin, as I discussed in the Introduction, focuses on the transition in the seventeenth and eighteenth centuries from the understanding of criticism as a mode of response on the part of playgoers and readers—such as heckling from the theatre pit, shouting over antagonists in the coffee house, or calmly taking turns to say one's piece in a polite social gathering—to a kind of writing that takes a variety of generic forms. Gavin thus distinguishes between ' "critical writing" ' as 'the generically heterogeneous mix of texts that engage arguments about poetry, plays,

[11] Johann Peter Eckermann, *Gespräche mit Goethe in den letzten Jahren seines Lebens*, ed. Christoph Michel (Frankfurt-am-Main: Deutscher Klassiker, 1999), 40. Further references to this edition are given after quotations in the text.
[12] Michael Gavin, *The Invention of English Criticism, 1650-1760* (Cambridge: Cambridge University Press, 2015), 1–23.

and prose fiction', on the one hand, and '"criticism"' understood 'in a much broader sense as *the socially realized exercise of judgment*', on the other. And., while critical writing in England emerged with the politically charged explosion in print during the 1640s and 1650s, the image of the critic as heckler persisted, Gavin notes, into the early eighteenth century at least, at which point '"criticism" was consistently associated with a mode of writing [and] acknowledged as a species of authorship'.[13] This reminder of Gavin's thesis, and the history onto which it is mapped, is in order here for a number of reasons. The first gives rise to a historical point. The contentious relation between the oral and social exercise of judgement, on the one hand, and criticism as a mode of authorship, on the other, continues to make its presence felt in literary-critical dialogue throughout the eighteenth century, but also into the nineteenth century and, indeed, beyond. As we also saw in the Introduction, the recognition that literary criticism can take place in conversation— however such a recognition may chafe against the understanding of literary criticism as a discipline—persists; the eighteenth century's questions of criticism continue to be ours. Second, the exact nature of the texts up for discussion and the way that they are disclosed to or concealed from other participants in the dialogue, is a significant index of the historical standing of literary criticism at the time of the dialogue in question (we will examine further the differences between manuscripts and other kinds of text sometimes discussed in dialogue when I turn to Wilde's 'The Decay of Lying' and Marcel Proust's *Contre Sainte-Beuve* below.) Last and most straightforward, Gavin's concern is, as he puts it, with the emergence of critical writing as 'the heterogeneous mix of texts that engage arguments about poetry, plays, and prose fiction' out of, and in more or less enduring relation to, the social exercise of criticism in the period from 1650 to 1760; my concern here is with the dialogue in particular as the form in which this relationship has continued long after the middle of the eighteenth century.

It is perhaps worth pausing to consider here that the role of text in dialogue has an ancient precedent in Plato's *Phaedrus*, a dialogue I touched on briefly in the preceding chapter where I discussed the lecturer's perception of her or his audience. Phaedrus' possession of the scroll on which a speech of Lysias (a celebrated Athenian speechwriter) is written out is pivotal to the opening of the dialogue. Phaedrus informs Socrates about Lysias' recently delivered speech, though he claims that he is not attempting to commit it to memory, but rather offers Socrates a summary instead. All the while, Phaedrus is concealing the text of the speech beneath his cloak. Socrates spots that Phaedrus is concealing something, correctly infers that it is the text of Lysias' speech, and consequently refuses to let Phaedrus practise what would be his own speech-making on him, demanding instead that Phaedrus simply read the speech out.[14] Although, as becomes clear in

---

[13] Gavin, 4.   [14] *Phaedrus*, p. 509 (228d).

the rest of the dialogue, Socrates is suspicious of the written word, in demanding that Phaedrus read out the text he is attempting to hide, Socrates refuses to connive at Phaedrus' fetishizing of the text as an item of property and refuses to accept his offer in its place of a dim recollection of Lysias' speech. 'Far better, then,' as G. R. F. Ferrari glosses Socrates' insistence that Phaedrus read the text out, 'to demystify the written word by bringing it into the open and reading from it directly; treating it only as tool, not talisman.'[15]

Phaedrus' possession and concealment of a text and Socrates' insistence on hearing it read out are central to the concerns of the *Phaedrus* as a whole—concerns with the emergence and status of writing, and with the relation between the oral practice of dialectical philosophy, on the one hand, and speech-writing for commercial gain, on the other. By means of the episode with the text of Lysias' speech, Plato negotiates a series of issues that are central to his philosophical project as a whole, including the still (at that date) contested standing of philosophy in relation to rival versions of public discourse and communication. There are a number of significant analogies with those dialogues that I want to examine here, then, since they too, despite their historical distance from the circumstances of the *Phaedrus*, likewise situate themselves in the context of changes to how new and emerging genres of writing are discussed and theorized, how critics come to establish their authority, and how an expanding print culture may be compared to a waning manuscript one. Though the historical differences between Socratic anxieties about script and eighteenth-century anxieties about print must be acknowledged, they should not blind us to equally significant analogies between the reception of what are, at their respective dates, innovations in methods of communication and its dissemination. The relation between a manuscript culture's associated scholarly practices and a print culture's less easily encompassed modes of reception and critical response is likewise comparable to the differences between speaking and writing that Socrates goes on to lay out later in the dialogue.

Significantly, it is on the basis of just such a recognition of what the eighteenth-century dialogues I examine in this chapter and the *Phaedrus* have in common, in fact, that a number of distinctions between the roles played by text in the *Phaedrus* and in those may more precisely be drawn. First, where Phaedrus conceals the scroll of Lysias' speech, the participants in the later dialogues I have been discussing, far from concealing the texts to which they have access, have ready recourse to them, even (so other participants sometimes suggest) flaunting them. Those texts, unlike the scroll of Lysias' speech, are often said to be written by the persons who have them in their possession and are frequently cast as unfinished or, at least, subject to revision. Also, the participants who have access to texts in the

---

[15] G. R. F. Ferrari, *Listening to the Cicadas: A Study of Plato's 'Phaedrus'* (Cambridge: Cambridge University Press, 1987), 209. Cf. Catherine Pickstock, *After Writing: On the Liturgical Consummation of Philosophy* (Oxford: Blackwell, 1998), 8–9.

dialogues I discuss need no second invitation to read from them (something, again, that other participants sometimes resent). Friedrich Schlegel's *Dialogue on Poetry*, published in the *Athenäum* in 1800, for example, stages a series of *Vorlesungen*—readings-out, though this is also the German word for lectures—of pre-prepared texts, which are in turn announced as conforming to different genres (a 'manuscript', a 'talk', a 'letter', and an 'essay'), followed by discussions among the various participants of the dialogue.[16] The host of these speeches and discussions, Amalia, was moved to propose them to the members of her coterie because, though 'the subject, the occasion, the center of their gathering' was usually 'poetry', '[s]he thought the friends did not realize clearly enough the diversity of their views'. And thus: 'Each [...] should speak from the bottom of his heart his thoughts about poetry or about a part, an aspect of it, or better still, write them down, so that they would have the opinion of each in black and white' (p. 56). In fact, although the reader is given access to opinions 'in black and white', the participants of the dialogue themselves are not: they must simply listen to pre-prepared texts being read out. It is the reader, then, who is the true beneficiary of Amalia's request (at one point, a party to the dialogue complains that another's 'tempo was a bit fast' in reading out his contribution (p. 89)). The dialogue's reader is thus in the position of judge or overseer, removed from the vicissitudes of spoken performance and able to read at her or his own pace, and to reassess, if necessary, what the participants in the dialogue may have only caught in passing. The text *in* the dialogue is the text *of* the dialogue and, though it has two readers, the reader in the dialogue and the reader of the dialogue, it is the latter whose reading is by implication the timelier and more measured.

Yet the privileged position of the reader of Schlegel's *Dialogue* is the exception rather than the rule when it comes to who has access to the texts that are revealed in dialogues. Clara Reeve's *The Progress of Romance* (1785) and Dorothea Veit Schlegel's 'Conversation on the Most Recent Novels by French Women' (1803) are signal instances of the compromised, rather than privileged, position of the reader. Both Reeve's and Veit Schlegel's dialogues are early attempts to theorize the novel, a form often anxiously associated with the expansion of print, the commercial mechanisms of distribution and circulation, and a critical free-for-all (including for women and other socially marginalized groups), ostensibly removed from a restricted culture of scholarly learning and manuscript circulation that it allegedly entailed. In addition, the novel's relation to the theatre, out of whose shadow it gradually and repeatedly emerges throughout the eighteenth and nineteenth centuries in the careers of a number of writers from Fielding to James, likewise evokes an anxious affinity of theorizations of the novel for the

---

[16] Friedrich Schlegel, *Dialogue on Poetry*, in *'Dialogue on Poetry' and 'Literary Aphorisms'*, trans. Ernst Behler and Roman Struc (University Park: Pennsylvania State University Press, 1968), 53–117 (60–80, 81–93, 94–105, 106–17 respectively). Further references are given after quotations in the text.

dialogue form.[17] Reeve's *Progress*, which attempts to establish romance on an equal footing with epic and to trace the emergence of the novel out of romance's ruins, is very much an endeavour among friends and among texts, to some of which those friends have access and to some of which they, significantly, do not.[18] In making the conventional apology for not having been able to take full account of other works on the topic that she is addressing, Reeve remarks that, '[t]o the perusal of these books [viz., Beattie's *Dissertation on Fable and Romance* and Warton's *History of English Poetry*], I was most strongly recommended by two friends, to whom I had shewn my own work, and to whose judgment I owe all possible respect and deference' (i, p. vii). Reeve's work was thus already, so it is claimed, in a form in which it could be 'shewn' to her here anonymous friends and thus become itself the subject of conversation. She slightly later gives an account of her exchanges with 'a learned writer, whose friendship does me honour' (i, p. xii).[19] This miniature exchange on quite a particular question, albeit one of some significance to the argument that Reeve will go on to make (namely, 'why the fictions of the Ægyptians and Arabians, of the Greeks and Romans, were not entitled to the appellations of Romances, as well as those of the middle ages, to which it was generally appropriated?' (i, p. xii)), is an important foretaste of Reeve's manner of proceeding in the dialogue itself. Notably, Reeve's correspondent, she records, responds to her question with a question: 'What did [she] know of the Romances of those countries?—Had [she] ever seen an Ægyptian Romance?' (i, pp. xii–xiii). And it is in response to this (slightly testy) enquiry that Reeve furnishes a text, which, revealingly, both is and is not her own: that is, *The History of Charoba Queen of Ægypt*, which will ultimately appear as an appendix to the *Progress*. Her correspondent's expression of mild bemusement (which Reeve quotes directly)—' "I return your Ægyptian story with thanks; whence you took it, or how far it is your own I know not" '—is apt, and does not admit of straightforward resolution. The text is Reeve's, for it is she who 'compiled and methodised' it; and yet it is not hers because '[i]t is extracted from a book called—', as she tells us, with fulsome display of scholarly scruple, '*The History of Ancient Ægypt, according to the Traditions of the Arabians.—Written in Arabic,*

---

[17] On the novel and theatre see, e.g., Mary Poovey, 'Creative Criticism: Adaptation, Performative Writing, and the Problem of Objectivity', *Narrative*, 8 (2000), 109–33 (113, 131 n. 22), and J. Paul Hunter, 'The World as Stage and Closet', in Shirley Strum Kenny (ed.), *British Theatre and the Other Arts, 1660–1800* (Washington: Folger Shakespeare Library, 1984), 271–86.

[18] [Clara Reeve], *The Progress of Romance, through Times, Countries, and Manners; with Remarks on the Good and Bad Effects of It, on Them Respectively; In a Course of Evening Conversations*, 2 vols (Colchester: printed for the Author, 1785). Further references are given after quotations in the text.

[19] The 'learned writer' was John Walker, Reeve's long-time correspondent, whose *Historical Memoirs of the Irish Bards* (London: printed for T. Payne and son, and G.G.S. and J. Robinson, 1786) attempted to furnish a comprehensive history for Irish poetry and song from their earliest records; like Reeve's *Progress*, which concludes with *The History of Charoba*, a short fiction adapted from a French version of an Arabic tale, Walker's *Historical Memoirs* concludes with instances of Irish song illustrative of his preceding discussion.

by the Reverend Doctor Murtadi, the Son of Gapiphus, the Son of Chatem, the Son of Molsem the Macdesian.—Translated into French by M. Vattier, Arabic Professor to Louis 14th King of France'. The question of how far anything is anyone's own is put into sharp relief by Doctor Murtadi's genealogy (all the way back to his Macdesian great-grandfather); by the fact that even the King of France is only one of fourteen; by the fact of translation; and by the mediation of the history of the ancient Egyptians by the 'Traditions of the Arabians'. Reeve's attempt to establish the critical credentials of the *Progress*, and hence of the theorization of the novel form as such, is undertaken through direct quotation from an esteemed correspondent and through the citation of an array of textual sources, to which, like the correspondence, Reeve has privileged access. This is an interplay of submission to an external authority in the person of the correspondent to which Reeve turns out to be equal, not least thanks to her own access to scholarly resources. Dialogue's relation to text is the means by which the novel's relation to criticism is articulated.

The reader, of course, does not know exactly what form Reeve's 'own work'— the work that she had shown her friends—had already taken. It is, in fact, frequently hinted throughout *The Progress of Romance* that there is much more to it than meets the eye—the reader's eye, that is, since Euphrasia's interlocutors do refer to the large number of papers she has brought along to their conversations: 'Artillery and fire-arms against the small sword, the tongue' (i, p. 5), objects Hortensius early on. Euphrasia's display of her papers serves to emphasize her erudition both to her interlocutors and to her readers, and it serves as well to remind us that the text we are reading could have taken a quite different form. The decision to render it in dialogue, then, is a decision that Euphrasia has taken, and thus it is her critical authority that the text—both the one we are reading and the one we are not—establishes.

The final, dialogical form of *The Progress of Romance* is the form in which it is cast, but not the form in which it originated. Reeve tells us in the preface that she was motivated to give the form of 'evening conversations' to her work thanks to what she says was its origin in just such conversations with friends as she has already referred to:

> While I was collecting materials for this work, I held many conversations with some ingenious friends upon the various subjects, which it offered to be investigated and explained. This circumstance naturally suggested to me the Idea of the dialogue form; in which opposite sentiments would admit of a more full and accurate examination, arguments and objections might be more clearly stated and discussed, than in a regular series of Essays, or even letters, not to mention, that the variety and contrast which naturally arise out of the Dialogue, might enliven a work of rather dry deduction, and render it more entertaining to the reader, and not the less useful or instructive.   (i, pp. vi–vii)

For all that the idea of the dialogue is 'naturally suggested' to Reeve, that it in turn 'naturally' gives rise to certain desirable features of the narrative, and, moreover, for all that the author claims she has learned from dialogue with friends who are more 'learned' and up-to-date with the relevant publications than she is, the selection of this form is nevertheless cast as a function of Reeve's authority over the text. Dialogue is at least as much a formal *setting* as it is the natural consequence of the origin of the work in conversation.

Of the fact that the dialogues have their real substance in the materials that their author, who has certain strong affinities with the character of Euphrasia, has gathered together, we are frequently reminded in the conversations themselves. As we have already seen, Euphrasia brings her papers along to her conversations with Hortensius (her gentleman antagonist) and Sophronia (the adjudicator), and it is Euphrasia who, early on, lets it be known that it is ultimately within her power to make their conversations public. Sophronia teases Hortensius with the prospect of what his gentlemen friends might say if they knew he talked to women:

SOPHRONIA What would your neighbour *Ergastus* say, if he should hear that you met weekly two women, to talk of Romances?

HORTENSIUS He would certainly indulge his splenetic humour at my expence [*sic*].

EUPHRASIA If you are afraid of him, it will be best to give over our meetings, for I am meditating to tell the subject of them to all the world.

HORTENSIUS That is indeed enough to alarm one. I find I must take care of what I say before you.

EUPHRASIA Take courage my friend.—I promise you never to make our conversation public, without your consent and approbation. (ii. 27)[20]

Since we are reading these conversations, we must infer that Hortensius has given his blessing to their publication—as, at the conclusion of the twelfth and final evening, he does, albeit with an important caveat: 'Why, if you will do it [i.e., offer "this work of ours" to the public] in your own name I have no objection,—but I should not choose that mine should appear in print' (ii. 98). The caveat is important, because it suggests that one solution to Hortensius' desire not to appear in 'this work of ours' would be for Euphrasia to take sole possession of it and not present it as a dialogue. That is not what she chooses to do. She opts for a third solution, not imagined by Hortensius, and presents it as a dialogue, thus

---

[20] For a helpful account of the gender politics of Reeve's *Progress*, see Jacqueline Pearson, *Women Reading in Britain, 1750–1835: A Dangerous Reaction* (Cambridge: Cambridge University Press, 1999), 199–200.

paradoxically exerting her control over the work, despite its apparently collaborative genesis and, even, its multivocal presentation.

As in Reeve's *Progress*, the central speaker of Dorothea Veit Schlegel's 'Conversation on the Most Recent Novels by French Women', published in 1803 in the first edition of the German Romantic journal *Europa*, has recourse to (lengthy) quotation from an unnamed textual source. Unlike Reeve's work, which addresses the history of romance and the emergence of the novel from it, Schlegel's dialogue concerns a single novel, Madame de Staël's *Delphine*, which had been published the year before in 1802. Constanze forcefully objects to *Delphine* on moral grounds, which draws an equally appalled response from Adelheid, who thinks it morally irreproachable, while Felizia insists there is merit in both Constanze's and Adelheid's positions and offers a number of philosophical reflections of her own on the novel as form. Albert, the one male participant in the conversation, while he may be credited with instigating the conversation in the first place, is marginal, although he does stir himself to demand quite insistently that Felizia decide which of Constanze or Adelheid is in fact right.[21] It is perhaps worth remarking here that, with the possible exception of Albert, it is not too hard to discern the characteristics of the different persons in Veit Schlegel's dialogue from their names: they are happy (Felizia), constant (Constanze), and noble (Adelheid). (Something similar may be said of Reeve's dialogue too, of course.)

Felizia does make a decisive intervention in the exchange of divergent views on De Staël's novel, and she does so through recourse to 'a passage from a manuscript [...] which contains some ideas relevant here'. The passage Felizia reads from the manuscript advances the crucial argument that the moral heroism and lofty idealism depicted in earlier poetic compositions has been replaced in 'contemporary life' with the novel's focus on more mundane and distinctly unheroic virtues. Felizia is thus in a position to claim that 'every virtue, every talent, every quality [*Eigenschaft*] of spirit and of character' (p. 100) is valorized in the novel. The dialogue's decisive argument is not, then, set forth directly by its (albeit reluctant) adjudicator, but rather indirectly, in the pages of a manuscript from which she is presented as reading. That the manuscript is anonymous; that it is, indeed, a manuscript and not a published text; and that, moreover, Felizia is in a position to 'share' it with her companions: all of these circumstances serve to indicate her standing as a properly informed critical authority (p. 98; and note that Felizia's learning is already intimated earlier when Albert is described perusing 'all the books that lay on the shelf and on the table' at her house (p. 89)). Rightly keen to

[21] 'D.' [Dorothea Veit Schlegel], 'Gespräch über die neuesten Romane der Französinnen', *Europa*, 1 (1803), 88–106, and see, e.g., pp. 89–96 for the dispute between Contanze and Adelheid and p. 96 for Albert's exhortation to Felizia to adjudicate between them and give her own view. Further references are given after quotations in the text. There is an English translation by Simon Richter of an excerpt from this text in Folger Collective on Early Women Critics (ed.), *Women Critics 1660–1820: An Anthology* (Bloomington: Indiana University Press, 1995), 339–42.

stress the construction of, in particular, Felizia's critical authority, the editors who introduce the translation of an excerpt from the 'Gespräch' in the anthology *Women Critics 1660–1820* claim that, '[a]lthough Felizia does eventually evoke the authority of print, the anonymity of her source also contributes to the authorization of the women as expert critics'.[22] While their second point is valid (and valuable), their first relies on a misidentification of 'manuscript [*Manuscripte*]' (p. 98) as 'print', with the consequence that Felizia's scholarly and critical authority is, in fact, underplayed. Felizia has authority as a scholar because her learning extends even to texts that have not (yet) been printed; she has authority as a critic because one reason she gained access to this text in the first place may well have been in order for her to give her judgement on it.

Her position of authority in the dialogue notwithstanding, Albert's attempt to extract Felizia's judgement on the quarrel between the moralist Constanze and sentimentalist Adelheid is initially rebuffed. The dialogue as a whole concludes, however, with the announcement of the end of the conversation and a speculation on what conclusions the reader may be able to draw. Who issues this announcement and ventures this speculation is not immediately clear, although the 'Gespräch' as a whole is signed 'D.', Veit Schlegel's own initial, at its conclusion. D. leaves the options open for the reader—that is, whether to add her or his judgement to those expressed in the dialogue or to form a composite judgement out of those encountered there—while herself adopting an Olympian attitude above the fray of contested opinions and casting herself as the reader of another text, namely, De Staël's *Delphine*, which had been the focus of the dialogue all along:

And with that the conversation ended.

————————

You, beloved, now have three judgements instead of one; perhaps, my friend, yours is yet a fourth, or is formed out of those three; I, however, will now be able to read *Delphine* with every wished-for impartiality.

D.

(p. 106)

Impartiality is precisely what the person of Felizia had sought to preserve in the dialogue in the face of Albert's insistence that she abandon it in order to be able to decide between the positions represented by Constanze and Adelheid. D.'s sign-off here reminds the 'friend' (explicitly figured as female: *Freundin*) of the purpose of the dialogue in facilitating an unencumbered reading of Mme de Staël's novel, while it also casts the practice of judgement as the adjudication of always

---

[22] Folger Collective on Early Women Critics, *Women Critics*, 339–40.

already competing opinions and the formation of a further opinion in relation to them. Impartiality does not entail mere ignorance of or disregard for the partialities of others but is rather the culmination of the mediation of opinions and the discursive formation of judgement out of them.

*

We do not know for sure who the friend addressed by 'D.' at the conclusion of Veit Schlegel's 'Gespräch' was. Simply to assume that it must have been someone in particular would in turn rest on a sexist assumption that an address to a friend gendered female (*meine Freundin*) must be an address to a specific friend, whereas one to a friend gendered male (*mein Freund*) may invoke the universal and time-less reader as such. The specificity or non-specificity, reality or unreality of D.'s friend is left, at the conclusion of the dialogue, crucially undecided. It is me, 'dear reader', who is always also not me but every other reader as well, and it is not me in a more radical sense still because it may be a single person, rather than every person in a group (readers) to which I belong. Dialogues frequently seem to invite the identification of one of their persons with the author of the dialogue—Plato with Socrates, for instance, Wilde with Gilbert in 'The Critic as Artist' or with Vivian in 'The Decay of Lying: An Observation: A Dialogue' (1891), Jerome McGann with the various bearers of anagrammatical versions of his own name in his dialogues (to which I turn below)—yet such identifications, even where they seem uncontroversial, soon bring numerous complexities in their own train. Does Plato make himself a mouthpiece for his venerated teacher or is Socrates a projection of Plato? If Wilde is so readily discernible as Gilbert and Vivian, are they really involved in dialogues at all? Which scrambling of 'Jerome McGann' represents the real Jerome McGann or is he really so radically undecided? I will try to answer some of these questions in what follows, but the point that I want to stress here is that the conclusion to Veit Schlegel's 'Gespräch' draws the identity, not of the participants of the dialogue, but of *the reader* into these questions. Am I the 'friend', the 'beloved'? If I am, could someone else be as well? Will the judgement that 'someone else' adds to the three we have been given be the same as mine or will the one she or he forms from those three judgements take the same shape as mine? Is the proliferation of judgement prompted by dialogue poten-tially infinite, therefore? The dialogue into which the reader is drawn is an imaginary and silent dialogue with other readers (who are real but also, in this respect, imagined) as well.

Writing over eighty years after Veit Schlegel, and hence after significant devel-opments in the theorization and criticism of the novel, as well as in the practice of the dialogue form, Vernon Lee (the pseudonym of Violet Paget) offered the fol-lowing account, worth quoting at length, of the 'friend' who gives his name to her *Baldwin*:

It would grieve me that any reader should question the real existence of my friend Baldwin; yet I confess also that I should be very sorry were any one to believe too implicitly therein. There is, in a hitherto unspecified part of this world, a borderland between fact and fancy; and in this borderland my friend has a very actual habitation. I dread misapprehension, and crave permission for a few words on this point. Ask yourself, my patient or impatient reader, how much you actually know of your own nearest and dearest; nay, of the nearest and dearest of all—of yourself. The question is one over which a judicious person might reasonably go mad, or die, without coming nearer to a complete solution. But this much of certainty would be acquired by the way, that the something to which we give the name of our friends is a creature somehow mysteriously born of ourselves and of them; a creature which exists not really in the exterior and concrete world, but in our mind, or, if you prefer, in that particular borderland of fact and fancy. I do not care to commit myself to stating on which side, nearer or farther, of that strip of borderland, lies the exact dwelling-place of the chief speaker in the following Dialogues. To any over-inquisitive person I would make this answer: Tell me precisely how much of yourself is real or imaginary; and you shall have the corresponding information respecting my friend Baldwin.[23]

Lee ends this passage by issuing an invitation to dialogue she knows will not be taken up in reality, though it may be in imagination—assuming, that is, that the reader knows the proportions of reality and imagination in their own constitution, which, as we saw with the conclusion to Veit Schlegel's 'Conversation', is hard for any reader to say. It is not simply the case that, as an author of dialogue, she does not 'care to commit [herself] to stating on which side' of a given argument she may come down; it is that there is a region between different sides of arguments to which dialogue itself gives access. Lee goes on to remark that he is a 'negative being, in many respects, my friend Baldwin, as you have already been told; and negative perhaps all the more that, as you see, there is much which is positive in his nature' (p. 13) As if prompted—and thus as if anticipating the dialogue form itself—she asks rhetorically 'My own relations towards him?' (p. 13), and the answer manages to be at once both decided and equivocal: 'Baldwin and I are distinct; he does not understand me quite; he stands outside me; he is not I' (p. 14).

Catherine Maxwell has usefully emphasized the direction given to Lee's dialogues by 'mentor figures'—especially the titular Baldwin and Althea of her two collections of dialogues—and the evocative settings, often described in some detail, in which they take place.[24] As Maxwell notes, in Lee's hands the dialogue

---

[23] Vernon Lee, *Baldwin: Being Dialogues on Views and Aspirations* (London: T. Fisher Unwin, 1886), 3–4. Further references are given after quotations in the text.

[24] Maxwell, 'Vernon Lee's Handling of Words', in Michael D. Hurley and Marcus Waithe (eds), *Thinking through Style: Non-Fiction Prose of the Long Nineteenth Century* (Oxford: Oxford University Press, 2018), 282–94 (286). See also Vernon Lee, *Althea: Dialogues on Aspirations and Duties* (London: John Lane, [1894]).

form allows for the reader to sympathize with a range of views, without necessarily arriving at a settled conclusion. The settings crucially 'remind us,' as Maxwell puts it, 'that our intellectual conversations do not take place in a vacuum but in particular places at particular moments in time and are affected by mood, emotion, and atmosphere, which add pattern and colour to our meditations'.[25] Some of these features of Lee's dialogues are especially pertinent to her 'On Novels', one of the dialogues of *Baldwin*, which addresses an abiding concern of Lee's with the moral duties (or lack thereof) of artworks—a topic that she had already explored in 'A Dialogue on Poetic Morality' between the characters of Cyril and Baldwin in *Belcaro* and that thus forms the blueprint for the more extensive experiments with the form in *Baldwin* and *Althea*.[26] Though Baldwin in 'On Novels' is most readily identified as one of what Maxwell calls Lee's 'mentor figures', it may not in fact be Baldwin with whom the reader feels a particular affinity at any given moment. The figure of Dorothy Orme seems a rather likelier candidate to fulfil that role, not least because throughout crucial phases of the dialogue it is she who, Lee tells us, 'had been listening attentively, and her face wore an expression of vague pain and perplexity'. Dorothy likewise struggles on occasion to make herself understood, at least by the rather more firmly opinionated and vociferous participants in the dialogue, but she is finally reassured by Baldwin's defence of the novel's capacity to balance the shrewd and tolerant, the generous and the austere. The dialogue concludes with the following exchange, which exemplifies Maxwell's point about the pertinence of particular locations to intellectual exchange:

'I don't know if it is you or the weather, but I feel less dismal about life, Baldwin,' said Dorothy.
   'It is the weather,' answered Mrs. Blake.
   The mist had gradually thinned, the luminous space about them had widened, the greyish-black vapour, gradually turning white, was rising into clouds, leaving the tree-tops distinct and green against a rift of moist, bright sky.   (p. 245)

' "It is the weather." ' But weather, perhaps especially on the moors above Haworth where this dialogue is set, is never just weather. This weather, with its dissipating vapours and the freshly distinct scene it reveals, is emblematic of the less dismal conclusion to which Baldwin's argument has brought Dorothy. One might also discern in the 'distinct' shapes of the treetops standing out 'against' a luminous, clarifying background a metaphor for the clarity of concluded debate and the settled position at which we may have arrived, but also, perhaps, a metaphor for the textual condition itself, the black marks against a contrasting background,

---

[25] Maxwell, 286.
[26] Maxwell, 284–7, where she emphasizes the dialogic character of the essays in *Belcaro* generally. See Vernon Lee, *Belcaro: Being Essays on Sundry Æsthetical Questions* (London: Satchell, [1891]), 230–74.

the means by which we, the readers, now have the dialogue before us. As text, dialogue has always already finished, and thus it is here at the finish that speech, cast as the negotiation of rugged terrain in misty weather, resolves into the clear vision of text. Yet the very fact that this interpretation of these closing lines risks being convicted as tendentious and wilful—and is admittedly speculative and tentative—itself intimates that the resolution of the back and forth, the cut and thrust, of dialogue into written form does not fix interpretations, though it surely provokes more of them.

*

In the episode of Lord Modish's experiment with the farmer's daughter, in Kant's 'young poet' who refuses to be swayed by popular opinion, and in Reeve, Schlegel, and Veit Schlegel, not to mention the Platonic precedent of the *Phaedrus*, we have seen how generational, social, and gender relations have played a significant role, not only in the course of the dialogues themselves, but in the formation of the position of the reader as well. While in concealing himself, the landed, titled Modish takes the part of the reader—who is likewise invisible to the farmer's daughter and is also the implied audience of Freeman's discussion with her—the reader in the dialogues we have been examining is not always recruited to the side of power and higher status. The reader takes the part of Kant's 'young poet' and of the judge who spurns the lessons that reading Aristotle, Batteux, and Lessing are supposed to yield, for example; the reader is explicitly addressed as female by Veit Schlegel and perhaps implicitly by Reeve. While the participants of these dialogues are given fictional names, their potential identity with real people, which is sometimes hinted at in prefatory or concluding paratexts, has an affinity with the reader's own position as both a real and an imagined personage. Lee, as we have seen, thus sites the reader along with Baldwin, the protagonist of her dialogues, in a region between imagination and reality. The fact that the reader is a reader and not a participant in the dialogue similarly finds its echo in the recourse many of the dialogues have to text and, specifically, to texts that are the special property of particular participants within the dialogue, who are thus both surrogates or proxies for the reader, but who are also the originators or orchestrators of the introduction of text into spoken discourse.

A number of the considerations that have been significant to our discussion of dialogues so far remain significant to the dialogues to which I wish to turn now. The relations between participants in the dialogues we have been examining are sociable relations among a group, and the reader, as we have seen, is drawn into those relations in a variety of ways. The relations upon which Wilde's 'The Decay of Lying' and, still more so, the dialogic fragments of Proust's *Contre Sainte-Beuve* are predicated are, however, of a markedly different kind. Like Plato's *Phaedrus*, Wilde's dialogues are not discussions among a group but rather between just two participants, one of whom advances an argument to which the other listens and which he occasionally questions. Proust's dialogical partner is his mother, the senior partner in the familial relationship, but at the same time essentially the respondent in the dialogue. These intimate, rather than more broadly convivial and sociable, relations are the context for the discussion of texts of different kinds from those discussed in earlier dialogues. Whereas Euphrasia in Reeve's *Progress*, various of the participants in Schlegel's *Dialogue*, and Felizia in Veit Schlegel's 'Conversation' read out from or otherwise refer to manuscripts, the protagonists of Wilde's 'The Decay of Lying' and Proust's *Contre Sainte-Beuve* have recourse to what are specified as articles in varying stages of preparation for publication. Now, in one sense, the distinction between manuscript and article may appear trivial. Euphrasia, certainly, and perhaps Felizia as well, produce texts that are planned for publication, and thus their discussion among friends is one important phase, we may say, of the drafting process. Vivian, in 'The Decay of Lying', and the son in the dialogic fragments of *Contre Sainte-Beuve*, are likewise working on something that they intend for publication. But the explicit identification of the texts in 'The Decay of Lying' and in *Contre Sainte-Beuve* as *articles*, rather than as *manuscripts*, more clearly evokes a professionalized critical field, complete with a system of relatively specialized publication. Moreover, in the earlier dialogues, texts are more or less freely circulated, discussed, and contested among a group that in many ways stands in for a broader public, whereas Vivian's show of wanting to be left alone to correct his proofs and his concession to reading out his article so long as Cyril does not interrupt too much, and the son's concealment of his article in a drawer in his bedroom only partially to share it with his mother, suggest instead a much deeper breach between a personal, intimate zone, on the one hand, and a professionalized, public sphere, on the other—the latter, a sphere about which both writers express principled misgivings in the articles that they share in only a limited way.

When Vivian commands Cyril to 'leave me to correct my proofs', he is both claiming the article as his own, private work and flaunting the fact that he has an article on the cusp of publication, thus reverse-psychologically inviting further enquiry about it. Cyril does not disappoint, and Vivian proceeds to read from the article—albeit on the important condition that Cyril will 'promise not to interrupt too often' (p. 74). In addition to the fact that the article is still subject to correction, Vivian does not simply proceed to read out all of 'The Decay of Lying: A Protest', but rather deploys certain sections of it in response to Cyril's questions. He even condescends to read sections out of the sequence in which they appear in his putative text, as when Cyril asks 'But what do you say about the return to Life and Nature?' and Vivian responds by reading the passage of his article addressing that topic, notwithstanding the fact that it 'comes later on in the article'. At one point in Schlegel's *Dialogue on Poetry*, the character Lothario declares that 'I wish I had put my thoughts about [the Elusinian mysteries] on paper, so that I could present them to you in the order and detail befitting the dignity and importance of the subject' (p. 91); Vivian, we are asked to believe, has put his thoughts down on paper, but he is willing to forgo the dignity and importance thus lent to them in order to respond to Cyril's enquiries in the order in which they come. What this betokens is the flexibility of Vivian's argument and its responsiveness to his interlocutor, which is counterposed to the fixed sequencing of its written form. The sense that the article anticipates the course of the dialogue may be taken to suggest that life really does imitate (the) art(icle).

Vivian accommodates Cyril's questions by distorting the ordering of his article, and, since this is also the only version of the article that we, the readers, have, we have it in an order that departs from that of the putatively underlying text. The case of Proust's *Contre Sainte-Beuve* is comparable but also different in some notable respects. As a matter of fact, and as John Sturrock attests in the introduction to his translation, *Contre Sainte-Beuve* itself emerged only gradually, and thanks to the labours of a number of editors, from the generic welter of Proust's own manuscripts.[27] Proust himself described his plans to write on Sainte-Beuve as tending in both traditional and experimental directions. Writing to his friend Georges de Lauris, for instance, he described how he would write a traditional article on Sainte-Beuve ('the Taine sort of essay, if less good', referring to Hippolyte Taine), but also 'the account of a morning and Mama coming to my bedside and my telling her about the article on Sainte-Beuve I wanted to do, which I would then develop'.[28] One of the draft prefaces to that envisaged text traces it to the discussion with the putative author's mother of another, ur-text:

> Mother left me, but my mind went back to my article and all of a sudden I had an idea for an impending *Contre Sainte-Beuve*. Recently, I had been rereading him, I had taken unusually for me numbers of short notes which I had there in a drawer, and I had important things to say about him. I began to construct the article in my head. New ideas came to me all the time. Not half an hour had passed, and the entire article had been constructed in my head. I wanted very much to ask Mother what she thought of it. I called, no sound in reply. I called again, I heard stealthy footsteps, a hesitation at my door, which creaked.
>
> 'Mother.'
>
> 'Did you in fact call me, darling?'
>
> 'Yes.' (*Against*, 8)

---

[27] John Sturrock, 'Introduction', in Marcel Proust, '*Against Sainte-Beuve*' *and Other Essays*, trans. Sturrock (London: Penguin 1988), pp. vii–xxix; *Against Sainte-Beuve* itself is on pp. 3–102. Further references are given to Sturrock's translation (abbreviated as *Against*) after quotations in the text; references to the French text (abbreviated as *Contre*) are to *Contre Sainte-Beuve*, ed. Pierre Clarac and Yves Sandre, Bibliothèque de la Pléiade (Paris: Gallimard, 1971).

[28] Marcel Proust, Letter XLIII (1908), in Proust, *Letters to a Friend*, trans. Alexander and Elizabeth Henderson (London: Falcon Press, 1949), 117. Sturrock also refers to this letter (see 'Introduction', in *Against*, p. xiii).

The dialogue between child and mother gets off to a hesitant, though highly literary, start: the mother goes on to quote from Racine's *Esther* in order to express her anxiety that she had in fact returned unbidden, before turning to Molière's *Amphitryon* in order to gloss her son's refusal of her offer to order the servant to bring a light, and then finally to the same writer's *Les Précieuses ridicules* to protest her own far-from-evident incompetence as a judge in matters of literature (*Against*, 8–9). So much literary badinage and false modesty this may be, but the thickly intertextual character of these opening exchanges—Racine, two plays by Molière, as well as a teasing reference to Madame de Scudéry's *Artamène ou le Grand Cyrus* and, indeed, the information that the son has already made his mother read essays by the critics Hippolyte Taine and Paul Bourget—is in keeping with the fact that this conversation between mother and son is to be a discussion of a text—namely, the narrator's rapidly conceived 'article' and the 'impending *Contre Sainte-Beuve*' that is to develop from it. That Proust at least conceived of *Contre Sainte-Beuve* as a dialogue—and there remain traces of this conception at several points throughout the book—becomes especially significant when considered against the background of Sainte-Beuve's own preferred critical form.[29] It is by no means inconsequential that Sainte-Beuve's reputation was founded on the series of *Causeries du Lundi—Monday Conversations* or *Monday Chats*—which from 1849 and for most of the next two decades he published chiefly (though by no means exclusively) in *Le Constitutionnel*.[30] Proust had earlier adopted pastiche as a form of criticism, assuming the persona of 'Gustave Flaubert', for instance, to write an extract from a putative novel, *L'Affaire Lemoine*, before in turn pastiching 'Sainte-Beuve' in a critique of that novel 'dans son feuilleton du *Constitutionnel*' (Proust's pastiche in fact appeared in the literary supplement to *Le Figaro* on 14 March 1908).[31] Proust's resort to dialogue in order to oppose Sainte-Beuve likewise appears to pastiche the latter's favoured critical form. As Proust argues, the popularly abbreviated title of these critical interventions—simply *Lundis*—should furthermore remind us 'that they were the hectic and delightful labour of a single week, his glorious Monday morning reveille-call' (*Against*, 17). Proust deplores both what he sees as conspicuous

---

[29] Traces of dialogue in *Against*, 34 and 56 are remarked by Sturrock ('Introduction', p. xiv), but there is perhaps another in connection with a discussion of Gérard de Nerval's *Sylvie*: 'This story, remember, which you call a naïve painting, is the dream of a dream' (p. 28).

[30] The word 'causerie' has been adopted in English, retaining the sense that it is quickly and regularly produced. See, e.g., Arnold Bennett, *The Truth about an Author*, 2nd edn (New York: George H. Doran, 1911), 46. For Anglophone versions of the form, see Andrew Lang, 'At the Sign of the Ship', *Longman's Magazine* (1886–1905), and A. R. Orage, 'Bookish Causerie', for the *Labour Leader* (1895–7). John Gross (*The Rise and Fall of the Man of Letters: English Literary Life since 1800* (Harmondsworth: Penguin, 1973; first pub. 1969) complains of the 'maundering velvet-jacketed causerie' in the period after Bagehot (p. 90) and notes that by the end of the 1870s 'the lay sermon was giving way to the causerie' (p. 148).

[31] See *Pastiches*, in *Contre*, 5–59 (12–21), and the useful commentary on Proust's critical practice of pastiche, esp. 688–9.

production (so to speak) and, more significantly, Sainte-Beuve's view of literature as it is implied by the adoption of the causerie. Sainte-Beuve, Proust alleges, 'saw all of literature as a sort of *Lundis* [...] which have had to be written in their own time heedful of the opinion of the good judges, in order to please and not relying too much on posterity' (*Against*, 19). Sainte-Beuve views literature 'on the same plane as conversation' (p. 16), of which, Proust claims, the journalistic form of the causerie is just one instance. 'It is,' Proust states, 'by the silences of the imagined approval of this reader or that that the journalist weighs his words and balances them against his ideas. Thus his work is written with the unconscious collaboration of others and is less personal' (p. 19).

The silence that betokens, for Sainte-Beuve, the imagined approbation of 'this or that' reader is far removed from the silence out of which, for Proust, literature emerges. Whereas the silence of Sainte-Beuve's reader is that of a mere recipient of the pronouncements of a critical authority who has pre-prepared those pronouncements for ready acceptation, the silence of the writer is, for Proust, the condition for the self's confrontation of the self out of which literature emerges. 'He drew no dividing line between the occupation of writing, in which, in solitude and suppressing those words which belong as much to others as ourselves, and with which, even when alone, we judge things without being ourselves, we come face to face once more with our selves, and seek to hear and to render the true sound of our hearts – and conversation!' (*Against*, 15).

We may also bring the difference between the role of silence in Sainte-Beuve and in Proust into focus if we return to the question of the text that forms the basis for dialogue in *Contre Sainte-Beuve*—namely, the 'article' on which 'the impending *Contre Sainte-Beuve*' is to be based. Admittedly, it happens that there is no way of knowing if Proust had formulated an article which then serves as the basis for his dialogue with his mother—yet that lack of knowledge is, in fact, significant. The chief participant in Proust's dialogue, that is, may simply be voicing views already given textual articulation, may be partially doing so, or may not be doing so at all. The invisibility to the reader of that supposed text is, therefore, crucial, as is the fact that Proust's interlocutor is not Monsieur This or Madame That upon whose approval Sainte-Beuve allegedly hung, but rather his mother, the most intimate (for Proust) interlocutor conceivable. The refuge and privacy of Proust's bedroom, into which even his mother only tentatively intrudes, contrasts sharply with the 'many Parisian bedrooms' (*Against*, 17) to which *Le Constitutionnel* is delivered. Those Parisian bedrooms ought to be the most intimate sanctuaries of their inhabitants, but they become the thoroughfares through which the traffic of the world passes, the venues if not for Sainte-Beuve's table talk, then for his bedside-table talk. It is central to Proust's case against Sainte-Beuve that Sainte-Beuve's causeries are by no means the product of the *moi profond*, by no means composed prior to their formation by the expectations of the fashionable chatter of the world. There is nothing in them that has not already been run through the minds of their readers; there is nothing in them that has truly emerged from the mind of their author. The traces of dialogue in *Contre Sainte-Beuve*, the awkward, intimate revelation of the article on which it is based, the halting discussion that surrounds it, is testament, in contrast, to the intricacies of the relations between writers and readers—and writers who are readers and readers who are writers—out of which genuine literary response, for Proust, emerges.

*

Proust's wildly tendentious account of Sainte-Beuve answers back to the elder, established critic, insubordinately offering a riposte to what had (Proust alleged) been a one-way discourse. For much of the ensuing century, in a dramatic fall from the eminence he had occupied in both nineteenth-century France and England, Sainte-Beuve featured in critical discourse as little more than Proust's foil. Subsequent scholarship has sought somewhat to rehabilitate him. Marc Fumaroli, for instance, notes that Sainte-Beuve and Proust operate with diametrically opposed conceptions of conversation arising, however, from their different historical moments. Where Sainte-Beuve, Fumaroli argues, in fact operated with a conception of conversation as a literary form developed through regular exchange with the dead—in essence, a conception of conversation as a dialogue with the dead—by the time Proust came to write, the possibility of such time-spanning, literarily informed conversation seemed (to Proust at least) to have receded, conversation having thus been debased by a worldly bourgeoisie, reduced to the merely transient and mundane.[32]

The potential for a dialogue with the dead—and indeed, the potential for dialogue in general—has been reaffirmed in recent years, albeit without necessarily offering a more optimistic view of the bourgeois subject, by a number of critics who have wished to develop historical modes for the understanding of literary texts. Michael Macovski pointed in 1997 to a 'recent resurgence and restructuring of dialogic criticism, a form that seeks to represent the multiplicity of current criticism in terms of discrete voices within a single text'. Macovski viewed this renewal of interest in the dialogue form as no less than 'the revitalization of a critical mode that has remained effectively dormant since the classical era'.[33]

[32] Marc Fumaroli, *Littérature et conversation: La Querelle Sainte-Beuve–Proust* (London: University of London Press, 1991), 18–19.

[33] Michael Macovski, 'Introduction: Textual Voices, Vocative Texts: Dialogue, Linguistics, and Critical Discourse', in Macovski (ed.), *Dialogue and Critical Discourse: Language, Culture, Critical Theory* (Oxford: Oxford University Press, 1997), 3–26 (12). Macovski's examples are: Geoffrey H. Hartman, 'The Interpreter: A Self-Analysis', in *The Fate of Reading and Other Essays* (Chicago: University of Chicago Press, 1975), 3–19; Michel Foucault, *The Archaeology of Knowledge* (1969), trans. A. M. Sheridan Smith (Abingdon: Routledge, 2002), 219–32; Stephen Greenblatt, *Renaissance Self-Fashioning: From More to Shakespeare* (Chicago: University of Chicago Press, 1980), 255–7 ('Epilogue'); and Alan Liu, *Wordsworth: The Sense of History* (Stanford: Stanford University Press, 1989), 500–2 ('Epilogue'). I discuss Greenblatt and Liu below.

As will already be clear from this chapter, the historical claim here does not stand up to scrutiny, but Macovski is nevertheless justified in pointing to renewed interest in the dialogue as critical form, suggesting (albeit somewhat mutedly) that it has an affinity with a commitment to plurality conducive to late-twentieth-century critical priorities.

Some contributors to Macovki's volume were keen to polemicize more vigorously for a quite generalized dialogical approach to the practice of literary criticism as such. Justifying what he describes as a 'symposium' in the specific sense of 'an *account* of previous utterances by a narrator', Don H. Bialostosky, for example, attempts to draw a distinction between scholarly orthodoxy, which requires that hats are tipped in the direction of critical predecessors, and the more dynamic requirement of what he calls '[d]ialogics', according to which the criticism of others is actively appropriated and thus critics are made 'answerable to the cosmopolitan critical community that enables and challenges their readings'.[34] Criticism practised in this way, according to Bialostosky, thus does not fulfil not a conservative scholarly duty but instead pursues the 'radical enterprise of producing new intellectual property through active appropriation of others' words and ideas'.[35] It is a vision far removed from Proust's encounter of the self with itself in the silence of solitude, heedless of the words of the world, but Bialostosky's 'active appropriation' is equally removed from what Proust cast as the 'unconscious collaboration' (*Against*, 19) governing Sainte-Beuve's criticism and underwriting the tacit assumption of assent on the part of his silent readers.

If Bialostosky's criticism does not quite mount to dialogue as such, other critics espousing a position strikingly akin to a commitment to 'cosmopolitan critical community' have had recourse to dialogue proper. In particular, the New Historicism—at least conceivable as a 'radical enterprise' aiming to produce 'new intellectual property' made from the words, ideas, and materials of others whose otherness, moreover, is a distinct critical concern for it—has shown a particular affinity for the dialogue form. In his penetrating early analysis of the New Historicism, Alan Liu emphasized how the movement 'complicated any faith in homogeneous culture with its instinct for fracture', with the result that 'there can be no secure over-Subject able to center the study of human subjects'. 'The tautology of universal explanation', Liu further remarks, 'must instead be made to branch into an endless quest for definition by alterity ("man is class-, state-, gender-, or ideological-struggle against other men")'.[36] Such an approach is opposed to the

---

[34] Don H. Bialostosky, 'Dialogics of the Lyric: A Symposium on Wordsworth's "Westminster Bridge" and "Beauteous Evening"', in Macovski (ed.), *Dialogue and Critical Discourse*, 101–36 (103, 127).

[35] Bialostosky, 'Dialogics of the Lyric', 127.

[36] Alan Liu, 'The Power of Formalism: The New Historicism', *English Literary History*, 56 (1989), 721–71 (732). On historicism (not necessarily New Historicism) and dialogue, see also A. Leigh DeNeef, 'Of Dialogues and Historicisms', *South Atlantic Quarterly*, 88 (1987), 497–517 (esp. 512–13), and Paul Hamilton, *Historicism*, 2nd edn (London: Routledge, 2003), 74–85.

specifically Socratic dialogue—'a "discussion" always implicitly presided over by a philosopher-king'—that Liu casts as the 'home form' of New Criticism.[37] I turn briefly to Liu's own experiment with critical dialogue below, but Jerome McGann's career is the signal instance here. McGann's early study *Swinburne: An Experiment in Criticism* (1972) is a major contribution to the late-twentieth-century recuperation of Swinburne's reputation; it is also probably the most sustained literary-critical dialogue written since the eighteenth century. In a 2006 reflection on his thirty-plus-year relation with the dialogue form, McGann remarks that the dialogue 'seemed to me—and still seems—a useful method for investigating a subject when uncertainties and contradictions pervade your field of interest. The dialogue form allows you to expose and play out those uncertainties and contradictions.'[38] Since uncertainties and contradictions surely pervade pretty much any field of interest, this is, notwithstanding its relaxed, personal tone, a bold claim for the sweeping relevance of the dialogue form. I quoted in the Introduction McGann's characterization of the essay and monograph as the dominant forms of criticism since the Enlightenment, and he goes on in this brief reflection on an aspect of his own writing career to claim that dialogue 'also encourages one to seek out lines of thought that the traditional critical essay, with its commitment to argument and exposition, discourages'.[39] The distinction between 'lines of thought', on the one hand, and 'argument and exposition', on the other, is suggestive of possibilities for the articulation of what remains 'thought', with various routes and potentials for its development ('lines'), which are not immediately reducible, however, to argument or exposition.

Yet one way in which dialogue can develop lines of thought is (as Bialostosky's vision of a radically productive and cosmopolitan criticism suggests) by incorporating and juxtaposing the arguments and expositions of others. The dialogue of McGann's *Swinburne* is conducted not among fictionalized protagonists (though there is fun to be had in imagining who they might have been in a discussion of *this* poet in particular—Lesbia, Flagellus, Mistheos, perhaps?), but rather 'among a group of Swinburne's contemporary men and women of letters'.[40] McGann's account of 'the characters' gives very brief thumbnail biographies of them, indicating, crucially, their writings on Swinburne (for example, 'COULSON

---

[37] Liu, 'Power of Formalism', 741–2. Liu evinces the conversations between Robert Penn Warren and Cleanth Brooks to which are dedicated the first 124 pages of Lewis P. Simpson (ed.), *The Possibilities of Order: Cleanth Brooks and his Work* (Baton Rouge: Louisiana University Press, 1976).

[38] Jerome J. McGann, 'Author's Note on the Work' (July 2006) <https://writing.upenn.edu/pennsound/x/McGann.php> (accessed 15 February 2022). For an informative treatment of McGann's dialogic criticism, see Till Kinzel, 'Literary Criticism as Dialogue: From Jerome McGann's Dialogical Confrontation with Swinburne to Meta-Dialogue', in Kinzel and Jarmila Mildorf (eds), *Imaginary Dialogues in American Literature and Philosophy* (Heidelberg: Winter, 2014), 259–67.

[39] McGann, 'Author's Note'.

[40] Jerome J. McGann, *Swinburne: An Experiment in Criticism* (Chicago: University of Chicago Press, 1972), publisher's cover copy. Further references are given after quotations in the text.

KERNAHAN (1858–1943) corresponded with Swinburne and wrote, among other things, *Swinburne as I Knew Him* (1919)' (p. 4)). In many respects, unlike McGann's later dialogues in which he either exchanges views with other living critics or comically reforms himself into anagrammatic versions of 'Jerome McGann' like 'Georg Mannejc', *Swinburne* is a late revival of the dialogue of the dead, a Classical form itself already revived in the eighteenth century in Fénelon's *Dialogues des morts* (1700) and Lyttelton's *Dialogues of the Dead* (from 1760), and developed further in Walter Savage Landor's massive sequence of *Imaginary Conversations* throughout a significant span of the nineteenth century. There are other, isolated versions of the critical dialogue of the dead—the occasionally testy 'Conversation in Limbo' between W. B. Yeats and H. G. Wells that forms the epilogue to Graham Hough's *The Last Romantics* (1949) is an important instance—but it is McGann's *Swinburne* that most extendedly revives the form and to which it is most critically significant, given, not least, the sentence of critical death imposed on Swinburne from the 1930s on.[41] The task of McGann's discussion of Swinburne is to recover a poet and his critics more than usually confined to the past, but also, in keeping with the approach to the historical past that McGann would come to develop throughout his career, not only to reconstruct the exchanges of the past but to enter into them as well.[42]

The cover copy's reference to those of McGann's characters who 'practice the New Criticism' might, though, give us pause. How is it that any of this cast of characters, whose works on Swinburne were written between 1900 and 1922, could have practised the New Criticism? Moreover, W. G. Blaikie Murdoch, who in reality lived from 1880 till 1934, has no trouble quoting from an article of F. R. Leavis's published in the *TLS* barely a year before the publication of *Swinburne* itself or from a work of Gilles Deleuze's (he has catholic critical tastes) translated at the same time (pp. 169, 281–2); Kernahan's judgement that '*Love's Cross-Currents* is a masterpiece' is acknowledged to have been anticipated by 'others before me' (pp. 284–5), including George Meredith, Randolph Hughes, and Edmund Wilson, the latter two writing well after the historical Kernahan had died.[43] This is neither the result of careless anachronism, nor indeed of the dialogic mask having to slip in order to reveal the stakes of the discussion. Bialostosky has claimed that 'the continued productivity of dialogue depends on our discovering mutual bearings among person-ideas that have not yet engaged one another as well as on our reconstructing the mutual bearings of those that have'

---

[41] For information and a selection from Fénelon, Lyttleton, and others, see Frederick M. Keener, *English Dialogues of the Dead: A Critical History, An Anthology, and A Check List* (New York: Columbia University Press, 1973), published, incidentally, the year after McGann's *Swinburne*. See also *The Complete Works of Walter Savage Landor*, ed. T. Earle Welby, 16 vols (London: Methuen, 1929–36; repr. 1969), i–ix, and Graham Hough, *The Last Romantics* (London: Gerald Duckworth, 1949), 263–74.

[42] Cf. Dominick LaCapra, *Rethinking Intellectual History: Texts, Contexts, Language* (Ithaca, NY: Cornell University Press, 1983), 50.

[43] As also remarked by Kinzel, 262.

and hence that 'there is no systematic or historical limit to the voices that may find a place in a given dialogue';[44] or, as McGann himself has put it, '[s]ince [the persons'] opinions expressed in this book [namely, *Swinburne*] may occasionally seem unlike what we might have expected, the present dialogues perhaps go some way to prove that, when we have crossed the bar, many things will be changed, in the twinkling of an eye' (p. 4).

Kernahan's claim that '[t]he critic cannot wait upon the good sense of his reader, which will probably not be there. He must, like the poet his mentor, help to develop through his own work that good sense of what aesthetic response entails' (p. 13) is crucial to McGann's commitment in this book and elsewhere to the principle that 'knowing's for the living', and it appears that a corollary of this commitment is that knowing can be neither straightforwardly nor neutrally imparted, but must be experienced.[45] Describing and defending Swinburne's own 'prose essays', Kernahan asserts that

[a]ll great criticism is creative and has in it, to a greater or lesser degree, the qualities proper to poetry. Impressionistic criticism is not more creative than, say, Arnold's or Johnson's. The difference is that impressionistic prose makes its own creative duties one of its primary themes. Its rhetoric aims to convince us that experience is more important than ideas, and that its own prose form—a vehicle customarily associated with discursive and philosophic purposes—also has obligations to foster the symbolic and creative values which we ordinarily associate with poetry.   (p. 14)

To which George E. Woodberry ('(1855–1930), prolific American writer and critic, wrote *Swinburne* (New York, 1905)' (p. 4)), responds that the consequence of Kernahan's position is 'that the most perfect act of aesthetic criticism could only be another work of art' (p. 23). It is perhaps pertinent here that McGann acknowledges a (qualified) debt to Schlegel's *Dialogue on Poetry*. 'Everyone's view of poetry is true and good as far as that view itself is poetry,' declares Schlegel in prefacing his *Dialogue*, thus lending support to Kernahan's insistence on the necessity for 'great criticism' to be creative and, implicitly, to McGann's own insistence on the multiplicity of 'true and good' views of poetry.[46] 'But since one's poetry is limited,' Schlegel continues,

just because it is one's own, so one's view of poetry must of necessity be limited. The mind cannot bear this; no doubt because, without knowing it, it nevertheless

---

[44] Don H. Bialostosky, 'Dialogics as an Art of Discourse in Literary Criticism', *PMLA* 101 (1986), 788–97 (790).
[45] See Jerome J. McGann, 'Dialogue on Dialogue', in Juliana Spahr et al. (eds), *A Poetics of Criticism* (Buffalo: Leave Books, 1994), 59–77 (60).
[46] For a subtle account of McGann's debts to and differences from Schlegel, see Kinzel, 261.

does know that no man is merely man, but that at the same time he can and should be genuinely and truly all mankind. Therefore, man, in reaching out time and again beyond himself to seek and find the complement of his innermost being in the depths of another, is certain to return ever to himself. The play of communicating and approaching is the business and the force of life; absolute perfection exists only in death.   (p. 54)

Schlegel's concluding apothegm might be taken one of two ways. Either death is the gate to the perfection that cannot be achieved in mortal life, or (and this, it must be admitted, seems more likely to be Schlegel's meaning here) death is itself absolute perfection in the sense of completion, termination, finish. But the more striking interpretative conundrum in the above passage arises in the statement that 'in reaching out time and again beyond himself to seek and find the complement of his innermost being in the depths of another, [man] is certain to return ever to himself'. Does he return to himself because he is nourished and improved by what he finds in the depths of others or because he is perpetually disappointed by them? Again, one strongly suspects that Schlegel means the former—and, in fact, what we take his meaning to be in this case is retrospectively influenced by how we interpret his view of the 'perfection' that is achieved in death. If death brings greater, final enlightenment, then, perhaps by means of a strange intimation of the riches of immortality, the partial insights of our fellow mortals are disappointing by comparison; whereas, if death is just a terminus, the discursive traffic with our fellow mortals is continuously, if not necessarily endlessly, sustaining.

*

McGann has found the dialogue form recurrently sustaining for his critical project from *Swinburne: An Experiment in Criticism* to the discussion that concludes *Byron and Romanticism*, with the many comic self-reflections in between—reflections of the self like those in a fairground hall of mirrors, which have the potential to be no less enlightening for the fact that they are distorting. In the 'Author's Note' in which he reflects on his dialogic practice, McGann remarks that a ludic strain of comic interventions was especially critically productive when turned towards (or against) the authoring self, 'producing what Arnold disparaged as a "dialogue of the mind with itself." Arnold', McGann concludes, 'had a somewhat undeveloped sense of humor'.[47] The truth-moment of Arnold's stricture, however, and the fact that, while they may be revelations, the reflections in the hall of mirrors remain distortions nevertheless, lies in the recognition that dialogue can indeed be a radically contingent affair. 'Marxism, Romanticism, and Postmodernism: An American Case History', by 'Anne Mack' and 'Jay Rome', ends by reflecting on itself as a partial, incomplete text, thus in keeping with the

---

[47] McGann, 'Author's Note'.

consciousness of dialogue's textual condition that we have encountered in a remarkable number of the dialogues examined in this chapter, and asks: 'Is this a case of multiple personality disorder, or is it a social text?'[48] It is a good question, to which the answer is that it is both, since a text's sociability is predicated to some degree on at least the reordering, if not the disordering, of personality. While this may be something that Proust resisted, even he, for instance, envisaged the solitary occupation of writing as that occupation in which 'we come face to face once more with our selves' (*Against*, 15), a formulation whose insistent redoublings—a gift of the grammatical requisites of the French in particular ('nous nous remettons face à face avec nous-mêmes' (*Contre*, 224))—places us in the hall of mirrors once more.

Proust's emphasis on silence is, nevertheless, surprisingly fertile for consideration of the dialogue as critical form—as, indeed, I suggested at the very outset of this discussion. The dialogue form may seem to insist on the essential talkativeness of the conduct of criticism, but, as we have seen at a number of points throughout this chapter, it is also acutely sensitive to the resources as well as the temptation of critical silence. The affinity of dialogue with the promises of silence is in evidence at the conclusion of McGann's *Swinburne*, where he is responding to Douglas Bush's judgement that Swinburne's poetry is 'forgettable':

> Odysseus meeting the ghost of his dead mother;
>   'Sky, and shore, and cloud, and waste, and
>   sea': is all this bleakness or is it beauty?
>   Swinburne reminds us how and
>   why it is and must be both.
>   For this, if for noth-
>   ing else, he too is
>   unforgotten.
>
> (p. 291) [49]

McGann glosses Odysseus' encounter with his mother's spirit in Swinburne's poem 'By the North Sea', and in particular its remonstrance that, the spirits having vanished,

> All too sweet such men's Hellenic speech is,
>   All too fain they lived of light to see,
> Once to see the darkness of these beaches,
>   Once to sing this Hades found of me
> Ghostless,

---

[48] 'Anne Mack' and 'Jay Rome', 'Marxism, Romanticism, and Postmodernism: An American Case History', in Macovski (ed.), *Dialogue and Critical Discourse*, 172–94 (191).

[49] See Bush, *Mythology and the Romantic Tradition in English Poetry*, rev edn (New York: Norton, 1963), 355; quoted by McGann, *Swinburne*, 286.

by attesting both to the lines' unflinching realization that the dead are beyond our embrace, even if they may not be beyond our discourse, and to the beauty of the lines, which itself owes something to their status as an act of remembrance of the disavowed vision of sky, shore, cloud, waste, and sea.[50] The dwindling of the book's conclusion to one word, 'unforgotten', like the 'Ghostless' isolated at the beginning of its line in Swinburne's 'By the North Sea', visibly records the resolution in silence of the book's dialogues, themselves conducted among critics who might themselves have been forgotten were it not for McGann's journey into the 'dark night' in which Swinburne's critical reputation had been plunged (p. 286).

In the seminal essay I briefly discussed above, Liu claimed that '[t]he New Historicist search for other subjective experience or *mentalité* is [...] doomed to a tragic recognition. Though *we* would understand *them* in all their strangeness, the forms of our understanding are fated at last to reveal that they are a remembrance or a prophecy of us.'[51] Remembrance and prophecy, however, are different, the one a recollection of what has gone past, the other a foretelling (frequently unreliable) of what is to come. To see ourselves remembered in the past is different from seeing ourselves prophesied by it. The journey to the underworld lies ahead of the hero at the beginning of his epic, but what he finds there is a remembrance not just of what has been but of what he, too, will be. Attempts to engage the past in dialogue foreshadow the silence that will fall on our own speaking. Evoking the mortal human need to approach and communicate with others that Schlegel described, as well as the destination of mortal humans in death, Stephen Greenblatt concluded his *Renaissance Self-Fashioning* by recalling a painfully awkward conversation during a flight he took from Baltimore to Boston.[52] The man in the seat next to Greenblatt is on his way to visit his son in hospital, where he is being treated for an unspecified (by Greenblatt) disease that has affected his speech so severely that he is able only to mouth words but not sound them, and, as a consequence of this debilitating condition, the man's son has lost the will to live. Were this information from one's fellow passenger not disturbing enough, Greenblatt's neighbour asks him to mouth the words 'I want to die. I want to die' in order that he might practise lip-reading a phrase that he thinks his son will, in all appalling likelihood, attempt to utter (p. 255). Greenblatt begins to try to oblige his neighbour but finds, unsurprisingly, that he cannot form such a terrible sentence. It is not easy to play-act the desire to die, perhaps especially so when the 'line' one is given both does and does not belong to a living human being (the man thinks this is something his son will be likely to say) and when one is asked to utter it not in a theatre, but in an aeroplane, where even for the frequent flier

---

[50] Swinburne, 'By the North Sea', in *The Poems of Algernon Charles Swinburne*, 6 vols (London: Chatto and Windus, 1911; first pub. 1904), v. 83–110 (part III, stanza 15 (96)).

[51] Liu, 'Power of Formalism', 733.

[52] Greenblatt, 'Epilogue', in *Renaissance Self-Fashioning*, 255–7. Further references are given after quotations in the text.

the shadow of catastrophe is more prominent than it is in a theatre. Greenblatt and his neighbour thus passed the flight in silence—or, rather, without verbal contact of any kind, since what the father had in any case requested of Greenblatt was precisely to speak silently. They did so not only because of Greenblatt's admittedly superstitious sense that mouthing 'I want to die' might have some sort of ominous force, but moreover because '[t]o be asked, even by an isolated, needy individual to perform lines that were not my own, that violated my sense of my own desires, was intolerable' (p. 256). There is something curious about that formulation—'to perform lines that were not my own' (Greenblatt had initially spoken of the man's request for him to 'mime a few sentences' and of his attempt to 'form the words')—since 'lines' that we 'perform' are rarely our 'own', unless we are, say, a playwright performing in our own play, and, even then, the lines may be said to belong, not to us, exactly, but to the character we have created. The oddity of that formulation, however, goes to the heart of Greenblatt's avowed reason for rehearsing this painful, abortive dialogue—a failed dialogue, moreover, that is meant to be the rehearsal for another, at least, desperately hampered one:

> As for myself, I have related this brief story of my encounter with the distraught father on the plane because I want to bear witness at the close to my overwhelming need to sustain the illusion that I am the principal maker of my own identity.
>
> (p. 257)

Albeit in drastically different circumstances, in his endeavour to assert control over his own personhood, Greenblatt is curiously akin to Kant's judge of taste. Greenblatt's attempt to sustain what he alleges is 'the illusion' of his own self-fashioning is made not only by refusing to take on the words—imagined and anticipated, if not yet actual—of another person but also by failing to converse altogether: 'we sat in silence for the rest of the flight.'

Liu's 'Epilogue' to *Wordsworth: The Sense of History* stages yet more dramatically the implication of the individual critic with his own specific and unshakeable inheritance, in the conduct of kinds of literary criticism that would question the role of an individual genius transcending the course of history. Whereas Greenblatt relates an abortive conversation, Liu's 'Epilogue' is a dialogue between a roman type 'I' closely identifiable with Liu and an italic, bluntly sceptical and insistently interregorative 'we', who seek to press their interlocutor on his emotional responses to '"facts"', on the one hand, and to literature, on the other, as well as on his putative motivation for writing as he has done. In particular, the 'we' alleges that Liu's study of Wordsworth and the French Revolution has served merely to romanticize his own sense of history, which is derived, via his parents, from the Cultural Revolution in China ('*that other revolution of culture in that land of your parents' origin*'). 'I' offers some plausible rejoinders to this imputed sequence of motives, but cannot, or at least does not, resist the force of the accusations advanced by '*we*': 'I am wordless.' The insistently contrarian response of '*we*'—'*No, you have much more to deny, whole books to write*'—may be the last word here, but it gives 'I'—and Liu—licence for the rest of his career.

The retreat to wordlessness at the end of Liu's 'Epilogue'—unsurprising, perhaps, at the conclusion to a 500-page monograph—serves to announce a hiatus in a self-critical debate that is to be continued. Likewise, Greenblatt's embarrassed recoil—and whoever has received an unwanted conversational advance in the confined space of an aeroplane cabin has surely experienced that feeling, even if not quite as the result of the singular and upsetting circumstance related by Greenblatt—provides only temporary comfort in the refuge of what Greenblatt himself avers is the 'illusion' of self-determined identity. The point of both of these brief but significant epilogues is that silence, wordlessness, is not the mere antithesis of dialogue, not its terminus and repudiation, but, as Kant himself recognized, vital to the very conduct of its critical form.

6

Letters

In a famous critical fragment from the *Athenäum* (1798), Friedrich Schlegel closely aligns dialogues and letters: 'A dialogue is a chain or a garland of fragments. A correspondence is a dialogue on a larger scale.'[1] Schlegel's floral imagery ('a garland of fragments') perhaps presents a rather verdant view of dialogue. As we have seen, dialogue is often prone to interruption and refusal, to the chain being cut, and to the fragments falling to the ground. The previous chapter began with a consideration of Kant's distinction between *Disputieren* and *Streiten*. *Streiten*, in contrast to the open-and-shut affair that is *Disputieren*, may conjure an image of the enlightened public sphere in which grown-up and respectful interchange of judgements nevertheless at variance with one another may tend to gradual convergence over time. Or it may conjure an image of fruitless striving to budge recalcitrant interlocutors from their absurd opinions that ends with them putting their fingers in their ears.

The expression and exchange of critical opinion often involve exertion of different kinds. In a review of William Empson's letters, Stefan Collini hits, in 'wrangling', on a good word for Empson's critical rough and tumble. Empson's love of wrangling can be felt throughout his work, but perhaps especially in his letters, which are in some ways unusually continuous with the character and interests of the rest of his writing. Collini remarks that '[o]ne reason why so little strain is involved in treating many of Empson's letters as extensions of his literary criticism is because as a critic he always wrote with a sense of his audience and where he had got to in an extended conversation with them.'[2] Collini quotes, for example, from a letter Empson wrote to his student Philip Hobsbaum in 1966, in which Empson is keen to restate his rejection of the anti-intentionalism that had, by that date, hardened into literary critical orthodoxy: 'it seems to me that the chief function of imaginative literature is to make you realise that other people are very various, many of them quite different from you, with different "systems of value" as well; but the effect of almost any Orthodoxy is to hide this, and pretend that everybody *ought* to be like Homer or Dr Leavis.'[3] It would certainly be a

---

[1] *Kritische Friedrich-Schlegel-Ausgabe*, ed. Ernst Behler et al., 35 vols (Munich: Ferdinand Schöningh, 1958–), ii (1967), 176.
[2] Stefan Collini, *Common Reading: Critics, Historians, Publics* (Oxford: Oxford University Press, 2008; repr. 2010), 98.
[3] 31 January 1966; *Selected Letters of William Empson*, ed. John Haffenden (Oxford: Oxford University Press, 2009), 396–8 (397).

Critical Forms: Forms of Literary Criticism, 1750–2020. Ross Wilson, Oxford University Press. © Ross Wilson 2023.
DOI: 10.1093/oso/9780198881117.003.0007

frightening world in which everybody strove to be like Homer or Dr Leavis (and a worse one still in which they succeeded). Collini does not remark it, but this formulation in the letter to Hobsbaum is the anticipatory expression of a tenet that Empson would repeatedly advance in his published work.[4] An essay on Jonson's *The Alchemist* (first published in the 1969–70 issue of the *Hudson Review*, and hence perhaps already in preparation when Empson wrote to Hobsbaum) is an especially crisp instance: 'The chief use of reading imaginative literature is to make you grasp that different people act on different ethical beliefs, whereas, the chief use of critical jargon is to obscure this basic fact, making you feel at home where you are not.'[5] Characteristically Empsonian in its eschewal of polite circumlocution, the 'you' here is 'you! reader! reading this'—and thus, in this particular case, *me*. But this 'you' also belongs at the same time to the category of 'different people'—people different, that is, both from me and from Empson, since 'you', obviously, cannot be Empson, and, when someone other than me is reading this passage (as *you* just have), neither is it *me*. The point here is that the phrase 'different people' does not name a faraway abstraction of whom we know nothing, but rather 'different people' are other *yous*, with their own real and distinctive characteristics.

In the above case, it is not so much that Empson's letters are an extension of his literary criticism, as the other way around. Collini's assurance that there is little 'strain' involved in reading Empson's letters as an 'extension' of his literary criticism (note also what Collini calls Empson's '*extended* conversation' with his audience) is perhaps itself rather at odds with the pugilistic, muscular straining that Collini identifies in Empson's writing. Strains of different sorts are crucial to the literary-critical letters investigated in this chapter. It is worth briefly recalling here Hohendahl's tentative definition of literary criticism that I examined in the Introduction. Hohendahl suggests, that is, that literary criticism be understood as '*public communication on literature* comprising both description and evaluation.'[6] Such a definition immediately poses problems for consideration of the letter as a critical form. It is true that a number of the literary-critical letters examined in this chapter are straightforwardly forms of public communication: what is in essence a treatise on romance that Richard Hurd nevertheless casts as a series of letters to an unnamed but occasionally invoked 'friend'; the correspondence between Lady Bradshaigh (who poses initially as 'Mrs Belfour') and Samuel Richardson that had its beginning in a public appeal to enter into correspondence; Hazlitt's vitriolic

---

[4] Christopher Ricks gathers a partial collection of Empson's reformulations of this principle in 'William Empson and "the Loony Hooters"', in *Essays in Appreciation* (Oxford: Oxford University Press, 1996; repr. 2004), 341–53 (350).

[5] William Empson, '*The Alchemist*', in *Essays in Renaissance Literature*, ed. John Haffenden, 2 vols (Cambridge: Cambridge University Press, 1994–95; repr. 2006), ii: *The Drama* (1994), 97–109 (97) (first pub. in *Hudson Review*, 22 (1969–70), 595–608).

[6] Peter Uwe Hohendahl, 'Introduction', in Hohendahl (ed.), *History of German Literary Criticism, 1730–1980* (Lincoln: University of Nebraska Press, 1988), 3.

open letter to William Gifford; the culmination of the correspondence between Vladimir Nabokov and Edmund Wilson; and the curious case of the adoption of the letter as form for *The Ferrante Letters* on Elena Ferrante's Neapolitan Quartet, which never were letters, but rather emails and blog posts. Perhaps Keats's letters are private, but, even then, they arise out of and enter into a context of sociable discussion. Where Schlegel had imagined correspondence (*Briefwechsel*) on analogy with dialogue, and Ignatius Sancho, one of the most celebrated letter-writers of the eighteenth century, prized 'conversable letters' above all, many letters are one-sided, sometimes by accident of history, sometimes (as in open letters and in treatises cast as letters) deliberately so.[7] While the letter does not conform simply to Hohendahl's definition of literary criticism as public discourse, therefore, neither is it reducible as such to sheer privacy. As we will see, the letter's middle position between publicity and privacy is a crucial aspect of it as a form of literary critical discourse.

*

It is worth taking up the issue of the letter's position between public and private by starting with an example taken, not from the period of widespread and habitual letter-writing, but from our own period, the period when the letter has increasingly lost out to alternative technologies of communication. Announcements of the death of letter-writing are frequent in its history and are always vulnerable to the counterexample of flourishing correspondences in the era of high-speed travel, the telephone, and perhaps even email and other forms of primarily textual electronic communication. Nevertheless, it is safe to say that such counterexamples are exceptions that prove the rule, and thus, in the most salient cases, the adoption of the letter form in the period when such rival modes of communication have achieved dominance must be explicated against the background of its historical circumstances, rather than just chalked up to the tenacity of the letter in the face of competition from other forms and media. In what remains one of the most prescient and penetrating accounts of the fate of letter-writing in the age of mechanical communicability, Theodor Adorno introduced a selection of the letters of Walter Benjamin (for whom the letter 'became a literary form') not only by remarking on Benjamin's gifts as a letter-writer, but by considering the mismatch between the historical fate of the individual and of the letter as form. 'Letter writing', Adorno wrote, 'announces a claim on the individual that it cannot do justice to nowadays, any more than the world is willing to honor it'. He explains the historical causes of this situation as follows:

---

[7] Sancho, letter XXIII, to Miss Leach, 7 August 1775, in *Letters of the Late Ignatius Sancho, An African*, ed. Vincent Carretta (Peterborough, ON: Broadview, 2015), 122.

In a totalized state of society that degrades each individual and relegates him to a function, it is no longer legitimate for anyone to report on himself in a letter as though he were still the unsubsumed individual the letter says he is: there is already something illusory about the 'I' in a letter.[8]

For Benjamin, then, 'the letter represented the wedding of something in the process of disappearing and the utopia of its restoration.'[9]

Adorno wrote his introduction to Benjamin's letters over half a century ago, before the development of still further technologies threatening the obsolescence of the letter, and before still further advancement of the totalized state of society that does likewise (and much more besides). One sphere of life into which the administered society has reached more deeply than even Adorno may have feared is the university and the practice of literary criticism within it. It is in part as a reaction to this situation that Sarah Chihaya, Merve Emre, Katherine Hill, and Jill Richards recently experimented with what they call 'collective criticism' in *The Ferrante Letters*.[10] Notably, *The Ferrante Letters* began not *as letters* but rather as a series of public blog posts on the site of the journal *Post45*, as well as of emails between the correspondents.[11] This may seem like a trivial point—after all, both the *Post45* and email format allow for something that has some of the trappings of traditional correspondence—but the explicit identification of the exchanges gathered in the volume with a form that at the very least remains under the shadow of the threat of obsolescence is vital to the specific critical enterprise Chihaya, Emre, Hill, and Richards want to pursue. That critical enterprise is centrally concerned with the relations between private and public response, personal, amical, and social criticism, and, somewhat contrastingly, with the professional work undertaken by employees of literature departments in universities. In their introduction, the authors (if that is quite the right word) of *The Ferrante Letters* cast the production of the book as secondary to 'the cultivation of a distinct model of criticism: one deliberately oriented to the ongoing labor of thought; one that would not insist on a static argument but embody a flexible and capacious process' and 'the slow, fractured, and creative accretion of ideas that underwrites all acts of criticism, both inside and outside the academy' (p. 3). The contrast between the rejection of insistence ('would not insist on') and the espousal of embodiment ('but embody a flexible and capacious process') may recall McGann's preference for the 'lines of thought' made available by the dialogue over the 'argument and explication' that are the province of the 'traditional essay' that we encountered in

---

[8] Theodor W. Adorno, 'Benjamin the Letter Writer' (1966), in *Notes to Literature*, trans. Shierry Weber Nicholsen, 2 vols (New York: Columbia University Press, 1992), ii. 233–9 (235). I thank William Holbrook for reminding me of the pertinence to this discussion of Adorno's tribute to Benjamin.

[9] Adorno, 'Benjamin the Letter Writer', 236.

[10] Sarah Chihaya et al., *The Ferrante Letters: An Experiment in Collective Criticism* (New York: Columbia University Press, 2020). Further references are given after quotations in the text.

[11] See <http://post45.org/2016/06/the-slow-burn-volume-2-an-introduction/> (accessed 13 January 2021).

the previous chapter. The adoption of the letter form seeks to recover the (in Adorno's words) 'unsubsumed individual' that is the inevitable basis of response to literary works, even as those responses are claimed as the raw materials of what is sold in measurable form in the marketplace of administered criticism. In her opening letter addressed, notably, to 'Dear Readers' (rather than to her fellow named correspondents), Chihaya describes the model of criticism she is interested in fostering as 'slow-form criticism: readings that happen on the back burner while your mind is mostly elsewhere, that, in their extended simmering, develop a different richness and depth over time from a quick-fired review' (p. 18; see also p. 123). Chihaya's opposition here between the kind of 'slow-form criticism' she wants to attempt and other kinds of critical writing that are cast as much faster ('a quick-fired review')—an opposition in which the review is the depreciated form and that we may therefore recognize from other attempts to elaborate suitable forms for criticism—is not the only way in which the temporality of critical correspondence is imagined in *The Ferrante Letters*. In the introduction, that is, the authors describe one of their aims as having been to depart from the 'standardized time of academic publishing' (p. 5). The achievement of that aim, however, is said to involve not slower-than-usual production of criticism, but rather quicker response to reading (so to speak) *in medias res*. One may thus write one's own criticism, and read the criticism of others, before it is subject to revision and thus before it is, in an academically accepted sense, finished. To be sure, the timescale of academic publishing reasserts itself somewhat, so that the authors work in what they call 'the hybrid temporality of contemporary critical writing'— a hybrid compounded of the fact that the collaborators on *The Ferrante Letters* read each other's 'letters' as they emerged, while knowing that they could (would) be read by others 'in the unknown future' (p. 5). This is not a mere inconsistency, however—and not least because the standard of consistency in the production of criticism is something that the authors of *The Ferrante Letters* deliberately suspend. Letters are answerable not only *by* their recipients but *to* the moment in which they come to be written: sometimes that moment allows for extended, considered discussion; sometimes not. As well as seeking to discover the situations of time and location in which literary criticism gets written—all of the letters in *The Ferrante Letters* are dated and located, even when those locations are themselves shifting and temporary: 'Sixth Car, Metro North, Just Outside of Stamford' (p. 58), for instance—the authors in general seek to push at the borders that are established between slow and fast, reader and writer, vacation and term, pleasure and work.

The scruple that reading for pleasure should be kept apart from reading for work, and vice versa, is a key target of *The Ferrante Letters*.[12] 'Our project', the

---

[12] See, again, Adorno, *passim*, but especially 'Free Time' (1969), in J. M. Bernstein (ed.), *The Culture Industry: Selected Essays on Mass Culture* (Abingdon: Routledge, 1991), 187–97. Rosa Mucignat is especially alive to this aspect of *The Ferrante Letters* in her review for the *Times Higher Education Supplement*, 20 February 2020 <https://www.timeshighereducation.com/books/ferrante-letters-experiment-collective-criticism-sarah-chihaya-merve-emre-katherine-hill-and> (accessed 13 January 2021). And on the

authors write in their introduction, 'was born out of a desire to reconcile shared pleasure with critical practice to produce an iterable model of reading and writing—a model that others could replicate through their prose or in their classrooms' (p. 4). Their project, moreover, arises from the effort to be faithful to what they describe (perhaps a touch optimistically?) as 'the rich and active social world of academic discourse' (p. 6), though the recollection that '[w]hat began as a pleasurable gamble emerged as a regimented practice of reading and writing' (p. 8) acknowledges that that social world is characterized by regimes as well as gambles, practices as well as pleasures. Indeed, the laudable 'desire to reconcile shared pleasure with critical practice' may have its origin as much in frustration and anxiety, as in desire or pleasure. In a letter that begins by upbraiding the string of men whose lives intersect, rarely happily, with the central pairing of Lila and Lenù throughout Ferrante's Neapolitan Quartet, Jill Richards gives eloquent expression to the persistence in herself of modes of reacting to a novel—'talking to characters, giving them advice, insulting them, sometimes out loud, in public places, where people will stare at you' (p. 84)—that she tries to drum out of her students. Confessor has become penitent here, owning up to the sins that are to be censured in others. The context of friendship and shared enthusiasms (as opposed, perhaps, to shared *interests* as such) conjured by the deliberate and anachronistic adoption of the letter form allows for the expression of the individual despite society's monitoring of reaction ('people will stare at you'). The deliberate if unthematized anachronism of the adoption of the letter form reinforces the sense that the kinds of critical response to which *The Ferrante Letters* aims to give expression are a thing of the past—but may be recovered for a different future of literary criticism. Reading someone else's correspondence is, in fact, rather like overhearing them talk to characters in books and then staring at them for their socially outré behaviour—but it is a stare that remains invisible, even if it is imaginable, to the writer and it may thus be borne in order to allow for the creation of 'a fiction of life within the medium of the frozen word'.[13]

*

The Ferrante Letters reprints an exchange among four female academics with posts at universities in the United States and United Kingdom, where they teach students whose reading habits they try to improve and where they pursue research careers in areas related to their teaching. Teaching students how to read a certain way, and pursuing research careers, are both good and bad things for the reasons that the exchange itself rehearses. The mention of gender here is pertinent for a

formation of different kinds of reading adjacent to professional literary critical reading, see Merve Emre, *Paraliterary: The Making of Bad Readers in Postwar America* (Chicago: University of Chicago Press, 2017), especially the trenchantly argued concluding reflections, pp. 253–61.
[13]   Adorno, 'Benjamin the Letter Writer', 234.

number of reasons, not only because all of the contributors to *The Ferrante Letters* have, to varying degrees, addressed questions of gender elsewhere in their work (as well as in the correspondence that constitutes the book itself) or because the letter is sometimes cast as the genre of care, which is in turn frequently cast as a burden for women to bear, but especially because the letter has historically been one form in which groups, including women, denied admission to institutions of criticism and their organs of publication, have been able to practise criticism.[14] The authors of *The Ferrante Letters* are not denied such admission, yet the letter as refuge for the professionally unsanctioned readings of particular individuals is, as we have seen, crucial to their endeavour in 'collective criticism'.

The affinity of the letter with those denied access to established modes of literary-critical communication was central to a series of literary-critical correspondences in the late eighteenth century. Ignatius Sancho, mentioned briefly above, was the first man of African descent to vote in a British parliamentary election and also the first in Britain to engage in literary criticism of a very specific kind—namely, the attempt to prevail upon a writer to write something in particular. Greatly influenced by Laurence Sterne's sentimental fiction, and ultimately celebrated as a sentimental writer in his letters himself, Sancho wrote (without prior introduction) to Sterne, both to applaud the consideration of slavery he had encountered in Sterne's *Sermons* and to enjoin him further to handle '[t]hat subject [...] in your striking manner'—a manner Sancho himself fulsomely displays—which would, Sancho claims, 'ease the yoke (perhaps) of many—but if only of one—Gracious God!—what a feast to a benevolent heart!'[15] Sancho's intervention arrived happily, we learn from Sterne's reply, as the author was indeed composing 'a tender tale of the sorrows of a friendless poor negro-girl', which would be included in volume 4 of *Tristram Shandy*.[16] Sterne's letter picks up on the sentimental tone of Sancho's—which, after all, had initially been his own—offering an affecting vision of the brotherhood of humanity (though Sterne's predication of a scale that 'descends from the fairest face about St James's, to the sootiest complexion in africa', in which it is clear who is at the top and who at the bottom, however connected they may be, is, though perhaps excusable by the standards of the time, unfortunate at best). The point, however, is that the facility the letter afforded not only to respond to the works of celebrated authors, but to attempt to steer their course, was readily exploited by writers whose responses (let alone interventions) would hardly have been entertained in a critical culture governed by hierarchies of rank, age, gender, and race.

As her correspondence with Denis Diderot had already shown, for instance, Madame Riccoboni's letters could not have been further from expressions of

---

[14] I owe the idea of the letter as 'the genre of care' to Tess Solomon.
[15] Sancho, letter XXXV to Laurence Sterne, 21 July 1776, in *Letters*, ed. Carretta, 128.
[16] Sterne to Sancho, 27 July 1776, in *Letters*, ed. Carretta, 312.

admiration (Sancho's attempted intervention in Sterne's writing career, after all, is couched in expressions of earnest admiration and, indeed, imitation) but were often criticisms in the starkest sense. Her teasing but earnest letter to Diderot begins with her refusal to offer him any compliments on his play *Le Père de famille* (1758) for fear of swelling his pride; Diderot's long reply sets out his own philosophy of 'dramatic action' (*l'action théâtrale*), which is, in no uncertain terms, starkly opposed to hers.[17] And, in writing to Choderlos de Laclos, Riccoboni opens by declaring that she is not surprised that he writes well, since 'the spirit is hereditary in his family'—an ambivalent compliment at best, since talents derived from one's parents and grandparents are less one's own for that reason, and it is certainly a compliment that serves to establish Riccoboni from the outset as the senior partner in this correspondence.[18] The implication that 'his talents, his facility, the graces of his style' are not exclusively his own, but are rather a familial inheritance, adds to the sting in Riccoboni's charge that Laclos has deployed these gifts to 'give to foreigners such an appalling idea [*idée si revoltante*] of the morals of his nation and of the taste of his compatriots' (p. 464): he has betrayed both his nation by depicting it in such a way and his ancestors by deploying to do so the talents bequeathed to him. Laclos responds with all the show of courtesy and compliment that would be expected, while nevertheless dissenting from Riccoboni's view: he has not embellished vice, but, he argues, only depicted it with all the charms with which it is very often adorned in actuality; he has wished to please only insofar as doing so assists him in attaining his primary object of being useful; and so on (p. 465). Perhaps already with an eye to the publication of this correspondence (which Laclos did publish, possibly without Riccoboni's permission, in the Nantes edition of 1787), Laclos attempts to assume control, issuing an invitation to 'his readers', among whom Riccoboni is tacitly not included, because his invitation is for them, once they are tired of the 'distressing images' they will find in *his* book, to re-peruse *her* works—to turn again, that is, to the 'gentler sentiments', 'embellished nature', to 'all the charms that spirits and grace can add to tenderness, to virtue' that are to be found there (p. 465). Riccoboni takes exception to this potential boost to her readership, however, accusing Laclos in response of having done her wrong in attributing to her 'the partiality *of an author*', and doubtless also takes exception to Laclos's dismissal, arrayed in gallantry, of her concerns (p. 466). Riccoboni wrote, rather, as a 'woman, as French, as a patriot zealous for the honour of [her] nation' (p. 466).[19] Keen as Riccoboni is

---

[17] See *Correspondance de Diderot*, ed. Georges Roth and Jean Varloot, 16 vols (Paris: Minuit, 1955–70), ii (1955), 86–103.

[18] 'Correspondance entre Madame Riccoboni et l'auteur des *Liaisons dangereuses*', in Pierre Choderlos de Laclos, *Les Liaisons dangereuses*, ed. Catriona Seth (Paris: Gallimard, 2011), 464–79 (464). Further references are given after quotations in the text. For a useful overview of the circumstances of the Riccoboni–Laclos correspondence, see Seth's note, 898–9.

[19] For commentary on this aspect of Riccoboni's self-depiction, see Terry Castle, 'Women and Literary Criticism', in *CHLC IV*, 434–55 (438).

to disavow the status of author in order to insist instead on her status as a reader of a particular (female, French, patriotic) kind, Laclos, as commentators on the correspondence have often remarked, sees the correspondence as an opportunity to extend his epistolary work from fiction into criticism, carrying on, for example, not only the 'flirtatious' mode of the letters in the novel but also their practice of quoting a correspondent's words back to them verbatim.[20]

Riccoboni's admonishment of Laclos is clearly intended to remedy (as she would see it) his writing in the future. Laclos immediately identified the resemblance of their critical correspondence to the epistolary form of his novel, such that criticism became an extension of, if not an intervention in, the novel itself in the Nantes edition. The correspondence between Lady Bradshaigh and Samuel Richardson in the course of the serial appearance of Richardson's massive epistolary novel *Clarissa* afforded rather greater opportunity for consequential intervention in the novel as it was being written. As Terry Castle has suggested, '[t]he "letter to the author" format'—one of the 'spontaneous and informal contexts' for criticism that Castle identifies, though even such informality can find expression in a 'format'—'seems to have unleashed in a number of women writers a subversive fantasy of rewriting received (male) texts.'[21] Both Bradshaigh—who wrote initially as 'Mrs Belfour', teasingly close to 'Belford', the chief correspondent of Lovelace, the anti-hero of *Clarissa* itself—and Richardson—who frequently deployed his characters as if they were real people, having escaped from the confines of their novelistic worlds and into the world of the correspondence—likewise exploited the affinity of their critical exchange with the form of the novels they were both addressing and, in some important ways, conspiring to write. Not only the pseudonym, but also Bradshaigh's intriguing (in the active sense) procedure of appealing for a reply from Richardson in the *Whitehall Evening Post* and her curse (no less) on him in the event that he chose not to end the novel happily—'May the hatred of all the young, beautiful, and virtuous, for ever be your portion!'—support Clare Bucknell's observation in her valuable essay on the Bradshaigh–Richardson correspondence that '[Bradshaigh] in particular, but Richardson too, found it difficult to exchange letters about *Clarissa* or *Sir Charles Grandison* without getting caught up in the formal equivalences between what they were doing and the epistolary world of the novel—without projecting themselves into the plot, say, or identifying more or less consciously with a particular character's letter-writing activity.'[22] But this way of putting it is perhaps to assume

---

[20] See Janie Vanpée, 'Dangerous Liaisons 2: The Riccoboni–Laclos Sequel', *Eighteenth-Century Fiction*, 9 (1996), 51–70 (54, 56–7), and François Migeot, 'Rapport de places et imaginaire dans les lettres de Laclos et Mme Riccoboni', *Semen*, 20 (2005) <https://journals.openedition.org/semen/2038> (accessed 28 July 2020) (para. 43 of 51).

[21] Castle, 443–4.

[22] See Bradshaigh's letter to Richardson, 10 October 1748, for the curse, in *Samuel Richardson: Correspondence with Lady Bradshaigh and Lady Echlin*, ed. Peter Sabor, 3 vols (Cambridge: Cambridge University Press, 2016), i. 5. Further references to this edition are given after quotations in the text.

that Bradshaigh and Richardson did indeed try to exchange letters 'without getting caught up in' the epistolary form for which Richardson's novels were celebrated, and that they were likewise keen to avoid projection and identification. It is, that is to say, to rely on a set of assumptions about reading and writing critically—the desirability of formal difference between imaginative and critical writing, the importance of resisting projection and refusing identification—that were only starting to establish themselves in the middle of the eighteenth century and are now, as we saw in the discussion of *The Ferrante Letters* above, once again being submitted to scrutiny by means of deliberate formal experimentation. The characteristics of the letter-as-form that Richardson found so conducive to the plots of his novels—their suitability to the expression of private views paired with their conventional and shared forms of address; the temporal lag between statement and response, question and answer; the evolving relationship between the discrete letter and the correspondence of which it comes to be part—were also deployed by Bradshaigh and Richardson for the purposes of criticism.

*

The correspondence between Bradshaigh and Richardson endured over a decade. Having begun with Bradshaigh's request for reassurance about the course of a novel still in the process of being written, Bradshaigh and Richardson went on to use their correspondence to share their views on a wide range of topics in the writing and culture of their (but not only their) time. One episode in their correspondence concerns the furore that had greeted the strictures on Jonathan Swift's character that Lord Orrery had articulated in his *Remarks on the Life and Writings of Dr Jonathan Swift*.[23] It is central to Orrery's work that he exploits the form of a series of published letters of advice to his son, a form that became especially celebrated with the publication in 1774 of Lord Chesterfield's *Letters to his Son* and was still being adopted twenty years later for discussion of literary and philosophical texts in, for instance, John Aikin's *Letters from a Father to his Son on Various Topics Relative to Literature and the Conduct of Life* (1794). Orrery's *Remarks* do have a named addressee in his younger son, Hamilton Boyle, from whom Orrery senior, as he writes in the opening letter, delights to receive letters, which he reads 'over not only with the fondness of a father, but with the affection of a friend' (Letter I, 1–2). Orrery draws an implicit contrast between his son's situation at

---

Clare Bucknell, 'I Can Scarce Hold My Pen' (review of *Correspondence of Samuel Richardson with Lady Bradshaigh and Lady Echlin*, ed. Peter Sabor), *LRB* 15 June 2017 <https://www.lrb.co.uk/the-paper/v39/n12/clare-bucknell/i-can-scarce-hold-my-pen> (accessed 13 January 2021). Compare Louise Curran's account of Bradshaigh's responses to *Clarissa* as 'both exposition and memoir in their mixture of combative literary criticism and fictional creativity' in *Samuel Richardson and the Art of Letter-Writing* (Cambridge: Cambridge University Press, 2016), 51–88 (p. 68).

[23] John Boyle, Earl of Orrery, *Remarks on the Life and Writings of Dr Jonathan Swift* [...] *in a Series of Letters* [...] *to his Son, the Honourable Hamilton Boyle* (Dublin: printed by George Faulkner, 1752). Further references are given after quotations in the text.

Christchurch, Oxford, 'that elegant seat of the muses', where he is sociably engaged 'amidst the best authors, and in a free conversation with men of letters', and his own unfortunate seclusion: 'early disappointment, the perplexed state of my affairs, an indifferent state of health, and'—as if that were not already enough to bear—'many untoward incidents, all contributed to make me, even in my earliest part of life, too fond of retirement' (p. 2) Again, the letter's negotiation of private and public, amateur and professional, lay and learned is crucial to Orrery's adoption of the form. Despite the adverse circumstances that have prevented him from taking an active part in the learned world, Orrery has nevertheless managed, as he tells us, to author a correspondence on Pliny's letters for his elder son (which, he notes, his younger son had praised).[24] It is, of course, impossible to miss in these early exchanges the considerable importance of letters in general to Orrery— Pliny's; his own about Pliny's; those he receives from his son; those he is writing to his son now—and their importance to him signals an attempt to compensate himself for having missed out on the 'free conversation with men of letters' that his son enjoys at Oxford. Letters in the sense of written communications addressed to a person serve as the compensation for his exclusion from letters in the sense of academic and literary culture more broadly. Orrery goes on to announce his intention to allow his younger son the benefit of what has been, the impediments to it notwithstanding, the 'real satisfaction and improvement' he has drawn from his 'acquaintance with the dead' (p. 3). While there is no doubt that Pliny is numbered among the dead, the reader soon learns that Orrery was acquainted with Swift (who is the subject of this correspondence) not quite in death but 'in the decline of life' (p. 4). While, in its intimation of mortality, this way of describing the time in Swift's life at which Orrery senior knew him preserves something of the distinction between youth and activity, age and retirement, that he has been drawing, it nevertheless also puts Orrery in a position of authority with respect to this particular subject. His son at Oxford would be pushed, certainly, to be able to claim acquaintance with such a man of letters as Swift. And, though Orrery opens his *Remarks* by displaying his gratitude for and enjoyment of the letters that his dutiful son writes home to him, the reader—the general reader, that is, not the named reader, Hamilton Boyle—sees only the paternal, not the filial, side of the correspondence. Orrery's *Remarks* have an addressee from whom he, he tells us, receives letters, but for us the correspondence is all one way. Even though he is named as the intended recipient of the *Remarks*, as far as the other readers of them can tell, Hamilton Boyle does not contribute or respond to them. The addressee, then, is just another reader, like us.

The epistolary guise was as important to the literary criticism of the eighteenth and early nineteenth centuries as it was to the literature of moral guidance and

---

[24] John Boyle, Earl of Orrery, *The Letters of Pliny the Younger. With Observations on Each Letter; and an Essay on Pliny's Life*, 2 vols (Dublin: printed for George Faulkner, 1751).

improvement—fields that, as in Orrery's *Remarks*, of course often overlapped. Unlike Orrery's *Remarks*, Richard Hurd's *Letters on Chivalry and Romance* have no named or fully characterized addressee, one only being invoked as 'my dear friend' (like the addressee invoked at the end of Veit Schlegel's 'Conversation' discussed in the previous chapter) on a couple of occasions near the beginning and end of the sequence of letters.[25] There is, then, something mysterious, or at least unexplained, about the identity of Hurd's addressee, but Hurd nevertheless explicitly deploys the episodic nature of the letter when he invites his reader 'to revolve this idea in your own mind' in the gap between the end of one letter and the beginning of the next (Letter II, 10; the idea is 'that Chivalry was no absurd and freakish institution, but the natural and even sober effect of feudal policy'), or when he promises to take up a particular theme in a following letter (Letter IX, 86). Perhaps these are features—the encouragement of individual reflection, the anticipation of what is to come—that may be shared (though they rarely are) by chapters in a treatise. But what Hurd especially emphasizes is the temporality of letter-writing, particularly as evinced in the gaps between instalments of a correspondence. Where treatises may have chapters or other suchlike divisions and subdivisions, their arrangement is fundamentally spatial, even where it is one of ascent or progress from one chapter to the next, whereas the gaps between letters are not spaces but instead temporal intervals. At the beginning of Letter IV, Hurd appeals explicitly to his imagined correspondent: 'What think you, my good friend, of my last learned Letter? Don't you begin to favour this conjecture, as whimsical as it may seem, of the rise and genius of knight-errantry?' (Letter IV, 23) 'But you ask me', his correspondent supposedly replies, 'where I learned the several particulars, on which I form this profound system. [...] Your request is reasonable' (p. 24). Again, later on, Hurd remarks that 'I am aware, as you object to me, that, in the affair of *Religion* and *Gallantry*, the resemblance between the hero and the knight is not so striking' (Letter V, 40); likewise, 'I have taken the fancy, with your leave, to try my hand on this curious subject [namely, "the general plan and conduct of the Faery Queen"]' (Letter VIII, 61); and, finally, 'Did the poet [Spenser] do right in this [namely, "to adorn a gothic story; and, to be consistent throughout, he chose that the form of his work should be of a piece with his subject"]? I cannot tell, but comparing his work with that of another great Poet, who followed the system you seem to recommend, I see no reason to be peremptory in condemning his judgment' (Letter IX, 76).

Who, in these examples, is it that objects, gives leave, and, indeed, seems to recommend a particular system for poetic composition? The suggestion that these may be the traces of Hurd's friendship and long correspondence with the

---

[25] [Richard Hurd], *Letters on Chivalry and Romance* (London: printed for A. Millar; Cambridge: printed for W. Thurlbourn and J. Woodyer, 1762), Letter I, 1, and Letter XII, 120. Further references are given after quotations in the text.

editor and critic William Warburton, though potentially informative, is, in this instance, beside the point.[26] While it is possible that the reader of Hurd's *Letters* may detect at such moments as those quoted above a series of potentially unintended acknowledgements of the other half of a correspondence only one half of which the reader can see, the effect of such moments is as likely, however, to be to recruit the reader her- or himself into the position of a participant in that correspondence. Even were the reader to respond simply by rejecting the imputation that she or he ever did object to something that Hurd has claimed, or that she or he propounds a certain system not aligned to the one Hurd is advancing, the result is to redouble the persuasiveness of Hurd's argument because such a reaction positions the reader on, as it were, Hurd's side. Though neither do they have an explicitly nominated addressee, nor do they, of course, integrate another side into the correspondence, Hurd's *Letters* do invite the intellectual collaboration, and thence the assent, of their reader.

What both Orrery and Hurd seek to exploit, in their different ways, are the distinctive features of epistolarity for criticism. As S. D. Chrostowska has observed in her indispensable overview of German (and Polish and Russian) literary criticism in the eighteenth and nineteenth centuries, the extraordinary efflorescence of literary criticism and theory in Germany in this period was characterized by the frequency with which it took an epistolary form. As Chrostowska notes, most examples of German epistolary criticism were written for a wide readership from the outset.[27] Letters and correspondences were often the mainstay of the leading literary journals, and frequently deployed an 'implicit or explicit addressee' who functioned as 'an imaginary stand-in for an intended reader [...], one of compatible intelligence or, on the contrary, exemplifying the qualities being criticized'.[28] Chrostowska adduces as instances of actual and supposed correspondences the correspondence conducted by G. E. Lessing, Friedrich Nicolai, and Moses Mendelssohn in 1756–7, the *Briefwechsel über das Trauerspiel* ('Correspondence on Tragedy'), and Herder's *Auszug aus einem Briefwechsel über Ossian und die Lieder alter Völker* ('Extract from a Correspondence on Ossian and the Songs of Ancient Peoples'), which she drolly describes as 'a fictitious excerpt from a non-existent correspondence' and which was first published in the collaborative and widely influential critical anthology *Von deutscher Art und Kunst: Einige fliegende Blätter* ('On German Character and Art: A Collection of Broadsheets'—or,

---

[26] See G. M. Ditchfield and Sarah Brewer, 'Hurd, Richard', *ODNB* <https://doi.org/10.1093/ref:odnb/14249>.

[27] S. D. Chrostowska, *Literature on Trial: The Emergence of Critical Discourse in Germany, Poland, and Russia, 1700–1800* (Toronto: University of Toronto Press, 2012), 62, 261 n. 53. For a thorough discussion of the same period in German criticism, with a particular focus on the critical letters of Johann Christoph Gottsched, see Thomas Nolden, *'An einem jungen Dichter': Studien zur epistolaren Poetik* (Würzberg: Königshausen & Neumann, 1995), 45–74.

[28] Chrostowska, 62.

perhaps better to evoke the ephemerality indicated by the subtitle, 'Some Leaves in the Air', of 1776).

These correspondences, like *The Ferrante Letters* with which I opened this chapter, are conducted among equal participants, whereas Johann Georg Hamann's playful *Fünf Hirtenbriefe, das Schuldrama betreffend* ('Five Pastoral Letters Concerning the School Play') (1763), Heinrich Wilhelm von Gerstenberg's long-running *Briefe über Merkwürdigkeiten der Literatur* ('Letters on the Oddities of Literature') (1766–71), August Wilhelm Schlegel's *Briefe über Poesie, Sylbenmass und Sprache* ('Letters on Poetry, Metre, and Language') of 1775, Christoph Martin Wieland's *Briefe an einen jungen Dichter* ('Letters to a Young Poet') (1782–4), and the *Brief über den Roman* ('Letter on the Novel') of 1800 by Friedrich Schlegel are, like Orrery's and Hurd's letters, the work of a single author writing to an addressee, sometimes named and sometimes not, sometimes explicitly offering her or him advice and sometimes not.[29] Central to the critical arguments of each of these texts is the invocation of an addressee, real or imagined, explicit or implicit, and the opportunities for deeper thinking and reconsideration off the page that the episodic nature of correspondence fosters. As Hamann puts it at the end of his first 'pastoral letter', for example, 'these are the rough preliminaries of my little correspondence, with which (hopefully) I'll go on and get ready for next time, si vacat & placidi rationem admittitis [Juvenal, *Satires* 1: 'if you have time and will listen calmly to reason']—. Now it is lunchtime. Keep well'; and at the beginning of his second letter: 'The longer I ponder the concept of a school play, the more fruitful it seems to me.'[30] The breaks by which daily life is routinely punctuated ('lunchtime') are allowed in turn to interrupt the correspondence as well, and the hiatus between instalments of the correspondence is explicitly acknowledged ('Keep well'); on the other hand, the continuity of the correspondence with a venerable discursive tradition is evoked by the citation from Juvenal (who also, incidentally, furnishes the epigraph to the whole correspondence), and it is resumed with an energetic emphasis on the results of the writer's contemplation in the meantime between letters.

It is perhaps Wieland's *Briefe an einen jungen Dichter*, however, that may be taken as the progenitor of a significant subgenre of epistolary criticism: the letter of advice to a poet starting out on a career in which the chances of success are at best uncertain.[31] As H. J. Meessen pointed out many years ago, Wieland's fiction that a young poet had asked him for advice may have served as a useful pretext

[29] Chrostowska, 62, 216 n. 56.

[30] Johann Georg Hamann, *Fünf Hirtenbriefe, das Schuldrama betreffend*, in Hamann, *Sämtliche Werke*, ed. Josef Nadler, 6 vols (Vienna: Thomas-Morus, 1949), ii: *Schriften über Philosophie, Philologie, Kritik, 1758–1763*, first letter (354–5) and second (356). Note that what Hamann had described at the opening of the first letter as 'my whims' have become, in the interval between that and the second letter, 'the concept' of a school play.

[31] For a discussion of the letter to a young poet as genre, see Nolden, esp. 23–42.

for issuing 'a blanket reply to the many budding writers who pestered him with letters and unsolicited manuscripts'; and, as Meessen also shows, one of the young poets addressed by Wieland's letters, especially the opening one, is clearly himself.[32] The young poet is allowed a spirited, impassioned voice in Wieland's opening letter (if not exactly a part in the correspondence as such) in response to the, in some ways, more worldly advice Wieland has been starting to bestow. But this is only a brief incursion, and, indeed, Wieland's response that the young poet's experience seems very close to his own lends credence to Meessen's reading.

The letter to the young poet certainly became a flourishing genre in the centuries after Wieland, perhaps the outstanding later instances being Rainer Maria Rilke's *Briefe an einen jungen Dichter* and, in England, Virginia Woolf's 'Letter to a Young Poet', which, though a one-off, was part of the Hogarth Press's series of letters to various figures.[33] This particular subgenre of epistolary criticism is criticism understood as advice—such as Woolf's advice that writing is learnt by imagining that you are someone different, rather in the manner that she herself imagines the situation of the young poet in order to be able to give him useful advice at all.[34] The provision of advice, of course, is one form in which the dialogue between the self-confident young poet envisaged by Kant and those seeking to disabuse him of his youthful regard for his own compositions might imaginably proceed. In keeping, in fact, with Kant's aesthetics, the letter to the young poet rarely seeks to lay down rules, preferring instead to build up over time estimable examples, persuasive arguments, and questions that might need to be answered in a way to which correspondence is conducive.

There are, however, few requests for advice in what are surely the most celebrated letters *from* a young poet—namely, those of John Keats. The rejection of, or defence against, advice is central to a number of Keats's most significant letters. For one who was supposedly killed by a review (as mentioned briefly in Chapter 3), Keats's declared attitude towards criticism from others is striking. Writing in October 1818 to thank his publisher James Hessey for having forwarded him letters published in the *Morning Chronicle* that sought to defend Keats from J. W. Croker's attack on *Endymion* in the *Quarterly Review*, Keats seeks explicitly to diminish the impact that such conspicuously public criticism has on him generally. 'Praise or blame has but a momentary effect on the man whose love of beauty in the abstract makes him a severe critic on his own Works.' He explains

---

[32] H. J. Meessen, 'Wieland's "Briefe an einen jungen Dichter"', *Monatshefte für deutschen Unterricht, deutsche Sprache und Literatur*, 47 (1955), 193–208 (198–9).

[33] Helmut Göbel et al. (eds), *Briefe an junge Dichter* (Göttingen: Wallstein, 1998), collects examples of the form, from the rather winning letter from 'Hexametron' in the early eighteenth-century German newspaper *Der Patriot*, to the exchange between Johann Voß and the celebrated poet Erich Fried, who is moved to apologize for the fact that his typewriter has no keys for the German ß or for umlauts, before telling Voß that, in Fried's view, he misunderstands what poetry is (p. 182).

[34] Virginia Woolf, 'A Letter to a Young Poet' (1932), in *Collected Essays*, 4 vols (London: Hogarth Press, 1966), ii. 182–95 (193).

further in a passage that is crucial for the self-presentation of his mode of working and is, as such, worth quoting at some length:

> My own domestic criticism has given me pain without comparison beyond what Blackwood or the Quarterly could possibly inflict. and also when I feel I am right, no external praise can give me such a glow as my own solitary reperception & ratification of what is fine. J.S. [one of the otherwise supportive *Chronicle* correspondents] is perfectly right in regard to the slipshod Endymion. That it is so is no fault of mine.—No!—though it may sound a little paradoxical. It is as good as I had power to make it—by myself—Had I been nervous about its being a perfect piece, & with that view asked advice, & trembled over every page, it would not have been written; for it is not in my nature to fumble—I will write independantly [*sic*].—I have written independently *without Judgment*—I may write independently & *without judgment* hereafter.—The Genius of Poetry must work out its own salvation in a man: It cannot be matured by law & precept, but by sensation & watchfulness in itself—That which is creative must create itself— [...] In Endymion, I leaped headlong into the Sea, and thereby have become better acquainted with the Soundings, the quicksands, & the rocks, than if I had stayed upon the green shore, and piped a silly pipe, and took tea & comfortable advice.—I was never afraid of failure; for I would sooner fail than not be among the greatest—But I am nigh getting into a rant.[35]

This letter bristles with the confidence—or at least the performance of confidence—in his own 'Genius of Poetry' that would lead Keats famously to declare to George and Georgiana Keats in a letter dated five days later that 'I think I shall be among the English Poets after my death' (i. 394). It is no coincidence that in that later letter Keats is relaying to his brother and sister-in-law the details of the hostile reviews he has received and the letters, including those in the *Chronicle* for which he had thanked Hessey, that had been written in his defence—a circumstance that somewhat dilutes his insistence on the relative insignificance to him of external, merely momentary criticism. Nevertheless, the twice repeated rejection of 'advice' in the letter to Hessey quoted above ('& with that view asked advice', 'and took tea & comfortable advice') is characteristic of Keats's letters, especially in the way that those rejections of advice develop into Keats's articulation of the priority of 'sensation & watchfulness' over 'law & precept'—an opposition that, in part via Christ's injunction to his disciples to be 'watchful' (something they conspicuously fail to be), hints at the supersession of the Old Testament by the New. Keats's distinctly *self*-critical admonition—'But I am nigh getting into a rant'—stops him from plunging any more deeply into the subjects of the mode of

---

[35] 8 October 1818; *The Letters of John Keats, 1814–1821*, ed. Hyder Edward Rollins, 2 vols (Cambridge: Cambridge University Press, 1958), i. 373–4. Further references are given after quotations in the text.

Endymion's composition or into the topic of his more general poetic ambitions. At the same time, the description of his own reflections as the beginnings, at least, of a rant also prompts the reader to reflect on whether what Keats has just said does in fact constitute a 'rant', or whether it was unlike, in fact, the kind of belligerent railing often dressed up as 'advice' and encountered in organs like the *Quarterly* (and sometimes, even, the friendlier *Chronicle*).

It is letters such as the one above, with its reflection on the mode of composition of one of Keats's own poems, that led B. Ifor Evans to declare of Keats that 'the letters are the truest criticism of the verse'.[36] Keats's image for the composition of *Endymion*—of having plunged into the sea, and thus into an element both potentially inhospitable and gloriously mysterious to humans, and one that other poets might have been keen to get out of as soon as possible—echoes what can only be miscalled his most famous critical concept, 'I mean *Negative Capability*' (to George and Tom Keats, 21, 27 (?) December 1817; i. 193).[37] The letter in which Keats heralds the capability 'of being in uncertainties, Mysteries, doubts, without any irritable reaching after fact & reason'—an image that juxtaposes not only uncertainty and so on with 'fact & reason', but also immersion ('being in') with grasping ('reaching after')—is certainly keen to display its own immersion in a specifically critical context. In describing the context of discussion in which '*Negative Capability*' 'at once [...] struck me', Keats draws a distinction that echoes Kant's distinction between *Disputieren* and *Streiten*: 'Brown and Dilke walked with me & back from the Christmas pantomime. I had not a dispute but a disquisition with Dilke, on various subjects; several things dovetailed in my mind, and at once it struck me [...]': unlike Kant, Keats does not specify what distinguishes a disquisition from a dispute—that would be irritably to reach for a definition—and, in contrast to '*Streiten*', 'disquisition' is more Latinate, less *echt* street-talking. But the distinction Keats is drawing nevertheless bears a significant resemblance to Kant's. Like the young poet of Kant's scenario (discussed in the previous chapter), Keats is hardly lacking in the confidence of his own judgements, with which this relatively short letter is brimming—from his opening praise for Kean's return to the stage as Richard III, the enclosure of his assessment of Kean's performance in Burges's *Riches*, which had been published in *The Champion*, his opinion of Benjamin West's painting *Death on a Pale Horse*, his allusion to *King Lear*, his animadversions on the 'mannerism in their very eating & drinking, in their mere handling a Decanter' of his irksome dinner companions

[36] B. Ifor Evans, *Tradition and Romanticism: Studies in English Poetry from Chaucer to W. B. Yeats* (London: Routledge, 1940), p. 133.
[37] On what Rollins has described as the 'very puzzling' transcript made of this letter by John Jeffrey (Keats, *Letters*, i. 91 n. 1), see Rollins's own brief discussion, 'Keats's Misdated Letters', *Harvard Library Bulletin*, 7 (1953), 172–87 (175), and, more recently and extensively, Brian Rejak and Michael Theune, 'Introduction: Disquisitions: Reading Negative Capability, 1817–2017' and Brian Rejak, 'John Keats's Jeffrey's "Negative Capability"; or, Accidentally Undermining Keats', in Rejak and Theune (eds), *Keats's Negative Capability: New Origins and Afterlives* (Liverpool: Liverpool University Press, 2019), 1–12, 31–46.

of a previous evening, his general assessment of Shakespeare's enormous capacity for 'Negative Capability', the concomitant contrast with Coleridge, to the brief, condescending assessment of '[p]oor Shelley'. While the tone of the letter's judgements taken individually is decided, their sheer profusion, their invocation of the host of discussants who called them forth (Kean, Reynolds, the merely witty rather than properly humorous fellow-diners, Brown, Dilke, Shakespeare, Coleridge, Shelley, and, of course, 'my dear Brothers' themselves), and the manner in which each topic for discussion gives way to the one that succeeds it, evoke not the 'irritable reaching after fact & reason' that a more sustained discussion of each judgement might have entailed, but instead precisely the capability of 'remaining content with half knowledge'.

It is useful to recall here Henry James's habit of following what have become the most celebrated pronouncements of his prefaces with what are, in some ways, apologies for, or qualifications of, them (examined in Chapter 1); likewise, Keats rounds off his articulation of 'Negative Capability', which had reached its verbally outlandish crescendo in 'a fine isolated verisimilitude caught from the Penitralium of mystery', by declaring that '[t]his pursued through Volumes would perhaps take us no further than this, that with a great poet the sense of Beauty overcomes every other consideration, or rather obliterates all consideration' (i. 194). Perhaps the pursuit of his insight through volumes would indeed take us no further than that—but, again like James, as soon as this halt has been called, consideration is resumed with the concluding comment on the incongruously quantitative 'Quota of good qualities' displayed by Shelley (i. 194). Where the previous paragraph had ended with what in fact appears to be the reasoned conclusion to an argument in the beautiful obliteration of consideration, here Keats has recourse, finally, to the exclamation 'in sooth la!!', before requesting his brothers' reply. As John Barnard remarks, '[t]he self presented [in letters] is a literary construct, but one which attempts through its own self-awareness to reach, genuinely, across time and space to his correspondents'.[38] Unlike the 'irritable reaching after fact & reason' that Keats casts as inimical to 'Negative Capability', his letters 'reach' instead to his correspondents—correspondents who include not only the letters' addressees but the letters' many implied interlocutors and discussants as well. The critical self is at once aware of itself and its own judgements, while simultaneously reaching beyond them, not to some final ground of rational judgement, but to other judges, with their judgements and their modes of being in uncertainties as well.

As Rollins, Roe, and Rejack all imply in their discussions of the letter to George and Tom Keats, the sheer chanciness of the survival and transmission of that letter is in keeping with the kind of criticism it practises. We have also seen that Keats's letters correspond not only with their addressees but with a wide array of

---

[38] John Barnard, 'Keats's Letters: "Remembrancing and enchaining"', in Susan Wolfson (ed.), *The Cambridge Companion to John Keats* (Cambridge: Cambridge University Press, 2001), 120–34 (131).

critical interlocutors as well. For all their apparent privacy, they arise from and are sent towards (as it were) a discursive, literary context. Both characteristics are exemplified in what Barnard describes as Keats's 'long journal letter' to his brother and sister-in-law, written intermittently from February to May 1819 (ii. 58–109).[39] This letter contains Keats's apothegm in which he again negatively compares a celebrated recent poet with Shakespeare—'Lord Byron cuts a figure—but he is not figurative—Shakespeare led a life of Allgeory; his works are the comments on it—' (ii. 67)—and it also contains, more or less verbatim, Keats's own review of Reynolds's *Peter Bell* for Hunt's *Examiner*, significant poems of his own, and his celebrated invitation to his correspondents to 'Call the world if you Please ' "The vale of Soul-making" ' (ii. 102).[40] It is perhaps inevitable that a letter of this length, composed over nearly a quarter of a year, should involve so much, but it is nevertheless characteristic of what we might call Keats's corresponding imagination that it is so profoundly immersed in its world. Much of this letter, like so many of Keats's letters, is touchingly intimate, expressive of the familial affection he feels for his now far-distant near-relations. But, as is made clear by Keats's disquisitions on the world as a vale of soul-making in which the individual is formed by the medium she or he inhabits, the expression of intimacy is, if not exactly dependent upon, then enmeshed with public networks of the transmission of writing. For instance, Keats describes the frustration of his hope 'of seeing some young Men who were to take some Letter for us to you [...]' (ii. 71). Not only has he missed this chance to send his letters to his brother and sister-in-law, but he has also missed 'the sail of the Post-Packet to new york or Philadelphia—by which last, your Brothers have sent some Letters' (ii. 71). He relays another frustration—'The weather in town yesterday was so stifling that I could not remain there though I wanted much to see Kean in Hotspur'—which, Rollins suggests in his note, is somewhat implausible, since the temperature on 11 March 1819 was not that hot. If it is not an accurate account of actual meteorological conditions, perhaps this description of the stifling weather was prompted instead by the verbal environment of Keats's letter itself—prompted, that is, by the desire to see 'Kean in *Hot*spur', a mechanism of verbal suggestion that one might also trace back from 'Kean' (*keen*) to 'wanted much'. Both the near-at-hand—town, yesterday—and the distant— New York, Philadelphia—are, in this letter, scenes of frustration. But they are frustrations that paradoxically bear considerable fruit, since, had Keats managed to meet the young men who could convey his letter to its intended recipients, the letter that would eventually fill another thirty pages or so (in Rollins's edition) might not have been written in the form it was at all.

---

[39] Barnard, 131.

[40] The accretion of quotation marks around 'The vale of Soul-making' is Keats's. For a recent virtuoso reading of this letter, see Yohei Igarashi, *The Connected Condition: Romanticism and the Dream of Communication* (Stanford: Stanford University Press, 2020), 149–54.

The vicissitudes of letter-writing—of the lags between writing, sending, receipt, and response, for example—can be productive, and can, as we saw with Hurd, be claimed for texts that little resemble letters other than in their designation as such. To relieve the sense of frustration that had settled on Keats's spring 1819 letter, Keats had recourse to the still more nearly at hand: 'I have by me at present Hazlitt's Letter to Gifford' (ii. 71). Barnard insightfully notices that the passage this announcement inaugurates, most of which is given over to fairly lengthy extracts from Hazlitt's *Letter*, concludes as it began with an evocation of the books strewn around Keats and on which he is physically pressing while he writes his letter: 'I am writing this on the Maid's tragedy which I have read since tea with Great pleasure' (ii. 73), an observation that lends an embodied, situated twist to the idea that criticism involves writing 'on' a text.[41] Commenting on a slightly later moment in this letter, Igarashi suggests that '[i]t seems that when Keats attempts to visualize his own life or the world he lives in, his mind turns to the idea of a medium, and when he thinks about a medium, he visualizes texts, often difficult ones'.[42] Having been frustrated by the failure to send his own letters and thus turning to Hazlitt's *Letter to William Gifford, Esq.*, Keats is turning not just to any of the texts lying about on his table or under his page, but to another critical letter, albeit, unlike the letter he is writing, an open one.[43] As is well known, Keats in his letters frequently draws on Hazlitt without explicitly acknowledging him—as he does, for instance, in the discussion of Benjamin West's painting in the letter to George and Tom Keats examined above.[44] Here, though, he is candid about his source, and liberally strews the ensuing passage with quotation marks (even if they do not always fall in the right places); in concluding his extracts from Hazlitt, moreover, he expressly praises '[t]he manner in which this is managed: the force and innate power with which it yeasts and works up itself—the feeling for the costume of society; is in a style of genius' (ii. 76). Keats had good reason to enjoy Hazlitt's 'feu de joie' (ii. 73) at Gifford's expense, having suspected Gifford (wrongly, as it happens) of being the author of an attack on his poetry in the Tory *Quarterly Review*. Keats's recourse to Hazlitt at just this point is a recourse not only to an amenable polemic (though it is that too) but to another mode of epistolary criticism at the moment when the delivery of his own letters has been frustrated. Keats's own familiar letter thus involves itself with another, public, polemical, critical missive.

Keats makes sure to begin his extracts from Hazlitt with the latter's implicit justification for responding to Gifford in the form of a letter:

---

[41] Barnard, 131, and also cf. Igarashi, 149–54.   [42] Igarashi, 152.

[43] In the following I quote Hazlitt as quoted by Keats; cf. William Hazlitt, *A Letter to William Gifford, Esq.* (1819), in *The Complete Works of William Hazlitt*, ed. P. P. Howe, 21 vols (London: Dent, 1930–4), ix: *A Reply to 'Z'*, etc. (1932), 11–59.

[44] See Keats, *Letters*, i. 192 n. 9, for details.

Sir, You have an ugly trick of saying what is not true of any one you do not like; and it will be the object of this Letter to cure you of it. You say what you please of others; it is time you were told what you are. In doing this give me leave to borrow the familiarity of your style:—for the fidelity of the picture I shall be answerable.   (Quoted by Keats, ii. 71–2)

It is Gifford's connection with the 'great and powerful' (in another extract quoted by Keats) who

do not like to have the privacy of their self love startled by the obtrusive and unmanageable claims of Literature and Philosophy, except through the intervention of people like you, whom; if they have common penetration, they soon find out to be without any superiority of intellect; or if they do not whom they can despise for their meanness of soul.   (Quoted by Keats, ii. 73)

The form of the open letter ideally suits Hazlitt's attempt to expose the 'privacy of their self love' betrayed by those Gifford calls 'wise and good'. What Hazlitt describes, in a phrase that surely appealed to Keats, as 'the obtrusive and unmanageable claims of Literature and Philosophy' are crucially enacted in the form of the open letter. It is obtrusive to have others read letters addressed to you (and it is notable how frequently Hazlitt deploys this little word, 'you', in his *Letter*, especially in those passages extracted by Keats), and the management of this correspondence is at the outset completely beyond Gifford's control (though recall, in contrast, Keats's praise for the way Hazlitt 'managed' his riposte to Gifford mentioned above). In a passage that Keats does not transcribe for his brother and sister-in-law, Hazlitt issues his withering judgement on Gifford's procedure, which is marked less by self-love, in fact, than by self-knowledge:

There is an innate littleness and vulgarity in all you do. In combating an opinion, you never take a broad and liberal ground, state it fairly, allow what there is of truth or an appearance of truth, and then assert your own judgment by exposing what is deficient in it, and giving a more masterly view of the subject. No: this would be committing your powers and pretensions where you dare not trust them. You know yourself better.[45]

In one sense, Gifford has heeded the demand of enlightenment: dare to know yourself. It is just that, for Gifford, that does not take much daring. Hazlitt's emphasis here on exposure, on Gifford's habit of keeping to safe ground, rather than 'committing your powers and pretensions where you dare not trust them', is in keeping with the selection of the form of the open letter for his riposte to

---

[45] Hazlitt, 16.

Gifford's attacks. The open letter exposes both Gifford, who refuses to expose himself even as he gleefully exposes others to criticism, and Hazlitt, whose strictures on Gifford are self-exposed, so to speak, to the scrutiny of a public tribunal who have no immediate part in this dispute, but who are drawn into it as observers and, necessarily, judges of it.

Keats's juxtaposition of his own familiar communication with his brother and sister-in-law with Hazlitt's public epistle against Gifford recruits Hazlitt to Keats's defence against his critics. Keats is, as it were, cheering himself up, since it is also via Hazlitt's *Letter* that he has overcome the frustration of missing the post-packet and come to share in the critic's 'feu de joie'. In one of the compelling verbal associations that are characteristic of Keats's letters, it is Hazlitt's *feu* that has burned brightly and thus consumed Keats's capacity to write on further: 'for the candles are burnt down and I am using the wax taper—which has a long snuff on it—the fire is at its last click' (ii. 73). But it has been worth it. The frustration of the passage of Keats's letters into the external network that would have conveyed them to his relatives is remedied by the inverse involvement into his letter of another letter, Hazlitt's, that is already and assertively public.

*

Keats's own 'domestic criticism' is, as we have seen, deeply intertwined with a wider world of literary and critical discussion—as is especially legible in his turn to the epistolary form of Hazlitt's criticism in the *Letter to William Gifford*. Epistolary criticism is thus often compacted of the intimacy of the letter and the publicity of criticism, even where it would seem to eschew the latter. I conclude this chapter by turning to a twentieth-century correspondence that spilled dramatically onto the letters' pages of some prominent literary journals. The correspondence between Vladimir Nabokov and Edmund Wilson is marked by numerous disagreements—'we have always been frank with each other,' as Nabokov remarks to Wilson when finding fault with the latter's *A Piece of My Mind: Reflections at Sixty*, 'and I know that you will find my criticism exhilarating'—but exhilaration became exasperation when Wilson reviewed Nabokov's translation of Pushkin's *Eugene Onegin* in the *New York Review of Books* in 1965.[46] Nabokov responded at length to Wilson's criticisms in a letter to the *NYRB* (as did others, though not at such length and without such an obvious investment). Nearly six years later, Nabokov wrote what would turn out to be his last letter to Wilson:

---

[46] The quotation is from a letter of 13 December 1956, in *Dear Bunny, Dear Volodya: The Nabokov–Wilson Letters, 1940–1971*, ed. Simon Karlinsky, rev. edn (Berkeley and Los Angeles: University of California Press, 2001), 338. Further references to this edition are given after quotations in the text. For a detailed account of the end of Nabokov and Wilson's friendship, see Alex Beam, *The Feud: Vladimir Nabokov, Edmund Wilson, and the End of a Beautiful Friendship* (New York: Pantheon, 2016).

Dear Bunny,

A few days ago I had the occasion to reread the whole batch (Russ., *vsyu pachku*) of our correspondence. It was such a pleasure to feel again the warmth of your many kindnesses, the various thrills of our friendship, that constant excitement of art and intellectual discovery.

I was sorry to hear (from Lena Levin) that you had been ill, and happy to learn that you were much better.

Please believe that I have long ceased to bear you a grudge for your incomprehensible incomprehension of Pushkin's and Nabokov's *Onegin*.

Yours,

Vladimir Nabokov

(2 March 1971; 372)

In some respects, it is a touching and affectionate letter. The retention of the term of endearment for Wilson ('Bunny', first adopted by Nabokov near the beginning of their correspondence thirty years earlier, though in fact Wilson's mother's name for him), the expression of sympathy at the news of his recent illness and of happiness at his recovery, and above all the rekindling of the old feelings, especially 'that constant excitement of art and intellectual discovery', are all evidence of an abiding and genuine affection. But this is a letter from 'Vladimir Nabokov', as he (especially in contrast to his familiar address to 'Dear Bunny') rather stiffly signs himself, and there is indeed a sting in the tail. The reassurance that Nabokov 'long ceased to bear [...] a grudge' towards Wilson for the latter's criticism of his translation of Pushkin also serves, as with any such reassurance, to remind Wilson that Nabokov did indeed once bear a grudge. Furthermore, Wilson's strictures are castigated as mere 'incomprehension'—itself 'incomprehensible', though it is perfectly clear which incomprehension is culpable and which simply inevitable—and they were strictures, Nabokov insinuates, aimed not just at Nabokov but at Wilson's beloved Pushkin as well: 'your incomprehensible incomprehension of *Pushkin's* and Nabokov's *Onegin*.'

Wilson responded ('I was very glad to get your letter' (8 March 1971; 373)), but, as noted above, Nabokov's was the last letter that he would write to Wilson, if not the last he would write about him. In his response to Nabokov's attempt to rekindle their correspondence, Wilson informed Nabokov that he had included an account of his visit to the Nabokovs' home in Ithaca (the town in upstate New York where Cornell University, Nabokov's then employer, is located) in a forthcoming book, *Upstate: Records and Recollections of Northern New York*. His forewarning to Nabokov is as much a foreboding: 'I hope it will not again impair our personal relations (it shouldn't).' It did. Ignoring the fact that he had actually been alerted to the imminent publication of *Upstate* by Wilson, his long-time correspondent, Nabokov's letter in response, addressed to the editor of the *New York Times Book Review*, opens by acknowledging a different 'kind correspondent' who 'Xeroxed and mailed me pp. 154–162 referring to my person as imagined by Edmund Wilson in his recent work *Upstate*'. Along with the condemnation of the 'Philistine imagination' and 'particularly repulsive blend of vulgarity and naïvité' of his 'former friend', Nabokov takes aim one last time at a habit of reading for which he had repeatedly castigated Wilson, though in less decidedly vitriolic terms, throughout the 'whole batch of our correspondence', the re-perusal of which had but lately given him such pleasure:

> First of all, the 'miseries, horrors, and handicaps' that he assumes I was subject to during forty years before we first met in New York are mostly figments of his warped fancy. He has no direct knowledge of my past. He has not even bothered to read my *Speak, Memory*, the records and recollections of a happy expatriation that began practically on the day of my birth. The method he favors is gleaning from my fiction what he supposes to be actual, 'real-life' impressions and then popping them back into my novels and considering my characters in that inept light – rather like the Shakesperian scholar who deduced Shakespeare's mother from the plays and then discovered allusions to her in the very passages he had twisted to manufacture the lady.[47]

Nabokov's attack on Wilson's 'method' is essentially a distillation of his numerous criticisms of Wilson's determination to trace literature to 'actual, "real-life" impressions'. At a rather happier, if hardly less contentious, moment in their correspondence, for example, Wilson expressed incomprehension (it is fitting that their correspondence should culminate in 'incomprehensible incomprehension') at what he took to be Nabokov's 'study of butterflies from the point of view of their habitat' while pretending 'that it is possible to write about human beings and leave out of account all question of society and environment' (15 November 1948; 238). Nabokov retorts that, in fact, 'biological and ecological characters have no taxonomic value *per se*. As a systematist, I always give priority to structural characters. [...] What you want me to do is to give superiority to ecology over morphology' (21 November 1948; 241). The dispute over the priority of (to adopt these terms) ecology or morphology in the case of literature is central to the whole of Nabokov and Wilson's correspondence, as it would be in Nabokov's barbs against Wilson at its end.

The correspondence is marked from very early not just by the frank exchange of views about each other's work, but also, more fundamentally, by the formulation of distinct literary principles intended to provoke response. These views are not only—not mostly, in fact—at the level of aesthetic principle or artistic procedure, but at the level of minute verbal particulars as well. In his response to *The Real Life of Sebastian Knight*, Nabokov's first novel in English, for example, Wilson moves from

---

[47] To John Leonard, Editor of the *New York Times Book Review*, 7 November 1971; repr. in Vladimir Nabokov, *Strong Opinions* (London: Penguin, 1973; repr. 2011), 187–9.

his opening expressions of enchantment and amazement to fine (but occasionally condescending) discriminations on Nabokov's English and his 'lamentable weakness for punning' (20 October 1941; 55–6); in praising *Laughter in the Dark*, Wilson seizes the opportunity to say that he 'noticed, by the way, that at one point the tip of somebody's cigar is referred to' (3 February 1942; 65), a usage in James's *The Aspern Papers* at which Nabokov had baulked in a letter two months earlier ('*Red tip* makes one think of a red pencil or a dog licking itself'; 28 November 1941; 59); and, on the thirty-seven pages of *The Person from Porlock* (which would become *Bend Sinister* and with which Wilson was ultimately disappointed) that Nabokov had sent him, Wilson expresses his liking, eagerness to see the rest, and view that 'there are three English verbs that you do not handle with quite a sure touch: *discern, reach* and *shun* (which you sometimes confuse with *shirk*). Otherwise, it is very well written' (24 January 1944; 138). There is something of Wilson's own sure touch in his handling of Nabokov's misuse of verbs all associated in one way or another with handling and touching, or with not handling and not touching. Few positive judgements in the Wilson–Nabokov correspondence are unqualified (that is less so with the negative ones), and '*otherwise*, it is very well written' comes to be their keynote. More important, though, is the cultivation throughout their correspondence of this kind of close discrimination. The request for and furnishing of opinions, the enclosure of texts for more or less immediate comment, the traffic of address and response essential to correspondence cultivates between Wilson and Nabokov this kind of focused critical commentary and judgement.

But the critical foci of Wilson and Nabokov's correspondence were not limited to their own works. The repeated expressions of sheer incredulity at the other's opinions concerning a vast range of literary work are what give Nabokov and Wilson's correspondence its sustained critical zest—and the fact that it is sustained across the intervals that inevitably come between the sending and receipt of the letters is part of what lends it its urgency. This is a quality that arises, moreover, from the fact that it is a correspondence, since it is inconceivable (to adopt a rather Nabokovian stance for a moment) not only without the clash of two unsociably social literary-critical personalities, but also without the insistence of question and answer, provocation and reaction, even of sometimes tactlessly proffered advice and its resentful rejection, to which correspondence can give rise. In the opening exchanges of their disagreement about the status of André Malraux, for example, Nabokov queries whether Wilson offers his contrary judgement in earnest, a query that brings to the fore a fundamental question of critical exchange:

> *Et maintenant—en garde!* I am at a loss to understand your liking Malraux's books (or are you just kidding me? or is literary taste so subjective a matter that two persons of discrimination can be at odds in such a simple case as this?). He is quite a third-rate writer (but a good kind man, a very decent fellow). *J'ai dressé* a little list of questions (regarding *La Condition Humaine*) which I suggest you answer. (27 November 1946; 202)

We saw in Chapter 3 Wilson's own propensity for the kind of rating to which Nabokov here subjects Malraux. Here is the opposition of literature, on the one hand, and ethical and political considerations, on the other, upon which Nabokov would continually insist. It is tempting, perhaps, to dismiss Nabokov's questions here as merely rhetorical, but questions as to whether judgements are in earnest or whether differences in 'literary taste' are ultimately irreducible are fundamental to the conduct of criticism. Just as tempting is to take sides, especially when a cherished writer is at issue between the belligerents. But a critical correspondence would thereby risk being reduced to a one-voiced polemic.[48]

Simon Karlinsky concludes his useful account of the Wilson–Nabokov correspondence by noticing the curious paradox that '[f]or all of Wilson's awesome scope as a literary critic' he did little publicly to establish Nabokov's reputation. 'Wilson had enjoyed *Speak, Memory*' (giving the lie, incidentally, to Nabokov's allegation that he had not bothered to read it), 'which had preceded *Lolita*, and he very much liked *Pnin*, which followed it, but he said so in his letters to Nabokov, not in critical reviews.'[49] This is to assume, of course, that any public pronouncement of Wilson's concerning Nabokov would have aided in establishing the latter's reputation: as Karlinsky goes on to note, Wilson did not deign to pass comment on *Pale Fire*, thought *Ada* unreadable, and never seems to have read *The Gift*; and he was unabashed about opening a letter of 30 January 1947 by declaring 'I was rather disappointed in *Bend Sinister*' (p. 209), a letter, incidentally, which, as it warms to its theme, contains the undying marker of the letter of complaint, 'Another thing [...]' (p. 210). Wilson's major public pronouncement on Nabokov's work, the review of his translation of *Eugene Onegin*, was hardly the puff from a powerful patron that would have sped it on its way. It was Nabokov himself who remarked of Wilson: '[a]s with most good critics, your war-crying voice is better than your hymn-singing one' (18 November 1950; 282). Karlinsky's opposition of 'letters to Nabokov' and 'critical reviews'—akin, incidentally, to the opposition between slow correspondence and quick reviewing entertained, as we saw near the beginning of this chapter, by Sarah Chihaya in *The Ferrante Letters*—may be taken to hint at a more pervasive distinction between criticism and letters that would not, however, be supported by their correspondence. The correspondence of Nabokov and Wilson was enmeshed in a network of critical discussion that traversed the distinction between private and public, personal and professional, amicable and critical, thus disabling any definition of literary criticism that would assign literary criticism, a priori, to public communication as such.

---

[48] I borrow elements of this phrasing from Christopher Ricks's assessment of John Clubbe's abridgement of *Froude's Life of Carlyle* (London: John Murray, 1979). See 'Froude's Carlyle', in Ricks, *Essays in Appreciation*, 146–71 (154).

[49] Karlinsky, 'Introduction: Dear Bunny, Dear Volodya; or, Affinities and Disagreements', in *Dear Bunny, Dear Volodya*, 1–29 (28–9).

7

Life-Writing

Describing his poetic formation in the opening chapter of his *Biographia Literaria*, Coleridge recalls the deflation of poetic fancy executed by his 'very sensible, though at the same time, [...] very severe' schoolmaster, the Reverend James Bowyer:

> In our own English compositions (at least for the last three years of our school education) he showed no mercy to phrase, metaphor, or image, unsupported by a sound sense, or where the same sense might have been conveyed with equal force and dignity in plainer words. Lute, harp, and lyre, muse, muses, and inspirations, Pegasus, Parnassus, and Hippocrene, were all an abomination to him. In fancy I can almost hear him now, exclaiming '*Harp? Harp? Lyre? Pen and ink, boy, you mean! Muse, boy, Muse? your Nurse's daughter, you mean! Pierian spring? Oh 'aye! the cloister-pump, I suppose!*'[1]

It is an amusing anecdote of the disenchantment of youthful poetic pretensions. It also serves as a useful reminder that critical forms frequently overlap with one another or contain elements of other forms within themselves: the stentorian voice of Mr Bowyer breaks into Coleridge's own recollection, if not exactly introducing an element of dialogue as such (it is hard to imagine Mr Bowyer brooking any sort of reply) then at least multiplying the voices to which the reader must attend. This kind of generic multiplicity is, of course, germane to *Biographia Literaria*, which, as is well known, was initially conceived as the preface to a collection of Coleridge's poems but which, by late summer 1815, 'had become far more than a preface and was fast turning into a book'.[2] It certainly seems that Coleridge derived what he called 'a maxim (*regula maxima*) of criticism' from Mr Bowyer's gruff common sense, which he articulated, not only in the *Biographia*, but elsewhere in his writing as well: 'Whatever is translatable in other and simpler words of the same language, without loss of sense or dignity, is bad. N.B. By dignity

---

[1] Samuel Taylor Coleridge, *Biographia Literaria; or, Sketches of My Literary Life and Opinions*, ed. James Engell and W. Jackson Bate, 2 vols (Princeton: Princeton University Press, 1983; repr. 1984), i. 9–10. Further references to this edition are given after quotations in the text.
[2] James Engell and W. Jackson Bate, 'Introduction', in Coleridge, *Biographia Literaria*, i, pp. xli–cxxxvi (li). For more detail on the emerging form of the *Biographia*, see Engell and Bate, 'Introduction', pp. xlv–lviii, and for a subtle account of the interplay between prefatory and biographical forms, see David Ferris, *Theory and the Evasion of History* (Baltimore: Johns Hopkins University Press, 1993), 49–51.

Critical Forms: Forms of Literary Criticism, 1750–2020. Ross Wilson, Oxford University Press. © Ross Wilson 2023.
DOI: 10.1093/oso/9780198881117.003.0008

I mean the absence of ludicrous and debasing associations.'[3] Glossing 'maxim' with the other and, not simpler, but more complex words '(*regula maxima*)' exceeds the strictures announced by the maxim itself—although Coleridge might respond to such a charge that this particular scholastic parenthesis is not quite from 'the same language' as 'maxim' and, more significantly, that its evocation of a tradition of systematic philosophical thinking lends greater dignity, if not sense, to what he is saying.

Coleridge's recollection of his schoolboy attempts at poetry and thus of his first encounter, at the hands of Mr Bowyer, with literary criticism is a good place to start a consideration of the relation between criticism and the writing of lives, because, while on the face of it that recollection seems to offer a biographical source for a critical principle that Coleridge would go on to espouse much later in his career, it also brings into view many of the tensions between literary criticism and literary biography. What Mr Bowyer is aiming to do when confronted with Pegasus, lutes, and so on is to bring flights of fancy down to earth, to rein in the productions of the imagination, keeping them to the tangible and near-at-hand. Yet, while Coleridge certainly finds Mr Bowyer's lesson conducive, both his own poetic practice and, moreover, the conjuring of his old schoolmaster in 'fancy'—a faculty that would surely have been suspected by Mr Bowyer—so that 'I can almost hear him now' undermines the very lesson that his teacher is said to have inculcated. Mr Bowyer's attempt at the biographical deflation of the young Coleridge's pretensions, at bringing his poetic ideals down to the realm of daily life, is nested in the older Coleridge's fancied evocation of his teacher. Mr Bowyer's lesson, it seems, was therefore not entirely effective. The apparent mundanity of biographical recollection does little, in this case at least, to restrain potentially idealizing accounts of the sources of poetic composition. Indeed, on closer examination, Mr Bowyer's own equivalences are themselves only imperfectly reductive. While we may grant that harp and lyre and muse are poeticizing transpositions of, respectively, pen and ink and Nurse's daughter, it is harder to see how the cloister pump performs any of the functions ascribed in the mythology of literary inspiration to the Pierian spring. Pen and ink are instruments of poetic composition, as harp and lyre are supposed to have been in a mythic and venerated poetic past; your Nurse's daughter is the unattainable and idealized feminine inspiration for poetry, and hence bears a distinct resemblance to the muse. But what comes out of the cloister pump cannot even approximate to the reputed inspirational powers of the waters of the Pierian spring. This is where Mr Bowyer's chain of deflating equivalences breaks down, because there is no imaginable equivalence between water from the cloister pump and water from

---

[3] Cited by Engell and Bate, i. 10 n. 1, from a note to *Biographia Literaria*, ed. H. N. and Sara Coleridge, 2 vols (London, 1847), i. 7, itself (Engell and Bate surmise) taken from Coleridge's annotations to his own copy of the published text.

the Pierian spring that is relevant to poetic composition. Poetic inspiration might turn out to flow from other sources after all.

Mr Bowyer's failure, in the end, entirely to explain the sources of poetic inspiration seems, therefore, to leave a literary residue that criticism must deal with by other means. It is perhaps no wonder, then, that an opposition between criticism and life-writing has often been insisted upon. It is widely acknowledged, to give just one example, that the protocols advanced by the adherents of the New Criticism rested in part on an express rejection of the relevance of biography to critical judgement. As Edward Mendelson, one of the most dedicated and thoughtful of literary biographers in recent years, has put it, for those who reject the critical salience of biography, 'a poem' (Mendelson's concern here is just with poetry, but his point could readily be extended) 'is the product of inner imaginative acts that are inaccessible to biographers and perhaps unknown even to the poet, generic and aesthetic forces that act independently of a poet's conscious or unconscious intentions, or impersonal cultural forces for which the poet is primarily the medium. Another view,' Mendelson goes on, 'holds that the meaning of the poem is created by its readers' interpretations of it, not by any of the personal or impersonal forces that caused it to be written.'[4] This is an even-handed summary of the challenges biography has faced in the history of twentieth-century literary criticism (though one might suggest that Plato had already insisted in his *Ion* that the poet was a mere 'medium', albeit for personal and divine, rather than impersonal and cultural, forces).[5]

Mendelson offers a restrained riposte to these objections to literary biography, suggesting that biography may 'offer valid cues to interpretation that would not otherwise be available and can illuminate patterns of implication in a poem that might not otherwise be accessible to readers and critics'. This is admirably undogmatic in its defence of biography, though its tentativeness, and the sense that biography yields 'cues to interpretation' but not interpretation itself, reinforces the sense that the benefits biography offers to criticism are slight. The second suggestion, that biography 'can illuminate patterns of implication in a poem', is admittedly stronger in this regard, though even here the emphasis is on implication, which again would require the intervention of 'readers and critics', instead of and in addition to biographers, to draw them out.

Yet it may be that biography is not an endeavour merely ancillary or preparatory to the real work of criticism but, rather, fundamental to its aim of understanding writers as distinct, (once-)living individuals, working in circumstances and from motivations, which, if not finally and wholly explicable, we must at least

---

[4] Edward Mendelson, 'Biography and Poetry', in Roland Greene et al. (eds), *The Princeton Encyclopedia of Poetry and Poetics*, 4th edn (Princeton: Princeton University Press, 2012), 140–3 (142). The following quotations are from the same page.

[5] See Plato, *Ion*, trans. Paul Woodruff, in *Plato: Complete Works*, ed. John M. Cooper (Indianapolis: Hackett, 1997), 938–49 (esp. 941–2).

try to comprehend as far as possible.[6] Something like this is the chief use of biography envisaged by Empson in his late collection of essays *Using Biography*. 'A student of literature ought to be trying all the time to empathize with the author (and of course the assumptions and conventions by which the author felt himself bound);' Empson continues: 'to tell [a student of literature] that he cannot even partially succeed is about the most harmful thing you could do.'[7] Empson's monitory 'you' (which we encountered in the previous chapter) is in evidence again here, and it is certainly important to recognize the force of Empson's statement, which draws much of its strength precisely from the imbalance of partial success, on the one hand, and the fact that to deny even that is 'about the most harmful thing you can do', on the other. Empson had been, if anything, more forceful when giving expression to this view at the very start of his career. 'If critics are not to put up some pretence of understanding the feelings of the author in hand,' he insisted in *Seven Types of Ambiguity*, 'they must condemn themselves to contempt.'[8] Glossing this statement, Alan Shelston shrewdly remarks that '"[u]nderstanding the feelings of" is very different, of course, from "recording the life of"'.[9] And, as Michael Wood has judiciously noted, 'the more strenuously [Empson] asserted the need for thinking about the author's mind, the more prodigiously varied and optional that place turned out to be'.[10] Shelston proceeds to half-censure, half-admire the fact that, in his actual attempts at biographical criticism in *Using Biography*, Empson 'moves from possibility to probability to certainty with a shameless ease that would horrify the professional biographer'.[11] Ultimately, however, the significance of biography for Empson is not exactly factual. As we saw when discussing Empson's letters in the previous chapter, his view is that '[t]he chief use of reading imaginative literature is to make you grasp that different people act on different ethical beliefs'.[12] It is the insistence—the belief, in fact— that writers have *beliefs* and that critics must try to account for them that draws together the most persuasive readings in the admittedly mixed bag that is *Using Biography*. Arguing, for example, that Fielding had something particular he wanted to say in *Tom Jones*, Empson bemoans the 'critical blind spot' produced by

---

[6] See William Empson, *Using Biography* (Cambridge, MA: Harvard University Press, 1984), pp. vii, 104. Empson is responding to (and rejecting) the argument advanced by W. K. Wimsatt and Monroe C. Beardsley in 'The Intentional Fallacy', in Wimsatt, *The Verbal Icon: Studies in the Meaning of Poetry* (Lexington: University of Kentucky Press, 1954), 3–18 (first pub. in *Sewanee Review*, 54 (1946), 468–88). Wimsatt and Beardsley open their essay by gesturing to the many consequences of their argument for 'inspiration, authenticity, biography, literary history and scholarship' and end it, famously, by declaring that '[c]ritical inquiries are not settled by consulting the oracle'.

[7] Empson, *Using Biography*, p. viii.

[8] William Empson, *Seven Types of Ambiguity* (London: Chatto & Windus, 1930), pp. xiii–iv.

[9] Alan Shelston, 'Biography and Criticism', *Critical Quarterly*, 27 (1985), 71–5 (73).

[10] Michael Wood, *On Empson* (Princeton: Princeton University Press, 2017), 18.

[11] Shelston, 73.

[12] William Empson, 'The Alchemist', in *Essays in Renaissance Literature*, ed. John Haffenden, 2 vols (Cambridge: Cambridge University Press, 1994–5; repr. 2006), ii: *The Drama* (1994), 97–109 (97).

the assumption on the part of '[m]odern critics' (not, note, on the part of a merely personified 'modern criticism') that preaching a doctrine is anti-artistic and that, in any case, 'the only highminded doctrine to preach is despair and contempt for the world'.[13] Or, with respect to Joyce: 'A critic is free to say that the advanced ideals entertained by authors around the turn of the century were silly; but if he won't even admit that they held such beliefs, what he says about them is sure to be wrong.'[14] Beliefs, as well as feelings, convictions, assumptions, and conventions, are things by which anyone may be bound and they are things that are varied, certainly, and may be optional. The use of biography to try, not simply to examine, but to empathize with them, is not thus like the use of a sledgehammer, a knife and fork, a plastic bag, or any other tool for the achievement of a clearly identified end established in advance. What it might actually be to grasp that different people act according to different beliefs and how we might then act on the basis of that realization in our turn is not the result of the single use of an established method, but is rather a process, perhaps doomed only to partial success, of *using*.

*

I touched above on the overlaps of biography with other critical forms (the example was the hint at dialogue in Coleridge's recollection of Mr Bowyer and the fact that *Biographia Literaria* had begun life as a preface), and, indeed, we have seen throughout this book that specific critical forms often adopt aspects of, emerge out of, or differentiate themselves from other critical forms. Just as Coleridge's *Biographia* must surely be confronted in any account of literary criticism and life-writing, so neither can any such account avoid discussing Samuel Johnson's *Lives of the Poets*. When considering Johnson's *Lives*, it is vital to recall this emphasis on the multiplicity and mobility of critical forms, since the *Lives* was not, at least originally, so titled. The process by which the *Prefaces, Biographical and Critical, to the Works of the English Poets* (1779–1781) became the *Lives* does appear to be one in which the relation of biography to criticism undergoes a revealing transformation, one whereby, in particular, 'Poets' rise as their 'Works' fall. The earlier title insists on the association of Johnson's pieces with the works that they address by emphasizing that they are prefaces, the nature of which is equally 'Biographical and Critical'; furthermore, what the prefaces preface are 'the Works of the English Poets', rather than, so to speak, the poets themselves. By 1781, works and poets, and hence, perhaps, criticism and biography, have been decoupled—and in the process the poets (not the works) are promoted: *The Lives of the Most Eminent English Poets; with Critical Observations on Their Works*. 'Lives', in 1781, occupies the main title, with criticism demoted to a subsidiary accompaniment: no longer does the whole work appear to be designated both biographical and critical.

---

[13] Empson, *Using Biography*, 131.   [14] Empson, *Using Biography*, 206–7.

That Johnson's *Lives* hardly addresses 'the Most Eminent English Poets', or, more precisely, does not address all of the most eminent English poets—no Chaucer, Spenser, or Shakespeare—while making room for many of the least eminent English poets—Broome, Duke, Fenton, Mallet, Sheffield, and so on—has, of course, been frequently remarked. Wordsworth excoriated what he acknowledged was not entirely Johnson's selection (an acknowledgement that he managed not to emphasize too strenuously, however) as having neglected 'the bright Elizabethan constellation' and 'the ever-to-be-honoured Chaucer', and as having included 'metrical writers utterly worthless and useless', who collectively give evidence of 'a small quantity of brain'.[15] Johnson defended the selection on the grounds that it was not he who chose the writers to be included in the edition for which he provided the prefaces, but his treatment of a number of minor figures, however, and his insistence on the inclusion of Richard Blackmore and Isaac Watts, whose claims to majority were tenuous, are more critically revealing than might initially appear to be the case. Freya Johnston has responded to the charge that Johnson's *Lives* addresses too many minor and too few major English poets by suggesting that

> it seems fitting that the *Lives* span a wide range of the poets' fraternity, since the presence of unaccomplished authors within the collection writes large Johnson's principled defence of including 'the minute details of life' in biography (*Rambler* 60, *Yale*, iii. 321). Representatives of the lower echelons of literature are made to exert pressure on the higher.[16]

The fact that this inclusion of minor writers 'writes *large*' Johnson's principle is apt—as is, albeit to a somewhat divergent effect, the sense that lowlier authors are '*made to* exert pressure': they pressure the loftier poets, but only because pressured (by Johnson) to do so. Or, as Johnson himself put it in reflecting on Dryden's parodic screed in response to Elkanah Settle's *The Empress of Morocco*: 'To see the highest minds thus levelled with the meanest, may produce some solace to the consciousness of weakness, and some mortification to the pride of wisdom' ('Dryden', ii. 87)

The slight controversy of the inclusion of minor poets at the apparent cost of the exclusion of major ones in Johnson's *Lives* is a question of the relative merits

---

[15] William Wordsworth, 'Essay, Supplementary to the Preface' (1815), in *The Prose Works of William Wordsworth*, ed. W. J. B. Owen and Jane Worthington Smyser, 3 vols (Oxford: Oxford University Press, 1974), iii. 62–84 (79). Roger Lonsdale provides a comprehensive overview of the reception of what was often taken (erroneously) to be Johnson's selection of poets in the edition of *The Works of the English Poets* that his *Lives* were to preface. See Roger Lonsdale, 'Introduction', in Samuel Johnson, *The Lives of the Most Eminent English Poets; with Critical Observations on their Works*, ed. Roger Lonsdale, 4 vols (Oxford, 2006), i. 1–185 (10–12). Further references to this edition (giving the title of the 'Life' cited) appear after quotations in the text.

[16] Freya Johnston, *Samuel Johnson and the Art of Sinking 1709–1791* (Oxford: Oxford University Press, 2005), 199.

of poetical works but also, as Johnson's remark in 'Dryden' itself suggests, of the relevance of minds and how they may be affected (solaced, mortified) by literary judgement. In 1783, the *Prefaces* became simply *The Lives of the Most Eminent English Poets*, a title that questionably (as we have been seeing) supposes the eminence of the poets discussed, but, perhaps more importantly, places the emphasis on their lives rather than their works. Criticism has (titularly, at least) disappeared, and so one can see why some have wished to insist on the initial published title of Johnson's work—namely, the *Prefaces*. That title would seem, above all, to preserve an avowal of the critical, rather than merely biographical, focus of the works. Johnson's preference for the critical *over* the biographical is the implication of Fanny (Burney) D'Arblay's recollection that '[t]he critical investigations alone he [Johnson] considered as his business. He himself never named them but as prefaces.'[17] But this estimation downplays Johnson's own commitment to biography and its significance. Moreover, the evidence simply does not support Burney's claim: Johnson routinely referred to his *Lives* and only rarely, in fact, to the *Prefaces* (i., 49 n. 80). However the *Lives* are most appropriately designated, Burney's sense that there is a distinction—and a fairly stark one at that—between 'critical investigations' and biography nevertheless continues to inform interpretation of Johnson's work. Lonsdale's own account of the typical structure adopted in the *Lives* emphasizes the transition from what he revealingly designates as 'biographical narrative' to 'critical discussion' by way (sometimes) of a central 'character' (i. 101–3). Like Burney, later commentators such as Lawrence Lipking and Lonsdale can often give the impression that the transition from biography to criticism is a jolting one.[18]

Any hope that this transition may be smoothed over by turning to Johnson himself is qualified at best, especially because the impetus to writing is cast as dependent upon contingent sources of explanation. Near the beginning of 'Cowley', which opens the *Lives*, Johnson famously remarks, for instance, on the young Cowley's happening to find a copy of Spenser's *Faerie Queene* '[i]n the window of his mother's apartment', and on how it was, by reading Spenser's poem, 'he became, as he relates, irrecoverably a poet' (i. 191). 'Such', Johnson asserts, establishing an important tenet for the *Lives* as a whole, 'are the accidents, which, sometimes remembered, and perhaps sometimes forgotten, produce that particular designation of mind, and propensity for some certain science or employment, which is commonly called Genius'. Genius is thus cast chiefly neither as a divine bestowal nor the gift of nature, but rather as the product of accident: 'The true Genius is a mind of large general powers, accidentally determined to some particular direction' (i. 191). Genius undirected by accident is simply not genius.

---

[17] Madame D'Arblay [Fanny Burney], *Memoirs of Dr Burney*, 3 vols (London, 1832), ii. 176, quoted in Lonsdale, 'Introduction', 49 n. 80.

[18] See, e.g., Lawrence Lipking, *The Ordering of the Arts in Eighteenth-Century England* (Princeton: Princeton University Press, 1970), 420.

Yet it is with genius that Johnson is ultimately concerned—ultimately, indeed, in the prosaic sense that each of his *Lives* begins with biography and concludes with an estimation of the genius of the poets he is dealing with. In one of the most astute treatments of the specifically critical stakes of Johnson's *Lives*, Fred Parker remarks that Johnson's chief concern is not in a 'strict sense' with biography, since his aim is not so much to 'draw from the life, but rather to memorialise the dead'.[19] Developing his view that Johnson 'writes his biographies as a stranger', Parker shows that the often sharp distinction between putatively biographical and critical sections in Johnson's *Lives* is not an awkward attempt to accommodate the demands of booksellers, but rather is necessary to the critical force of the texts themselves. It is a function, that is, of 'Johnson's format' to express the view 'that the value of poetry lies in what escapes the biographical, what stands undiminished by the sense of temporal diminution and the vanity of human achievement'.[20] The contrast between Pope's worldliness and vanity and the achievement of his poetry, or the fact that *Paradise Lost* could be composed by 'the obstinate, impudent, unreasonable, ungrateful, egotistical bigot that is almost all that Johnson shows us in Milton the man', serve to prove Parker's point. Johnson's concern, then, is to transmit 'the sense of an encounter with a complex, vigorous, living mind'—a living mind, moreover, belonging to an individual who is, in all other respects but this most vital one, usually dead.[21] Parker suggests that the best label for this 'third thing' between biography and criticism is 'literary biography', not understood merely as the biography of literary writers, but rather as a distinct form of biography that attends to the life evinced by texts as much as to the life once lived by a person.

*

As Johnson recognized in a more than merely routine way, people die. While that is the fundamental and unhappy fact of mortality, it is a boon for the conventional biographer. Lives have beginnings, middles of varying lengths, and ends that happily delimit the biographer's task. But, as Parker argued with respect to Johnson, the specific concern of the form of 'literary biography' in the distinctive meaning Parker lends to that label is not to draw from the life but to memorialize the dead—and to do so by making a space for what escapes reduction to the lived record of a particular individual.

This may seem to run counter to Empson's insistence (rehearsed earlier) on empathy and on the usefulness of biographical detail to the cultivation of it. Yet Empson's emphasis on understanding different people acting on different ethical

---

[19] Fred Parker, 'Johnson and the Lives of Poets', *Cambridge Quarterly*, 29 (2000), 323–37 (328). The literature on Johnson's *Lives* is, of course, vast, but, for additional consideration of their relation specifically to literary criticism, see also Stephen Fix, 'Distant Genius: Johnson and the Art of Milton's Life', *Modern Philology*, 84 (1984), 244–64.
[20] Parker, 333.   [21] Parker, 336.

beliefs is frequently in the service of allowing the dead to live again, to refuse their consignment to oblivion—to reanimate them, even. The striking conclusion to his essay on '*Ulysses*: Joyce's Intentions' in *Using Biography* quotes the anecdote of Nora Barnacle refusing the offer of a Catholic funeral for Joyce and goes on to reject the Christianization of Joyce's work at the hands of a number of later-twentieth-century interpreters. 'He would regard it as an enormous betrayal that, since his death, everything he wrote has been twisted into propaganda for the worship of the torture-monster,' Empson wrote. 'It is pitiful to think of his ghost for ever dancing in fury.'[22] Empson reanimates Joyce in fury at the betrayal of his work, even though he does not believe that Joyce has a ghost or that it is condemned to any kind of existence 'for ever'—precisely, of course, the belief he has been arguing against. But the imagination of the dead writer's afterlife often presses on the attempt to recuperate the vitality of her or his mind, even in such latter-day, disenchanted accounts as Empson's is. For instance, at the end of *The Quest for Corvo*, the account both of the life and work of Frederick Rolfe and of his own fascination with it, A. J. A. Symons reflects as follows:

> It was a deeper satisfaction still to know that every one of the works which had been left and lost in obscurity when Frederic William Serafino Austin Lewis Mary Rolfe died suddenly and alone at Venice had been collected together by sympathetic hands, and that, alone of living men, I had read every line of every one. Nothing was left to be discovered; the Quest was ended. Hail, strange tormented spirit, in whatever hell or heaven has been allotted for your ever-lasting rest![23]

Rolfe is dead, and, among the living, it is Symons alone who bears the memory, not of Rolfe, but of every single line of every one of his works. That was what Symons had sought to discover, and the 'spirit' hailed in the book's final sentence is as much the spirit of that work as it is that of a shade among the damned or an angel among the blessed.

Far from being the boon it is to the merely conventional biographer, death is the challenge the literary biographer must confront and overcome. Needless to say, literary biographers do this in many different ways, and the author of the biography I want to examine now, *The Life of Charlotte Brontë* (1857) by Elizabeth Gaskell, would never have dreamt of countenancing the imagination of her subject in hell. Gaskell's biography is especially pertinent here, since I have so far been relying, at least implicitly, on something akin to Empson's account of empathy with the beliefs of writers writing at other times and from perspectives quite different from our (or, as Empson would put it, *your*) own. Gaskell's is a perspective sharply

---

[22] Empson, *Using Biography*, 216.
[23] A. J. A. Symons, *The Quest for Corvo* (London: Penguin, 2018; first pub. 1934), 250–1.

different from Empson's because, while she shares a commitment to recovering a literary imagination from what subsequent criticism may have made of it, she does so by means radically distinct from those entertained by a figure like Empson in, for instance, his rescue of Joyce from critical perversions of his work and person. The presiding critical intelligence of Gaskell's *Life* is, in many ways, God (Empson's 'torture-monster'). This is intimated by the book's epigraph from Elizabeth Barrett Browning's *Aurora Leigh*, which had been published earlier in 1857. The epigraph, which quotes lines spoken by Aurora, appears as follows:

> O my God,
> —————— Thou hast knowledge, only Thou,
> How dreary 'tis for women to sit still
> On winter nights by solitary fires
> And hear the nations praise them far off.
>
> AURORA LEIGH[24]

The most immediate point of placing these lines from *Aurora Leigh* at the head of Gaskell's *Life* is to emphasize the seclusion of the woman artist and her alienation from the praise she deserves, as well as, more subtly, to hint that Brontë is the equal of a much more celebrated writer like Barrett Browning, whose work was, in 1857, insistently current and living. They are intriguing lines in themselves, but just as intriguing are the lines that Gaskell does not quote—lines whose absence is indicated by the long dash, which in the context of the epigraph itself may appear to mark not so much an elision but the time in which the speaker's general appeal to God comes to crystallize around a specific, articulable concern, or, alternatively, to hint at the fruitless mental casting around for others, in addition to God, who have knowledge of what it is like for women to sit secluded, far from the praise they deserve. In addition to a second 'my God', which renders the exclamation a clear echo of Christ's cry of abandonment on the cross (Matthew 27:46 and Mark 15:34), these are the lines that Gaskell omits:

> O supreme Artist, who as sole return
> For all the cosmic wonder of Thy work,
> Demandest of us just a word . . a name,
> 'My Father!'
>
> (v. 435–8)

---

[24] Elizabeth Gaskell, *The Life of Charlotte Brontë*, ed. Angus Easson (Oxford: Oxford University Press, 1996), 1. Further references are given after quotations in the text. Quotations from *Aurora Leigh* in what follows are by book- and line-numbers from the Norton Critical Edition, ed. Margaret Reynolds (New York: Norton, 1996).

There are a number of plausible reasons that may be given for Gaskell's having passed over these lines, potentially including uneasiness at the suggestion of equivalence between the Divine Artist and the woman artist. The omitted lines, though, do in fact capture something central to Gaskell as biographer. One of the repeated and major concerns of *The Life of Charlotte Brontë* is precisely to do with what 'return' the 'wonder' of 'work' (even if it is not, in Brontë's case, 'cosmic work') can hope for. Where God demands 'just a word . . a name', the return yielded to human artistic work in criticism is usually more extended, though, in Brontë's case, settling on 'a name' for the pseudonymous Currer Bell had of course been a preoccupation of responses to the initial publications.[25]

The epigraph's concern with God is central to understanding the conception of criticism, which is, as intimated above, at work at a number of crucial junctures in the *Life*—or, if not criticism exactly, then judgement, for throughout her *Life of Brontë* Gaskell repeatedly disdains critics, mocks their priorities, and abjures criticism itself, while judgement remains the eschatological horizon within which she sets Brontë's works. Something comparable to such a distinction between judgement as well-grounded, considered reflection and criticism as ill-informed opinion is certainly to be encountered, for instance, in Johnson *Lives* as well: 'So little sometimes is criticism the effect of judgement,' Johnson notes aphoristically in relation to Addison's adverse account of Spenser, whose work Addison had not, at the point he ventured that criticism, actually read ('Addison', iii. 3). But, for Gaskell, the distinction between criticism and judgement is mapped onto another distinction—namely, that between the mass of carping humanity, and the inscrutable, yet perfectly just judgement exercised by God.

Gaskell's distinction between God-as-judge and humanity-as-critics also determines the particular structure of another key opposition in her *Life*—namely, that between the woman—dutiful daughter, eldest surviving sister, and, eventually and briefly, wife—and the author.[26] Gender is clearly a significant consideration in Gaskell's distinction between Brontë as woman and artist, but the distinction between life and work, and, crucially, how each is to be known and judged, also exercised literary biographers working on other writers as well. In his *The Life of Goethe* (1855), for instance, George Henry Lewes chose as his epigraph a statement attributed to 'Jung Stilling' (that is, Johann Heinrich Jung): 'Goethe's heart, which

---

[25] See, e.g., the positive notice of *Poems by Currer, Ellis, and Acton Bell* in the *Critic*, 4 July 1846, 6–8, repr. in Miriam Allott (ed.), *The Brontës: The Critical Heritage* (London: Routledge & Kegan Paul, 1974), 59–61 (59), and the review of *Jane Eyre* in the *Christian Remembrancer*, 15 (April 1848), 396–409, repr. in Allott (ed.), 88–92 (88–9).

[26] For further discussion of this distinction, see, e.g., Deirdre d'Albertis, ' "Bookmaking Out of the Remains of the Dead": Elizabeth Gaskell's *The Life of Charlotte Brontë*', *Victorian Studies*, 39 (1995), 1–31 (esp. 20–7); Maria H. Frawley, 'Gaskell's Ethnographic Imagination in *The Life of Charlotte Brontë*', *Biography*, 21 (1998), 175–94; Lucasta Miller, *The Brontë Myth* (London: Cape, 2001), esp. 34–7; and Linda Peterson, 'Elizabeth Gaskell's *The Life of Charlotte Brontë*', in Jill L. Matus (ed.), *The Cambridge Companion to Elizabeth Gaskell* (Cambridge: Cambridge University Press, 2007), 59–74 (67–8).

few knew, was as great as his intellect, which all knew.'[27] Lewes goes so far as to suggest—albeit again at the remove offered by citation—that Goethe's life was in fact worthier of notice than his work: 'Merck said of him that what he lived was more beautiful than what he wrote; and his Life, amid all its weaknesses and all its errors, presents a picture of a certain grandeur of soul, which cannot be contemplated unmoved.'[28] This way of putting it, however, subtly undermines the distinction between life and work. Goethe's life, already described as 'beautiful', 'presents a picture', and is thus itself one of his own artistic productions—like his writings. In the case of Gaskell's Brontë, the distinction between life and work turns out to be similarly difficult to maintain, not for the reason that the work must always be referred back to the life, but for the opposite reason that it is the life *of the work* that asserts itself as the real focus of the book. In an important passage, Gaskell recounts how, with the publication in 1847 of *Jane Eyre*, 'Charlotte Brontë's existence becomes divided into two parallel currents—her life as Currer Bell, the author; her life as Charlotte Brontë, the woman.' While the flow of 'currents' into 'Currer', and even the parallel of 'parallel' in 'Bell', suggest the priority of author over woman, the switch into the present tense here, and even the choice of the processual 'becomes' over the decisive 'is' (or 'was'), suggest the fluid and provisional nature of any such division and hence of any prioritization predicated upon it. Gaskell describes how the duties of the two roles were not in opposition, but were nevertheless difficult to reconcile (p. 271), going on to argue that this difficulty does not arise in the case of male authors, whose other employments—in law, medicine, trade, or business—may more easily be set aside or changed than those of a woman, since she may not 'drop the domestic charges devolving on her as an individual, for the exercise of the most splendid talents that were ever bestowed' (p. 272). Since Gaskell does not claim that Brontë did escape the tasks imposed upon her as the woman of the house, this is as much an account of why someone might not have written, of what stood in the way of her writing in the first place, as it is of what caused her to write as she did. Again, therefore, it is as much what has managed to escape the life as what is finally traceable to it that literary biography witnesses.

While Gaskell gives more space to the duties of a woman, it must be recalled that both of Brontë's roles—as woman and as author—entailed duties. The first duty of the author was '[i]n a humble and faithful spirit [...] to do what is not impossible, or God would not have set her to do it'. Then comes a significant reflection on the ultimate confluence of the duties of woman and author, worth quoting at length:

---

[27] Quoted from George Henry Lewes, *The Life of* Goethe, 2nd edn (London: Smith, Elder, 1864), title page. I have been unable to trace the epigraph in Jung-Stilling's works; W. T. Hewitt attributed the same statement (without making any reference to Lewes's attribution) to Jean Paul (see Hewitt, 'Goethe as a Man', in Marion V. Dudley (ed.), *Poetry and Philosophy of Goethe* (Chicago: Griggs, 1887), 252–8 (252)).

[28] Lewes, 2.

I put into words what Charlotte Brontë put into actions.

The year 1848 opened with sad domestic distress. It is necessary, however painful, to remind the reader constantly of what was always present to the hearts of father and sisters at this time. It is well that the thoughtless critics, who spoke of the sad and gloomy views of life presented by the Brontës in their tales, should know how such words were wrung out of them by the living recollection of the long agony they suffered. It is well, too, that they who have objected to the representation of coarseness and shrank from it with repugnance, as if such conceptions arose out of the writers, should learn, that, not from the imagination—not from internal conception—but from the hard cruel facts, pressed down, by external life, upon their very senses, for long months and years together, did they write out what they saw, obeying the stern dictates of their consciences. They might be mistaken. They might err in writing at all, when their afflictions were so great that they could not write otherwise than they did of life. It is possible that it would have been better to have described only good and pleasant people, doing only good and pleasant things (in which case they could hardly have written at any time): all I say is, that never, I believe, did women, possessed of such wonderful gifts, exercise them with a fuller feeling of responsibility for their use. As to mistakes, they stand now—as authors as well as women—before the judgement-seat of God.   (p. 272)

The passage opens with Gaskell's description—a one-sentence, ten-word paragraph—of what she is doing in comparison to what Brontë did: 'I put into words what Charlotte Brontë put into actions.' The difference in tense between the two 'put's—Gaskell's present and Brontë's past—marks the distinction between the living witness to the life and the dead liver of it. But the fact that it is the very same word also attests to the common endeavour to make writing itself a 'living recollection'. Gaskell may initially appear to be downplaying her activity as biographer at the outset of this passage: she is offering a merely *verbal* description of Brontë's *active* life. Yet the action of Brontë's that Gaskell has just been considering at the end of the preceding paragraph is precisely the deployment of her talents, the rendering of her 'gift' to 'the use and service of others'—that is, the putting of her gift into words by writing. It is Brontë's words that are active, and it is to the condition of verbal activity that Gaskell herself aspires in this passage. It was the Brontës' 'living recollection' of their sufferings, not the mere recording of them, that prompted their fiction to take the shape it did and to which 'thoughtless critics' objected, and it is 'living recollection' that Gaskell is likewise attempting here.

Gaskell proceeds to develop this emphasis on the forces that drove the Brontës to write the way they did into a clearly articulated (if brief) psychology of composition that is meant to absolve the Brontës of any blame that may attach to them by dint of their works. And 'forces' is the right word here, since Gaskell is not, now, concerned with the often-subtle influence of social and geographical context, but rather with suffering, its living recollection, and what it is capable of wringing out of people. Thus, Gaskell claims, it is not imagination that is chiefly at work in the novels of the Brontës—at least not so far as the coarse elements of those novels are concerned—but rather conscience. Gaskell's envisaging of the directions of the different forces to which the Brontës may be said to have been subject—in particular, her deployment of the language of inner and outer, up and down—is especially revealing in connection with the relative roles of imagination and conscience as (respectively) inner and outer faculties. Rather than accepting that the writing of the Brontës 'arose out' of them, Gaskell avers instead that it was in response to 'the hard cruel facts, *pressed down*, by *external* life, *upon* their very senses' (emphases added) that they 'did [...] *write out* what they saw'. This route 'out'—by writing—is quite different from the upward trajectory assumed by imagination.

None of this, however, amounts in the above passage to finally decisive exoneration. In contrast to 'thoughtless critics', Gaskell thoughtfully refuses to assume the role of judge herself. Christopher Ricks remarks (in connection with a passage from somewhat earlier in the *Life*) that Gaskell's understanding of Brontë—understanding as both conception of and sympathy with her—is 'inseparable from its imaginative intelligence and principled puzzlement about her searchability and unsearchability'.[29] There are two important conjunctions here: imaginative intelligence *and* principled puzzlement; searchability *and* unsearchability. Neither is detachable from the other. Gaskell's puzzlement, and her recognition that Brontë is at least in part unsearchable, found her conviction that any final assessment of Brontë, woman and author both, cannot be made by human judges. It is her self-limiting self-announcement—'all I say is,... I believe,...'— that licenses her sure and certain belief that 'they stand now—as authors as well as women—before the judgement-seat of God'.

It is with a similar expression of the limitations of what she has to say and, in particular, of her inability to judge that Gaskell's *Life* ends. 'I cannot measure or judge of such a character as hers' (p. 457). The ends of biography are not, for Gaskell, explanation through recourse to circumstance but acknowledgement that measurement and judgement can proceed only so far. Gaskell then quotes from a letter by Mary Taylor, Brontë's friend, which concludes pessimistically— nihilistically, even—that Brontë had sought the judgement of the world but had been ill-served by it: 'They heartily, greedily enjoyed the fruits of her labours, and then found out she was much to be blamed for possessing such faculties. Why ask for a judgement on her from such a world?' Gaskell does not answer

---

[29] Christopher Ricks, 'E. C. Gaskell's Charlotte Brontë', in Ricks, *Essays in Appreciation* (Oxford: Oxford University Press, 1996; repr. 2004), 118–45 (133). Ricks is commenting on the passage at the beginning of chapter 7 in which Gaskell reflects on Brontë's youthful correspondence with Ellen Nussey (*Life of Brontë*, 94–5).

that question but suggests instead that there may be another world whose judgement it is worth having:

> But I turn from the critical, unsympathetic public,—inclined to judge harshly because they have only seen superficially and not thought deeply. I appeal to that larger and more solemn public, who know how to look with tender humility at faults and errors; how to admire generously extraordinary genius, and how to reverence with warm, full hearts all noble virtue. To that Public I commit the memory of Charlotte Brontë. (p. 457)

Easson's gloss of this concluding response to Taylor's letter, which is also the conclusion to Gaskell's own narrative of Brontë's life, suggests that the 'Public' that Gaskell envisages is now equipped, thanks to her, to offer a creditable judgement of Brontë: 'she herself concludes,' Easson remarks, 'by challenging a new judgement from a world she deems more ready to understand, because of what they have read, than that characterized by Mary Taylor' (p. 568). There are reasons to suspect that Gaskell has in mind something not entirely identifiable with a direct appeal to her readers for informed judgement, however, despite the fact that Easson is right to claim that she is schooling her readers in how to judge and implicitly reminding them of everything she has told them. Turning from 'the critical, unsympathetic public' via 'that larger, more solemn public', Gaskell finally entrusts Brontë's memory to an upper-case 'Public' that is more than a merely uncritical, blandly sympathetic readership from which she has by now won admiration for Brontë. It is a 'Public' that is in a position to see and think 'deeply', one that does not look away from 'faults and errors', or demur from identifying them as such, but that countenances them with its own 'tender humility'. It is such a Public, whose judgements would arise from a comprehensive understanding both of what is being judged as well as of the qualifications of human judgement itself, that might, for Gaskell, finally be capable of Criticism.

The Winding-Up

WILSON I'm hoping you've titled this 'the winding-up' because you're only *winding us up* about actually writing your conclusion as a dialogue. I mean, *really*?! For a start, isn't the dialogue the form that everyone goes for when they want to try their hand at something that isn't an article or a monograph? Let me tell you: you're too late. In case you hadn't noticed, you've just written a pretty straight monograph and there's nothing you can do to change that now. You're just tired of listening to yourself—and to be honest, I can't blame you. But the thing is, it's still *you* you're going to have to listen to.

ROSS Precisely—which means it was *you* just as much as it was *me* who chose the title and, worse, form for this conclusion. And I'm—sorry, *we're*—not winding anyone up. 'The Winding-Up' is what Charlotte Brontë calls that strange, tormented final chapter of *Shirley*. And, as you know, we've been interested in Brontë's endings for a while.

WILSON Let's stick with this project until *it* has ended, shall we?

ROSS We were just talking about Brontë's endings, remember? But fair enough. By the way, thanks for pointing out that I've written a monograph—which, again, you had a pretty major hand in too. I hope you're not implying either that dialogues are predictable or that monographs are dull, though I suspect you are. If you are, I don't agree.

WILSON You've already told us how much you love academic writing. Which is a bit self-regarding, if you ask me.

ROSS I'm not asking you, but in case you're wondering, it's other people's academic writing I love rather than *ours*. And I'm actually rather glad that literary critics have turned to dialogue. We wrote a whole chapter on it, remember. Anyway, what other form are we going to adopt here? It's too late for a preface; we began with a bit of autobiography; this book at least partly has its origin in lectures; even bits of reviews we've written have crept into the footnotes here and there; I can't quite see how a selection would work at this point (though it really does work at the end of Eric Hayot's paean…)—and who writes letters anymore? So—dialogue it is.

WILSON I'd rather write a letter. But if you insist…

ROSS I do. And in any case, isn't dialogue actually the fundamental critical form? Remember that thing Leavis said?

WILSON Go on.

Critical Forms: Forms of Literary Criticism, 1750–2020. Ross Wilson, Oxford University Press. © Ross Wilson 2023.
DOI: 10.1093/oso/9780198881117.003.0009

ROSS Let me find it…Here it is: 'a critical judgment has the form, "This is so, isn't it?". And the concurrence appealed for must be real, or it serves no critical purpose, and, if he suspects insincerity or mere politeness,'—remember Kant's young poet, pretending to go along with his friends to get them off his back while his own judgement sharpens itself?—'can bring no satisfaction to the critic—to the critic *as* critic.' Then the bit just after that is really important too: 'What, of its very nature, the critical activity aims at, in fact, is an exchange, a collaborative exchange, a corrective and creative interplay of judgments. For though my judgment asks to be confirmed and appeals for agreement that the thing is *so*; the response I expect at best will be of the form, "Yes, but—", the "but" standing for qualifications, corrections, shifts of emphasis, additions, refinements.'

WILSON Wonder what he means by 'at best' there…

ROSS You mean: is it 'that's as much as I can hope for', which is a bit despondent, or is it 'the best kind of response, the response you'll get when you really know you're engaged in *criticism*', which is a bit more promising?

WILSON Yes, that's what I'm asking.

ROSS It's the latter. It isn't like he just wants the other person to say 'Yeah, sure, whatever you say'. Though I suspect that was the effect of quite a few of Leavis's pronouncements, to be honest.

WILSON Well in any case, you're right: Leavis did say all of that about critical exchange—and he said it *in a lecture*. So, before we get too excited about dialogue (I'm still trying to get you off this notion—perhaps I should just stop saying 'I' and 'you')—

ROSS—and appropriate the authority of impersonal academic discourse all for yourself? Nice!

WILSON All right, all right. As I was saying: before we get too excited about dialogue, we've encountered a number of claims (and even more implications) to the effect that certain forms bespeak the essence of criticism. The selection, for instance, which fulfils the ultimate task of the critic just to indicate worthwhile work. Or what about Clive Scott's statement that 'good interpretation is a shareable spiritual autobiography of the reading self, and, as readers of criticism, we are readers of other readers, who make available to us modes of response we have yet to explore ourselves'.

ROSS We tried autobiography too, remember. We're ticking all the boxes!

WILSON You're the one who has an autobiography. If you'd have got that job, we would have been me. But anyway, if we are going ahead with this madness, then *I* insist on at least a little bit of method. First, let's try to describe what you think you can say about criticism after going through these different forms of it: prefaces, selections, reviews, lectures, dialogues, letters, and life-writing.

ROSS There are more forms of criticism than those, of course.

WILSON Of course. It's clearly playing on your mind. But back to what you think you have shown, rather than what else, were there world enough and time, you might have wanted to discuss. The most obvious point is that different forms of criticism have different critical priorities and even, as it were, different critical personalities. And those priorities and personalities go missing as soon as literary criticism is taken to be a body of opinions and doctrines that develops progressively instead of being a writing practice situated in broader contexts of and for discourse. Is that true?

ROSS That's true, Socrates.

WILSON Very funny. But also, we had to work quite hard—

ROSS —ah! 'we': when there's credit for hard work to be had...

WILSON —we had to work quite hard to identify the formal aspects of quite a lot of the texts that we examined because, precisely as a consequence of the deemphasis of critical writing practice (even where it is vaunted in opposition to the strawman of 'theory'), those formal aspects often appear invisible: the selection is of course the emblematic case here, but it's worth remembering the fact that most of the texts we discussed have undergone a process of essayification or treatisification.

ROSS '-ification'. Good 'method'. And yes, true—though I'm a bit unsure whether anything can '*appear* invisible'. Isn't that a contradiction in terms precisely of the kind that makes you anxious? But, if you mean that the formal features of literary-critical texts tend to fade from view, then I think you're right. Which, though understandable, is a pity, because it obscures those characteristics— 'critical priorities and personalities', I think you said—

WILSON You've just scrolled up the page to check, so you know I said it.

ROSS You're determined to ruin this, aren't you?

WILSON Just carry on.

ROSS ...because it obscures those critical priorities and personalities (as you said) that attention to form brings to light.

WILSON Well, I have to say I'm glad you've gone beyond merely protesting the literary dignity of criticism.

ROSS Where did I 'merely' do that? If what you mean is my advocacy for literary criticism as writing, well, I stand by it. But haven't we wanted to argue instead that the forms of critical attention and judgement are substantially fostered by the forms of critical writing in which they are practised?

WILSON I suppose we have. But let's move on, shall we? Wasn't this also where you were going to talk about some of the turns that criticism has taken most recently—Twitter, Amazon reviews, the whole digital critical landscape—all of that.

FOOTNOTE Hello hello, nice to see you again![1]

WILSON Bit informal for you, Footnote...

---

[1] WILSON I thought it was just us two! We got away with that Leavis quotation and so on. Anyway, isn't this 'Footnote' character a device you've stolen from Jerome McGann's 'Dialogue on Dialogue', in

FOOTNOTE I'm loosening up here at the end. Perhaps I'm turning into Endnote? They're less formal than I am. Sorry if this is a bit previous, but I think it's right that your reader should know that there are a number of considerations of these questions.

ROSS Your reader too, of course. But do we have to do this here? I mean, aren't we breaking the mould? And what about anti-communicative tactics aiming at communication?

WILSON Yes, we do; no, we're not; I'm not convinced. I think we should pay our dues.

FOOTNOTE Thank you, Wilson.

ROSS Go on then.

FOOTNOTE There's Phillipa K. Chong's book on recent reviewing practices.

WILSON We mentioned that in Chapter 4.

FOOTNOTE You did.

ROSS Yes, but doesn't Chong downplay the democratizing effect of online reviewing and the like? She says 'the critics' circle remains relatively closed'.

FOOTNOTE Phillipa K. Chong, *Inside the Critics' Circle: Book Reviewing in Uncertain Times* (Princeton: Princeton University Press, 2020), 144.

WILSON Right. I've read that book too. But Chong's interest isn't in any case really in the impact of digital media on the *forms* of criticism in the way that we've been thinking about it, is it? What about all those listicles? Live Tweeted readings? What is there to say about those? Personally, they don't strike me as especially interesting, to be honest. What's so exciting about the fact that puffs and blurbs and reviews, selections and reading lists, and even the odd essay are written and read on little glowing confections of toxic metals and plastics, rather than on paper?

ROSS You might have a point—up to a point. But I'm not sure that's *all* there is to it. There's Louis Bury's cautionary account of what he calls 'topical criticism'—

FOOTNOTE—'Topical Criticism and the Cultural Logic of the Quick Take', in Houman Barekat et al. (eds), *The Digital Critic: Literary Culture Online* (New York: OR Books, 2017), 86–101 (87).

Julianna Spahr et al. (eds), *A Poetics of Criticism* (Buffalo: Leave Books, 1994), 59–77? In which case, don't you think you'd better acknowledge your source?

ROSS They'll hear you. And you just have acknowledged our source—thanks! I liked your intonation there to show that some of what you said was in parentheses, by the way. But much as I like our friend Footnote, there might be something to be said for the view that '[s]uppression of footnotes may be one instance of the justified secret, in that it can at a particular opportunity be almost the only way of getting a hearing for ideas which might otherwise be at once destroyed by being referred back to a prior set of stories about them. It can be an anti-communicative tactic which aims at communication, a withholding of information for the sake of thought.'

WILSON Who said that?

ROSS I did.

WILSON It didn't sound like you—and you did the quotation-intonation. I'll let you get away with it because I want to get out of this dungeon now, please.

ROSS—thank you—in which Bury acknowledges that topical criticism (by which he means 'critical takes' characterized by being in and of the moment) 'has always existed in one form or another'—

WILSON—Ah, so it isn't a form as such, then, but rather a mode that exists across different forms?

ROSS—That would seem to be the implication. But if I may? Bury goes on: 'it has newly distinguished itself as the characteristic, if hitherto unnamed, form of criticism in the digital age, the form that embodies a prominent strain of values in online critical practice today.' 'It is', he says, 'the form par excellence of putting one's foot down in cyberspace'.

WILSON That sounds a bit more like a form than it did a moment ago. Doesn't Bury end that essay rather pessimistically? 'The vogue for topical criticism might therefore seem harmless enough—expedient and inevitable, even—but, as it conditions audience expectations and authorial sensibilities, it erodes the middle ground between vernacular criticism and the scholarly ideal' (100).

FOOTNOTE Oh...

ROSS True. But at the start he's a bit more even-handed—the section where he talks about how digital response just speeds up 'the process of consensus-building disputation that has always, from the pages of Addison and Steele's *The Spectator* to the open-air debates of the Greek agora, been the Zenonian endpoint towards which critical discourse tries to refine itself'.

FOOTNOTE 89!

ROSS Thank *you*. He does say that the speeding-up is both 'beneficent and frightening'—though, as you're implying, Wilson, he perhaps comes to give a bit more emphasis to the frightening side of things.

WILSON I can't help thinking there's something strange about that formulation—from *The Spectator* to the Greek agora—from later to earlier, instead of the more usual other way around. Perhaps there's something like an inkling that digital communication has more in common with modes of communication from before print and thus that contemporary literary criticism (and intellectual exchange generally) has certain things in common with the cacophony, publicity, and competition for attention of the agora? You certainly hear enough about the 'marketplace of ideas' these days.

ROSS And enough of people suggesting their adversaries should go away or drink hemlock. It isn't like a real marketplace, though, in which there's someone (at least in theory) who ensures that people don't get ripped off. But that invocation of Addison and Steele is telling in its own right. Kasia Boddy—

WILSON—we work with her!

ROSS—I thought you were supposed to be the professional one? Yes, we do, but that isn't relevant. Kasia Boddy invokes Tobias Smollett's 1755 account of the 'true spirit' of criticism in her foreword to *The Digital Critic*. It doesn't matter, she says, that Smollett's context 'is a world away from the open-to-all digital land-scape' and that 'we should also be skeptical of the more recent authority of imme-diacy and self-expression'.

FOOTNOTE Kasia Boddy, foreword to Barekat et al. (eds), 7–10 (8–9).

WILSON I subscribe to that view, certainly.

FOOTNOTE Ignoring me now?

WILSON Hardly! Sorry. Thanks!!

ROSS We're in agreement, then—though perhaps it's worth introducing a couple of caveats.

WILSON Go on.

ROSS So, N. Katherine Hayles says at the end of her chapter on 'Intermediation' in *Electronic Literature* that literature conceived as the whole process and network of literary production, including criticism, 'is permeated at every level by compu-tation'. And, for her, it's clear who still wants to deny this: 'The bellelettristic trad-ition that has on occasion envisioned computers as the soulless other to the humanistic expressivity of literature could not be more mistaken. Contemporary literature, and even more so the literary that extends and enfolds it, is computa-tional'. Footnote?

FOOTNOTE Ooh, thanks! *Electronic Literature: New Horizons for the Literary* (Notre Dame: University of Notre Dame Press, 2008), 85. And see also the accom-panying website: <https://newhorizons.eliterature.org/index.php> (accessed 27 January 2021).

ROSS Fastidiously done. Anyway, what Hayles says is probably undeniable, as far as 'contemporary literature' is concerned—I mean, the computer has been pretty important to us in writing this book, hasn't it?—though what Bury and Boddy have also made us see is that the 'bellelettristic tradition' (if that's what Addison, Smollett, et al. belong to, which is certainly, let's say, arguable) is far from dead yet.

WILSON I see what you mean, I think. So, Hayles is right to criticize a lazy, anti-digital humanism assumed by some critics—

ROSS—and let's be honest, we've hardly been immune from that ourselves.

WILSON You're over-sharing. We haven't really betrayed such a view here, have we?

ROSS I guess not. Sorry—ignore that. And what she says about computers is certainly true. You and I only exist in a computer!

WILSON I'm not sure I'm cheered by that thought. Perhaps we'll get out one day. Anyway, Hayles's statement is salutary as far it goes, but we've also seen that certain views and practices of criticism have proved rather more abiding than might perhaps have been expected.

ROSS Yes, I think that's right.

WILSON What was the other caveat?

ROSS Well, where Boddy talks about the 'open-to-all digital landscape', we need to question how 'open-to-all' it really is. There are still some gatekeepers, aren't there? Lots of them! And that's to say nothing of digital poverty—yet another form of the poverty that society inflicts on some of its members.

WILSON I think that claim about the digital being 'open-to-all' arises from the contrast between the kind of people that had access to criticism—to doing criticism, I mean—in the mid-eighteenth century and those that have access to it now. It's hard to argue that it isn't a more diverse field now, even if there's still a long way to go, and even if, yes, the structures of inequality and exclusion that still characterize society also still characterize access to criticism. But perhaps the contrast between those who tended to do criticism in the eighteenth century and those who are permitted to do criticism now doesn't map straightforwardly onto the contrast between print and digital after all.

ROSS OK, but let's nevertheless acknowledge that, as a matter of fact, if not of destiny (if you see what I mean), people have done formally innovative things with literary criticism on computers.

WILSON Like?

ROSS Thank you. Though I thought you were averse to all those social media reactions?

WILSON I am! I mean: like what? What literary-critical innovations have computers enabled?

ROSS Ah, I see. It would be much easier if we were doing this in writing! Well, like *CommentPress*, 'a WordPress plugin for social texts in social contexts […] that allows readers to comment paragraph-by-paragraph, line-by-line or block-by-block in the margins of a text.' Footnote?

FOOTNOTE You don't have to say 'Footnote'. See <https://futureofthebook.org/commentpress/> (accessed 27 January 2021) and the insightful account of *CommentPress* in the context of broader arguments in textual studies by Kathleen Fitzpatrick, '*CommentPress*: New (Social) Structures for New (Networked) Texts', *Journal of Electronic Publishing*, 10 (2007) <https://doi.org/10.3998/3336451.0010.305> (accessed 5 April 2023).

WILSON Interesting. That's where Fitzpatrick has important things to say about book production too, isn't it? Her point (borrowing from Peter Stallybrass—no need Footnote: just let them look it up if they're really determined) that authors don't produce books but rather sentences and that even printers don't produce books but rather pages is a good one.

ROSS And it's one we can appreciate, isn't it? I mean, let's hope these sentences become a book—but that isn't up to us, is it?

WILSON What are you holding in your hand?

ROSS Nothing. I'm sitting at a desk looking at a computer screen.

WILSON Not you—*them*. [*Silence*] Well, back to our sentences…It seems to me that there's been a resurgence of interest in commentary—and I suppose one might instance the excellent *Glossator* here, a journal concerned with 'the practice and theory of commentary', and whose history seems entwined with the turn to computational modes of criticism (though we should admit that it also takes the form of a print edition). [*An expectant pause*]

FOOTNOTE Ah—me? Yes: <https://glossator.org/about/> (accessed 27 January 2021).

ROSS There are different ways you can be 'entwined' with something…

WILSON Indeed. And again, the various forms of commentary are venerable indeed. Also, if we admit the whole, rich history of annotations in the margins, on napkins and the backs of receipts stuffed between pages, and not to mention the furtive history of the defacement of library books—

ROSS—don't make it sound heroic!

WILSON—no, of course not! Arrant vandalism. But anyway, commentary as annotation seems to come as close to being 'open-to-all' as digital criticism.

ROSS 'Vandalism'…that's a *touch* strong, maybe. We've always enjoyed good annotations. And we have to admit that the pencilled note in the margin is where most of our literary-critical writing at least begins.

WILSON Most of it ends there too.

ROSS Trust you! But maybe you're right…Anyway, that's where literary criticism begins, often in response to other literary criticism, for lots of the users of the English Faculty Library at Cambridge. Remember the title page of the copy of Earl R. Wasserman's book on Keats, *The Finer Tone*, in that library? Thickly annotated in several hands. The apparent instigator writes in inky block capitals: 'THIS BOOK IS A BIBLE'. Then 'A BIBLE' is crossed out and replaced (but just in pencil this time) with 'very monotonous', before a more circumspect reader (though confident writer: ink) suggests merely 'limited' instead. One annotator, while taking the point of the original critic, objects to its blasphemous comparison of a volume of literary criticism to Holy Scripture, to which another responds 'I do believe we have a Christian in our midst'. I love the hauteur of that 'I do believe…'. Perhaps they'd been reading Empson—for the anti-Christian aspect, but not quite the hauteur. And then at the bottom there's the person who's just had enough who writes—

WILSON—well, you can leave that to our imaginations.

ROSS Yes, probably best to. Good place to stop?

WILSON Yes. I think you've gone far enough.

Bibliography

Adorno, Theodor W., 'Benjamin the Letter Writer' (1966), in *Notes to Literature*, trans. Shierry Weber Nicholsen, 2 vols (New York: Columbia University Press, 1992), ii. 233–9.

Adorno, Theodor W., 'Free Time' (1969), in J. M. Bernstein (ed.), *The Culture Industry: Selected Essays on Mass Culture* (Abingdon: Routledge, 1991), 187–97.

Adorno, Theodor W., 'On the Crisis of Literary Criticism' (1952/3), in *Notes to Literature*, trans. Shierry Weber Nicholsen, 2 vols (New York: Columbia University Press, 1992), ii. 305–8.

Allott, Miriam (ed.), *The Brontës: The Critical Heritage* (London: Routledge & Kegan Paul, 1974).

Anderson, Randall, 'The Rhetoric of Paratext in Early Printed Books', in *The Cambridge History of the Book in Britain*, 7 vols (Cambridge: Cambridge University Press, 1999–2019), iv: John Barnard and D. F. McKenzie (eds), *1557–1695* (2002), 636–44.

Armstrong, Isobel (ed.), *Victorian Scrutinies: Reviews of Poetry 1830–1870* (London: Athlone, 1972).

Arnold, Matthew, 'The Function of Criticism at the Present Time' (1864), in *The Complete Prose Works of Matthew Arnold*, ed. R. H Super, 11 vols (Ann Arbor: University of Michigan Press, 1960–74), iii: *Lectures and Essays on Criticism* (1962), 258–85.

Arnold, Matthew, 'The Literary Influence of Academies' (1864), in *The Complete Prose Works of Matthew Arnold*, ed. R. H Super, 11 vols (Ann Arbor: University of Michigan Press, 1960–74), iii: *Lectures and Essays on Criticism* (1962), 232–57.

Ashton, Jennifer, 'Our Bodies, Our Poems', *American Literary History*, 19 (2007), 210–31.

Ashton, Jennifer, 'The Numbers Trouble with "Numbers Trouble"', *Chicago Review* 53 (2007), 112–20.

Aubrey, John, *Brief Lives, with An Apparatus for the Lives of Our English Mathematical Writers*, ed. Kate Bennett, 2 vols (Oxford: Oxford University Press, 2015).

Bagehot, Walter, 'The First Edinburgh Reviewers' (1855), in *The Collected Works of Walter Bagehot*, ed. Norman St John-Stevas, 15 vols (London: The Economist, 1965–86), i (1965), 309–41.

Bagehot, Walter, *Literary Studies*, ed. Richard Holt Hutton, 2 vols (London: Longmans, 1873).

Bagehot, Walter, 'The Morality of the Coup d'État' (1852), in *The Collected Works of Walter Bagehot*, ed. Norman St John-Stevas, 15 vols (London: The Economist, 1965–86), iv (1964), 35–44.

Baker, Nicholson, *The Anthologist* (London: Simon & Schuster, 2009).

Baraka, Amiri, and Amina Baraka (eds), *Confirmation: An Anthology of African American Women* (New York: William Morrow, 1983).

Baraka, Amiri [LeRoi Jones], and Larry Neal (eds), *Black Fire: An Anthology of Afro-American Writing* (New York: William Morrow, 1968).

Barnard, John, 'Keats's Letters: "Remembrancing and enchaining"', in Susan Wolfson (ed.), *The Cambridge Companion to John Keats* (Cambridge: Cambridge University Press, 2001), 120–34.

Barrett Browning, Elizabeth, *Aurora Leigh*, ed. Margaret Reynolds (New York: Norton, 1996).

Bate, Jonathan, 'Reckless Eric' (review of Eric Griffiths, *If Not Critical*), *TLS* 22 August 2018, 3–4.

'B.D.', 'On Prefaces', *Athenæum*, 31 October 1919, 1113–14.

Beam, Alex, *The Feud: Vladimir Nabokov, Edmund Wilson, and the End of a Beautiful Friendship* (New York: Pantheon, 2016).

Benjamin, Walter, 'The Concept of Criticism in German Romanticism' (1920), trans. David Lachtermann, Howard Eiland, and Ian Balfour, in *Walter Benjamin: Selected Writings*, ed. Michael W. Jennings, 4 vols (Cambridge, MA: Belknap Press, 1996–2003), i. *1913–1926* (1996), 116–200.

Benjamin, Walter, 'Notes (II)' (*c.*1928), trans. Rodney Livingstone, in *Walter Benjamin: Selected Writings*, ed. Michael W. Jennings, 4 vols (Cambridge, MA: Belknap Press, 1996–2003), II.i. 285–7.

Benjamin, Walter, 'On the Image of Proust' (1929; rev. 1934), trans. Harry Zohn, in *Walter Benjamin: Selected Writings*, ed. Michael W. Jennings, 4 vols (Cambridge, MA: Belknap Press, 1996–2003), II.i. *1927–1930* (1999; repr. 2005), 237–47.

Benjamin, Walter, *Walter Benjamin: Gesammelte Briefe*, ed. Christoph Gödde and Henri Lonitz, 6 vols (Frankfurt-am-Main, 1995–2000).

Bennett, Arnold, *The Truth about an Author*, 2nd edn (New York: George H. Doran, 1911).

Bennett, Paula Bernat, *Poets in the Public Sphere: The Emancipatory Project of American Women's Poetry* (Princeton: Princeton University Press, 2003).

Benson, Steven, and Clare Connors (eds), *Creative Criticism: An Anthology and Guide* (Edinburgh: Edinburgh University Press, 2014).

Bernstein, Charles, 'The Revenge of the Poet-Critic; or, the Parts Are Greater than the Sum of the Whole', in *My Way: Speeches and Poems* (Chicago: University of Chicago Press, 1999), 3–17.

Bersani, Leo, *Thoughts and Things* (Chicago: University of Chicago Press, 2015).

Bialostosky, Don H., 'Dialogics as an Art of Discourse in Literary Criticism', *PMLA* 101 (1986), 788–97.

Bialostosky, Don H., 'Dialogics of the Lyric: A Symposium on Wordsworth's "Westminster Bridge" and "Beauteous Evening"', in Michael Macovski (ed.), *Dialogue and Critical Discourse: Language, Culture, Critical Theory* (Oxford: Oxford University Press, 1997), 101–36.

Boccaccio, Giovanni, et al., *The Early Lives of Dante*, trans. Philip H. Wicksteed (London: Chatto and Windus, 1907).

Boddy, Kasia, 'Foreword', in Houman Barekat et al. (eds), *The Digital Critic: Literary Culture Online* (New York: OR Books, 2017), 7–10.

Borges, Jorge Luis, 'Pierre Menard, Author of the Quixote', in *Collected Fictions*, trans. Andrew Hurley (Harmondsworth: Penguin, 1998), 88–95.

Borges, Jorge Luis, 'Prólogo de prólogos', in *Prólogos con un prólogo de prólogos* (Buenos Aires: Torres Agüero, 1975), 7–9.

Boswell, James, *Boswell's Life of Johnson*, ed. George Birkbeck Hill, rev. L. F. Powell, 6 vols (Oxford: Clarendon Press, 1934; repr. 1971).

Bourget, Paul, 'Charles de Spoelberch de Lovenjoul', in *Pages de critique et de doctrine*, 2 vols (Paris: Plon, 1912), i. 294–304.

Bowlby, Rachel, 'Introduction', in Virginia Woolf, *Orlando: A Biography* (1928), ed. Bowlby (Oxford: Oxford University Press, 1992; repr. 2000), pp. xii–xlviii.

Braithwaite, William Stanley, *The Book of Elizabethan Verse*, 2nd edn (Boston: Herbert B. Turner & Co., 1907; first pub. 1906).

Braithwaite, William Stanley, *The Book of Georgian Verse* (New York: Brentano's, 1909; London: Grant Richards, 1909).

Brinkman, Bartholomew, *Poetic Modernism in the Culture of Mass Print* (Baltimore: Johns Hopkins University Press, 2017).

Bromwich, David, 'Wilson's Modernism', in Lewis M. Dabney (ed.), *Edmund Wilson: Centennial Reflections* (Princeton: Princeton University Press, 1997), 39–52.

Browning, Robert, *The Agamemnon of Aeschylus* (London: Smith, Elder, 1877).

Brontë, Charlotte, *The Clarendon Edition of the Novels of the Brontës: Charlotte Brontë: 'The Professor'*, ed. Margaret Smith and Herbert Rosengarten (Oxford: Clarendon Press, 1987).

Brontë, Charlotte, *The Letters of Charlotte Brontë: With a Selection of Letters by Family and Friends*, ed. Margaret Smith, 3 vols (Oxford: Clarendon Press, 1995–2004).

Brontë, Emily, *The Clarendon Edition of the Novels of the Brontës: Emily Brontë: Wuthering Heights*, ed. Hilda Marsden and Ian Jack (Oxford: Clarendon Press, 1976).

Bucknell, Clare, 'I Can Scarce Hold My Pen' (review of *Correspondence of Samuel Richardson with Lady Bradshaigh and Lady Echlin*, ed. Peter Sabor), *LRB* 15 June 2017 <https://www.lrb.co.uk/the-paper/v39/n12/clare-bucknell/i-can-scarce-hold-my-pen> (accessed 13 January 2021).

Burgess, Anthony, 'Bagehot on Books' (review of *The Collected Works of Walter Bagehot*, ed. Norman St John-Stevas, i, ii), *The Spectator*, 7 January 1966, 15.

Burton, Robert, *The Anatomy of Melancholy*, ed. Thomas C. Faulkner et al., 6 vols (Oxford: Clarendon Press, 1989–2000).

Bury, Louis, 'Topical Criticism and the Cultural Logic of the Quick Take', in Houman Barekat et al. (eds), *The Digital Critic: Literary Culture Online* (New York: OR Books, 2017), 86–101.

Butler, Marilyn, 'Culture's Medium: The Role of the Review', in Stuart Curran (ed.), *The Cambridge Companion to British Romanticism* (Cambridge: Cambridge University Press, 1993), 120–47.

Byron, George Gordon, Baron, *The Vision of Judgment*, in *Lord Byron: The Complete Poetical Works*, ed. Jerome J. McGann, 7 vols (Oxford: Oxford University Press, 1980–93), vi: ed. McGann and Barry Waller (1991), 309–45.

Cappello, Mary, *Lecture* (Oakland, CA: Transit, 2020).

Castle, Terry, 'Women and Literary Criticism', in *CHLC IV*, 434–55.

Chesterton, G. K., *Appreciations and Criticisms of the Works of Charles Dickens* (London: Dent, 1911).

Chihaya, Sarah, et al., *The Ferrante Letters: An Experiment in Collective Criticism* (New York: Columbia University Press, 2020).

Chong, Phillipa K., *Inside the Critics' Circle: Book Reviewing in Uncertain Times* (Princeton: Princeton University Press, 2020).

Chrostowska, S. D., *Literature on Trial: The Emergence of Critical Discourse in Germany, Poland, and Russia, 1700–1800* (Toronto: University of Toronto Press, 2012).

Cicero, Marcus Tullius, *Letters to Friends*, ed. and trans. D. R. Shackleton Bailey, 3 vols (Cambridge, MA: Harvard University Press, 2001).

Clausen, Christopher, 'The Palgrave Version', *Georgia Review*, 34 (1980), 273–89.

Coleridge, Samuel Taylor, *Biographia Literaria; or, Sketches of My Literary Life and Opinions*, ed. James Engell and W. Jackson Bate, 2 vols (Princeton: Princeton University Press, 1983; repr. 1984).

Coleridge, Samuel Taylor, *Coleridge's Lectures on Shakespeare*, ed. Adam Roberts (Edinburgh: Edinburgh University Press, 2016).

Coleridge, Samuel Taylor, *The Watchman*, ed. Lewis Patton (Princeton: Princeton University Press, 1970).

Collini, Stefan, *Common Reading: Critics, Historians, Publics* (Oxford: Oxford University Press, 2008; repr. 2010).

Connors, Clare, 'Creative Criticism: A Histori-Manifesto', in Irving Goh (ed.), *French Thought and Literary Theory in the UK* (New York: Routledge, 2020), 46–62.

Cooper, Isabella M., and Margaret A. McVety, *Dictionary Catalogue of the First 505 Volumes of Everyman's Library* (London: Dent, 1911).

Corney, Bolton, *Curiosities of Literature, by I. D'Israeli, Esq., Illustrated by Bolton Corney, Esq.* (London: Schobert, 1837).

Crane, R. S., 'On Writing the History of Criticism in England 1650–1800', in *The Idea of the Humanities and Other Essays*, 2 vols (Chicago: University of Chicago Press, 1967), ii. 157–75.

Curran, Louise, *Samuel Richardson and the Art of Letter-Writing* (Cambridge: Cambridge University Press, 2016).

d'Albertis, Deirdre, '"Bookmaking Out of the Remains of the Dead": Elizabeth Gaskell's *The Life of Charlotte Brontë*', *Victorian Studies*, 39 (1995), 1–31.

Danson, Lawrence, *Wilde's Intentions: The Artist in his Criticism* (Oxford: Clarendon Press, 1997; repr. 1998).

Dee, James H., letter to the Editor, *TLS* 29 May 2009, 6.

Deleuze, Gilles and Félix Guattari, *What is Philosophy?*, trans. Hugh Tomlinson and Graham Burchell (New York: Columbia University Press, 1994).

Demata, Massimiliano, and Duncan Wu (eds), *British Romanticism and the 'Edinburgh Review': Bicentenary Essays* (Houndmills: Palgrave Macmillan, 2002).

DeNeef, A. Leigh, 'Of Dialogues and Historicisms', *South Atlantic Quarterly*, 88 (1987), 497–517.

Derrida, Jacques, *Dissemination*, trans. Barbara Johnson (London: Continuum, 2004; first pub. 1981).

Diderot, Denis, *Correspondance de Diderot*, ed. Georges Roth and Jean Varloot, 16 vols (Paris: Minuit, 1955–70), ii (1955), 86–103.

Dillon, Brian, *Essayism* (London: Fitzcarraldo Editions, 2017).

D'Israeli, Isaac, *Curiosities of Literature: Consisting of Anecdotes, Characters, Sketches, and Observations, Literary, Critical, and Historical*, 3rd edn (London: John Murray, 1791).

D'Israeli, Isaac, *The Illustrator Illustrated* (London: Edward Moxon, 1838).

Ditchfield, G. M., and Sarah Brewer, 'Hurd, Richard', *ODNB* <https://doi.org/10.1093/ref:odnb/14249> (accessed 5 April 2023).

Dove, Rita (ed.), *The Penguin Anthology of Twentieth-Century American Poetry* (New York: Penguin, 2011).

Dove, Rita, 'Defending an Anthology' (letter to the Editors), *New York Review of Books*, 22 December 2011 <https://www.nybooks.com/articles/2011/12/22/defending-anthology/> (accessed 1 February 2021).

Duras, Marguerite, *Marguerite Duras: Suspended Passion*, trans. Chris Turner (London: Seagull Books, 2016).

Durham Peters, John, *Speaking into the Air: A History of the Idea of Communication* (Chicago: University of Chicago Press, 1999).

During, Simon, 'Henry James and Me', *Modern Language Notes*, 118 (2003), 1278–93.

Eagleton, Terry, *The Function of Criticism* (London: Verso, 2005; first pub. 1984).

Echtermeyer, Theodor, *Auswahl deutscher Gedichte für die untern und mittlern Classen gelehrter Schulen* (Halle: Buchhandlung des Waisenhauses, 1836).

Eckermann, Johann Peter, *Gespräche mit Goethe in den letzten Jahren seines Lebens*, ed. Christoph Michel (Frankfurt-am-Main: Deutscher Klassiker Verlag, 1999).

Eliot, T. S., 'A Note of Introduction to *In Parenthesis*, by David Jones' (1961), in *The Complete Prose of T. S. Eliot: The Critical Edition*, ed. Ronald Schuchard and others, 8 vols (Baltimore: Johns Hopkins University Press, 2014–19), viii: *Still and Still Moving, 1954–1965*, ed. Jewel Spears Brooker and Ronald Schuchard (2019), 479–81.

Empson, William, 'The Alchemist', in *Essays in Renaissance Literature*, ed. John Haffenden, 2 vols (Cambridge: Cambridge University Press, 1994–5; repr. 2006), ii: *The Drama* (1994), 97–109 (first pub. in *Hudson Review*, 22 (1969–70), 595–608).

Empson, William, *Seven Types of Ambiguity* (London: Chatto & Windus, 1930).

Empson, William, *Selected Letters of William Empson*, ed. John Haffenden (Oxford: Oxford University Press, 2009).

Empson, William, *Some Versions of Pastoral* (London: Penguin, 1995; first pub. 1935).

Empson, William, *Using Biography* (Cambridge, MA: Harvard University Press, 1984).

Emre, Merve, *Paraliterary: The Making of Bad Readers in Postwar America* (Chicago: University of Chicago Press, 2017).

Engell, James, *Forming the Critical Mind: Dryden to Coleridge* (Cambridge, MA: Harvard University Press, 1989).

Evans, B. Ifor, *Tradition and Romanticism: Studies in English Poetry from Chaucer to W. B. Yeats* (London: Routledge, 1940).

Ferguson, Frances, 'Now It's Personal: D. A. Miller and Too-Close Reading', *CI* 41 (2015), 521–40.

Ferrari, G. R. F., *Listening to the Cicadas: A Study of Plato's 'Phaedrus'* (Cambridge: Cambridge University Press, 1987).

Ferriar, John, *Illustrations of Sterne, with Other Essays and Verses* (London: printed for Cadell and Davies, 1798).

Ferris, David, *Theory and the Evasion of History* (Baltimore: Johns Hopkins University Press, 1993).

Ferris, Ina, 'Antiquarian Authorship: D'Israeli's Miscellany of Literary Curiosity and the Question of Secondary Genres', *Studies in Romanticism*, 45 (2006), 523–42.

Ferry, Anne, 'Palgrave's "Symphony"', *VP* 27 (1999), 145–62.

Ferry, Anne, *Tradition and the Individual Poem: An Inquiry into Anthologies* (Stanford: Stanford University Press, 2001).

Fitzpatrick, Kathleen, '*CommentPress*: New (Social) Structures for New (Networked) Texts', *Journal of Electronic Publishing*, 10 (2007) <https://doi.org/10.3998/3336451.0010.305> (accessed 5 April 2023).

Fix, Stephen, 'Distant Genius: Johnson and the Art of Milton's Life', *Modern Philology*, 84 (1984), 244–64.

Focillon, Henri, *The Life of Forms in Art*, trans. Charles B. Hogan and George Kubler (New York: Zone, 1989; repr. 1996).

Folger Collective on Early Women Critics (ed.), *Women Critics 1660–1820: An Anthology* (Bloomington: Indiana University Press, 1995).

Forest, Phillipe, 'Marginalité de la préface autoriale', in Forest (ed.), *L'Art de la préface* (Nantes: Defaut, 2006), 11–23.

Forster, Antonia, 'Book Reviewing', in John Barnard et al. (eds), *The Cambridge History of the Book in Britain*, 7 vols (Cambridge: Cambridge University Press, 1999–2019), v: Michael F. Suarez, SJ, and Michael L. Turner (eds), *1695–1830* (2009), 631–48.

Forster, Antonia, *Index to Book Reviews in England 1775–1800* (London: British Library, 1997).

Foucault, Michel, *The Archaeology of Knowledge*, trans. A. M. Sheridan Smith (Abingdon: Routledge, 2002).

Fowler, Alasdair, *Kinds of Literature: An Introduction to the Theory of Genres and Modes* (Oxford: Clarendon Press, 1982).

Frawley, Maria H., 'Gaskell's Ethnographic Imagination in *The Life of Charlotte Brontë*', *Biography*, 21 (1998), 175–94.

Fumaroli, Marc, *Littérature et conversation: La Querelle Sainte-Beuve–Proust* (London: University of London Press, 1991).

Gardner, Helen (ed.), *The New Oxford Book of English Verse, 1250–1950* (Oxford: Oxford University Press, 1972).

Gaskell, Elizabeth, *The Life of Charlotte Brontë*, ed. Angus Easson (Oxford: Oxford University Press, 1996).

Gates, Henry Louis, Jr, 'Mister Jefferson and the Trials of Phillis Wheatley', 23 March 2002 <https://www.neh.gov/about/awards/jefferson-lecture/henry-louis-gates-jr-biography> (accessed 19 January 2022).

Gaugain, Claude, 'Les Préfaces dans le roman policier', in Phillipe Forest (ed.), *L'Art de la préface* (Nantes: Defaut, 2006), 187–99.

Gavin, Michael, *The Invention of English Criticism, 1650–1760* (Cambridge: Cambridge University Press, 2015).

Genette, Gérard, *Paratexts: Thresholds of Interpretation*, trans. Jane E. Lewin (Cambridge: Cambridge University Press, 1997).

Glen, Heather, *Charlotte Brontë: The Imagination in History* (Oxford: Oxford University Press, 2002; repr. 2004).

Göbel, Helmut, et al. (eds), *Briefe an junge Dichter* (Göttingen: Wallstein, 1998).

Goetschel, Willi, *Constituting Critique: Kant's Writing as Critical Praxis*, trans. Eric Schwab (Durham, NC: Duke University Press, 1994).

Goetz, William R., 'Criticism and Autobiography in James's Prefaces', *American Literature*, 51 (1979), 333–48.

Goffman, Erving, *Forms of Talk* (Oxford: Oxford University Press, 1981).

Goldie, David, 'Literary Studies and the Academy', in *CHLC VI*, 46–71.

Gorra, Michael, 'Introductions: A Preface', *Sewanee Review*, 116 (2008), 124–7.

Grant, Allan, *A Preface to Coleridge* (London: Longman, 1972).

Greenblatt, Stephen, *Renaissance Self-Fashioning: From More to Shakespeare* (Chicago: University of Chicago Press, 1980).

Gregory, George, *Essays Historical and Moral* (London: J. Johnson, 1785).

Grierson, Herbert J. C. (ed.), *Metaphysical Lyrics and Poems of the Seventeenth Century* (Oxford: Clarendon Press, 1921).

Griffiths, Eric, 'The Disappointment of Christina G. Rossetti', *Essays in Criticism*, 47 (1997), 107–42.

Griffiths, Eric, *The Printed Voice of Victorian Poetry*, 2nd edn (Oxford: Oxford University Press, 2018; first pub. 1989).

Griffiths, Eric, *If Not Critical*, ed. Freya Johnston (Oxford: Oxford University Press, 2018).

Groom, Nick, *The Making of Percy's 'Reliques'* (Oxford: Clarendon Press, 1999).

Gross, John, *The Rise and Fall of the Man of Letters: English Literary Life since 1800* (Harmondsworth: Penguin, 1973; first pub. 1969).

Gross, John, 'Naming Names', *TLS* 7 June 1974, 610.

Guillory, John, 'Canon', in Frank Lentricchia and Thomas McLaughlin (eds), *Critical Terms for Literary Study*, 2nd edn (Chicago: University of Chicago Press, 1995), 233–49.

Gwynn, R. S., 'Approaching a Significant Birthday, He Peruses *The Norton Anthology of Poetry*', in *No Word of Farewell: Poems 1970–2000* (Ashland, OR: Story Line Press, 2001), 42–3,

Hadley, David, 'Public Lectures and Private Societies: Expounding Literature and the Arts in Romantic London', in Donald Schoonmaker and John A. Alford (eds), *English Romanticism: Preludes and Postludes: Essays in Honor of Edwin Graves Wilson* (East Lansing, MI: Colleagues Press, 1993), 43–57.

Hale, Dorothy J., 'Henry James and the Invention of Novel Theory', in Jonathan Freedman (ed.), *The Cambridge Companion to Henry James* (Cambridge: Cambridge University Press, 1998), 79–101.

Hamann, Johann Georg, *Fünf Hirtenbriefe, das Schuldrama betreffend*, in Hamann, *Sämtliche Werke*, ed. Josef Nadler, 6 vols (Vienna: Thomas-Morus, 1949), ii: *Schriften über Philosophie, Philologie, Kritik, 1758–1763*, 353–69.

Hamilton, Paul, *Historicism*, 2nd edn (London: Routledge, 2003).

Hardwick, Elizabeth, *The Collected Essays of Elizabeth Hardwick*, ed. Darryl Pinckney (New York: New York Review Books, 2017).

Harrison, Patrick, 'Downing after the War', in Ian McKillop and Richard Storer (eds), *F. R. Leavis: Essays and Documents* (London: Continuum, 2005), 244–63.

Hartman, Geoffrey H., 'The Interpreter: A Self-Analysis', in *The Fate of Reading and Other Essays* (Chicago: University of Chicago Press, 1975), 3–19.

Hay, Ian, *A Safety Match* (Edinburgh: William Blackwood, 1911).

Hayles, N. Katherine, *Electronic Literature: New Horizons for the Literary* (Notre Dame: University of Notre Dame Press, 2008).

Hayot, Eric, 'Academic Writing, I Love You. Really, I Do', *CI* 41 (2014), 53–77.

Hayot, Eric, *The Elements of Academic Style: Writing for the Humanities* (New York: Columbia University Press, 2014).

Hazlitt, William, *A Letter to William Gifford, Esq.* (1819), in *The Complete Works of William Hazlitt*, ed. P. P. Howe, 21 vols (London: Dent, 1930–4), ix: *A Reply to 'Z'*, etc. (1932), 11–59.

Herder, J. G., *Ueber Thomas Abbts Schriften*, first part ([Leipzig]: [Hartknoch], 1768).

Herford, Oliver, *Henry James's Style of Retrospect: Late Personal Writings, 1890–1915* (Oxford: Oxford University Press, 2016).

Hewitt, W. T., 'Goethe as a Man', in Marion V. Dudley (ed.), *Poetry and Philosophy of Goethe* (Chicago: Griggs, 1887), 252–8.

Hierocles, *Hieroclis Philosophi Alexandrini Commentarius in Aurea Carmina*, ed. Peter Needham (Cambridge, 1709).

Hohendahl, Peter Uwe, *The Institution of Criticism* (Ithaca, NY: Cornell University Press, 1982).

Hohendahl, Peter Uwe, 'Introduction', in Hohendahl (ed.), *A History of German Literary Criticism, 1730–1980* (Lincoln: University of Nebraska Press, 1988), 1–12.

Holland, Laurence B., *The Expense of Vision: Essays on the Craft of Henry James* (Princeton: University of Princeton Press, 1964; Baltimore: Johns Hopkins University Press, 1982).

Horkheimer, Max, 'Fragen des Hochschulunterrichts' (1952), in *Gesammelte Schriften*, ed. Alfred Schmidt and Gunzelin Schmid Noerr, 19 vols (Frankfurt-am-Main: Fischer, 1985–96), viii: *Vorträge und Aufzeichnungen, 1949–1973* (1985), 391–408.

Hough, Graham, *The Last Romantics* (London: Gerald Duckworth, 1949).

Hugo, Victor, 'Preface to *Cromwell*', in *The Essential Victor Hugo*, trans. E. H. and A. M. Blackmore (Oxford: Oxford University Press, 2004), 16–53.

Hunt, Leigh, 'On Periodical Essays', in *The Selected Writings of Leigh Hunt*, ed. Greg Kucich and Jeffrey N. Cox, 6 vols (London: Pickering and Chatto, 2003), i: *Periodical Essays, 1805–14*, 35–57.

Hunter, J. Paul, 'The World as Stage and Closet', in Shirley Strum Kenny (ed.), *British Theatre and the Other Arts, 1660–1800* (Washington: Folger Shakespeare Library, 1984), 271–86.

[Hurd, Richard], *Letters on Chivalry and Romance* (London: printed for A. Millar; Cambridge: printed for W. Thurlbourn and J. Woodyer, 1762).

Igarashi, Yohei, *The Connected Condition: Romanticism and the Dream of Communication* (Stanford: Stanford University Press, 2020).

Jackson, Kevin, *Invisible Forms: A Guide to Literary Curiosities* (London: Picador, 1999).

Jackson, Virginia, *Dickinson's Misery: A Theory of Lyric Reading* (Princeton: Princeton University Press, 2005).

James, Felicity, 'Charles Lamb', in Peter Holland and Adrian Poole (eds), *Great Shakespeareans*, 18 vols (London: Continuum, 2010–13), iv: Adrian Poole (ed.), *Lamb, Hazlitt, Keats* (2010), 10–63.

James, Henry, *The Art of the Novel: Critical Prefaces*, ed. R. P. Blackmur (New York: Scribner's Sons, 1947; first pub. 1932).

James, Henry, *The Letters of Henry James*, ed. Leon Edel, 4 vols (Cambridge, MA: Harvard University Press, 1974–84).

James, Henry, *Literary Criticism: Essays on Literature, American Writers, English Writers*, ed. Leon Edel (New York: Library of America, 1984)

James, Henry, *Literary Criticism: French Writers, Other European Writers, the Prefaces to the New York Edition*, ed. Leon Edel (New York: Library of America, 1984).

James, Henry, *The Princess Casamassima*, ed. Adrian Poole (Cambridge: Cambridge University Press, 2019).

Jarvis, Simon, 'Criticism, Taste, Aesthetics', in Thomas Keymer and Jon Mee (eds), *The Cambridge Companion to English Literature, 1740–1830* (Cambridge: Cambridge University Press, 2004), 24–42.

Jarvis, Simon, 'The Future of Monologue', *New Formations*, 41 (2000), 21–30.

[Jeffrey, Francis], 'Art. VIII. *Thalaba, the Destroyer*: A Metrical Romance. By Robert Southey', *Edinburgh Review*, 1 (October 1802), 63–83.

[Jeffrey, Francis], 'Art. II. *Thalaba the Destroyer*; a Metrical Romance. By Robert Southey', *Monthly Review*, 39 (November 1802), 240–51.

[Jeffrey, Francis], 'Art I. The Excursion, being a portion of the Recluse, a Poem. By William Wordsworth', *Edinburgh Review*, 47 (November 1814), 1–30.

Johnson, James Weldon (ed.), *The Book of American Negro Poetry*, rev. edn (New York: Harcourt, Brace, 1931; first pub. 1922).

Johnson, Samuel, *The Lives of the Most Eminent English Poets; with Critical Observations on their Works*, ed. Roger Lonsdale, 4 vols (Oxford: Oxford University Press, 2006).

Johnson, Samuel, *The Yale Edition of the Works of Samuel Johnson*, ed. Robert DeMaria, Jr et al., 23 vols (New Haven: Yale University Press, 1958–2019), xx: *Johnson on Demand: Reviews, Prefaces, and Ghost-Writings*, ed. O. M. Brack, Jr and Robert DeMaria, Jr (2018).

Johnson, Samuel, *The Yale Edition of the Works of Samuel Johnson*, ed. Robert DeMaria, Jr et al., 23 vols (New Haven: Yale University Press, 1958–2019), vii and viii: *Johnson on Shakespeare*, ed. Arthur Sherbo (1968).

Johnston, Freya, 'Introduction', in Eric Griffiths, Eric, *If Not Critical*, ed. Johnston (Oxford: Oxford University Press, 2018), 1–7.

Johnston, Freya, *Samuel Johnson and the Art of Sinking 1709–1791* (Oxford: Oxford University Press, 2005).

Kamuf, Peggy, *Book of Addresses* (Stanford: Stanford University Press, 2005).

Kant, Immanuel, *Critique of Judgement*, trans. James Creed Meredith, rev. and ed. Nicholas Walker (Oxford: Oxford University Press, 2007).

Karshan, Thomas, and Kathryn Murphy (eds), *On Essays: Montaigne to the Present* (Oxford: Oxford University Press, 2020).

Kazin, Alfred, 'Writing for Magazines', in *Contemporaries* (London: Secker and Warburg, 1973), 471–4.

Keats, John, *The Letters of John Keats, 1814–1821*, ed. Hyder Edward Rollins, 2 vols (Cambridge: Cambridge University Press, 1958).

Keble, John, *Keble's Lectures on Poetry 1832–1841*, trans. Edward Kershaw Francis, 2 vols (Oxford: Clarendon Press, 1912).

Keble, John, *Praelectiones Academicae: Oxonii Habitae Annis MDCCCXXXII–MDCCCXLI*, 2 vols (Oxford: Parker, 1844).

Keener, Frederick M., *English Dialogues of the Dead: A Critical History, An Anthology, and A Check List* (New York: Columbia University Press, 1973).

Kelley, Theresa M., *Wordsworth's Revisionary Aesthetics* (Cambridge: Cambridge University Press, 1988).

Kelly, Gary, 'Reeve, Clara (1729–1807)', *ODNB* <https://doi.org/10.1093/ref:odnb/23292> (accessed 5 April 2023).

Kennedy, William J., 'Petrarchan Poetics', in *CHLC III*, 119–26.

Kermode, Frank, *Pleasing Myself: From Beowulf to Philip Roth* (London: Allen Lane, 2001).

Kermode, Frank, *The Uses of Error* (London: Collins, 1990).

[Kierkegaard, Søren], *'Prefaces' and 'Writing Sampler'*, ed. and trans. Todd W. Nichol (Princeton: Princeton University Press, 1997).

Kinzel, Till, 'Literary Criticism as Dialogue: From Jerome McGann's Dialogical Confrontation with Swinburne to Meta-Dialogue', in Kinzel and Jarmila Mildorf (eds), *Imaginary Dialogues in American Literature and Philosophy* (Heidelberg: Winter, 2014), 259–67.

Klancher, Jon, *The Making of English Reading Audiences 1790–1832* (Madison: University of Wisconsin Press, 1987).

Klancher, Jon, *Transfiguring the Arts and Sciences: Knowledge and Cultural Institutions in the Romantic Age* (Cambridge: Cambridge University Press, 2013).

Klancher, Jon, 'Transmission Failure', in David Perkins (ed.), *Theoretical Issues in Literary History*, Harvard English Studies, 16 (Cambridge, MA: Harvard University Press, 1991), 173–95.

Kramnick, Jonathan, 'Criticism and Truth', *CI* 47 (2021), 218–40.

Kramnick, Jonathan, 'Literary Criticism among the Disciplines', *Eighteenth-Century Studies*, 35 (2002), 343–60.

Kramnick, Jonathan, and Anahid Nersessian, 'Form and Explanation', *CI* 43 (2017), 650–69.

LaCapra, Dominick, *Rethinking Intellectual History: Texts, Contexts, Language* (Ithaca, NY: Cornell University Press, 1983).

Laclos, Pierre Choderlos de, *Les Liaisons dangereuses*, ed. Catriona Seth (Paris: Gallimard, 2011).

Lamb, Charles, *Specimens of English Dramatic Poets, who Lived about the Time of Shakespeare. With Notes*, 2nd edn, 2 vols (London: Edward Moxon, 1835; repr. Cambridge: Cambridge University Press, 2013).

Landor, Walter Savage, *Imaginary Conversations*, in *The Complete Works of Walter Savage Landor*, ed. T. Earle Welby, 16 vols (London: Methuen, 1929–36; repr. 1969), i–ix.

Lang, Andrew, 'At the Sign of the Ship', *Longman's Magazine* (1886–1905).

Lavery, Jonathan, 'Philosophical Genres and Literary Forms: A Mildly Polemical Introduction', *Poetics Today*, 28 (2007), 171–89.

Leavis, F. R., *The Great Tradition: George Eliot, Henry James, Joseph Conrad* (Harmondsworth: Penguin, 1977; first pub. 1948).

Leavis, F. R., *English Literature in our Time & the University* (Cambridge: Cambridge University Press, 1979; first pub. 1969).

Lee, Vernon, *Althea: Dialogues on Aspirations and Duties* (London: John Lane, [1894]).

Lee, Vernon, *Baldwin: Being Dialogues on Views and Aspirations* (London: T. Fisher Unwin, 1886).

Lee, Vernon, *Belcaro: Being Essays on Sundry Æsthetical Questions* (London: Satchell, [1891]).

Leighton, Angela, *On Form: Poetry, Aestheticism, and the Legacy of a Word* (Oxford: Oxford University Press, 2007; repr. 2008).

Lewes, George Henry, *The Life of Goethe*, 2nd edn (London: Smith, Elder, 1864).

Liddle, Dallas, 'Salesmen, Sportsmen, Mentors: Anonymity and Mid-Victorian Theories of Journalism', *Victorian Studies*, 41 (1997), 31–68.

Lipking, Lawrence, *The Ordering of the Arts in Eighteenth-Century England* (Princeton: Princeton University Press, 1970).

Lipking, Lawrence, 'Poet-Critics', in *CHLC VII*, 439–67.

Liu, Alan, 'The Power of Formalism: The New Historicism', *English Literary History*, 56 (1989), 721–71.

Liu, Alan, *Wordsworth: The Sense of History* (Stanford: Stanford University Press, 1989).

Locke, Alain (ed.), *The New Negro* (New York: Boni, 1925; repr. New York: Atheneum, 1975).

London, April, 'Isaac D'Israeli and Literary History: Opinion, Anecdote, and Secret History in the Early Nineteenth Century', *Poetics Today*, 26 (2005), 351–86.

Lowth, Robert, *Lectures on the Sacred Poetry of the Hebrews*, trans. George Gregory, 2 vols (London: printed for J. Johnson, 1787).

Lowth, Robert, *De Sacra Poesi Hebræorum* (Oxford: Clarendon Press, 1753).

McCue, Jim, letter to the Editor, *TLS* 8 May 2009, 6.

McGann, Jerome J., 'Author's Note on the Work' (July 2006) <https://writing.upenn.edu/pennsound/x/McGann.php> (accessed 15 February 2022).

McGann, Jerome J., 'Dialogue on Dialogue', in Julianna Spahr et al. (eds), *A Poetics of Criticism* (Buffalo: Leave Books, 1994), 59–77.

McGann, Jerome J., *The Point Is to Change It: Poetry and Criticism in the Continuing Present* (Tuscaloosa: University of Alabama Press, 2007).

McGann, Jerome J., *Swinburne: An Experiment in Criticism* (Chicago: University of Chicago Press, 1972).

Mackail, J. W. (ed.), *Select Epigrams from the Greek Anthology* (London: Longman, 1890).

Macovski, Michael (ed.), *Dialogue and Critical Discourse: Language, Culture, Critical Theory* (Oxford: Oxford University Press, 1997).

McWhirter, David (ed.), *Henry James's New York Edition: The Construction of Authorship*, (Stanford: Stanford University Press, 1995).

Mandell, Laura, *Misogynous Economies: The Business of Literature in Eighteenth-Century Britain* (Lexington: University of Kentucky Press, 1999).

Manning, Peter J., 'Manufacturing the Romantic Image: Hazlitt and Coleridge Lecturing', in James Chandler and Kevin Gilmartin (eds), *Romantic Metropolis: The Urban Scene of British Culture, 1780–1840* (Cambridge: Cambridge University Press, 2005), 227–45.

Mason, Nicholas, '"The Quack Has Become God": Puffery, Print, and the "Death" of Literature in Romantic-Era Britain', *Nineteenth-Century Literature*, 60 (2005), 1–31.

Maurer, Oscar, Jr, 'Anonymity vs. Signature in Victorian Reviewing', *Studies in English*, 27 (1948), 1–27.

Maxwell, Catherine, 'Vernon Lee's Handling of Words', in Michael D. Hurley and Marcus Waithe (eds), *Thinking through Style: Non-Fiction Prose of the Long Nineteenth Century* (Oxford: Oxford University Press, 2018), 282–94.

May, Derwent, *Critical Times: The History of the Times Literary Supplement* (London: HarperCollins, 2001).

Meessen, H. J., 'Wieland's "Briefe an einen jungen Dichter"', *Monatshefte für deutschen Unterricht, deutsche Sprache und Literatur*, 47 (1955), 193–208.

Mendelson, Edward, 'Biography and Poetry', in Roland Greene et al. (eds), *The Princeton Encyclopedia of Poetry and Poetics*, 4th edn (Princeton: Princeton University Press, 2012), 140–3.

Meyer, Steven, 'Gertrude Stein', in *CHLC VII*, 93–121.

Mieszkowski, Jan, *Crises of the Sentence* (Chicago: University of Chicago Press, 2019).

Migeot, François, 'Rapport de places et imaginaire dans les lettres de Laclos et Mme Riccoboni', *Semen*, 20 (2005) <https://journals.openedition.org/semen/2038> (accessed 28 July 2020).

Miller, Lucasta, *The Brontë Myth* (London: Cape, 2001).

Moretti, Franco, 'Conjectures on World Literature', *New Left Review* (January–February 2000), 54–68.

Morrison, Toni, 'The Future of Time: Literature and Diminished Expectations', 25th Jefferson Lecture in the Humanities, 25 March 1996 <https://neh.dspacedirect.org/bitstream/handle/11215/3774/LIB39_002-public.pdf?sequence=1&isAllowed=y> (accessed 22 March 2022).

Morrison, Toni, *Goodness: Altruism and the Literary Imagination* (2012 Ingersoll Lecture on Immortality), online video recording, YouTube, 14 December 2012 <https://www.youtube.com/watch?v=PJmVpYZnKTU> (accessed 22 March 2022).

Morrison, Toni, *Goodness and the Literary Imagination: Harvard's 95th Ingersoll Lecture with Essays on Morrison's Moral and Religious Vision*, ed. David Carrasco et al. (Charlottesville: University of Virginia Press, 2019).

Morrison, Toni, 'Nobel Lecture', 7 December 1993, audio recording <https://www.nobelprize.org/mediaplayer/?id=1502> (accessed 22 March 2022).

Morrison, Toni, 'Nobel Lecture', 7 December 1993, text <https://www.nobelprize.org/prizes/literature/1993/morrison/lecture/?_ga=2.30313530.46266796.1647959409-500863312.1647959409> (accessed 22 March 2022).

Morrison, Toni, *Playing in the Dark: Whiteness and the Literary Imagination* (New York: Vintage, 1993; first pub. Cambridge, MA: Harvard University Press, 1992).

Morrison, Toni, 'Unspeakable Things Unspoken: The Afro-American Presence in American Literature', The Tanner Lectures on Human Values, delivered at the University of Michigan, 7 October 1988 <https://tannerlectures.utah.edu/_resources/documents/a-to-z/m/morrison90.pdf> (accessed 21 March 2023) (first pub. in *Michigan Quarterly Review*, 28 (1989), 1–34).

Mucignat, Rosa, review of *The Ferrante Letters* by Sarah Chihaya and others, *Times Higher Education Supplement*, 20 February 2020 <https://www.timeshighereducation.com/books/ferrante-letters-experiment-collective-criticism-sarah-chihaya-merve-emre-katherine-hill-and> (accessed 13 January 2021).

Mullan, John, *Anonymity: A Secret History of English Literature* (London: Faber and Faber, 2007).

Mullan, John, 'Beastliness' (review of Eric Griffiths, *If Not Critical* and *The Printed Voice of Victorian Poetry*, 2nd edn), *LRB* 23 May 2019 <https://www.lrb.co.uk/the-paper/v41/n10/john-mullan/beastliness> (accessed 14 January 2021).

Multigraph Collective, *Interacting with Print: Elements of Reading in the Era of Print Saturation* (Chicago: University of Chicago Press, 2017).

Myers, Mitzi, 'Mary Wollstonecraft's Literary Reviews', in Claudia L. Johnson (ed.), *The Cambridge Companion to Mary Wollstonecraft* (Cambridge: Cambridge University Press, 2002), 82–98.

Myers, Mitzi, 'Sensibility and the "Walk of Reason": Mary Wollstonecraft's Literary Reviews as Cultural Critique', in Syndy Conger McMillen (ed.), *Sensibility in Transformation: Creative Resistance to Sentiment from the Augustans to the Romantics* (Rutherford, NJ: Fairleigh Dickinson University Press, 1990), 120–44.

Nabokov, Vladimir, *Dear Bunny, Dear Volodya: The Nabokov–Wilson Letters, 1940–1971*, ed. Simon Karlinsky, rev. edn (Berkeley and Los Angeles: University of California Press, 2001).

Nabokov, Vladimir, *Strong Opinions* (London: Penguin, 1973; repr. 2011).

Ngai, Sianne, *Our Aesthetic Categories: Zany, Cute, Interesting* (Cambridge, MA: Harvard University Press, 2016).

Nolden, Thomas, '*An einem jungen Dichter*': *Studien zur epistolaren Poetik* (Würzberg: Königshausen & Neumann, 1995).

Ogden, James, *Isaac D'Israeli* (Oxford: Oxford University Press, 1969).

Orage, A. R., 'Bookish Causerie', *Labour Leader* (1895–7).

Orrery, John Boyle, Earl of, *The Letters of Pliny the Younger. With Observations on Each Letter; and an Essay on Pliny's Life*, 2 vols (Dublin: printed for George Faulkner, 1751).

Orrery, John Boyle, Earl of, *Remarks on the Life and Writings of Dr Jonathan Swift* [...] *in a Series of Letters* [...] *to his Son, the Honourable Hamilton Boyle* (Dublin: printed by George Faulkner, 1752).

Orwell, George, *The Collected Essays, Journalism, and Letters of George Orwell*, ed. Sonia Orwell and Ian Angus, 4 vols (London: Penguin, 1970).

Palgrave, Francis Turner, *The Golden Treasury*, ed. Christopher Ricks (London: Penguin, 1991).

Palgrave, Gwenllian F., *Francis Turner Palgrave: His Journals and Memories of his Life* (London: Longmans, Green, and Co., 1899).

Parini, Jay, 'The Disappearing Art of Reviewing Books', *Chronicle of Higher Education*, 23 July 1999, 4–5.

Parker, Fred, 'Johnson and the Lives of Poets', *Cambridge Quarterly*, 29 (2000), 323–37.

Parker, Herschel, 'Deconstructing the Art of the Novel and Liberating James's Prefaces', *HJR* 14 (1993), 284–307.

Pearson, Jacqueline, *Women Reading in Britain, 1750–1835: A Dangerous Reaction* (Cambridge: Cambridge University Press, 1999).

Pearson, John H., *The Prefaces of Henry James: Framing the Modern Reader* (University Park: Pennsylvania State University Press, 1997).

Peterson, Linda, 'Anthologizing Women: Women Poets in Early Victorian Collections of Lyric', *VP* 37 (1999), 193–209.

Peterson, Linda, 'Elizabeth Gaskell's *The Life of Charlotte Brontë*', in Jill L. Matus (ed.), *The Cambridge Companion to Elizabeth Gaskell* (Cambridge: Cambridge University Press, 2007), 59–74.

Phillips, Caryl, *The European Tribe* (London: Faber and Faber, 1987).

Pickstock, Catherine, *After Writing: On the Liturgical Consummation of Philosophy* (Oxford: Blackwell, 1998).

Plato, *Complete Works*, ed. John M. Cooper (Indianapolis: Hackett, 1997).

Poovey, Mary, 'Creative Criticism: Adaptation, Performative Writing, and the Problem of Objectivity', *Narrative*, 8 (2000), 109–33.

Potter, Lois, *A Preface to Milton* (London: Longman, 1971).

Price, Leah, *The Anthology and the Rise of the Novel: From Richardson to George Eliot* (Cambridge: Cambridge University Press, 2000).

Prince, Michael, *Philosophical Dialogue in the British Enlightenment: Theology, Aesthetics, and the Novel* (Cambridge: Cambridge University Press, 1996).

Proust, Marcel, *'Against Sainte-Beuve' and Other Essays*, trans. John Sturrock (London: Penguin 1988).

Proust, Marcel, *Contre Sainte-Beuve*, ed. Pierre Clarac and Yves Sandre, Bibliothèque de la Pléiade (Paris: Gallimard, 1971).

Proust, Marcel, *Letters to a Friend*, trans. Alexander and Elizabeth Henderson (London: Falcon Press, 1949).

Quiller-Couch, Arthur (ed.), *The Oxford Book of English Verse* (Oxford: Oxford University Press, 1900).

[Ramsay, Allan], *A Dialogue on Taste*, 2nd edn (London, 1762).

Redfield, Marc, 'Appendix 1: Courses Taught by Paul de Man during the Yale Years', in *Legacies of Paul de Man*, ed. Redfield (New York: Fordham University Press, 2007), 179–83.

[Reeve, Clara], *The Progress of Romance, through Times, Countries, and Manners; with Remarks on the Good and Bad Effects of It, on Them Respectively; In a Course of Evening Conversations*, 2 vols (Colchester: printed for the Author, 1785).

Regis, Amber K., 'Interpreting Emily: Ekphrasis and Allusion in Charlotte Brontë's "Editor's Preface" to *Wuthering Heights*', *Brontë Studies*, 45 (2020), 168–82.

Rejak, Brian, and Michael Theune (eds), *Keats's Negative Capability: New Origins and Afterlives* (Liverpool: Liverpool University Press, 2019).

Richardson, Samuel, *Samuel Richardson: Correspondence with Lady Bradshaigh and Lady Echlin*, ed. Peter Sabor, 3 vols (Cambridge: Cambridge University Press, 2016).

Richetti, John, *Philosophical Writing: Locke, Berkeley, Hume* (Cambridge, MA: Harvard University Press, 1983).

Ricks, Christopher, *Essays in Appreciation* (Oxford: Oxford University Press, 1996; repr. 2004).

Ricks, Christopher (ed.), *The Oxford Book of English Verse* (Oxford: Oxford University Press, 1999).

Riding, Laura, and Robert Graves, *A Pamphlet against Anthologies* (1928), in *'A Survey of Modernist Poetry' and 'A Pamphlet against Anthologies'*, ed. Charles Mundye and Patrick McGuinness (Manchester: Carcanet, 2002), 151–256.

Robbins, Bruce, *Secular Vocations: Intellectuals, Professionalism, Culture* (London: Verso, 1993).

Rollins, Hyder Edward, 'Keats's Misdated Letters', *Harvard Library Bulletin*, 7 (1953), 172–87.

Ronell, Avital, *Dictations: On Haunted Writing* (Lincoln: University of Nebraska Press, 1993; first pub. 1986).

Roper, Derek, *Reviewing before the 'Edinburgh': 1788–1802* (London: Methuen, 1978).

Rousseau, Jean-Jacques, *Eloisa; or, A Series of Original Letters Collected and Published by J. J. Rousseau*, trans. anon., 4th edn, 4 vols (Dublin: P. Wilson, 1766).

Rowe, John Carlos, *The Theoretical Dimensions of Henry James* (London: Methuen, 1984).

Rundle, Vivienne, 'The Prefaces of Henry James and Joseph Conrad', *HJR* 16 (1995), 66–92.

Saintsbury, George, 'Appendix I. The Oxford Chair of Poetry', in *A History of Criticism and Literary Taste in Europe*, 3 vols (Edinburgh: William Blackwood, 1900–4), iii: *Modern Criticism* (1904), 615–29.

Sancho, Ignatius, *Letters of the Late Ignatius Sancho, An African*, ed. Vincent Carretta (Peterborough, ON: Broadview, 2015).

Sanders, L. C., 'Gregory, George', rev. Philip Carter, *ODNB* <https://doi.org/10.1093/ref:odnb/11463> (accessed 5 April 2023).

Schlegel, Friedrich, *'Dialogue on Poetry' and 'Literary Aphorisms'*, trans. Ernst Behler and Roman Struc (University Park: Pennsylvania State University Press, 1968).

Schlegel, Friedrich, *Kritische Friedrich-Schlegel-Ausgabe*, ed. Ernst Behler et al., 35 vols (Munich: Ferdinand Schöningh, 1958–), ii (1967).

Schwiegershausen, Erica, 'Eileen Myles on the Book that Made Writing like Talking', *The Cut*, 29 August 2017 <https://www.thecut.com/2017/08/eileen-myles-on-lectures-in-america-by-gertrude-stein.html> (accessed 14 January 2022).

Scott, Clive, *The Poetics of French Verse: Studies in Reading* (Oxford: Oxford University Press, 1998).

Shattock, Joanne, 'Spreading it Thinly: Some Victorian Reviewers at Work', *Victorian Periodicals Newsletter*, 9 (1976), 84–7.

Shattock, Joanne, *Politics and Reviewers: The 'Edinburgh' and the 'Quarterly' in the Early Victorian Age* (London: Leicester University Press, 1989).

Shattock, Joanne, 'Contexts and Conditions of Criticism 1830–1914', in *CHLC VI*, 21–45.

Shattock, Joanne, 'The Culture of Criticism', in Shattock (ed.), *The Cambridge Companion to English Literature 1830–1914* (Cambridge: Cambridge University Press, 2010), 71–90.

Sheed, Wilfrid, 'The Good Word: The Politics of Reviewing', *New York Times*, 7 February 1971, 15–16.

Shelley, Percy, *Shelley's Poetry and Prose*, 2nd edn, ed. Donald H. Reiman and Neil Fraistat (New York: Norton, 2002).

Shelston, Alan, 'Biography and Criticism', *Critical Quarterly*, 27 (1985), 71–5.

Shesgreen, Sean, 'Canonizing the Canonizer: A Short History of *The Norton Anthology of English Literature*', *CI* 35 (2009), 293–318.

Simpson, Lewis P. (ed.), *The Possibilities of Order: Cleanth Brooks and his Work* (Baton Rouge: Louisiana University Press, 1976).

Smith, Charlotte, *Emmeline, the Orphan of the Castle*, 4 vols (London: printed for T. Cadell, 1788).

Smith, Zadie, 'Introduction', in Hanif Kureishi, *The Buddha of Suburbia* (London: Faber and Faber, 2017; first pub. 1990), pp. v–xiii.

Southey, Robert, *The Collected Letters of Robert Southey*, part III (1804–9) <https://romantic-circles.org/editions/southey_letters/Part_Three/HTML/letterEEd.26.1283.html> (accessed 29 December 2020).

Southey, Robert, *The Remains of Henry Kirke White, with an Account of his Life, by Robert Southey*, 2 vols (Cambridge: printed for Vernor and others; Nottingham: printed for Dunn and Tupman, 1807).

Southey, Robert (ed.), *The Works of William Cowper*, 15 vols (London: Baldwin & Cradock, 1835–7).

Spahr, Juliana, and Stephanie Young, 'Numbers Trouble', *Chicago Review*, 53 (2007), 88–111.

Sprat, Thomas (ed.), *The Works of Mr Abraham Cowley* (London: printed for Henry Herringman, 1668).

St Clair, William, *The Reading Nation in the Romantic Period* (Cambridge: Cambridge University Press, 2004).

Stein, Gertrude, *Lectures in America* (London: Virago Press, 1988; first pub. 1935).

Steiner, George, *Lessons of the Masters* (Cambridge, MA: Harvard University Press, 2003).

Sterne, Laurence, *The Life and Opinions of Tristram Shandy, Gentleman*, ed. James A. Work (New York: Odyssey, 1940).

Sterne, Laurence, *The Life and Opinions of Tristram Shandy, Gentleman*, ed. Melvyn New and Joan New (London: Penguin, 2003).

Stevenson, Anne, 'Why Palgrave Lives', *VP* 37 (1999), 211–14.

Stevenson, Robert Louis, *An Inland Voyage* (London: Kegan Paul, 1878).

Sussman, Henry, 'Criticism as Art: Form in Oscar Wilde's Critical Writings', *Studies in Philology*, 70 (1973), 108–22.

Sutherland, Keston, *Stupefaction: A Radical Anatomy of Phantoms* (London: Seagull Books, 2011).

Swinburne, Algernon Charles, 'By the North Sea', in *The Poems of Algernon Charles Swinburne*, 6 vols (London: Chatto and Windus, 1911; first pub. 1904), v. 83–110.

Symons, A. J. A., *The Quest for Corvo* (London: Penguin, 2018; first pub. 1934).

Taine, Hippolyte, 'Sainte-Beuve', in *Derniers essais de critique et d'histoire*, 7th edn (Paris: Hachette, 1923), 91–8.

Tillotson, Kathleen, 'Palgrave's *Golden Treasury* and Tennyson: Another Source', *Tennyson Research Bulletin*, 5 (1988), 49–54.

Thaventhiran, Helen, *Radical Empiricists: Five Modernist Close Readers* (Oxford: Oxford University Press, 2015).

Thompson, David, and Alan F. Nagel (eds), *The Three Crowns of Florence: Humanist Assessments of Dante, Petrarca and Boccaccio* (New York: Harper & Row, 1972).

Thomson, James, *Biographical and Critical Studies* (London: Reeves and Turner, 1896).

Tregear, Theodore, 'Anthologizing Shakespeare, 1593–1603' (unpublished doctoral thesis, University of Cambridge, Trinity College, 2019), in *Apollo—University of Cambridge Repository* <https://doi.org/10.17863/CAM.40256> (accessed 23 December 2020).

Trescott, Jacqueline, 'Toni Morrison, Reading Ahead', *Washington Post*, 26 March 1996 <https://www.washingtonpost.com/archive/lifestyle/1996/03/26/toni-morrison-reading-ahead/baa0c80f-3769-47a7-9fda-551ec79fc89d/> (accessed 22 March 2022).

Trilling, Lionel, *The Experience of Literature: A Reader with Commentaries* (Garden City, NY: Doubleday, 1967).

Trilling, Lionel, *Prefaces to 'The Experience of Literature'*, The Works of Lionel Trilling (Oxford: Oxford University Press, 1981).

Ulmer, Gregory L., 'The Object of Post-Criticism', in Hal Foster (ed.), *Postmodern Culture* (London: Pluto Press, 1985; first pub., as *The Anti-Aesthetic*, 1983), 83–110.

Vanpée, Janie, 'Dangerous Liaisons 2: The Riccoboni–Laclos Sequel', *Eighteenth-Century Fiction*, 9 (1996), 51–70.

[Veit Schlegel, Dorothea], 'Gespräch über die neuesten Romane der Französinnen', *Europa*, 1 (1803), 88–106.

Vendler, Helen, 'Are These the Poems to Remember?' (review of Rita Dove (ed.), *The Penguin Anthology of Twentieth-Century American Poetry*), *New York Review of Books*,

24 November 2011 <https://www.nybooks.com/articles/2011/11/24/are-these-poems-remember/> (accessed 1 February 2021).

Walker, John, *Historical Memoirs of the Irish Bards* (London: printed for T. Payne and son, and G.G.S. and J. Robinson, 1786).

Wallinger, Hanna, 'Toni Morrison's Literary Criticism', in Justine Tally (ed.). *The Cambridge Companion to Toni Morrison* (Cambridge: Cambridge University Press, 2007), 115–24.

Walton, Izaak, *The Lives of John Donne, Sir Henry Wotton, Richard Hooker, George Herbert, and Robert Sanderson* (London: Oxford University Press, 1927; repr. 1966).

Wardle, Ralph M., 'Mary Wollstonecraft, Analytical Reviewer', *PMLA* 62 (1947), 1000–9.

Wasserman, Steve, 'Goodbye to All That', *Columbia Journalism Review*, 46 (2007) <https://archives.cjr.org/cover_story/goodbye_to_all_that_1.php> (accessed 23 February 2020).

Watson, George, *The Literary Critics: A Study of English Descriptive Criticism* (London: Penguin, 1986; first pub. 1973).

Weinberg, Bernard, *Critical Prefaces of the French Renaissance* (Evanston, IL: Northwestern University Press, 1950).

Wellek, René, 'Literary Theory, Criticism, and History', in *Concepts of Criticism*, ed. Stephen G. Nichols, Jr (New Haven:; Yale University Press, 1963; repr. 1969), 1–20.

Wellek, René, 'The Poet as Critic, the Critic as Poet, the Poet-Critic', in Frederick McDowell (ed.), *The Poet as Critic* (Evanston, IL: Northwestern University Press, 1967), 92–107.

Wenzel, Christian, *An Introduction to Kant's Aesthetics: Core Concepts and Problems* (Oxford: Blackwell, 2005).

Wenzel, Christian, 'Kant Finds Nothing Ugly?', *British Journal of Aesthetics*, 39 (1999), 416–22.

Wilde, Oscar, 'The Critic as Artist with Some Remarks on the Importance of Doing Nothing' (1891), in *The Complete Works of Oscar Wilde*, ed. Russell Jackson and Ian Small, 10 vols to date (Oxford, 2000–), iv: *Criticism: Historical Criticism, Intentions, The Soul of Man*, ed. Josephine M. Guy (2007), 123–206.

Wilde, Oscar, 'The Decay of Lying: An Observation: A Dialogue', in *The Complete Works of Oscar Wilde*, ed. Russell Jackson and Ian Small, 10 vols to date (Oxford, 2000–), iv: *Criticism: Historical Criticism, Intentions, The Soul of Man*, ed. Josephine M. Guy (2007), 72–103

Wilson, Edmund, *Literary Essays and Reviews of the 1930s & 40s*, ed. Lewis M. Dabney (New York: Library of America, 2007).

Wimsatt, W. K., and Monroe C. Beardsley, 'The Intentional Fallacy', in Wimsatt, *The Verbal Icon: Studies in the Meaning of Poetry* (Lexington: University of Kentucky Press, 1954), 3–18.

Winny, James, *A Preface to Donne* (London: Longman, 1971).

Wirth, Uwe, 'Das Vorwort als performative, paratextuelle und parergonale Rahmung', in Jürgen Fohrmann (ed.), *Rhetorik: Figuration und Performanz* (Stuttgart: Metzler, 2004), 603–28.

Wollstonecraft, Mary, *The Works of Mary Wollstonecraft*, ed. Janet Todd and Marilyn Butler, 7 vols (London: Pickering, 1989).

Wood, Michael, *On Empson* (Princeton: Princeton University Press, 2017).

Woolf, Virginia, 'A Letter to a Young Poet' (1932), in *Collected Essays*, 4 vols (London: Hogarth Press, 1966), ii. 182–95.

Woolf, Virginia, 'Why?' (1942), in *Collected Essays*, 4 vols (London: Hogarth Press, 1966), ii. 278–83.

Wordsworth, William, *The Prose Works of William Wordsworth*, ed. W. J. B. Owen and Jane Worthington Smyser, 3 vols (Oxford: Oxford University Press, 1974).

Wright, Richard, *Early Works* (New York: Library of America, 1991).
Wright, Richard, 'How "Bigger" Was Born', *Saturday Review of Literature*, 1 June 1940, 3–4, 17–20.
Wright, Richard, 'Introduction: How "Bigger" Was Born', in *Native Son* (London: Vintage, 2000), 1–30.
Zimmerman, Sarah, 'Coleridge the Lecturer, A Disappearing Act', in Alexander Dick and Angela Esterhammer (eds), *Sphere of Action: Speech and Performance in Romantic Culture* (Toronto: University of Toronto Press, 2009), 46–72.
Zimmerman, Sarah, *The Romantic Literary Lecture in Britain* (Oxford: Oxford University Press, 2019).

Index

For the benefit of digital users, indexed terms that span two pages (e.g., 52–53) may, on occasion, appear on only one of those pages.